# Forward

Your Honor,

With reference to the case of James Kopp, I have enclosed an analysis according to the science of ethics for your information.

I understand that the court made a valiant attempt to dispense justice during the proceedings. I shall not attempt to comment on whether it was prudent or not for Mr. Kopp to enter into the kind of action for which he has been already judged.

Although the court has decided that he was objectively gravely erroneous, his perspective is such that Mr. Kopp may have judged this act to be licit and appropriate under these particular circumstances. Nevertheless, all that one can hope for now is that he be accorded clemency. May I take the liberty, Your Honor, of strongly requesting that you allow the strains of mercy and clemency to guide your most prudent judgment in according Mr. Kopp the sentence you consider to be fitting.

I have the honor to be your humble servant,
Raphael T. Waters, Ph.D., L.Ph., Ph.C.
Professor of Philosophy
President, Scholars for Social Justice
Registrar, Catholic Academy of Sciences in the USA. Director, Aquinas School of Philosophy.

## Dedication

This book is dedicated to sidewalk counselors, rescuers, crisis pregnancy center workers worldwide, moms and babies who could catch a break today, and to a tiny handful of helpers who are named at the end.

*All things bright and beautiful*
*The Good Lord made them all.*

# THE CASE OF JAMES KOPP

A great deal of publicity has been given by the media to the case of James Kopp. Much injustice has been involved, for the assumption of his guilt is widespread. It is not the intention of this analysis to claim that he is guilty or not guilty but is an effort to bring out aspects which seem to have been neglected. In order to clarify the moral principles involved, let us consider the following cases:

FIRST CASE: Joseph is brutally attacked by a man who quite evidently has the intention of doing him great bodily harm, possibly even up to the point of his death. There is no time to call the police, who are responsible for the defense of the community, so Joseph defends himself and has to use such force, while rejecting the attack of the other, that the assailant dies. This is in accordance with the principle of double effect and its four conditions, for the death of the attacker is indirect and not intended.

The principle of double effect is enunciated as follows: If an act is followed by two effects, one good and the other evil, it is morally permissible to do the act provided the following four conditions are met: II-II, 64, 7.

a) The act itself is morally good or at least indifferent. The act is properly and formally the removal of the attack by rejection of the attacker. Removal of the attack is a good act. The removal may be considered the killing of the attacker if it is considered physically (materially).

b) The two effects, one good and the other evil, follow with equal immediacy: Joseph's safety (his life is preserved) and the others death occurs at the same time.

c) The good effect alone is intended--the safety of Joseph's life, not the assailant's death, which is merely tolerated.

d) There is due proportion between the good and evil effects; Joseph's safety (goods equivalent to life) and the death of the other have equal value.

This is morally permissible, for, at that moment, since authority for self-governance is a property of human nature, which is usually delegated to the civil authority, Joseph rightly exercises that property of his human nature, which is social self-governance, in the absence of those who have care of the community. He chooses the means for effecting the good end, but in causando, the evil effect also results. The act is chosen for the good effect while tolerating the evil effect. No doubt, the court also will acknowledge the right to defend oneself, completely exonerating Joseph. Of course, there should be no more action by Joseph than is necessary.

In popular superficial thinking, the above action would be described as the killing of a man. This is a physical description whereas a moral description upholds the defender's action as the rejection of an attack (or preservation of the victim's safety) which is appropriate whether the attacker is a man, a dog, a shark, or a lion.

SECOND CASE: Robert sees a young girl being attacked by a man, and fearing for the child's life, he calls the police, who treat the matter indifferently. Robert insists that the child is in great need of help but the police and others all totally ignore his plea for help. Then Robert decides to defend the girl even up to the point of causing the death of the man. No doubt the defender would receive a commendation by authorities for risking his own life in order to save another. Indeed, if he had ignored the plight of the girl, everyone would have judged him adversely. Morally, he is innocent even though the attacker lost his life. It would be ludicrous to argue that the attacker was the father of a family or that the defense took place in front of his family, notwithstanding that regretful but unavoidable circumstance.

THIRD CASE: Consider the assassination of a tyrant in which case there is no authority other than the tyrant to prevent the tyranny imposed on society. The action has as its good end, the direct removal of the tyrant for the safety or integrity of the common good, and indirectly, the death of the tyrant. With certain conditions being observed this action is morally permissible if it also meets the requirements of the principle of double effect even though it is evident that there would be legislative prohibition against such assassination.

FOURTH CASE: In the case of the assassination of Dr. Slepian, the following should be noted:

The assassin would have had full knowledge that attacks are being made on the life of innocent babies, notwithstanding this, that the authorities are fully aware of the attacks and indeed condone them by establishing laws permitting abortion, which laws are invalid laws since they are in utter conflict with the natural moral law. Moreover, he would have realized the enormity of the injustice since the direct killing of innocent babies is taking place in great numbers. Furthermore, having pleaded with civil authorities to stop the slaughter -- or at least, knowing that others have done so -- Mr. Kopp sets out to stop the attacker. If he meets the four conditions of the principle of double effect (e.g. revenge is not intended), he is acting according to the principle and that he is, in fact, removing a danger to the infants in their mothers' wombs. His action is formally an act of removal but only materially can it be described as the killing of the attacker who functions as the killer of innocent babies.

Analysis of the Principle of Double Effect: If the attacker's intention (motive) was good (not intending death as death but as removal for the sake of the innocents), it seems that the four conditions apply, as follows:

a) The act of removing an attack or attacker could be described as, at least, an indifferent act or a laudable action.

b) The two effects proceed with equal immediacy from the act, the safety of innocents from his attack, and the loss of the life of the assassin.

c) The good effect alone was intended.

d) There is due proportion between the good and evil effects, the safety of innocents from his attack and the loss of the life of the assassin.

Objection: Should this action of assassination be condemned as an act of murder?

Reply: It should be stated that murder is defined as the unauthorized and direct killing of an innocent human person. Cf. note that Abraham, when he intended to sacrifice Isaac, was acting with the authority of God.

It must also be said that authority is vested in human nature (as a property of man's rationality) and delegated by the people to those appointed to take care of the community (the government). Then at the moment of his action, the assassin, exercising his authority for self-preservation as well as social preservation, represents the government while defending the innocent person. Hence, the act of defense is authorized by reason of human nature and the circumstances of the act of defense, that is, the deliberate neglect or opposition of the governing authority, or its instrument, the police.

Objection: Perhaps it can be claimed that excessive force was used.

Reply: The question should be raised concerning other available means; other means have all been rejected by courts and other defenders of abortion; this constant rejection would be known to Kopp.

Objection: Dr. Slepian was killed in his own home and in front of his family.

Reply: The fact that the victim was killed in his own home and in front of his family is a rhetorical argument and accidental to the moral consideration of the action.

Objection: If it is claimed that the assailant intended the death of the other, the following should be said in reply.

Reply: The teaching of a famous moralist, De Lugo, states that the state can intend the death of the other. Moreover, St Thomas Aquinas states that it is laudable for the state to execute certain types of criminals (II-II, q.64, a. 2). Now at the time of the assassination of Dr. Slepian, if the assailant decided to remove the attacks on the innocents, then at that time, he represents the state as said above.

Objection: However, it has been objected that his use of stealth vitiates his act.

Reply: No one should judge this case because the assailant used stealth. The generals who attempted to assassinate Hitler during World War II also used stealth yet no one judged their attempts as evil, but regretted their failure.

If an intruder was in my home and I was alone to defend myself, stealth might be one of the few advantages in my defense. Even if the assailant had not used stealth, no doubt his action would still be judged as culpable in the eyes of the media and public opinion.

Objection: Some have argued that Kopp has given credence to his guilt by reason of his flight to Europe.

Reply: On the other hand, he must have known that he would be judged in a biased fashion based upon the news releases immediately after the assassination and the injustices established by the state with the invalid laws established by the state. We cannot judge motives or know his reasons for flight until there is some evidence.

CONCLUSION:

It seems that the assailant is removing a deadly threat to innocent lives while death is an indirect effect of removing that danger, if his motives are good.

However, in the public mind, the action of Mr. Kopp was a violent act and therefore, immoral. This failure to distinguish an act of force from an act of violence springs from the lack of education in ethical matters. A police officer or soldier may employ acts of force to prevent an evil doer from his activities just as a man ought to use force to remove a loaded pistol from the hands of a child who is wielding it irresponsibly.

On the other hand, to employ an act of violence would involve injustice as can be found in someone removing candy from a child who was given this by his parents. It would be otherwise if the child was diabetic. Failure to make suitable distinctions, such as between force and violence, has allowed public reporting even to declare some act, an accident, to be an act of murder because someone died in the accident. It is obvious that Mr. Kopp's action was forceful rather than an act of violence.

Furthermore, one might claim that Kopp used excessive force which is contrary to the fourth condition of the principle of double effect, namely, that the evil effect and the good effect ought to have due proportion to each other. Then it becomes a question of Kopp's motives. Again in keeping with this objection, it has been stated that Kopp used a rifle suitable only as an attack weapon rendering his claim doubtful. One would have to know if any other rifle was available for his use and, moreover, whether he had sufficient understanding of firearms to realize the power of such a weapon. [*Here in the Forward, in the Afterword, and in the six chapters, I will comment. Comments and brackets will be in italics -- to carry out his plan to wound only, Jim had to place a bullet at least through glass and perhaps through wood as well and be very precise. To do this he needed a high-powered rifle, not something like a 22.*] If Mr. Kopp pleads that he intended only to wound Dr. Slepian rather than kill him, as the sole means available to impede the physician's activities, which are manifestly contrary to the natural moral law, then admittedly it all comes down to his motives which are impossible to judge.

There appears to be no sound argument which demonstrates the immorality of the act and culpability of the assailant -- whether Kopp or another. But in view of the above analysis, it must be said that since there are doubts about the guilt of Kopp, namely that he intended a violent act, an act contrary to the virtue of justice, then he should be given the benefit of the doubt. This is a tenet of the natural moral law as well as the civil law which is subordinate to the natural moral law. Hence, leniency at least should be apportioned to Mr. Kopp.

The medley of voices, especially the media, have clamored for judging Mr. Kopp to be guilty, based on acceptance of abortion, a heinous social crime contrary to the common good and threatening the lives of the unborn citizens in the name of a spurious freedom. Public opinion is at a very low level as some citizens opt for every activity destructive of the common good and undermining the very fabric of civil society.

The court has found Mr. Kopp guilty while others might see him as a hero inasmuch as he has stopped one physician performing abortions while this seems to have even caused a drop in the numbers of physicians willing to perform abortions.

However, Kopp is being judged now by those opting for abortion and who have permeated the political scene with their teachings aiming at the destruction of the unborn innocents, which is supported by the clamor of those seeking their own political and financial advantage.

It is reasonable to request that the court in the very least ought to show leniency in apportioning penalty to a citizen who, manifesting great enthusiasm for the preservation of delicate lives at risk from the widespread destruction of American children in their mothers' wombs need only be accused of over-enthusiasm and perhaps keen activity with poor judgment at the very most.

The above has been written to elucidate the case in view of principles of the natural moral law to which civil law is sub alternated. Civil law, which is positive law, is merely the particularization of the natural moral law, the principles of which are discovered by an adequate understanding of human nature. Therefore, any law which conflicts with the natural moral law is invalid law. This is clearly taught in the science of ethics and applies to civil laws permitting abortion. Raphael T. Waters

# Affidavit of James Charles Kopp

## IN RE: Waters Letter Provenance

1. In 2007 Dr. Raphael T. Waters was Associate Professor at Genesee College, Western New York, and President of the US Thomas Aquinas Society;

2. Upon knowledge and belief, in Spring 2007 Waters sent the letter titled "THE CASE OF JAMES C. KOPP" to HH Judge Richard C. Arcara, USDC - WDNY in advance of the sentencing of Kopp;

3. At or about the same time Waters sent a copy of the letter to Thomas A. O'Conner, MD, Eggertsville, New York;

4. Upon knowledge and belief only, Professor Dr. Bonette was a mutual acquaintance of both O'Conner and Waters;

5. O'Conner sent a copy of the letter to Kopp;

6. In June 2007 a paralegal in the employ of Bruce Barket, Esq., Garden City, NY, met Waters in Western New York and personally verified the contents of his letter to Judge Arcara;

7. Dr. Waters died in 2009. He is survived by numerous professional colleagues who will attest to his competence in philosophy and moral theology.

I affirm under the penalties and pains of perjury and I declare pursuant to 18 USC Section 1746 and "Houston v. Lack" that the foregoing is true and correct.

*Executed at (BOP - FCI), 5 June 2022 (OSB) James C. Kopp*

## Table of Contents

Chapter 1: Childhood, Cheryl, Switzerland . . . . . . . . . . 1

Chapter 2: Education, Fullerton, Dr. Rosenberg . . . . . . . . . . 57

Chapter 3: From Academia to Operation Rescue . . . . . . . . . . 117

Chapter 4: Keith Green, Rome, Catholicism . . . . . . . . . . . . 166

Chapter 5: The Life and Death of Rescue . . . . . . . . . . . . . 232

Chapter 6: Shooting Slepian . . . . . . . . . . . . . . . . 280

Chapter 7: France, the Vito Squad, Lavender Hill . . . . . . . . . . 299

Afterward: James Kopp, In Defense of Others . . . . . . . . . . . 352

## Chapter 1

## Childhood, Cheryl, Switzerland

Standard Disclaimer -- I mention tons of people in this book. Famous people, not-so-famous, and lots of nobodies. I want to hereby save them all a lot of trouble by stating categorically that all of them don't believe in the Thomistic use of force to save children. If any of them disagree with that, they can write their own damn book. But I'm saying it now. That means, as you are reading this, cowardly mainstream prolifers and just average couch potatoes of America, don't write me to yell about it. You are off the hook right now. And you celebrities, read this part to your lawyer before you yell at him. Or, let him read it to you. I'm quit of you. See you at the finish line, win or lose.

Who knows how these things happen. Maybe it was a "Harps and Angels" kind of thing, an angelic visit, but I found myself turning the wheel of my bike toward the slough that day after school. The slough itself doesn't have much to recommend it: scarcely five or ten acres of channels and marsh grass, all completely dominated by the overarching smelly, noisy shadows of the concrete freeway exchange. I did not know what I was looking for as I dawdled by that swamp but I knew what it was the instant I saw it. A blue heron, right there in front of me, barely fifty feet away, more dignified than a prophet. Great Blue Herons (GBH) live in a world of their own, especially when they are fishing. They aren't afraid, they know you are there, and if you get too close, they'll scoot. They'd just as soon dine alone, nothing personal. Unless.

Unless you slide just a little onto the edge of their comfort zone and then just zone out so very completely, as if you didn't exist. Four and a half decades later I can't help but wonder if all quiet times and the healings and silent resolution that came from that, and all of quiet surveillance and all of the success, from a baby's and mom's perspective, didn't all come from that silly bird who was just hanging out. My own personal spiritual quiet time guide, with feathers.

I did slide up, and he did assess the situation and decide I was a suitable dining/contemplation companion, and we've been talking ever since that first meeting of an hour or so. A few months after that I spotted him fishing close by that spot, right next to the Don Quixote statue just across the same exchange. On that occasion I didn't need to maneuver. I was pushing my bike over the freeway exchange. This time, he was fishing differently. It was a proper mud flat connected to the embayment of the creek. He had a much bigger space to work in than the original slough banks where I first saw him on the other side of the exchange. The sun was just going over the yardarm -- must've been a late rehearsal that day, or swim team practice. After a minute of watching I saw the whole story. He faced into the sun so his shadow was entirely behind him. He would put one foot forward delicately and then pause, perfectly still. Tiny minnows at his feet would return to the shallow space over his toes from where they had scurried away only a second before. Those minnows! Short-term memory issues for them are the bread and butter of our fisherman pal. He never came up empty. A one hundred percent efficient fisherman, our heron is, and the motion of his head, still, all of three feet over the water, to down, snatch, and up, was invisibly quick. When it's time to wait, he waited. When it was time to move, it was so quick you miss it. He had no hesitation or false move, and he fished with supreme confidence.

This confidence in his own fishing abilities ramified through the rest of his birdy life. The heron has a leisurely pace in his life, especially among so many usually frantic birds. So often he's just daydreaming, when most birds are always scrounging around for something to eat, right? Or speed-dating, anxious flighty and nervous. Not our gentleman heron. I didn't know it at the time but I learned a lot from him about pace, timing, work, preparation, surveillance, calmness, and confidence.

Up at our house just a little bit from this, my mom had a poem on the kitchen wall: Said the Robin to the Sparrow as he sat upon the bough,/ Tell me, why do all these humans rush about and worry so?/Said the Sparrow to the Robin as he flew down from the tree,/They must have no Heavenly Father, such as cares for you and me. We all rush around so much, but for what? Is the width and breadth of all we do really worth it? Is it worth the loss of heaven, the only mudflat that counts? Focus. Make haste slowly. Look for the substance and meaning, or lack of it, at all times in everything we do and don't do. We must seek the Lord's will the whole time, but we need to be careful, or "we'll wind up having nothing to talk about in the locker room." Kardashian cosmetic surgery? Pimp My Ride? Say Yes to the Dress? Bizarre Foods? Please. Life is short. Eternity beckons.

In the same view from my room across the Ross Valley you could see a tiny Lutheran church, stop Number One on our search for a new church up north. We went there for a while, and I remember an awfully cute quiet girl. I did my Eagle project there, making plywood lecterns that would sit on a table for Sunday school, but our family never jelled at that church. Mom looked around; she probably checked out every church in Marin, not a huge task, but I don't remember the rest of us going with her. She finally settled on a Lutheran church in Novato, Good Shepherd. She seemed to be happy but the simple fact is that there was no Pastor Mees in Marin. Not even close. If there had been, she would have found him, especially since we'd all gotten such a deep draft of real faith down south. By the time Mom found the Novato church, our family had gotten used to the idea of not going to church on Sunday. Even the Quantico "every Marine in chapel on Sunday" vibe didn't cut it anymore. One very good thing Good Shepherd did was introduce Mary to some neat charismaniacs who seemed to treasure her in a way beyond the family circle. This stood her in good stead since she came to a saving adult faith with the charismatic crowd a few years before her horrible death from leukemia when she was only nineteen.

Glen Danley, the Good Shepherd organist, and I used to gossip shamelessly in the organ loft during services. She was so good she could do it even while she was playing, and tell jokes, saying "hang on" if she needed to concentrate on something. She could even throw on a perfect poker face in a millisecond if the pastor happened to look up. Betty White doing brain surgery, all day long. Other than that, I can't think of a single eventful thing there, spiritually speaking, between when I first got to Marin in '68 when I was fourteen and when I had almost graduated from college in 1976. Not a thing. Marin is full of pop stories about metal bands that partied there, but spiritually it was a wasteland. Were there any evangelicals in South Marin, below the cowtowns, in the '60s and '70s? If there were, I never knew it. Ditto for college at Santa Cruz. Spiritually speaking everything was dead, right up until a day in the spring of '76, the year I graduated. I was standing in my girlfriend's apartment, in the kitchen by the refrigerator in fact, and…

Wait. Let me back up just a scooch. This'll just take a minute. As I write this, I regularly denounce our promiscuous age and all its accouterments such as perennial divorce, pulling the heads off helpless children, Frankensteining of helpless embryo kids, perennial in vitro murder of helpless children to cover the infertility from abortions that come from promiscuity…

I can't "fast forward" to the conversation with my girlfriend in senior year at Cal Santa Cruz without a little comment. Yes, I'm now against cohabitation. It tends to be based on child killing, either surgical or by poison and suffocation of a child the size of your little finger, meaning, the Pill. But I did have a girlfriend. Both of us since then have become Christians and, in that process, do denounce cohabitation. Christians will instantly comprehend what I mean, since ours is a faith of second chances and also preaches the acknowledgement of sin and repentance.

No matter what I say, however, I will always have a truckload of accusers who point and say: See? He's a hypocrite! He doesn't practice what he preaches! This, from people who are threatened even by my telling of the story, and obviously have no notion of sin in their own lives. And it's not like I'm a plaster saint now (I'll buy you a beer and tell you about it if you're interested). Then my accusers will proceed, by impeccable logic, to dismantle everything I've ever said or done about saving a handful of babies and moms from the disaster that even many women acknowledge. I'm very familiar with this crowd dynamic, by the way. I remember well the -- literal, trust me -- witches in Burlington Vermont who drank blood from babies killed in their mill there in their black masses and then bragged about it in the newspaper. Then they chanted at us while we were silent, locked in on their precious holy ground, with a few supporters nearby who silently held pictures of the witches' handiwork.

We held the pictures, and our ground, in silent argument; they chanted: "Anti-women, anti-gay/Born-again bigots, go away. I bring this up now, out of sequence, because we could say it belongs in the "prolife" chapter of this book, but I do it to use as an example of what I mean when I say I had a girlfriend in school. The chant of hypocrisy will then start up.

There will be zero comprehension of the extremely wise view of these things by the likes of say Teresa Tomeo who comments on stories like this by saying "your misery is your ministry." They will never call up or write or visit the gentle Jennifer O'Neill or any of the other women of Silent No More who bravely tell their stories. The neo-chanters will never understand the forgiveness of God, barring some kind of miracle, and the Christians always will. The attackers will always cite studies by Bill Baird that "Catholics" are X percent of the people who trot off to the mills, and they will never understand when I try to tell them that in many ways the prolife movement was started precisely by sadder-but-wiser women, whom they now denounce the same way they denounce the femaleness of, say, Sarah Palin or the blackness of Ben Carson or Alan Keyes, all of whom would make perfect presidents.

When my attackers read the story of the Palo Alto VA Hospital ward of 48 beds filled with nothing but women who went clinically insane the instant they realized they had hit menopause and were sterilized by the only abortion they had, and killed the only child they had ever conceived, as I tell it elsewhere in this book, they will plug their ears and say I'm making it up. They say that even as they sign the consent forms for abortion, which they don't read. If they had read them, they would see right there where it says precisely that can happen, from one abortion alone. Sadly, there will be many women who, in their twenties or thirties, think something that might happen ten years down the road is irrelevant. They don't expect to make it that long, and in any event, the partying of the moment trumps any such consideration.

For my attackers, it's all perfectly embodied by an article I read once about a "street party" phenomenon carried out by a gaggle of people with coordinated boom boxes saturating a public area with techno music: don't ever let the party stop. The party must go on. Quietly, these people will find out, from VD, from suicide, from the emptiness of the cradles in their houses and lives, exactly what happens when the party stops, but they don't want to hear it now. They are stopping their ears and chanting. It is a one hundred percent perfect, iterating disconnect. Walker Percy predicted this disconnect of the public square flawlessly just before he died and it has now come to pass. He might as well have quoted a scene in Flannery O'Connor where four kids on a double date come to the point where the two Catholic kids begin singing "Tantum Ergo" and the Protestant kids sing "Jesus Loves Me." At the same time, right past each other.I appeal to Flannery and Walker, now, as my judges, and the loving Judge behind them. Yes, I resist abortion. Yes, I had a girlfriend. It was a sin, and I was and am a sinner. I wish I had never done it. But now I resist abortion. Deal with it. I approach Jesus on this subject first, not anyone else, and I listen to His take on it. The real God, the living God, not the fake human construct that exists in your mind and does your bidding on demand when you want to live as you want. The real God works in real time. Thank Him. The time of my college days is the past, which past, in a way, doesn't exist anymore. All evil itself will cease to exist in just a few years, for you and me, like it or not.

But now, in this moment, you and I are responsible for the kids who will get their heads torn off by nine AM tomorrow morning. We are just as responsible as the Germans who sat by and watched it happen, singing in their churches all the while. I'm going to continue my story now with full awareness of the chanting in the background. If you'd like to say something more intelligent than satanic chanting, by all means, state your case. Write your own damn book. Speak up. Fill this room with your intelligence. I'm agog with anticipation.

So. back to UCSC…let's say it was the Spring of 76 since Cheryl and I were about to graduate. I doubt we were the only students who were wondering quo vadis at that point since the end of school is a natural fledging point for kids, especially the middle class suburban kids for whom college is often a mere extension of home, responsibility wise. Now, really, is the time we would have to decide what we would do with our lives. But, spiritually speaking, one last glimpse backward: was all of high school and college a waste, spiritually? Well, not to put too fine a point on it, but yes, especially when compared to the heart-warming faith of Pastor Mees. Our poor little rich family living in fancy-pants Marin never had a church with the likes of him in it. In college I don't recall anyone every inviting me to church and, up until the spring of '76, if they had, I suppose I would have snorted at them with scorn like all the rest of us hippies, the seemingly infinite tolerance of New Age liberalism and openness slams shut resoundingly at the sound of anything that sounds like real doctrine, especially the Real God Who, interesting as He is, just might ask you to do something you don't want to do one day. ABC I call it. Anything But Christianity. New Age makes me think about a New Orleans graveyard on Halloween, decorated with bits of colored paper or gaudy ornaments but inside filled with dead men's bones. New Agers love the artifice or accidental tangents of disembodied spirits but only provided that substance is absent.

Don't take the Christians' word for it. Hindu and Buddhist priests, gurus, swamis, and scholars have been turning back the breathless, excited, starry-eyed backpacker types for generations now, but they won't listen. Even before they left the West, they fought, dabbling over substance or commitment, in any tradition. "Go back home," the teachers have been saying, for two generations now. But the dilettante backpackers won't listen. Kind of the like the people Flannery O'Connor was talking about. Disconnect. Talking past. So. One afternoon in the Spring of 1976 my girlfriend and I were talking in the kitchen of our tiny apartment on the beach in Santa Cruz. "Do you believe in God?" she asked. Uh, I don't know." As you can see, four years of chi-chi NPRish Marvelous Marin and another four years of secular university of California had had their effect on the Pastor Mees, Boy Scouts, Luther's Short Catechism, simple child-like faith of my youth. "But are you sure you don't believe in God?" she persisted, "not even a little?"

If I had abandoned God, my girlfriend had also abandoned New Age, apparently, without any memo coming across my desk, because New Agers are perfectly contented with "maybe" as an answer to a question like this. When she came to college, she had been overwhelmed by the pressure of studying and exams. Her response to this was to "put God in a box," temporarily, at least, as she put it, while she was in college, and take on a boyfriend as a way of coping with it all. Now, graduation was here. Time to decide what to do next. God had been in the box long enough. She was honoring a contract she'd made with Him earlier that putting Him in a box would only be for four years, after which He would be released on good time. A kind of Lion in Winter thing where the king lets his wife out of the tower once a year to see how she's doing. OK, so, the outline of Cheryl's backstory -- all of this was news to me, and I had lived with this wonderful woman for four years -- was starting to emerge.

She used to be in a Bible study in high school, ostensibly, with some measure of faith. She'd put "God in a box" for the last four years, and lived with me, as a kind of emotional coping mechanism for the pressure of classes and exams in school. God was now out of the box again, and did I believe in Him? Just when you're thinking it couldn't get much worse, boyfriend-wise -- surprise! There was more. Cheryl and I had paid for school at least partly with summer jobs, preferable to jobs during the school year that cut into study time. We were both scientists, and that's a lot of studying and labs and field trips. During this outpouring of emotion and intent from Cheryl, it came out that in addition to the God's-out-of-the-box revelation, a second theme emerged. In between the summer jobs Cheryl had managed to scrounge and save away a sizable bit of money for the purpose of a round-the-world trip which she wanted to take immediately after graduation.

But wait, shoppers! There's more! Further, that this round-the-world trip would culminate in a visit to some kind of ashram in Europe -- a perfectly logical place for an ashram, don't laugh. And (she was breathless) she wanted me to come with her on this trip around the world. Now, from the distance of years and encounters with all kinds of people, I wonder if this small, sad story wasn't a universal fable, played out as it was in the sunny kitchen of that tiny flat, with the last lazy bends of the San Lorenzo River winding past the kitchen window, and the salt air of the Santa Cruz Boardwalk surf wafting through the front door. There's a little something for everyone in this tale.

For my dear evangelical brothers and sisters, including Mom and my sister Anne, they would probably nod their heads wisely and intone: So, Jim. You had a free ride, there, for a few years, but now the party's over. Time to turn from sin and come to the Lord. For my dear charismatic Catholic brothers and sisters, you can almost hear them say: join her religion and marry the girl. We do it all the time. Cynics: chime in here anywhere you want. My dear Byzantine brothers and sisters might weigh in: a nice Armenian girl you couldn't find? Who'd never leave you high and dry like that? And you had to get all involved with some girl of no people? Some geschicksa that caught your eye? Nothing from the old world? Tchah. (Pat on cheek). You come by for dinner on Sunday, meet my Sophie. Such a girl! The girl for you, young man! Nice church wedding, you'd make the perfect couple, so beautiful.

My New Age friends and extended family members, they are legion, would listen for a second in an NPR haze, and then cut in, "Who is this girl?" Well, whoever she is, she picked an awfully elaborate way to break up with her college boyfriend. Trip around the world? Ashram? Who's she kidding? I'm going to a rave tonight. You're coming too. Plenty of fish in the sea, and they're ready to party. Get over it.

The real meaning of this backed-up-against-the-reefer conversation for me didn't become clear until years later, but back then, the first thing I said was that I really had not thought very much about God and it was unfair to expect a snap decision from me on the subject when her deep feelings about Him were news to me. Side note: during our relationship I had now and then lamely bruited the idea of getting married. Every time I did that she would screech in my ear the sound of a baby crying, with great sarcasm. She was the eldest of a large family and I was the youngest. A huge diaper-smelling differential there, if you think about it. After I defended my agnosticism though and Cheryl persisted in laying out all her plans, a chill crept into my spine. The ax is laid to the root of the tree. It was the beginning of a feeling that would haunt me for the next several years. Panic and fear. What I had taken for granted was now being taken from me, and it was a huge wakeup, all the more since I had no idea it was coming. Men are galactically stupid that way, of course. Plus, I didn't have the bucks for Tahiti. I'd put it all in school, every penny.

Why didn't I take out a loan, then, if Cheryl was so precious to me? I was touched, actually, that she had in fact invited me to go on the trip; when you throw in the destination of the ashram, it was clear she wanted me to go with her and she wasn't breaking up at all. She still wanted me to experience all these things with her, including anything God might want to do now that He was kicked loose. Whatever else Cheryl or I was thinking at the time, I don't recall any animosity. From her side I now know that she was relieved God was set free again. Just what had He been up to, out of sight for so long, you could ponder, of course. I had a fuzzy mix of panic, but also, the German impulse, arriving at the scene of a disaster, of Don't Worry, This Is All Under Control. Why my Irish genes didn't surface at the time I don't recall, but I don't recall drinking, philosophy, or improvised blank verse shouted into the night or "Dublin In The Rare Auld Times."

I will mention Newport, Oregon from the science perspective but here I'd like to tell you the spiritual side of what happened up there. Come to think of it, the blarney may have surfaced after all, because Newport is where I learned the Dizzy Gillespie habit of playing with a whisper mute and headphones. If no one but you hears anything, it's a great way to learn improvisation. I learned backup on the job with Sinatra At The Sands and the Nat King Cole memorial set. And, it was a huge consolation. In Newport I had a Christian housemate who probably exerted an invisible influence on me simply by virtue of his profound cheerfulness. Not that cheerful Protestants are always well-received by me; in fact, usually I run the other way. But for whatever reason, he was not irritating as they so often are, God bless 'em. His guilelessness was no obstacle to what followed. We lived in a house on a bluff north of town. You could see the breakers from the front porch. The jazz and the surf combined into a feel of that house and that time. There was a measure of healing or calmness which cushioned the shock of a remote small town being the place of my first job as a professional biologist, a huge difference from the congeniality of a college campus. A buffer also to the sadness and panic about Cheryl.

To her credit, we were not officially broken up at that point and I guess that was because she was letting me down gently or still considered me a contender. Cheryl is one of those people who simply cannot lie, so I am convinced the two of us were still in the running even if it was up in the air. This ray of hopefulness combined with the German crisis management meme served to make a day-to-day feeling that was not too depressing though it was depressing enough.

Work wasn't that hard. It was scientific journal research for an EPA white paper on intertidal pollution indicator species in the wake of the Exxon Valdez crash of a few years earlier. Us techs from the marine lab on the south bank of the river would shoot pool at night since it was usually raining up there. If I did have to move on with my life, this was as good a start as any. In all its low-profile pleasantness none of this was a warning for what happened one day when I was standing in the kitchen, flipping through a book.

So, what was this book that caused so much trouble? It was *He Is There and He Is Not Silent* by Dr. Schaeffer. Why would i, a functional atheist, be looking in a book written by a Christian? Love does funny things to you, I'm reliably told, and in a phone call from Europe, Cheryl had mentioned the Swiss "ashram" and Dr. Schaeffer as the head beagle over there. A quick trip to the library showed up this book as the shortest one he had written. I wonder if at this point Cheryl was still hoping for a reconciliation or not; I really don't know. I found out years later that the California evangelical churches had really become battle-scarred warriors in the matter of dealing with all the wreckage of the sexual revolution of the late 60's and 70's, especially when the Jesus Movement came along shortly after. I also found out from these brave West Coast Christians that the odds of a "live-in" relationship surviving one or the other of the couple's converting were not so hot. Had someone told Cheryl this same news in Switzerland? Was it a "God or the boy" crisis for her? Certainly by now it is known among honest agnostics that with a live-in relationship, there is a psychic bond that develops even if there is no contractual marriage. Atheist shrinks have finally publicly agreed that little girls grow up way the hell too fast. This is the disaster of the sexual revolution, in which absence of commitment and awful precocity are the cornerstones. I grieve for her, that she may indeed have had to struggle through all this alone. But, meanwhile, she was kind enough to point me in the right direction with good books.

Over the phone I do remember, however, a note of humble hesitation creep into Cheryl's voice, who normally wouldn't have a problem commanding the Seventh Fleet. "I'm not really a good one to talk to about all this, Jim," she said when I asked her about Christianity, "I'm just figuring it out myself." This was a big changeup for her, too. She was definitely a jump-on-the-surfboard, grab-the-wheel-of-her-mom's-airplane; i-can-do-this kind of gal. My Cheryl was changing, there, in Switzerland, at the other end of the phone line, and I could only watch from afar. Even at that late moment, however, we were still a little like Thisbee and Paramus whispering hopefully through the hole in the garden wall. For her love was changing to something heavenly, but for me back in Oregon, I was still looking at something much closer to earth, my little Earth Angel.

So. A long way 'round to explain how a book written by a Christian had gotten into my hands and I was motivated to read it. But it needs telling. In the same phone call Cheryl had recommended He Is Not There And He Is Not Silent and I had chased off to the Christian bookstore, a new experience for me, as I was chasing off after Cheryl. I brought the book back home and started flipping through it, an old speed-reading habit. I was standing in the kitchen, dusk coming on, rollers booming just off the porch, thoughts of hope about Cheryl still swimming in my head, looking down at the beach and back to college and home. But it all went straight out of my head when my eyes casually fell on a single phrase in the Introduction. I can't remember the entire sentence, I can't even remember the subject of the sentence, but this phrase hit me like a sledge hammer: ". . . intellectually and exegetically satisfying to the enquirer," or something like that. I think the context of the sentence was musing on a possible answer to a question; i.e., would such an answer be both exegetically and intellectually satisfying to a hypothetical enquirer? Hmmm… one minute, here I was, cynical male, flipping through my little cram-course book, the Cliff Notes I needed to get Cheryl back, and the next minute, any thought of Cheryl, poor thing, went straight out of my head. On top of it, I had to scramble around the house to find a dictionary: exegesis, it turns out, had something to do with Bible preaching. Huh! So this obscure weird Christian guy who hung out at an ashram in the Swiss alps, who'd stolen my girlfriend's attention, so to speak, was now proposing something to me: there is such a thing as something that is both a Christian/Bible thing, and at the same time intellectually rigorous?

Well, chazzan. You could've knocked me over with an extremely tiny feather. In Redwood High School I recall an exchange between my English teacher and a student: when the teacher thought about Darwinism, he did it with his head; when he thought about God, he did it with his heart. Glasnosty enough, and honest; still, the teacher's reaction was typical. No interface between the two camps, Christians and scholars. They sailed past each other like ships in the night. Did heart and mind sail past each other, too? Was it Darwin and a-bombs and Agent Orange and DDT and redline mortgages six days a week, and hearts and flowers Sundays, Christmas and Easter? Was it white and colored drinking fountains, and Founding Fathers owning slaves, and Cheney's no-bid Halliburton contracts in Iraq Monday through Friday, and Smurfy "Jesus," my Huggy Wuggy Teddybear, on Sunday to irrationally square it all up, somehow? Was it kick the Cherokees out of Appalachia and the Utes out of Colorado and massacre the babies at Sandy Springs when it came to that little matter of where to put the log cabin, but then roll into church on Sunday and thank God you weren't a heathen savage?

Was it buy a gun, depopulate Africa, Norestryn force-implanted or IMF tease/abandon, and then write First Things articles about Christian love for our brother the black man? Was it Dutch slaver ship profit, ignoring the pope about slavery, throwing up the Spanish Inquisition Black Legend as a smokescreen and then raise your hands and shout hallelujah on Wednesday Night Bible study? as it FDR passing up a chance to bomb rail tracks to death camps with a phone call, and then, quick, off to synagogue with you, it's Friday night? For all the wonders of the faith of Pastor Mees, I don't suppose anyone could ever have accused him of being an intellectual, except for the tiny inconvenient fact that he was one, in his sturdy journeyman way, just without the fancy schmancy vocabulary. "Vas yoo dere, Charly?" he used to always say in catechism class when evolution came up. We weren't there to witness the Creation and the Garden of Eden, but neither was Darwin, was the idea. Couldn't call him a charismaniac, either. Too practical. And I mean charismaniac in the nicest way. My family is thoroughly infested with 'em. They prayed me into the faith, and, for completely inscrutable reasons; in Asia I am regarded as one myself. Anyway, there I was standing in the kitchen in the beach house in Newport, my world getting messed up real good over a handful of words in one of the most underappreciated books ever written.

If there was such a thing intellectually and Christian-wise compatible, it meant that I was no longer able to dismiss Christianity as something only emotional people such as my mom and sister would mess with. It could not be discounted out of hand if it made this new claim to intellectual rigorousness. With a casual unpresumptuous handful of words, this Schaeffer guy had neatly nudged my bust of Darwin off of my New Age plinth and set a crucifix in its place as casually as an innocent cat creating havoc, prowling along the mantelpiece. Well, huh.

You know what? I could go on and on about that moment, the beginning of all kinds of change for me, but having vigorously waved the flag of reason I find myself at the same time retreating. Well, no, advancing, into the heretofore creepy world of metaphysics. I'm not at all sure what the hell happened that night in the kitchen in Newport. Just because a heartsick scientist of this-and-that soft California suburban upbringing reads these or those magic words, it does not at all necessarily follow that he'll drop to his knees, crawl to the King and shout Mercy! Hallelujah! Even writing about it now you'd think i'd have a clue but I must say the whole thing is bewildering. I can guarantee you it was all that and a bag of chips in 1977, even with Dizzy and the Chairman of the Board and Satchelmouth in close attendance.

Viewed from the currently invisible side, a psychic shift like the epiphany in the beachside kitchen looks as simple as an ice cream cone. Viewed from the visible world something as profound and substantial as the real laughter of God is no more complicated than the flight of a hummingbird. If you really watch. And feel. If you think you can hang out on one side of the fence at the expense of the other, you're wrong, dear soul. If you look at nothing but halves of apples all your life you can resoundingly and completely forget that each one started out as a whole, round, red fruit. You think you got the whole thing, but you ain't. OK, Chuck?

In the science part of this book, I tell about what happened in the labs there, but this chapter here could be a good place to try to describe the spiritual stuff. Why did I go to Austin? Well, Cheryl was there, for starters. She was now back from Europe with her newly edified faith, no longer the will-o'-the-wisp Sunday religion of her high school years, but something here to stay. God wasn't just out of the box, he was on the throne, dawg! and she told me so. Like all the other tricky males in the history of the world, I showed interest in my face and nodded and said, "Gee, that's great for you, honey"… but then promptly acted as if she hadn't said a thing. Come on, guys. Confess. To her credit as a newly retreaded Christian she was awfully nice about it, even if at least part of it was lingering pity. Whatever may have been concluded on her part, we still had a small amount of amiable communication, even if it was strained by the new Presence in the middle of it all. Of course it's embarrassing and humiliating to admit I'd traipsed half-way across the country to see my old girlfriend but, as Joseph II used to say,"there it is." I'm embarrassed. I wonder if it's better to get that all over with in this life. While there's still time. Beats incurable embarrassment on the other side, I bet.

Embarrassing to recount or not, I needed a job and a place to stay in Austin. The job you'll know about in the Science chapter but for a place to stay I wound up in Deutsche Haus, a room-and-board residence just off the shady, leafy old avenues of the UT part of Austin. It was nice old house in a mini-plantation style; an old frat house or some old oil baron's place, either one. I lived in the garret, an unfinished attic where you had to watch your head, and you could see out of the roof shingles. But it was redeemed by a tiny window door that led out onto the roof of the large porch, a favorite drinking spot. I made a birdfeeder that swung out like a bowsprit over the front of the house. The birds were happy.

Deutsche Haus really takes me back. Quirky university culture is not confined to the campuses of the University of California, Ann Arbor and a few other nutty spots I could mention, thank God for that. The Deutsche Haus residents were all that and a set of new spark plugs. Hell, they were all spark plugs, over there. At dinner if someone accidentally spoke English -- Deutsche Haus did have a theme -- the lanky bespectacled and pleasant Irish majordomo would interject. "Sprichst du denn Chinesich. Was ist'los hier denn?" I'm so dumb it took me a month to even figure out what he was saying. Why couldn't they speak the King's English down there in Texas? This is America, dammit! I\ even remember some on-campus science seminar where I met a Chinese geologist who could speak not one word of English, to match my own not one word of Mandarin. But we carried on all night in German. We had to.

Saturday nights were a trip at Deutsche Haus. Austin was one of "those cities" which have been playing the Rocky Horror Picture Show once a week since it was originally fomented. Fermented? Wedding dresses, rice thrown at the screen, etc., were only the start of it! You could hear any resident of Deutsche Haus instantly break into song at any moment, day or night, thus: "I'm just a sweet transvestite/From Transsexual,/ Transulvaniaaaaaaaah...." But on Saturday night the transsexual Greek chorus really picked up. On slow days I'd hang out in the attic and listen to Lani Hall and Newman's silver album, the one with "Baltimore" on it. Hall is one of the most underappreciated singers of all time: "There are women and there are women/Some will hold you tight/And some leave you counting/Stars in the night." It's funny. I wonder if Austin was where I started to make the shift from being a music performer to being a music listener. Also, from classical to pop or jazz. Another solace about the whole girlfriend thing.

I met Scott Austin in Austin, Texas in the Newman Center on campus. How did I get there, a place that was like a church, when I was still in sunny California agnostic hippie mode? Well, that's a poser. I don't know. I do recall a nice large lounge catty-corner from the chapel where people could hang out and talk. This was where most of my conversations with Scott took place. Scott was a grad. student there at UT in religion or philosophy, I forget which. At about the same time I met Scott I started reading Mere Christianity by C.S. Lewis. When I would have a question about what I was reading, I would ask Scott and his answers seemed to be quite confident and knowledgeable, even though Scott himself told me often that he was not a Christian. This is something academia is well-used to now in the last half-dozen centuries, the idea of a teacher who does not believe, but in Scott's case it was also true. I think Cheryl was the first one to recommend this book. Come to think of it, the story of my conversion to Protestantism could be easily divided into the time before I read it, and after. I must disclose that in successive years I've discovered that Lewis might not be all he's cracked up to be by his adoring US evangelical fans. Don't get me wrong: he's a great dude, a great thinker, an obviously great Christian who suffered much, especially with his heroic act of marrying Joy Davidman.

The strongest point in favor of Lewis is that before him, English apologetics could get a little dry. I mean, Ronald Knox was so much more extensive, but also so much more boring. Lewis generated tremendous excitement in his World War II radio speeches and in his public speeches also. Once at a public speech, when the guy defending the atheist position was done, a crowd member shouted, "Go get him Jack!" as if it were a rugby scrum. Knox, bless him, never was one to generate enthusiasm like that. My only microscopically tiny bone to pick with Lewis is gossip to the extent that at the end of his life Lewis possessed completely sufficient information to know the Catholic position was true and replete, even as it included everything in the Anglican tradition.

The gossip further states that Lewis only refrained from converting due to fear of backlash from his Belfast roots which were vehemently anti-Catholic, Magisterium be damned. His autobiography gives extremely palpable hints as to the honest fear he had of his own father's derision, who was a completely unregenerate Granger, just like my own Gramma Leonard. I can hardly blame Lewis. I just wish he'd found a way, for his own peace of mind. Chesterton and Newman are only two examples of English intellectuals who had to brave massive scholastic and religious backlash when they moved over, and Lewis knew all about them. It's so important to remember that barely a century or two earlier priests and even laypeople were executed just for going to Catholic Mass in both England and Ireland.

All of this is to say that despite my tiny wishes about the end of things, Mere Christianity really put a line in the sand about in or out with regard to Christianity of any denomination. Lewis is so reasonable, pleasant, winsome, not bitter, quaint, homey and practical about all the usual objections people raise about Christians, that not only was the book a watershed for me, but I have recommended it to a ton of enquirers ever since.

Before I read Mere Christianity, the idea of possibly becoming a Christian was mixed up with unorganized and compulsive feelings in every direction. The strong desire to somehow regain Cheryl was there, of course, but there were other strong impulses scattered through my life. Only a year or two earlier many people I love had died: my dear Gramma Leonard who laughed and smoked her way through life, my brother-in-law Rick, leaving my sister Annie with two little babies, and my own sister Mary. This close manifestation of mortality cast a deep pall over my youth. I was barely eighteen when Mary died, and the other deaths came in a cluster at the same time. Then there was the on-and-off fleeting memory of Pastor Mees' intensely sincere and simple faith, and that of my own mother's Auntie-Mame-like intensity, which tended to gather up all stragglers, especially lazy dreamers like myself.

These were scattered feelings about people who had faith, what Mother Teresa called the "catching influence," and the sympathetic attraction of Christians nearby, even if they didn't preach at you but lived life well and as such they are heavenly. But they were only unorganized feelings. Mere Christianity set all those feelings into a lovingly and jovially prepared sconce which was in no way restraining or oppressive or excluding, but now cast a steady illumination over what had been a smoky existence. You can be nudged here and there all day long but sooner or later the human heart wants "to drive the bus home." Unpresumptuous Mere Christianity does exactly that. Before I read it, I was vaguely interested, emotionally, with wisps of feeling here and there. After I read it, the slow thought descended on me: well, why not? Someone has satisfactorily dealt with all the standard objections to Christianity that we hear all about all day long, so…why not? The problem with thinkers, or wannabee thinkers, is that after receiving the warm-hearted impulse in their souls, and even after receiving obviously complete and satisfactory intellectual information required to remove all rational and even irrational obstacles, it's just never quite that simple to step through the open door. Jesuits would say that a motion of the will is needed. Schaeffer would say it is a leap, but not a leap in the dark, a leap in the light. There will always be something holding you back, and you always need to leap past it, but it's not as if you are ignoring your brain. My brain was very well fed during the entire process, but in the end it was not pure reason that pushed me across, as if it were like solving an equation. The quirkiness of each human spirit comes into play in an extremely personal way. God is not calling widgets into eternity. He calls you and me.

We always seem to come up with things we can't let go of, or, that we are afraid we must let go of, even if it isn't so. Cheryl put it like this in a letter from Europe: "I always want to be 'Boss of the turns,' like my niece Suzy would shout in the games they would play sledding when they were little." In his subtle and underappreciated way, Benedict XVI covered this exact point with extreme sensitivity and delicacy in one of his shorter popular books to the tune that when we surrender to heaven, we actually increase our freedom rather than diminish it, sin being such a slave master.

Recently I found myself mulling this idea: inquirers or possible converts hanging on the fence love to linger over the prerogative of the freedom they will have to surrender when really what we're thinking about is nothing more than our desire to continue sinning. And sin is such a taskmaster. Ask any junkie. Or, translating for New Agers: compulsive partying as a mode of existence is what we don't want to lose. It's a testimony to the horribly and incredibly compressed horizons of our current era that the vast majority of the people who read these words would instantly pump their fists in the air and shout, "Yeah!" to the partying. It took me only a short decade to fully realize that Christians party as much as pagans, only so much better.

We don't have to worry about trips to the vomitorium, trips to the abortion mill (just a modern day vomitorium), trips to AA, trips to the lawyer to deal with that pesky little DUI in Cleveland last summer, trips to the fertility clinic to fix the partial sterility secondary to some history of abortion or VD, trips to the bank to pay for all that, trips to the liquor store to soften the edges of the trips to the bank, trips to the VD clinic to pick up the results of that little test that they said they "couldn't say over the phone, you better stop by," trips to the other lawyer to pay for the divorce, child custody and TROs to keep back Husband Numero Dos, checks to the carpenter to cover the holes that showed up in the walls in the scary light of hungover Saturday dawn, trips to the shrink to deal with that old abortion guilt that just won't go away (ask any liberal shrink, ka-ching!), trips to the florist to buy "something really nice" for your next-door-neighbor's daugheter's funeral, the one that OD'd last week just about eighteen months after that abortion in the next town over you're not supposed to know about. Pagan "freedom" is just so enslaving.

Catholic Nightclubbing, FYI, and damned expensive. She got me going to the bank, the only rap video I absolutely love, it says it all. Compulsive, selfish freedom's got you goin' to the bank every day and you can barely keep up. Christian partying has all the great stuff the pagans have without all the damned trips to the bank and here and there. True, Christian parties are a little different. We tend to hang out in parks on a Sunday afternoon, not skanky smoky bars or lasery raves. Instead of the smell of gangaweed wafting over the place, you're more likely to detect the smell of diapers and nicotine. Instead of your 11-year-old boy running into a wall imitating a scene from Jackass, he pulls off at the last moment, knowing already without your telling him that he can't tear the place up too much or he'll wake the baby. Instead of trading divorce lawyer business cards, women tend to affectionately re-tell all the shortcomings of their husbands, but within limits. Divorce is off the table. The husbands put up with all this. Divorcees, men and women, will never know about C.S. Lewis' idea of how couples break through to a higher level of companionship when they get past smaller disappointments, instead of just throwing in the towel when they encounter problems, which is the current a la mode. I could go on but back in Texas in the Spring of '78 the journey for me had entered a phase which took the form of a retrench of the lingering pagan side of me. Unlike the warm, Irish heart impulses of before, now, intellect seemed to be skipping lightly ahead in the theology department while a vaguely defined heart desire to retain selfish control, which all of us deal with all the time, was keeping the boat tied to the dock. You like my mixed metaphors?

But I remember stops on the way. A few years after I'd left Texas, I visited Scott Austin on-campus at his new job, teaching religion and philosophy at Boston College in Cambridge. It was late spring then, also, and we walked down the main pathway between the lecture halls.

"What's the latest?" I asked him. He knew I meant, about God.

"Grace. Grace is the phase I'm in now, Jim. Just nestling my head against big huge fluffy pillows of grace. I know it's probably all wrong (he admitted cheerfully) but I cant help it and I'm loving it. Grace, grace, tons of grace, all day long grace." We walked a little farther and after a while he said something like, did I have any comment about all this grace stuff. "Not really," I said. "Then I stand completely refuted by your silence."

It's not very often you get to win a debate with a professional egghead, and on the cheap, too. Actually, I'm also a big fan of grace, but what Scott didn't know that day in Cambridge was that in the intervening months I had run into a heart and mind called Keith Green who did have something to say about big fluffy "pillows of grace." Real grace included the grace to follow and obey in hardship. But wait. I'm getting ahead of the story.

I mentioned Scott and Cambridge because it perfectly illustrated Scott's suggestions to me back in the city of Austin when I had sought him out for advice in the casual-friendly foyer of the Newman Center. At that time in the Spring of '78 Scott was in a different phase, a eucharistic phase. He wanted me to come to Communion even though I was not yet officially a Christian. He had come to believe that the eucharist had an in se spiritual medicinal value and that I obviously, with my hesitations, needed strength added to my faith. Yes, I was attracted to Christianity even beyond the hope of regaining Cheryl, but I also was hanging back for what I now know are the usual reasons, all connected to the fear of letting go. Scott was probably the one who pointed out to me C.S. Lewis's observation that some people convert from their heart first, in an impulsive rush (think charismatics, say) and later in their walk could find themselves reading Aquinas. Others, no less loved by God, come in through the door almost reluctantly, but forced by the crushing ontological logic of an Augustine, or even Aristotle, and later in their walk they find themselves weeping uncontrollably over the let-go admonitions of a heart specialist such as Leo Buscaglia.

One other milestone in Texas that spring that I remember was a casual discussion that took place on a Saturday night at Deutcheshaus. There were a bunch of us in the tiny front parlor hanging out and now I think of it, it was probably the Rocky Horror Picture Show pre-party. Since the flick didn't show till midnight -- that's how they were able to keep it going so long: it didn't interfere with the regular flicks -- there was time to kill.

I couldn't make the Rocky Horror viewing since I had a date on back-up in a jazz bar downtown with my silver Civil War Boston Three Star cornet with the Harmon stuffed into it for a small club sound. But that wasn't 'till later. In the parlor we were all just kicking it, an unusual thing since students usually don't like to gather in largish groups outside of lecture halls. One-to-one, yeah, but not groups. They get enough of the sheep feel in lectures. I simply cannot remember how it arrived there but at one point the conversation took the form of a philosophical discussion about whatever. The topic of Christianity was broached. Not Jesus, mind you. Just religion.

At the time of this writing I would say, in a similar situation that anytime Christianity as a topic was broached it would only be with the intellectually and scintillating pagan buzz attached to it, thus: religion is the cause of all wars, and always has been, the current oh-so-clever extension of the old saw, how could a good God exist in an evil world? Both propositions, of course, unanswerable in the mind of the belligerents. Wow. Deep, huh? Whatever. Chesterton said any church will do to beat the Catholic Church with when really a pagan is not interested in the truth and all he wants to do is get back to his ganjaweed and his girlfriend and this tired, tired and obviously false but oh-so-chic au courante NPR meme is the most efficient way to do it, silencing all unquestioning enemies, provided some pesky Christian doesn't dare to raise his head. I could train decerebrate rats to bring more intellect into the public square in moments like this.

But back to Deutcheshaus. We don't want to miss a second of this fascinating debate (zzzzz), but even if it wasn't that exact line of baloney toss-off, it was another one like it that had raised its head in the wide-ranging conversation that day. Once that happened, even more deeply shallow truisms were tossed out and buffeted back and forth the way all college kids do. Anything to get Mom and Dad's religion out of their lives now that they were kicking up their heels away from home. This bantering went back and forth for quite a while but then there was a lull embedded in the smiling agreement and satisfaction with the empowerment to partying as the purpose of life that they had put forth, and the trashing of all obstacles. Nothing to see here. Move along. I was as surprised as anyone else to hear a timid but steady voice speaking into this lull: "There seems to be a possibility no one is considering, and I think intellectuals of any stripe should be open to all possibilities." Um…it was my voice. "What's that, Jim?" someone asked. "Well…isn't it possible that despite the numerous and abundant abuses and problems with it all, that in its inception Christianity could in fact be true? Jesus could be a historical figure, and all the historical sources could point to an effect that flowed from something a little more substantial than what you'd expect from a mere sage or wise teacher, or even a prophet. I mean, He could really be God, right?"

The liberal tea-sipping, kicking-their-heels-up crowd was stunned. I was more stunned than they were at the sound of my own voice. I was so, so, so, so, wrong, they didn't know where to start to straighten me out! One of them finally found his voice. It was loud, "Don't tell me you actually believe in all that Jesus shit!" In all my diffidence and cerebral calm and back and forth discussions with Scott and others, no one had ever put the question to me quiet so eloquently. "I do," I hear myself saying, and again, I was as surprised as they that I or anyone would have found anything wrong with the popular and oh-so-provable received knowledge of the day.

Thinking back on it now I recall a feeling at the time. I'm not sure how to describe it. It showed up in many instances later in my life, especially in rescue trial kangaroo courtrooms, especially the pretrial in limina hearings. One way to try to describe this feeling would be if you and I tried to "channel" fourth century Christians just before they got to the part about the lions and the coliseum. Back up just a smidge, to the "pinch of incense" part where they are asked to worship Caesar by offering a pinch of incense before his statue. If you throw the pinch of incense onto the fire, that's OK, and they let you go. If you refuse, it's African Safari time.

There's a moment where a timid soul quavers, eh? "Its just a little pinch. Go ahead. God won't care," says the little jinn on your left shoulder. But then the thought of betraying the One Who has been so faithful, Who died on the Cross for us, kicks in, and in a wonderful miracle known to repeat itself a million times since then, a spirit gently invades. Shoulders are squared. I can do this through Christ Who strengthens me, and the lions, bless their little pea-pickin' hearts, get a little snack. It also reminds me of the feeling when you're waiting for a wave in winter at Manhattan Beach or Huntington Beach, and you are in the series, and you see a good one coming, but you aren't quite sure. Go? Or stay? And something says, go for it.

The next day a microscopic ripple passed through the tiny ad hoc clique of Christians I had been talking to on campus.

"Is it true?" Scott asked, and others. "Yes," I told them, and I felt great, as if a burden had been lifted off my shoulders. The cynic can always say it was simply the desire to be able to tell Cheryl I was now a card-carrying member of the true faith that fueled the front parlor incident. But truth be known, at some point in all this sojourn, I started to be more interested in the card than in the girlfriend, much as I was still crazy about her. And this attraction to God, which had had such a quirky start in the kitchen in the beach house in Oregon, had actually been continuing apace. By the time of the Deutcheshaus front parlor incident, without really being aware of it, I had started to be more interested in God than Cheryl, even though God was essentially an invisible or non-present Personality and Cheryl was still the real deal. Cheryl was still in the mix, but it's just that subsequent events proved that the shift from one to the other was substantial. When a huge oil supertanker pulls away from a dock, there's a moment, a perceivable movement, where it's definitely undocked and free-floating, but definitely not under way, either. Or, it's like a transition compound in inorganic chemistry. I was that tanker, that transitional compound, there, in Austin.

After a couple of weeks of the detente I bumped into Cheryl on campus. "Is it true?" she asked, like everyone else had. "Yup," I told her, but any notion of mission accomplished was quickly scuttled by those piercing eyes fronting the piercing intellect. Plus, she just knew me. The gist of that conversation was that if it were really true, there would need to be an incoming ritual vis-s-vis the "Body of Christ" in Austin. I would be baptized, I would make a public profession of faith in a church, and I would be formally received into the fold. All of which is true, of course, but up until then I had had no interaction with a church as such, even if I did read Schaeffer and Chesterton and even a little George MacDonald. Scott, as an example, was a brilliant intellectual but he was hardly a card-carrying church member anywhere I was aware of, and as part of his own journey he'd try on doctrinal subjects as you and I'd try on a suit coat. Not exactly church material, Scott was, even as he deftly scored points on subtle things like the ex opera operation healing effect of the Real Presence, or grace, etc.

So. German-Irish-Cherokee Marines are determined, though, and after a pause to dress my wounds, so to speak, I kept up inquiries, even if it occasionally meant more non-church stuff. One night this took the form of a public lecture on-campus. I can't remember if I was invited or if I'd seen a notice on a billboard. I suspect it was an invitation because I did not recognize the name of the speaker at all. Plus, the feel once I got there was quite strange. I hadn't darkened the door of any church since our family moved away from my beloved Trinity Lutheran in San Gabriel ten years earlier. To attend a lecture by a Christian was the closest I'd gotten in all that time. I sat in the back, a little embarrassed. Endless discussion with independent spirits like Scot and others was one thing, but this was different. This was a public assembly. Would lightning strike me dead as I was reaching inside the badger skin tent? Me, the infidel disgracing the holy places?

I can't remember a word of it, but after the lecture I found myself in the gaggle of lingerers at the podium that always accompanies such events. The speaker was a man with a British accent and obvious kindness and humility despite brains enough for a dozen Grays. He dealt with each questioner one at a time with complete absorption even though it was late and he was Heathrow jet-lagged. I don't have the slightest memory of what I asked, but I remember the sensation. I had doubts in my mind about God and even His existence and I had a strong intuition that this man would set me straight or send me packing, one way or the other.

Now, when I see other inquirers do the same thing on just about any topic, not just a sojourn of faith, I recognize this feeling perfectly. I also grieve for those people so much. Yes, all of us, even after the fortunate ones are called to Christ, can experience some species of legitimate doubt. Yes, there are the real and deep pains of perpetual growth, the ongoing conversion process and everyday sanctification. But for the pagan the doubts can rise to the point where there is a crushing loss of peace, of confidence. If I am a Christian, even if I die today, I do not doubt the hope I have, even if the hope itself is an inexact quantum or species. I didn't even have that, before, and so the doubt could rise so high I would risk the embarrassment of queuing up in a public place to talk to a speaker, an obvious petitioner, cap-in-hand.

I needn't have worried. When I got to the podium the speaker gave a quick answer to me and a quick glance at his watch and then he asked me if I would like to come to the place he was staying to talk more. Cynics will say the only motivator here was that the poor man could hardly keep standing, but I beg my dearly beloved pagan readers to please follow the idea carefully: This is how it works. You can keep chanting your "coincidence, coincidence" mantra till the day you die but a wise pastor once told me that coincidences happen when we pray. "But coincidences don't happen when we don't pray" she intoned, with much metal, at my casual response. I've never forgotten this advice. Plus, there's always Pascal's Wager, don't forget that! Ooooops! I'm getting ahead of the story again. The people who were hosting the visiting speaker had a very nice house just off-Cray's. IVCF types, if I had to guess, they very kindly and quietly retreated while the speaker and I continued our conversation in the front room. At one point I think I alluded to a fine point I'd garnered from one of the C.S. Lewis books I'd been reading. "Well, you're right, in a sense, of course, but that's not really what Jack meant there." "Oh?" He glanced at me. "Well, we talked about that exact point. Several times. On a country pub crawl time-to-time, you know?" It turns out I was talking with a fellow faculty member of Lewis's from the Oxford years, and a good friend of his of many years.

Pagans, dear hearts, let's review the bidding: the against-the-reefer incident in Santa Cruz; leaning on the kitchen counter at the Oregon beach house; traipsing off to Texas, brokenhearted; the quirky thing in the Deutcheshaus parlor, a "coincidence" if ever there was one, considering my Darwinist roots and professional entanglements; persisting even after I got shot down by Cheryl; why go to this lecture at all? why did the speaker feel like talking to me at length, when he was already exhausted? why did I hang around after the lecture and even ask him anything?

Without each and every one of these happy coincidental serendipities, I would never have met C.S. Lewis's extremely nice and intelligent drinking buddy, Dr. James Houston. We talked until two or three a.m., poor guy! He told me in no uncertain terms that he was convinced that I already had what Aquinas types would call sufficient salvific knowledge as of that moment and he repeatedly asked me to "pray with him." You know what that means! but I refused. Gun-shy from the other thing, I wouldn't be surprised. But I recall one thing he said to me despite all my fears and doubts, including the ongoing fear that I'd apostatize after conversion. "Job," he said. "Yes?" "Lord, though Thou slay me, yet will I follow Thee." It took a few years to grasp the full import of this but it's a Marine's verse, all day long. When the landing craft front hatch drops in the assault on the heavily protected pacific island, defiladed with tons of machine guns -- Move. Don't stand there. Even if you know you are going to die. My much beloved pagan readers, try to pry yourselves away from the raves and computers and TVs and endless smart phone thumbing, even if only for a few hours a day or week, and sit. You could get the truth, as I did with this dear old guy with the funny accent, and still miss it if you aren't quiet.

If you sit still long enough, life will come to you. You don't need to chase after it with the next story on the fake news, or some electronic drug. If you sit quietly enough, I promise to you most solemnly that the center of the universe will slowly stand up from where it is seated, and slide and shift and creep until it is right where you are. You will lack for absolutely not one thing. You don't need to go anywhere. You don't need to say anything. You will not need to do anything. Sit long enough with the weak idea of rejecting the evil one and being open to the Good God as you understand Him, and you will get it all. Everything.

 I was just about to leave Texas and wing my way to Switzerland where I wound up that summer, the summer of 1978, but I just remembered something. Something embarrassing! Remember when I talked about the hypocrisy accusation I expect from my enemies, God bless 'em, when I told you about my live-in girlfriend of four years, in school. Well, uh, wait till you hear this one: Bless me, Father, I have sinned. Your last confession? Uh, actually, Father, it's the Wayback Machine this time…Sorry. [inward groan from priest, long sigh.] 1978: Austin, Texas. I was a tech., there. [Priest peeks out "windshield" to see how long the line is. Settles brow on fist. Shoulders sag. Fleeting temptation to wonder where he'd be now if he hadn't given up that golf pro finals spot.] I'm not sure how to say this, so I just have to say it and get it over with: I was in Austin from the fall of '77 to the summer of '78. That spring was very rough. God was knocking on the door pretty loud but a very practical section of my male brain (admit it, guys) was starting to get the message on all six cylinders: it's over. But I still hoped, and I was obviously in denial, I was carrying the torch. Converting to Christianity couldn't quite happen fast enough, as the false start in the parlor at Deutsche Haus would testify. I was a transitional compound, not quite fish or fowl. Ol' Nick is an expert at exploiting moments like this, especially if he sees signs he could be on the delicate edge of Losing Another One, and I fell off the wagon further from happy Christine morals than having a live-in girlfriend in school. This fall took the form in Texas of a microscopically small but intense round of night-clubbing.

 There. You happy? "Nightclubbing?" "Uhhh, women, Father." "[sigh] a half dozen, you say?" "Less. Or so," Priest glances at his watch and makes a rapid calculation: He could get the veal parmesan in the rectory and still catch the same tee-time. Martinis at the club after that. Straightens up in seat, clears throat. "Mystery a night, make it, um, maybe a round half-dozen." "After all. Padre. Sorry." Counting on fingers, "make it a sorrowful." Stares straight ahead. "Say your Act of Contrition, now." Insert Latin here: old absolution formula. Priest lifts eyes to horizon manfully, the glowing tones of the cardinal virtues of Hope and Fortitude shining from his features.

I only drag you through this so I can tell what came after: One night for whatever reason, but certainly including despair about Chreryl, and conflict between the half-dozen, and God, and what Schaeffer and Lewis had been teaching me -- actually, I have no clue where this came from -- I suddenly dropped to my knees by the side of rny garret bed and clenched my hands together like that painting of George Washington at Valley Forge in the snow. Where the hell did this schoolboy at prayer vibe come from? 1 have no idea. I tend to be a strolling Buddhist monk prayer when it comes to body posture, I found out later, but back there in Austin, that was it, the George Washington thing. Protestant, you could say. I was disgusted with it all and I angrily begged God to just take it away, whatever "it" was. I was sick of it all. I needed peace.

1 didn't realize it at the time, especially with all my selfish motives, but I had just accepted Pascal's. The chips were on the number and the wheel was already spinning and the line was closed. The pack was already past the first turn and the ticket was in my hands. The last kiss goodbye was over and the doors of the surgery had swung closed. The trunk was hot as a pistol and the blue lights were already pinging off the headliner of my car. The smoke was billowing up and you could hear sirens already. Your ears are ringing and you still got a helluva lot of work to do. Is this reaching out to the invisible irrational? Obviously not. It's a well-defined belief that not all things can be stuffed into a finite human head, or programmed into a computer for that matter, which program we call reason, by itself.

The first thing someone does when he stops going to church is that he starts listening to Coast-to-Coast about channeling dead pets, ghosts, and Area 51, and the next thing you know he's hanging out with the charisrnaniacs. The totality of truth is partially visible, even if reductionists deny it. Even the Modern reductionistic science that got us this far, got there by being open to the invisible, even if the invisible in centuries past was something like electromagnetisrn, or radiation, or gravimetric attraction. An open-minded scientist is open minded to the invisibles of the human heart, which is attached to the mind of every reductionist scientist.

If I stop to let the feeling of a wonderful sunset or a sundog soak into my heart, and I raise my eyes to the possibility of something unseen, I expect to sense something unseen. Something invisible even to an electron microscope. Something undetectable by a radiation counter. If I wanted to see another human and nothing else, I wouldn't be looking for something transcendent, I would just go to the local coffee shop or knock on my neighbor's door. But if I do not lift my eyes to Beauty, beauty of any kind, there's no cause to complain about the dreariness or pettiness of humans doing each other in. When I look to watch the door of a Tramalqavorian spaceship open, I know what will step out is not a human

On my knees, there in Texas, like some schoolboy saying his prayers at night, I was just a few horses away from grabbing the brass ring on the carousel. But instead of pulling the ring to myself, I hung on and the ring pulled me into another universe, like the back wall of the Ward Robe in Narnia. And not just one universe, cascading tiers of numbers of universes stretching off into infinity, bigger than you or I can think of, even in science fiction. I thought i'd get a brass ring but the brass ring got me. He heals you where you are, keeping you as the unique creature that other gods would sweep aside like a child angry with a broken toy. The God I ran into was the only One Who fixes things instead of condemning them. And it's perfectly confusing because He is the only god Who is disguised as a man, and not some big shot either, but a simple carpenter with sawdust in His hair and scars on his hands.

I heard an interview with a Dr. Aaronreit about this interesting book. She describes childhood mystical experiences she had even though she is an atheist and a reductionist scientist. But she believes she was contacted by the invisible world, in a neutral way. She thinks it's possible there are beings in an invisible world, but not necessarily friendly, as Christians might say. Asked if it was unknowable if this world existed, she said it was knowable, an important distinction for a scientist to make. At one point all her atheist friends said she must be nuts, and her reductionism pointed to that, but in the end she said, "I chose sanity," meaning that there could be an alternate explanation for her experiences. She was also a solipsist when younger but not so when she was older. When her atheist friends read her book, she was afraid of a backlash, but many of them called to tell her of similar experiences. It's amazing to me that the experiences she had happened about the same time as mine; schoolyard experience, even though we were of different ages. Also, her experiences took place barely a hundred miles away from my schoolyard. She says she hates the word belief in connection with experiencing the invisible, but I wonder if for all we know Christians mean simple knowledge when they use the word belief to describe something invisible that they experienced. The Christians are afraid of backlash, and it gave them a little buffer, perhaps. Also, that Christians are knowing about something only just outside the range of acceptable experiences about the unseen world. This range is artificially established by modernist scientists. Also, that the modern scientist would believe, as Clint Eastwood recently said, if only someone would bring him proof. But Jesus came, plenty of proof there! And we accept his historicity, just not His divinity, which has aspects of invisibility to it.

I was pleasantly surprised to hear about Martin Buber's "Other" coming from a totally different direction. Yes, Aaronreit denies that she thinks she has contact with a deity. Yes, her anthropology is more inclined to think there are somethings like aliens or angels, who don't mean us harm or good, since we are not that important, but the main thing is that she is acknowledging an Other, of whatever dimension, an other that comes to us out of what we think are invisible regions, just like Germ theory, radiation, gravity and electromagnetism came to us out of invisible regions and then took their places in even the reductionists' world view of acceptable evidences. Perhaps the world will always be divided between those who accept invisible but very real heart indications as part of their universe, and those who don't, but maybe not forever. Aaronreit describes her atheist friends with similar experiences. I wonder if God isn't so generous that He comes to everyone at one point or another. He knocks at the door. Will we open? What a shame if we don't open the door simply because our reductionist world view won't take into account this or that invisibility. Then we run off, slumming, listening to coast to coast or hanging with Coast-to-Coast to fill that other need, and if so, great! As Schaeffer said, for all we know it is a step in the right direction of truth, even if is not replete. Life is a journey.

The UCSC program administered two off-campus areas: one in Daufusky Island, South Carolina, and one in North Richmond, Ca. At the time anyone who was picked for North Richmond was very disappointed, since the sea islands seemed so much cooler and a bigger switch from California. But looking back I don't regret a thing about going just up the road, barely ten miles from where I went to high school in Marin. What a difference that simple crossing of the San Rafael-Richmond Bay Bridge was, I would soon find out. To this day I've never seen downtown Richmond. I spent all my time in North Richmond, tucked as it is in between the town and the massive Chevron refinery, dock and train yard. You hear the trains switching and huffing and puffing all night long in North Richmond, but it's soothing after a while, even the long concatenated bumps of all the cars when the mule trains hit them to join them up. Boats, ships, planes and trains can be relaxing that way.

As I hopped off the bus, North Richmond looked like something I might identify with: tiny, neat houses on straight streets with perfect lawns, everything flat just like the humbler parts of San Fernando Valley or a post World War II San Gabriel or Glendale, my Swiss grandmother's neighborhood. The lilting feeling of this could work, I can do this vaporized the instant the police rolled up on me as I was walking from the bus station to the home of my hostess where I would be staying while I was there. No policeman had ever turned his gaze upon me, or spoken one word to me, in my entire life before that day, unless it was at church or a political fundraiser, and he was out of uniform and being polite to my folks. This was the year I turned twenty-one.

"Where ya headed, pal?" There were two in the cruiser, one black, one white. It turned out they didn't know anything about the UCSC program and they were completely flummoxed why a white boy from Marin would be on their turf, unless it was to buy drugs. This last part I figured out later because they managed to get through their interrogation of me without mentioning it specifically. This must be some new line of bullshit the dealers tell 'em to say ran through their minds a hundred times before they reluctantly let me go, fearful to the last that they were being had. When I produced the name and address of my hostess, they slowed down just a little bit. They didn't even believe it when I walked through the front door and she waved, though she was known as a churchgoing widow with a son who stayed out of trouble. Strange, but of all the crimes they suspected, they had zero concern that a stranger would do harm to an elderly taxpayer on their watch.

Mattie Shields is a dear dear lady who lived with her adult son in a tiny painfully neat house whose backyard bordered on the train yard. I connect all the things I saw in Richmond schools with the sound and feel of the trains switching and building all night long, especially the bang of the engine against a long line of tankers and the answering but diminishing bangs as all the cars down the string banged back. Then, the slow acceleration of four ganged diesels to make the windows rattle, but a nice low sound that rattled pleasantly in your chest like when I'd advance the throttles on the twin Cummings' engines on the landing craft on Angel Island when I worked there. Our own little San Francisco Bay rolling diesel thunder, right there, Richmond was, on dry land. It's a beautiful sound. For all the evils and blood connected with oil, it's still the sound and smell of commerce, wealth, power. Before I could get to the Tutoring Center or be a teacher's aide in the local elementary school, which were my official posts, I had to get through the unofficial one of being "dumb suburban white guy gets a taste of ghetto life,"

Sunday. What's the big deal about Sunday? Sleep in, eat too much, fall asleep watching a ball game? No. Not in Mattie Shields' house. Anyone living in her house would be in church on Sunday morning, best clothes, bright eyed and cleaned up. I doubt the sending program back down at UCSC knew about this little bit of political incorrectness. Come to think of it, I doubt Mrs. Shields would have insisted if I didn't want to go. But I went. When in Rome, plus, I hadn't been seen in church regularly since I was fourteen back at San Gabriel Trinity Lutheran. A little church wouldn't kill me. Right? Oh, sinners, take heed. Beware the Point of No Return. There Be Dragons Here. I couldn't have been more wrong about my devaluation of the dangers of hanging out in church with Mattie Shields' homeys. That Sunday I most nearly died. I suppose if you have to die, church is a good place for it, still. If I had to guess, I'd say it was an AME Zion church. But it doesn't matter. It might as well have had a huge sign over the front door, "We eat skinny white suburban boys for breakfast." Ayup. One hundred percent of what polltakers call African Americans. And there were no light skinned folks in here. Nothing but the real deal. 1865. Ford Theatre. Not a day later.

Bear in mind that my entrance into the cosmopolitan Roman Catholic Church was still ten years in the future and the Lutherans were not known for a big African presence in their Nordic churches, more's the pity. OK, so, a black church. Fine. I would just do what any geeks do in a stressful public situation: hide. The church was built in such a way that there were half a dozen eight inch steel columns in it. I found one in the back and sat behind it. The column was painted white. I am white. Get it? Camouflage. Oh, gentle suburban student out a-wandering in ghetto sensibility programs, beware! Beware the Deacons, the ushers who lurk and prowl and watch the back of churches ferreting out slackers. The usher who was the cause of my misery waited and waited and waited. He saw the skinny white boy slinking behind the pillar. He saw Mrs. Shields up front hanging with her buds. He waited until the music started and the swaying started. Hmmm, a little Oscar Peterson stride thing, going on there? Nice. A little Phoebe Snow lilt to the singing? This might not be so bad after all. Just when the choir director got everybody up and swaying and clapping, the deacon pounced, a swooping falcon demolishing the helpless victim. I didn't have a chance.

"Come on up to the front," he grabbed my elbow." You can hear better up there. You're welcome up front with the rest of us. Come on." Doomed. I was doomed. It was bad enough that the Lord was thoroughly capable of finding the back row for an accurate lightning strike to punish the slacker who hadn't darkened the door of a church in seven years, but the thought of the humiliation of my charred, smoking carcass being perched up front for everyone to see? Doom and shame, both together. A kind of divine Two-fer. The closer I got the more the music pounded. The usher wouldn't let go until he'd shepherded this lost soul into the safe pastures of a seat not only up front, but the only seat in the church that was absolutely in the front row and in the center, directly under the pulpit. Hellfire and brimstone have no chance at all to diminish when they are distributed from up there and you are the target. You get the full whack all in one go, no chance to run. No missing from that distance, either.

I was a geek. I was shy. My usual companions were a microscope or a sep. funnel or a computer or a book. This was bad. Very bad. I was desperate. It was enough to make you get religion, just in self-defense. "A Ha! My mistake! I'm born again, brothers and sisters!" accompanied by rolling around on the ground, were the words that never seemed to find their way to speech. Once I surrendered in helplessness to my fate, everything about that service was a blur, with me trying and failing to look like a misplaced fire hydrant. Nice Lutheran boys don't do shouting in church. We rarely do it anywhere else, for that matter. The infinitely powerful God we believe in is thoroughly capable of hearing sermons and prayers and responses from the congregation spoken in a normal civilized tone of voice.

Not so in the African Episcopal Methodist Zionist church, oh no. God obviously needs to be woken up! Hear it again! Hear it shouted back and forth from the brothers and sisters! In fact, with the AME's, it's clearly a Horton Hears A Who scenario: God cannot hear until all are on their feet, screaming. OK, the terrified white boy possessed by the mortal sin of originating from the evil suburbs thought to himself: Can you get slain in the spirit? standing a little too close to the action? I mean, what if you don't really want to? Nothing personal, but this wasn't covered in Luther's Small Catechism, you know? The fight-or-flight response had already been drowned in waves of adrenaline. Maybe I'll survive and just kind of slink out of there when they're done shouting, I began to hope. Maybe this church service will come to an end before Jesus returns again, despite the obvious wishes of these nice people that they just hang around until He does. If he did come back again, I hoped he would do it before I got slain. Or zapped. Or died of old age. Or gone deaf.

It was a foolish hope. AME preaching has a shout-and-response rhythm to it and this builds to a fever pitch the emotional high point of the service, the day, and the week. I must confess. Bless me Father, I'm a Lutheran. In all the denial and survival of that experience and mind-shifting myself to serene Himalayan slopes and valleys with quiet monks chanting away in them, I can't remember a single word of that sermon. Until IT happened. There I was, hapless, beyond all hope, hoping it would be quick, whatever it was, whatever form the end of my life came in, hoping God and or His chosen ones had perhaps made a little clerical error and missed the fact that such a reprobate would get so close to the Holy Ark of the covenant when I heard a voice thundering from On High, high above the band amplifiers, high above 300 people screaming:

"And I tell you brothers and sisters, God made both BLACK AND WHITE!" I shrunk down into my seat, the church erupted in the loudest shouting and screaming and banjo strumming I'd ever heard in my entire life. I peeked up at the pulpit to see what the fuss was about and there the preacher was reaching over the front of the pulpit, pointing at me, his pointing arm stretched out over the front of the pulpit, no more than two feet from my cowering head just in case there might be one person in the place who did not know the exact location of the specific white person under discussion. He was pointing at me. Little old me, the butterfly-chasing geeky science major from the hippie school in the hobbit forest who really had no problem at all with black people, thank you very much, thought they were just fine folks, but…can't we just all get along together? Pretty please? Not quite so much noise? Scientists, find another way to get those sociology credits. Get a starry-eyed adoring look on your face when someone tells you Joyce loved his cat a little too much. If you do ever walk past an AME Zion Church on your way to pick up a Nobel Prize or something, be sure to handcuff yourself to the radiator in back in case you get dragooned in the door, and tell the usher it's a condition of your parole on a charge he doesn't want to hear about.

You know what, though? Looking back on the day I finally became born-again (not the same as Lutheran as a kid, exactly) and Switzerland was a mere three years away. Maybe a little something rubbed off in that little church, despite my protest. Hmmm. I mean, maybe we can just all get along together, in the Lord's economy. But don't tell me that, in 1975, in North Richmond AME Zion. Get me out of here and get me a drink. And I don't even drink. Mattie and her homeys? After they knew how it all came out in Switzerland a few years later they would say it took a Keeping It Real church in the hood to slap the devil outta this white boy. They'd be right, too. Probably got a gold circle drawn around that scorch mark in the carpet. Wanna join us for worship, young man? If I ever go back, I'd offer to testify, and tell the story in great detail. I bet we'd all have a big laugh in the Lord. Who loves us and works in mysterious ways.

North Richmond elementary school fifth grade class was under the tutelage, no, refereeing, of a short, white, dark-haired teacher of long experience, Miss Jones. Miss Jones had two speeds to her transmission: the soft Quiet Voice of NPR Reason and the screaming Don't Mess with Me. Five miles an hour golf cart, and whining redlining in fourth in a Formula One. The principal of the school, even shorter, blacker than Duke Ellington's "Indigo Blues," very athletic, never went anywhere in the school for one second without a three-foot ruler in his right hand. Let me make a tiny carpenterial point here. If you went to a lumberyard in the old days you could get a soft pine yard ruler for free, an inch wide and barely an eighth of an inch thick. You could break it absentmindedly slapping it against your leg or stepping on it. The principal, by contrast, had a yardstick. It was every bit of five sixteenths thick by three inches wide. Bolt six of them together and you've got two supports for the roof of your front porch. Also, there are hardwoods and there are hardwoods. This was California orange stick. When the principal slapped it against his leg when he was talking to a troublemaker, his leg gave, not the stick. He'd shake a little, and so would the kid.

His eyes were humorless, intense, and completely in control. He was twitchy, too. And fast. Not even a twitchy fifth grader with enough testosterone in his veins to float an aircraft carrier, wing fleet, could out-twitch him. If the kid flinched, the principal would meet him halfway before he got there. We're talking faster than Quick Draw McGraw. Faster than thought. Faster than quarks in a hurry. To get somewhere and do what they do. Whatever that is. I sat in the back of the class as I'd wanted to in church. The suburban white boy may have attracted some attention at first, but when the students saw that I was quiet, they ignored me. Occasionally in between tirades the teacher would ask me to "help" the students while they were "studying." The cycle time from soft-spoken NPR announcer intelligent kindness to the next and only other stop was just about seven or eight minutes. Not quite time enough to solve an algebra problem or figure out a mnemonic for some state capitals, but you could try. One day the teacher decided I should "tutor" the half dozen loudest boys so the rest of the class could get something done. As near as you could tell from the absence of fathers in these boys' lives, they had never done a single thing wrong. To do something wrong you absolutely have to have someone in your life who is capable of identifying this problem and then communicating this to you in no uncertain terms. In my own case this never required violence, shouts or threats. Marine officers, hell, the enlisted men, too, carry a presence all their own and at an early age I clearly understood the hierarchy, and cast-iron principles such as You Don't Talk To Your Mother Like That.

There was no Marine in the lives of these boys. They sat in the back of the class and talked constantly in a normal tone of voice, not whispering even, unafraid, unashamed. Many of the topics they talked about would make a sailor blush. Or retch. A sailor with five tours of duty near Bangkok, Tokyo and Saigon. It came out of their mouths effortlessly, without stint, a constant stream, like water in a mountain freshet in early spring. They teased the girls, who didn't quite know how to damper it. The girls never had a mother to tell them that this is not how you talk to a girl. That it is unacceptable.

The teacher decided I should "tutor" the trouble boys out of the room. This would enable the rest of the class to learn something for a little while. She opened a spare classroom for me and the half-dozen troublemakers. In the time it took for me to turn toward the teacher, say goodbye and close the door, the troublemakers, all of them, had scrambled to the top of a row of closets and cupboards along the back of the empty classroom. Looking back I gather this is something they had always dreamed about doing if they ever had a chance to get the run of a room without a teacher in it. By their logic, the skinny white boy from the suburbs was obviously not a teacher. I didn't scream and I didn't have a big stick like the principal's. Eventually they came down and started playing the board games they had found up there but not before I had a heart attack imagining what it would be like trying to explain to some school board how a helpless innocent underprivileged minority ten-year-old kid got paralyzed from the neck down after 3.7 seconds under my supervision. Pay It Forward, Goodbye Mr. Chips or To Sir With Love this was not. More like World Wide Wrestlemania. Without even the fake referee.

Any teacher who even tries to be a dad to kids without dads should get a medal. And liability insurance. And a big stick, I guess, like the principal. Oh, and the black skin. Don't forget that. Believe it or not being assistant teacher in the public grade school was not my main gig in North Richmond. That spot was at the North Richmond Tutoring Center, a charity installed in a one family house which had been remodeled a little for teaching. They had bake sales and church drives and maybe grants to keep it going. The tutoring center was everything the public school was not in terms of loving control of the kids. This was because when you first walked in the building you entered a large central room, the old living room of the house, and in that room was a state population at all times of half-a-dozen large, dark, matronly females Who Tolerated Absolutely No Bullshit.

Any antsy twitchy anger management dropout fifth grader with an attitude against authority was made to understand at an autonomic nervous system level that it was a privilege to come to the Center, and that they were there for one purpose only and that was to learn, and if they didn't do that, and behave in the process, they would be kicked out and not only that, their mothers and schoolteachers, and for all I know, their parole officers, would receive a nasty report. Even a "trouble" kid, for whom any learning had become pain, might reconsider tutoring if only as an escape from the conventional classroom. All the time I was there I never never ever heard even so much as an impolite word uttered by a student to me or anyone else. Ever. In fairness to the public schools, everything in the Center was one-on-one, but even so, the backbone of the British public system (meaning private) and all of Oxford and Cambridge should not be tossed out lightly as it has been in the States. (The closest thing to it here is something like B B, and they don't teach.) But the wonderful and beautiful strength of the Center even went beyond these No Nonsense angels in the lobby. Even outside of the daily operation of the Center there was a support structure that any NGO would weep over the beauty of, and I have some experience in this matter.

There always seemed to be a potluck lunch, a bake sale, a covered dish dinner, a field trip, a zoo outing or something going on and the feeling of all these things was not merely to push the center mission or raise money. At these functions something else came out, something I hadn't seen in a while. The Center supporters, donors and staff not only loved the Center, but they loved hanging out with each other. It's almost as if their love for each other, solidarity under stress and easy of companionship preceded the building of the Center. As if they were all good buds to begin with notwithstanding God knows how many horrific divorces, abandonments with children, domestic miseries, poverty, etc., and then said, hey, let's make a tutoring center. And not as a cushy boondoggle either. That center did its job and worked hard all day long on chiefly volunteer labor. I simply cannot imagine any "ghetto" in the world, and I include the worst: Nairobi and Manila, and most especially Kolkata and Lima, that would not receive huge blessings from a place like this one. But it started with a benign sisterhood; and I certainly felt welcome as a big bad man.

Come to think of it, the last time I recall seeing white folks enjoying each other as much as the Center staff did would have been big rescues out East. But before then it would have been at the parties in the late 50's and early 60's in South Pasadena where they blocked off the street. Or the fairs at the elementary school, the kind where you try to throw a ping pong ball into a little goldfish bowl. Or some scouting function or a company picnic in the park by the LA River near Arroyo Seco Park in S. Pas. Massively extended pool parties, beach parties, surfing parties, scouts award dinners, scout jamborees and Order of the Arrow campouts, or Friday night football at the South Pas High School, where the only electronics to be seen was a PA system older than Marconi for the play-by-play, which blew a tube half the time anyway. All of these times had that feeling. Since then even the tiny remnants of white folks' socialness is haunted by quick hellos, a nibble and quick goodbyes, or so much drinking it amounts to the same thing. Somewhere, something else more important is going on, and it involves a Facebook, a flat TV, an MP3 player or some other e-presence of total strangers.

# RALPH M. GABRIEL

Since the 50's the only remnant of a Center-like solidarity I saw, outside of prolife stuff and rare Old Mass gatherings was the love my sister Marty had for her pals and her pals for her in Santa Barbara, especially in the 20 years she survived her cancer, and every day struggled to provide for herself and Breezy with a day job she hated and her ongoing cancer pain and fatigue. Marty had a deep sisterhood, there. Other than that, white folk may have money, and even jobs, but they never had the love of that Center community. Teaching in that structured tough love environment was the second greatest joy of my life, terminal care at the hospital being the other. Well, and big rescues, in the clink. That part. Helluva party, that.

OK, there's the False Start in the Deutscheshaus front parlor in the winter of 77-78. Then there was the desperate unbelievably impulsive and unexpected disgust with sin in the garret upstairs and the amazing late-night conversation with Dr. Houston, C.S. Lewis's drinking buddy. All of this pointed to Switzerland. As in the "ashram" Cheryl had gone to, to find an answer or resolution. But I have to ask, why? Any dope could see that Cheryl and I were over. And if a brilliant interlocutor like Scott Austin were to get his PhD and leave town that summer, there were more like him where he came from, one could hope, in that university environment. I could've hung out in Austin, gone to med. school in Galveston like Dr. Folkers wanted me to, gone back to California, or gone anywhere in the world to pursue studies in Christianity, so why Switzerland? Reader, I've asked so much of you. But if you ever do run into the Living God, and I hope you do, ask Him, will ya? And let me know, OK?

After the standby flight from Houston I made a side trip to a Welsh fisheries station near Bangor and then it was off to a route that became a familiar one later on, hitchhiking east off the French/Belgian debark of the Dover boat. But something happened in London on the way to Dover that I remember distinctly. As you know, people drive on the "wrong" side of the road in England. When they'll catch up to shining, progressive Africa I have no idea, but until then you have to look carefully before you cross a street in the UK. They even have huge signs painted on the tarmac to warn us dumb visiting yanks who keep looking the wrong way. No matter how many times I knew this, the childhood reflex of many years to look in the American direction was a strong habit, and I did, one day, anxious to cross a London street to get to, probably Victorian station for the Dover train, or to find some travel agent.

wham! The nasty bare steel flat bed of a deuce-and-a-half truck fully loaded came barreling past my left cheekbone as my head was stuck out into the street, looking to the right. I don't think it was six inches, and it surprised both the driver and me. I had stuck my head out so suddenly and with such a strong reflex. He didn't even have time to honk or swerve, poor guy. Probably needed an extra bitter, that night. The whoosh alone of the truck pushed me back, and I was deeply shattered as they say. One-minute standing on the street in a strange land and the next, a truly near-miss. The truck was a click away before I recovered myself to even think about trying to get across that street, but once on the train a funny feeling came over me: death, the idea of it, was no stranger to me, at age 23. My own dear Irish Cherokee gramma, my own dear sister Mary and dear brother-in-law Rick had all died in close succession just a few years earlier. Mortality was a strong meme in me by the time I got to the London sidewalk. But a few more clicks and clacks down the rail to Dover, and it occurred to me: 1 wasn't afraid of death alone, back on that sidewalk in Westminster, the near miss. I had a new fear. I was afraid of hell. Whatever had gone on in my head about Cheryl, God , dead white European intellectuals, nightclubbing or the loathing of it, the false starts, the lingering memories of Pastor Mees and other sincere Christians and the so-so-imminent fear of harness. Somewhere in all that mix I had just discovered by "accident" that I now had a healthy belief in hell, and that I could go there. No-fooling, fire and brimstorm, irritating Deep-South TV Evangelist Big-Hair, sho-nuff paid-to-be-there H-E. Double Hockey Sticks. The Big One. Hell. Burning. Devils, pitchforks, scary as, no fooling, Ol' Nick's gotcha-by-the-neck hell.

For all the doubts I'd had about yes or no, to go to Switzerland, by the time the train hit the beach I was actually quite glad I was headed east to Europe instead of west back to California. A British soldier returning from leave with his family was good for as far as Essen in northern Germany but that still left the drop south through Bavaria and the Munich area to Switzerland. By a miracle I got picked up by some eccentric genius who missed the boat to Silicon Valley. He was inventing or re-inventing the digital pixel, there, in Bavaria. What a rip. That got me to Geneva. Within Switzerland, hitchhiking is like looking for bluegreen algae in a black hole in deep space. You stand a better chance of finding an intact atom at the cyclotron at CERN. That left the train. The train rolled along the north shore of Lake Geneva, past Challot's "Lady of the Lake" castle and those marvelous US spinoff side-wheel paddleboat steamers. The milk-run wheezed to a halt in Aigle, where the east end of the lake meets the southern end of the Rhone valley and river. Turning left and heading north up the valley, the Matterhorn is thirty clicks up, on your right. But 15 clicks up, from Aigle, on your left, is a ski spot up the mountainside known to Europeans -- Huemoz-sur-Ollon.

Immediately south of Villars on the same winding alpine road, windier and alpinier than a fire trail in the Grand Tetons, was the microscopic village of Huemoz-sur-Ollon. The taxi left me at the center of the village, a place so small it couldn't have had more than a few dozen houses, and many of them were smaller than chalets. It was so small it couldn't even afford its own boulangerie, a bakery, and in French-speaking Europe, that's small. I still remember the first thing that happened when the taxi drove away. It was an event of momentous significance to an American: silence. Perfect, total, ear-stuffing silence. After five thousand miles of jet engines, ferry boat whistles and clinkety-clank trains and chatty hitchhike hosts, it was a deafening silence. After a while I noticed a tiny sound, always refreshing, of trickling water. There was a public spring that emptied into a stone pony tray on the side of the only intersection in the town, an intersection smaller than an American suburban driveway. After an even further lull -- I was frozen by the pleasant anodyne joy of the silence, and relief at finding the place -- I heard another small sound that I did not recognize and only learned later what it was. It was the random tinkle-bong-bonging sound, the casual symphony of a cow herd slowly making its way across a meadow. Each cow had her own bell tied around her neck but the size of the bell varied with the size of the cow, ranging from a shot glass size for a veal on up to teapot size bells for bigger cows. The cows simply must have been well-paid members of a union. I've never heard anything more wonderful in all the width and breadth of the American Federation of Musicians.

L'Abri ministry in Huemoz, Switzerland, Vaca Canton, was started in the early 1950's by Francis and Edith Schaeffer, Francis being at that time an unknown American Presbyterian minister from Detroit. The young Francis heard a call from God to go to Switzerland and preach to and evangelize a country that had first heard the Gospel all of 14 centuries earlier. Novice students at the L'Abri community listened to "The Romans Tapes" on creaky old cassette playsrs in the basement of the chapel, there, perched on the hillside in Huemoz, with the gorgeous Sound of Music Rhone valley displayed below, and across the valley, the Alps. The Matterhorn was just to the left as you looked out into the valley, to the north, in the range of Alps there. To this day I don't understand why these tapes were never edited and published: if these wonderful tapes were merely excellent theology, a real help to any new or inquiring Christian especially in today's feel-good pew-sitter environment, they would be brilliant. But they were so much more than that. Here was a man who was preaching in the early '50s but he was ahead of his time. Or really, outside of time, in an eternal way.

Let me explain. The '50s was a time of smoothies, wasn't it? Perry Como, Norman Vincent Peal, Norman Rockwell, Nat King Cole, Sarah Vaughan, Robert Schuller, Ike, Sinatra…smoothies, all of them, with a smooth message. Understandable after the war, of course. On the Roman's tapes, all was not smooth. The teaching was clear as a bell and forthright, sprinkled liberally with micropolemics that deconstructed humanist existentialist and atheist baloney which, up until them, had suffered no resistance from Protestant evangelical circles. This was a pleasant surprise to me, to hear someone stand up to the Sorbonne/NYU/Columbia/Berkeley/Ann Arbor cafe circuit of Marxist/Existentialists and attack them on their own ground as unsubstantial. Most especially, to tear up their pompous anti-Christian arguments which so often were mere assertion based on false atheist presuppositions and cheap false anti-histories fabricated for convenience and not based on fact. Many of these false histories are several centuries old and very entrenched, made up to begin with as smokescreens to distract from the obvious failings of atheism and human selfishness untouched by an eternal perspective of grace.

My favorite anti-history to hate is the fake story about the Spanish inquisition. It was put in place to distract from Dutch Protestant slavery of Africans after the pope said knock it off in 1550. It's a Stalinist thing, to fiddle with history on purpose like that. But Schaeffer's Roman tapes were even better than this. Now and then Schaeffer would simply let loose a tirade against hypocrisy, weakness, corruption, the soft American lifestyle, cowardice, sloth, narcissism, spiritual cravenness and more. His target? Not the militant atheist Marxists. Not the effete coffee shop humanist existentialists. Not the corrupt Catholics who were basket cases anyway as far as a Reformation type was-concerned. No. His target was his own, fellow born-again Protestant Christians. The hypocrisy of this group, his own, enraged him more than that of any other, by far. I got a little ahead of my story again! Tchah.

Before I arrived at Huemoz, I'd glanced at one of their prayer newsletters I had gotten from Cheryl. Of all the organizations I've known I'd have to say L'Abri, Wycliffe Bible Translators, and the Missionaries of Charity family of orders are the three tops in the area of trusting in the living God and not in human bureaucracy or striving to raise money. In the case of L'Abri this trust took the form of the nature of their reservation policy: they had none. Here was a group on a hillside in Switzerland who had extended an open invitation over decades to any travelling hippies, college students, beatniks, Eastern Block and Asian Communists, bikers, European Existentialists…an open invitation to drop by, to anyone, to the whole world. And they did all this without anyone calling ahead. Just drop in. And all of this, with the offer of hospitality that included a room and a bed in an achingly clean really nice chalet in the Alps, three hot home-cooked meals at essentially no cost other than a token pitch-in to help with groceries that was less than a backpacker would spend on a loaf of bread.

When I got there, all the student places were full but after an interview they quickly put me in a local place and asked me to wait for a few days to see if something opened up. They trusted God, about everything, I suppose, at L'Abri, but especially about this. Right up front I saw an interesting little glimmer of faith in action. I still remember perfectly that first interview. I was invited into an Inklings-era furnished room in a gorgeous chalet in the Alps. When I sat down I was exhausted and a mess from hitching and no shower for five thousand miles.

The first thing my hostess, a US college student, as I recall, asked me was when was the last time I'd eaten? Uh, I'm Scotch. I drink Scotch, I speak Scotch and I am Scotch, and I'm a bad liar. And cheap about restaurants on the road. I cast my eyes up to the ceiling and started to formulate a prevarication, but my hostess just smiled and held out her hand to make me stay. She immediately got up and came back in a few minutes carrying a large, heavy ceramic bowl with hot oatmeal in it, and brown sugar, and raisins and butter, just like your mom used to make. Sorry sports fans, but this is class, all the way. She was good-looking, too, as I recall, and very kind.

We talked a short while and I surprised myself with the amount of information that had piled up in a mental buffer, somewhere, so to speak, of a lot of specialized knowledge that most folk just wouldn't be interested in: Cheryl; The Deutscheshaus parlor false-start incident; The James Houston conversation; My own family's charismatic/Pentecostal faith; Pastor Mees and the memory of his sincere faith. It was a jumble sale/dog's breakfast of information that just would not make sense to most people, like cyclotron target pictures always look like random squiggles to anyone except a high-energy jock, you know? It's just all Greek. But this young lady of no particular training or experience, instantly saw the significance of the bigger picture, the sojourn, and told me so right off the bat. Between us, however, we agreed that the top of the list in terms of a problem would be the fact that despite all these low-level stirrings of the soul, I still had a bunch of questions about God and to date I had not received satisfactory answers. Were these honest questions? Or simply a smokescreen my conscious mind was throwing out to distract from the fact that I, hippy that I was, was unwilling to "sign up for the 30 long haul" into a religion which, despite any ostensible connection to the real and existential personality of Jesus himself, also had obvious rules. Rules like, uh, just to pick one: you can't sleep with your girlfriend.

Heart Christians who've hung out with the Lord a while laugh at the fears of people who only view religion as a list of don'ts and then either resist conversion altogether, or maybe shop for something looser, like Unitarianism, or just-enough-religion but not too much New Age, or liberal Methodists. Whatever. These souls know that a short list of don'ts actually opens the door to an infinite list of Do's. A list inaccessible if we stubbornly insist on confining our lives to carrying out the short list of don'ts. You can believe it or not, but sex, drugs, rock and roll and nothing else can get old. Ask Mick Jagger. Don't take my word for it. Ask anybody. But there still is the matter of getting over the hump at the front end of all this. My hostess in Switzerland that morning was not laughing at all. She took it all in very seriously and after ten minutes or so, she stopped me and declared she would do everything she could to find me a place quickly in the program. "It's for someone like you, with the questions like yours, that L'Abri is here," she said and these words instantly and forcefully had an effect on me. How to put it? I knew I was finally in the hands of professionals, after having wasted a lot of time bouncing from here to there and encountering nothing but well-meaning amateurs.

By contrast with this reception in Switzerland, I can remember a well-meaning US Protestant pastor who, after having heard my questions, said, "Well, it's obvious that you do not believe. You don't have faith. People who have faith just don't ask questions like this. You need to pray that you will get faith. Then you won't keep asking these questions." There is actually merit to this position, but suffice it to say that Schaeffer and his ministry took all questions quite seriously, and he went way out of his way to avoid ending a conversation with only a reference to a subjective or purely personal experience, which is effectively what the US Protestant pastor had done. "If you only had experienced what I've experienced, you wouldn't be asking these silly intellectual questions. You'd just believe." This is probably why Schaeffer was characterized as a "missionary to intellectuals," in a milieu, era, and cultural denominationalism which had no time for it. Years later I would discover that the Catholics are chock-a-block with people like Schaeffer in this regard, but people like that tended to be shunted aside at the phase I was in, a kind of bare-bones basic entrance into faith at the threshold, the raw border between atheism and creed. Catholic eggheads I think tended to focus on retreading childhood Catholics who'd fallen away. In any event, there was a Protestant/Catholic disconnect in place that was four centuries old. No help there.

L'Abri is actually as famous for the warmth and Good Sam practicableness of its ministry, as much as for the writings and speeches of Schaeffer. I was as grateful for one as for the other that morning at the end of a long dusty trail that had started way back in the kitchen in Oregon. Actually, the kitchen in Santa Cruz. Kitchen theology, we're about here, I suppose. After a week in the loft of a pig barn for a franc a day---luxurious by Scotch standards, and lots of nice hay--I was moved into a guesthouse in Huemoz. I had already been listening to the Romans tapes during the days when I slept nights in the barn loft, but eating in a chalet you could see even more clearly the Good Sam approach to faith there. Great care and detail and love went into serving meals. It was as if all three meals were "for company," and I was the company.

Everything was immaculate. The food was very carefully cooked and nice recipe-kind-of food that I hadn't really seen since I left home for school years earlier. All the plates and dishes were thick ceramic and homey and nice, and probably even matched, most of the time. Always a table cloth, always cut flowers, always grace before meals and nice table manners all around, no matter if you were sitting between an enquiring Asian Marxist on one hand and a French Existentialist on the other.

Done that. You can say that you just felt as if you were at home eating your Mom's food, and it was a fancy dinner, for guests, as formal as a house gets, but if you did conclude that, it's worth considering how they put that feeling across to a constant stream of strangers who came and went, in a foreign land. And, doing it in their own houses. This was a feeling uncreatable in the fanciest hotels in Europe, but they did it on zero budget, zero fundraising (another trust thing) in private residences, there at L'Abri in Huemoz.

I should explain a little about the structure of the ministry. Back in the 50's when Francis and Edith started out, they found a way, without fundraising, to buy a house for each daughter as she married. There were four daughters, and each of them, in a kind of miracle, not only married pastors, but they all married pastors who were interested in L'Abri. This is saying a lot when you consider the ferociousness of the "P.K." syndrome with all pastors' kids, who are in a huge hurry to distance themselves from their dads ASAP as soon as they grow up. As each daughter grew up, married, and with her pastor husband moved into a chalet in Huemoz, this added to the capacity of the ministry to accommodate guests, and all of them in a homey way. With any mission, quality, the personal touch, is everything. Just ask Mother Teresa's spiritual daughters, 4500 of them, all of them right there in plain view.

The way this all happened with the chalets is not a small point. They could have just built a dorm and a chapel and a mini-school and accommodated that many and more people for less money, and saved the stress on their own families in the process, coming and going from work like any working stiff, but the way it happened with each new chalet gathering around a host family was much more personal and homey, and this hominess was part of the entire mission and ministry. Schaeffer did not preach in a vacuum. He and his extended family walked the walk to make myself and visitors at home, and not a few of them were something like hoboes, wandering around Europe with nothing to do, and in the early days they were definitely biker/Jack Kerouac types. This was quite obviously a burden to the families, raising their children and grandchildren with strangers constantly underfoot, but it was a burden borne with a stunning level of sincere kindness and cheerfulness, no bitterness that I could see. For all of Schaeffer's cheap-seats critics in academia, not one of them ever did anything even remotely like this. The whole thing added up to a spoken and unspoken message of a loving God who cares.

I was assigned a tutor, Barry Seagren, husband of one of the Schaeffer daughters, and himself an ordained Presbyterian minister. Barry was British but he was as far from a loud Monty Python stereotype of them as it is possible to imagine. He was humble, quiet and thoughtful. Toward the end of my stay there, which turned out to be about three months, he almost casually shared with me that he had also been the tutor of one Cheryl, graduate of UCSC, and that he'd heard a little bit about the two of us and all that. I think he was low-key talking about her due to any cleric's natural reticence to reveal confidences. He never did, but simply stated that he knew Cheryl and understood a little about the backstory. Strange to relate Barry and 1 did not spend that much time talking about Cheryl even after he told me he'd met her. It turned out Seagren was something of an amateur theoretical scientist. I think he had an engineering background before he took up the collar. True or not, he was certainly fluent in science shoptalk. In addition to his knowledge of the Cheryl connection, it turned out that this science capacity on his part was very providential. At the start I had no idea how much. Click, click, click. The coincidences just kept accumulating. How I wish everyone could have some in their lives.

One day 1 was invited up to Chesalet, Francis and Edith's house on the southern border of Villars-sur-Ollon. From the chapel in Huemoz it was a pleasant 20-minute walk. The invitation was for lunch, and there were about a dozen of us students there plus Dr. and Mrs. Schaeffer. There were also students specifically connected with Chesalet who were helping to put on the meals, but that morning everyone got drafted, as was the way in L'Abri. Formal? Yes. Company manners, plates, dress? Yes. But everyone pitched in, too. All of this came about effortlessly, pleasantly and without rancor, even though you could tell that some of the students there did not have a let's-pitch-in upbringing. This cooperative effort explains how at one point I was chopping carrots in the kitchen, standing next to Mrs. Schaeffer, and we got talking. Somehow the conversation got around to why I was there, and my sojourn, etc. In that conversation I asked her a question and she said, "That's a great question for Fran. Why don't you ask him? "Who's Fran?" "My husband. You could ask him at lunch."

A little later, lunch started with all of us going around the table and introducing ourselves. In terms of getting to ask Dr. Schaeffer a question, this was scary to me because anyone of the guests could conceivably launch off into an elaborate discussion, and i'd never get a chance! I watched, a little worried, as they took turns introducing themselves. I was very near the end of the circle. Finally it was my turn. I said the usual, my name, where I was from, etc., and then I sat silent. I wasn't sure if this was the time to ask a question or not. Schaeffer pointedly held his hand up, stopping the circuit around the table and looked at me. "Jim, do you have a question you'd like to ask?" What a relief to hear these simple words. It turns out Mrs. Schaeffer had mentioned to her husband our little conversation in the kitchen. OK, sue me. Call me a groupie, but how nice it was, barely a year and a half after I'd read words written by this man, the words which had, humanly speaking, brought me up so short in the seaside kitchen in Oregon, and now I could ask that same man a question.

"Does God answer prayers from non-Christians? Is this possible?" I was thinking of the desperate night back in Austin when I had knelt by the side of my bed in the garret and begged God to help me with the whole nightclubbing thing. It was a Pascal's Wager kind of prayer since at that point in Texas I simply was not sure if God even existed. Pascal's idea was -- what've you got to lose? The worst thing that could happen, assuming you do not know for certain if God is there, and it turns out he isn't, is that you waste a few minutes and look foolish to yourself, "talking to the ceiling." On the other hand, if God really were to exist and you did not call out to Him at one point at least, paralyzed instead by your doubts, you stood to lose a lot, and the loss would be of an iterative and uncorrectable nature.

Schaeffer's answer to my question was surprisingly precise and careful. I could have instead imagined just about any of the US TV evangelist/ Big Hair types answering a question like that with either a hearty clap on the back and "Heck , yes, brother! Hallelujah!", or, "Hail, no, you rotten sinner! First ya gotta accept Jaysus Chrast as your . . . " Well, I'm sure you know the rest. But in Chesalet that day in the summer of 1978 Schaeffer was at great pains to make a subtle distinction: yes, God could answer a prayer from a non-Christian, but it was not the same as how he related to a question from a Christian, in which case he had bound himself to answer. "If you call upon Me, I will answer" could be a scripture Schaeffer could cite on the one hand, and that verse and a jillion like them have got to be the most elegant contract ever written, unlike in so many other religions. One stunningly simple condition, and one equally simple promise. Would that presidents or emperors talk like this!

In the case of that scripture, Schaeffer might have gone on to say that the context was a conversation with the Psalmist, David, and through him with all the Israelites. In the New Covenant dispensation, the promise ostensibly would be extended toward all believing Christians. By this exegesis, myself, as an atheist, could be excluded from getting an answer to my prayer. But that still left open the idea of God's largesse which most certainly could be on tap for little old matheist me. The overall impression Schaeffer gave was one of positive hope on the point, but I suspect he also did not want at the same time to extend past what scripture would endorse. Either way, I was grateful for the answer, even if qualified. I believe heart speaks to heart, and Schaeffer never let his learning or even his wisdom interfere with the main event, which, even if at times cerebral, most certainly includes simple invitation to friendship with God, no matter how we arrive there. Now that 1 think of it, maybe that was the reason for the enormous success, within its own hidden circles, of his ministry.

Yes, he went out of his way to study and refute the gasbag European eggheads that gifted us all with God Is Dead, horse manure impractical Existentialism, mass-slaughtering Marxism, the Great Endarkenment, and a few other little intellectual gems. But in all that, and in all of his personal confrontations with those types, he never lost the simple personal touch, and it grieves me to say how few academicians I can say that about. In fact, guess what? Zilch. Zip, zero, nada. I can't think of a one who fills his shoes that way. Every other academic or professional Christian pastor I ever met didn't have it; the simple personal touch. Well, OK, except Pastor Mees and a few priests I met years later, but I wonder if those exceptions just prove the sad rule. Mother Teresa wouldn't count, because even if she could be called a professional -- disgusting, that word applied to her -- no one would ever accuse her of being an academic. Even if she could handily refute each and every one of them, fake "christian" flavor or atheist flavor, with a handful of words. Or a small handful of heartfelt actions. And a Big Smile.

I suppose the only reason the world doesn't know this is that the academicians knew full well she could do it. They were scared, quite simply. Better to thuggerize helpless students in a lecture hall with droning vapidities, encyclopedic stupidity and pompous insubstantial books. I guess part of the insight to all of this for us in trying to interpret or understand the L'Abri phenomenon and all of its spiritual children and grandchildren would be to dwell for a moment on what it must have been like for Schaeffer in the early, coffee shop days. I wonder how many US evangelicals would truly understand the price to be paid for even so much as attempting to interact with the ivory tower types – argumentativeness, for its own sake, all day long. I'm perfectly acquainted with how scientist dogs-eat-dogs, being a battle-scarred veteran my own self, but in science there is at least the hope that sooner or later the process would find itself devolving around a fact, which could be established or denounced. But even that thin reed is further weakened by the spiritual cloud Darwinists have cast over happy biology. Then there's physics and the A-bomb, geology and Uniformitarianism, psychology, and Freud. Any academic who wants to stay human has his work cut out for him.

But think about Schaeffer's task: everything he did, effectively evangelizing no less than all of academia, even if indirectly, through its students, was aimed at the squishiest areas of intellectual pursuit, philosophy and theology. There are even worse areas like literature and psychology, but in philosophy and theology, everyone's got an opinion, an idea that Schaeffer embraced even as egghead nitwits tried to shoot him down. The nitwits are peevish, off-point, argumentative, and ad homs. All that and extra fries. Schaeffer paid the dues of studying the Modern big guns of atheism and refuting them, point by point, but any jackass can take a stab at shooting him down without any reasonable thinking at all. Let me give you an example. In the 70's Schaeffer and his son Frank made a series of documentary films, How Shall We Then Live. Schaeffer 52 spoke openly in the films about the decay of the West and the partial cause of it: bonehead Modern philosophers beginning with Descartes and slouching quickly past Locke. Sooner or later, and it was inevitable for someone with such a wide range of endeavor, Schaeffer made some trivial error of fact, either on or off-camera, off-camera being the speeches he made on the film premieres around the country.

I don't know what this error is and I don't care. I'm not even sure there was an error but if there was, so what? It's the exact kind of thing you would expect and forgive coming from a gifted amateur who's got a Bigger Point. But the professional academic who nastily attacked Schaeffer completely missed the Big Point and focused on the little boo-boo. In the mind of the pinhead moron professional, this error justified ignoring everything Schaeffer had ever said. Atheists get desperate when they sense substance on the horizon. Never mind that even the pros since then have all granted Schaeffer's Big Point in spades. I recognize this sterile nit-picking from prolife public debate on a sidewalk or in a lecture hall, and also, in court. There's a vibe to it, argumentation purely to tear down, not an honest seeking of the truth. No one in academia ever made a nickel saying "I agree wholeheartedly with my colleague" even on simple stuff. Everyone has to put himself ahead of the other guy at his expense. And it dovetails into the Modern habit of fake novelty for its own sake.

A story from the Romans tapes puts this all in perspective. When he first got to Switzerland in the 50's and preached in the coffee shops, I bet Schaeffer got back chatter from atheist European intellectuals who bothered to listen. As a result, Schaeffer went and read all the thinkers they were referring to and in an interesting phase, before the ministry was so busy later, he paced up and down in the hayloft of a barn and thought about it all. The result was a series of intelligent and aggressive answers that went beyond the simple fideism I had encountered in the US before I went to Switzerland. Yes, Augustine and the other early church fathers had all arrived at the same conclusions, and no Jesuit in the world was unfamiliar with it, but Schaeffer will always be credited with bringing the specific apologetics into the fundie Evangelical theater of battle, which, after all, is the battlefield of the New World. This work of mercy is impossible to overestimate.

Add to it the personal homey touch of L'Abri in Huemoz and it was a tremendous blow struck for good which ramifies and goes on to the present, even if behind the scenes. I was not aware of any of this, eating lunch at Chesalet that day in 78, but I was grateful for a kind thoughtful answer to something that had been bugging me: Yes. Yes, God could have answered my prayer back in Austin as I had felt the burden and the sadness of the whole nightclubbing thing lifting off me from that moment on. Schaeffer confirmed it, as far as I was concerned. God had communicated with me and not just through the Bible, which is good enough, to be sure. He answered prayers too. Got to remember things like that because as much as we beg for an answer for things, so often we forget the blessing two seconds later, like the baby you give the Hope Diamond to who looks at its sparkle for three seconds and then drops it in the mud.

There is another L'Abri chalet, this one located back down in Huemoz, in the southwest corner in the direction of the Panay pathway. The host may not have been one of Schaeffer's sons-in-law, but I seem to recall that he was a vegetarian. After dinner I'd float around the village a little bit. On one of the dinner invitations I recall a conversation with a young woman student. I wonder if she was the same one who did the startup interview? Because she seemed to have a bead on my sojourn. I had asked her one of my remaining questions, the list of questions I had about Christianity had dwindled down over the summer as I talked with all the people there, students and pastors. But I still kept asking a few. I can't recall all of them, but the problem of evil and a good God was one of them. The greedy capitalism/ historical Christianity connection was another. So, I'd asked the young lady a question and she answered it, but then she very gently and politely challenged me. "You've learned a lot about Jesus and Christianity here this summer and you say you're closer to a decision, but actually you are no closer to Christ than when you first came here." I was stunned. Not only by the holy boldness of these words, but by my reaction to them. The effect of what she said was to silence me and bring me up short, almost as Cheryl had done in Austin a few months earlier.

What the heck do you think you are doing? was the sound of it to me, in the nicest way. Did I know what I was doing? Or was I just fooling around, using repeated questions as a smokescreen to avoid real commitment, commitment being the logical denouement to a sustained inquiry. After a while any lower division physics students can be asked, do you believe in the Second Law of Thermo? Or don't you? They better have a ready answer, and a defense for their position. "No matter how much you debate or even think about it, you will always be separated from a living faith by one single act of making a decision, until you do just that," the student at the chalet dinner added. "Sooner or later you have to decide one way or another." Since then I've seen the same hanging-on-the-fence messing around in so many others and it grieves me to think that they never had the benefit of an environment gently and lovingly concentrated just enough, like L'Abri, to help someone off the fence and into faith. Instead, we live in an anonymous, stranger culture. We love machines like the TV and treat people like machines, even our own spouses and kids and parents.

There is never a personal awareness of our steady-state vacillation; it just goes on and on, and even becomes fixed and institutionalized, laughed and joked about. How can we be aware of playing hide-and-seek with God, a subtle thing, if we are so busy with TV we can't even tell if the house is on fire, Bobby's on drugs, and Suzie's at a rave? How many times have you heard a cheap MS-LSD-type rejoinder to someone's ardent sincere proposition of faith, which sounds like this: "Well, I don't know about all that Christina stuff, but I do know that they're all hypocrites since the Spanish Inquisition." See? a commonplace lie is used to distract from the speaker's emotional sloth or disengagement. You don't know about Christianity? In this culture? Well, you should! It's not like it's a secret.

And yet, aside from the institutionalized stupidity of TV culture, so often, in the everyday world the people we run into have a stock arsenal of "gotchas" about Christianity but all they really want to do is get rid of the annoying buzzing fly of the Holy Spirit so they can get back to blowing crack and cheating on their wives. They don't have the slightest interest in the truth, or even a meager means toward a right way. The only "truth" they know is their stock of lies that they preserve and cultivate as if there were sincere questions to trot out if they happen to bump into something real, something reaching out to The Other. A hard-enough enterprise as it is, since our benighted culture so well deserves His crushing silence. Which Joe-Six Pack thinks is just fine, sadly. Back in L'Abri, this young lady's gentle challenge set me back in a good way. She was right. This pleasant interlude could not go on forever without a decision. It was painful to hear, a little, but so's the dentist's drill.

l could write ten books about that summer at L'Abri -- the walks to Panay; the old TB sanitarium surrounded by graves from an old epidemic that reminded me so much of Grandfather's unofficial TB clinic in Blue Jay; long talks with a converted Buddhist monk about Eastern vs. Western contemplation; the story of the student of Jean-Paul Sartre whom he sent down to Switzerland to straighten out Schaeffer, but who called back to Paris a couple weeks later: "Surprise! I'm born-again!" the fascinating East European and Asian Communist intellectuals with their long-as-Tolstoy questions drenched in Marxist lingo that Schaeffer fielded without blinking an eye, and great sympathy for what could be a noble impulse buried under tons of misguided socialism; the Saturday nights Schaeffer casually hopped up on to a stone inglenook in the fireplace in the chapel and answered questions from anybody on any topic: science, Darwin, Marxism, Great Enlightenment, French Revolution, Catholicism, etc., and subtler categories, like the heartlessness of modern technology, the lostness of modern man alone in the midst of all his toys, the collapse of art as a window to eternity, the hypocrisy of the US evangelical community, the original impulses of the Reformers. Then there were all those meals, lovingly prepared and creating pleasant semi-formal environments for serious discussion. I could go on! How I wish the world could see it. I think L'Abri's gone now, perhaps, except for one near Boston.

Toward the end of my stay there in Huemoz my list of remaining questions, especially after the chat with the brave student, burned down to two clinkers that would not go away. Clinker #1 was an obsession with my false start experience in Austin: if I did become a Christian, now, there in Switzerland, would I have enough faith to stay? Or would it just be another false start? Was I pushing myself into it just to please people, or Cheryl in particular? This possibility frightened me. It fatally offended my German sense of loyalty or decisiveness. Why, or how, my Irish side, the happy-go-lucky, let's give it a whirl genes didn't rise up and clobber the German side (they are at each other all the time anyway) I don't know. But the Stodgy German DNA was winning, so far, back in Switzerland. The second clinker in the grate that wouldn't burn up took me completely by surprise. Remember Barry Seagren, the tutor/pastor, and his engineering background? One day I must've said something about my undergraduate Darwinist major advisor whom I admired so much, or maybe I just said something about Darwin.

If you love a life on the fence, dabbling with any sloppy lifestyle and sloppy thinking, bless your heart, and at the same time do what Schaeffer called "stealing from the cookie jar," beware! Don't read the book Barry gave me! "Stealing from the cookie jar," I should explain, was Schaeffer's way of describing so many fence sitters. They strain out a gnat and swallow a camel. They go to Midnight Mass Christmas Eve and get a warm fuzzy feeling from all the smells and bells and then Monday morning they trot off to the mill to take care of that little Christmas party problem like it was a car wash. They hold their hands up and sway back and forth to get a buzz on Sunday morning, but if you ask them to even so much as hold up a baby picture at a rally they look at you like you're from Cygnus X. They call themselves Vice President, or Speaker of the House, or

Senate majority leader and spare no effort to get tax dollars for abortions, but they still want to trot up to Communion. They go on and on about "deciding for Christ" and how much they love Jesus but if you ask them to take a single mom into their house you'd think you just infected them with the plague. Stealing from the cookie jar, Schaeffer would cry. Half in, half out. A foot on both sides. Take what you want from either camp to please yourself. Get the perceived benefits of both sides, and the commitment of neither. If I could pick one way to describe the reality of American fake spirituality I'd say this is it: we all steal from the cookie jar all day long, and we've institutionalized it and formalized it and made a science out of it and every one of us does it all day long and no one challenges it. Except for the lone voice from Switzerland that was stilled too early, in 1984.

"Phew" "Where was i? Oh. Sorry." Don't read the book Barry gave me that day in the chapel 35 years ago, especially if you are a typical cookie-jar-stealing scientist as I was. You will be blown away and you just might have to climb off that upholstered air-conditioned perch on the fence. You just might have to stop cookie jar stealing and make a spiritually honest person out of yourself. If you do ever read the book, don't come complaining to me. I warned you. I could write a hundred books about the solid science in that book and how it affected me, the scientist. I've read plenty of anti-Darwin polemics since then, but that tiny book packs a tremendous punch, and Barry wasn't even a natural history scientist, Darwin's area and the area of most scientists who defend Darwinism. The author was simply an honest biochemist who saw "irreducible complexity," not just in DNA -- this is important, if you ever talk to a scientist about it -- but also in the jillion other complexities of what makes a cell run, even for simple energetic metabolism, the tertiary folding of proteins into delicately functional enzymes and other places like that where no one had looked. And this all preceded the natural law argument or Intelligent Design that runs around now, which tends to ontology, which is fine, but the biochemist simply said, look. Look at this complexity. So far past Stanley Fox's experiment it's ridiculous. In fact, it is an insurmountable obstacle, even if you allowed a fake setup of the Fox experiment. There are plenty of good books about Darwinism. Suffice it to say that the current debate is finally getting around to where it should have been a hundred and fifty years ago: Darwinists accuse fundie Christians of not having enough science when the world is only slowly waking up to the fact of how much (fake) religion is embedded in Darwinism, which is so incredibly unsubstantiated. The very fact that supposed cool and calm "scientists" get so torqued up about it is prima facie evidence about it. Real scientists don't get torqued up about the Second Law of Thermo. They either just explain it again, or assume they are in the presence of imbeciles, and stop talking.

You have to have intense religious fervor to buy even the stratigraphic column as received from geologists, when a fossilized tree, a single tree, was found growing up through all the strata. You need more than Jimmy Swaggert sweating 6 at the piano-like intensity to believe you can go from mud to the thousand-Pentagons-like complexity of a living cell with only one stop off in between mud and the Fox experiment. Even so, without knowing the details at all, 99.99% of our culture have that precise level of religious abandon. Gotta be money in that, somewhere. Pray, put your hands on the TV, and send your checks to Ivy League, NOW! Your tax dollars too. It's a big topic and I won't cover it here. If you think carbon dating has ever kicked out an un-massaged number bigger than seven thousand years, please don't write me! Read Barry's book. I'm real tired of Darwinists preaching as if they cared about science when really all they want to do is get back to their club, their bimbo, and their crack pipe; they won't deal with these simple, appraisable problems, and paid-to-be-there ontology, an area Darwin himself respected, gets you deer-in-the-headlights. But they sure as heck will count the number of adapted and naturally selected angels on the head of a pin! And burn you at the stake if you don't shout hallelujah when they do. I know. Because I don't. Not anymore. More like, laugh.

There is a saying I learned from the Catholics a few years down the road: all heresies begin below the belt. Darwinism is not substance. It's just one more flimsy excuse to continue with the Grand Coalition of the Status Quo, which, however empty it is intellectually and in terms of true heart and spirituality and solidarity, always seems to maintain hourly child decapitation on its list of must-haves. And we all know where babies come from, huh? We make Attila the Hun look good. Real good. At the time I was completely unaware of how much my religious belief in Darwin had been holding me back but Barry in his quiet way reached through all the questions I was kicking out and put his finger on the one idea that was needful. I read the book and completely changed my mind all in the space of a week, amazing when you consider I'd believed

Darwinism for a good twelve years or more up until then. Much more could be said about Darwinism but that would not be true to the situation as it happened. In real time, my religious fervor of Darwinism clicked off in the space of a few days; it turned out -- I only think this in retrospect -- to have been the last durable obstacle to a totally liberating swing over.

How could this be? How could it happen so fast? Again, as in the kitchen in Oregon, I really can't say for sure how. But when the living God is part of the story and when the idea of Him is allowed into the picture, an invisible side of the universe swings into alignment with the visible part and not in any way that always makes sense. Especially, it does not make sense if you confine yourself to explanations that only you, as a human, can generate, based on your own experience. Also, it doesn't make sense if you are a reductionist and confine truth to only what you see or think you can see. By that light, of course, science would never have found out radiation, gravity attraction, or electromagnetism, either, but don't tell the scientists that! Rainbows and sunsets and even "the smile on a dog" are certainly visible but to the non-transcendentalist they might as well be invisible. The reductionist claims he's confined to what he thinks he can see, but his vision is even smaller than that. God could slap him upside the head and he'd still miss it. No one is so blind as someone who doesn't want to see. These limitations to only what we think is visible are crushing, and taken as a whole, explain our currently so completely broken modern world, but back then I took these limitations as normal. Something any good scientist does as a matter of course, as a matter of good Modern "scientific" practice and discipline. It was only decades later that I would discover that this visible-only thing was alien to all people, including true scientists before the Great Endarkenment.

Two days after I finished Man's Origin Man's Destiny, I chatted with Barry about it. It was my birthday, August 2. One day after that, at night, two minutes after eleven p.m. local time I felt a nudge to kneel by my bed again as I had in Austin six months earlier. As soon as I knelt I was overcome by a feeling hard to describe. The only way I know how to describe it is to say that the feeling was as if I were standing on the ground next to a massive carousel, the kind children ride at a carnival at a state fair, the kind with "painted ponies that go up and down" as it spins in a circle.

But this carousel was infinitely bigger than that, bigger than an aircraft carrier, bigger than a thousand aircraft carriers big as a universe, but you could see clearly the edge of it near you, and it was slowing down almost to the point of stopping.

## Chapter 2

## Education, Fullerton, Dr. Rosenberg

The First Time I Saw Nature. . . I think it was because it was the part of it visible to a two-year-old. That would be Callita Street -- a redundancy, but don't tell the blancos that -- in San Gabriel, California, the town George Patton and I were both born in, the same town his family still had a ranch in. Back then our house was tiny and sunny, but it was the outside that always drew me. Family pictures show my brother and me sitting on miniature ponies in cowboy gear. No one ever makes those pictures anymore. The duck in our backyard was Mrs. Dingles. She had her little pond behind the garage. This was still the 50's: Sex and the Single Girl had yet to hit the scene, so there would be no single unchaperoned females in our backyard, thank you very much. I was only in San Gabriel for four years, from my birth until 1958 when we moved to South Pasadena, but the memories seem huge. Everything was a symbol for something bigger. Usually, something now gone.

One day my Mom took me across the street and down a few doors. For a long time I only remember a big metal top, the kind you spin, not with a string, but a handle you push down like a Yankee screwdriver.

There was an incredibly kind silver-haired lady there who would push the handle down for me. I think she was my babysitter. I don't remember Walt being there; I don't know why. Baby eye-level nature caught my eye: there was an abundant section of baby's breath against the back wall of her yard; the sun came in over that yard and hit the side of her yellow house making a bright cheery place; combined with the shade and the baby's breath, it was like a secret garden. But it was the first of a later theme in life: man has made a shady cool, natural spot in the middle of relentless sun, and this is good. LA was a desert at first, but is a garden now, in little pockets like this. But it takes doing.

Thinking back, I'm convinced this nice lady was a war widow, maybe even from World War I, if not II. Also, from the distance of time, I realize now that this poor lady had to subdivide her lot and build on the back to make some money; that's why her backyard was crammed between the back of her house and the fence only a dozen feet away. To see something cheery at the moment, but then, realize later, there's a story…this hits me now. How much of life has secret sadnesses like this? And so many more in LA; they came from all over the country, but once the war was over and Uncle Sam deposited them on US soil there in California after the Pacific Campaign, they could never face going back all the way to Peoria. They stopped right where they were. All went to tiki bars together; all PTSD'd about a-bombs craters and survivors and machine guns above the beaches together; only talked to each other; became drunks together; got divorced together; felt Tom Waits was the only one who understood them, together; and were sent to shrinks together. Everyone calls California "crazy" but we came by our status honestly. We cleaned up everyone else's mess, and this, also, haunts me.

This part of the book was supposed to be about nature. I found a corner of nature in the nice lady's backyard, but musing a little, I found a whole lot more. Sadness, recovery, moving forward, solving a problem. Now I'm told San Gabriel is all "mezkun." I've grown tired of telling all my white friends, when they say this, that "Mezkuns" have babies, and don't divorce as we do. We kill our babies and divorce like Henry the Eighth. So don't cry to me about immigration. You can't hold the ground you're standing on, even with a thousand a-bombs and drones, if you won't have kids. Stop crying. And, class dismissed. That's enough for today!

In 1958 when I was four our family moved from San Gabriel to South Pasadena, much closer to downtown LA for my commuter Dad. South Pasadena is not the southern part of Pasadena, a separate city. South Pasadena is its own city. Between when I was born and when I went to college, our family only moved twice. For many that's nothing, especially Army brats. Even those two moves were a big shakeup, though, for me. The South Pas. house was bigger than the San Gabriel one, but the big draw about our new town was the schools, even though it was not that wealthy an area. In first grade I was called "Mr. Science." In fifth grade for Show and Tell, I imported a 50 kV Tesla coil into the classroom, with a five-foot coil and capacitors a yard square. I arced it through the air and lit up a hand-held florescent tube. On another day I did water electrolysis and ignited pure hydrogen gas generated from that. No, I didn't blow up the school, either. Somewhere in about third grade I stopped raising my hand if the teacher asked a question. If the silence went on long enough sometimes the teacher would just look at me and say, "Jim?" Go ahead, hate me. Get it out. Discuss amongst yourselves. But I have an excuse. In the fifth grade I had a ham radio station in my bedroom with an antenna that stretched over our entire property. It pulled in Russia and the Philippines. In junior high I did drafting and print shop, we had real drafting boards, and set cold type by hand, just like Ben Franklin.

I know this all could be making your blood boil. Me too! but hang on just a second. My sister Mary taught me how to read when I was four. "It's easy! Look…see? Jack and the Beanstalk." Beginning about fourth grade when homework started, I would go downstairs early in the morning before anyone was awake. There was a heating grille in the floor at the bottom of the stairs in an inglenook: perfect. Southern California, a desert, can get cool nights. I would set up books and papers in a circle, like props. It looked as if I was studying. Then under cover of early morning darkness, I'd carefully crawl across the room to the bookshelf under the piano where there was an old edition of the Encyclopedia Britannica. Sneaking back to my study spot I'd slowly flip through the crackling coated pages that no one else had read yet. At that time in school we were barely past "See Dick and Jane" but thanks to Mary at home, there before dawn, a whole new world opened up before me. My little fingers would trace under the captions of the pictures of exotic locations, sounding out the words I had never heard, not even in school: Istanbul. Hong Kong. Moscow. Paris. Rome. Jakarta. Singapore. Kuala Lumpur.

Hinduism. Jainism. Sufism. Shintoism. Atomic table. Injection molding. Jet engine. Hydroelectric turbines. Brahms. Saint-Saens. Middle Ages. Ancient Greece. Robert Frost. Ezra Pound. Eliot. Joyce. Tang Dynasty. Copepods. Feather duster worms happy at eight thousand feet. Guadalcanal. Iwo Jima. Winston Churchill. Dwight Eisenhower. Einstein. Bohr. Fleming. Pascal. Alger Hiss. Did I understand any of this? With my eight-year-old brain? Of course not. But I got enough of it, cheating on my homework time, to know for a certainty; there's' a whole world out there they don't teach you about in school. "Don't let schooling get in the way of your education" was my favorite saying, and later I taught it to my nieces and nephews.

My best friend in junior high school was Ken Witgers who lived up on Monterey, the same street that the founder of the Navigators lived on just a few years earlier. Ken actually got his ham license and transmitted while I never did. But we had a gas doing radio stuff together. He grew up to become an engineer like a bunch of kids in South Pas. who didn't grow up to be docs and lawyers. Ken was Mormon; he had a dozen or so brothers and sisters in a house much smaller than ours. I'm not sure even his longsuffering and very cool parents actually knew how many kids there were; they would never sit still long enough to count them. That family probably went to triple or quadruple bunk beds about the time other families were going up to four-bedroom houses, a room for each kid. Ken's folks were wonderful. They always had an aura of Iowa farmer patience. Nothing upset them, and the kids figured out long ago that they should probably be good if for no other reason than an ambulance gurney couldn't get to them in time through the sea of humanity of all their brothers and sisters if they really messed up. Ken's mom and dad never rushed around or yelled or scolded. They both would smile calmly, sitting in the kitchen or near it, and speak in a low voice, very slowly, as if they knew that if they sat long enough, a kid could be rushed off to the hospital, get sewed up, and come back before anyone really got too excited, just in time to say, "Well, then. Some tea, Jim?" Anything less than a hospital trip might rise to the level of a parental suggestion, more musing to each other than spoken to the kids, but one kid would transmit the message to another, on down through the ranks, until the three year old finally shouted at the eighteen month old: "Be good! Mommy said so!" and another crisis was averted with nothing even remotely close to a parental heart attack. A hush would reign over the set of the Exodus scene in the Ten Commandments for every bit of six, or even seven minutes before it picked up again. Gotta love that family, broke but happy as heck.

One day Mr. Witgers took us sailing, probably off San Pedro. Raised to try to be of use on a project, I jumped up and "rigged" the sheet block to the end of the boom, two things I'd never seen in my life, out on the water on a strong tack. Mr. Witgers happened to notice for the first time my rigging job. In my anxiety to be useful I had hastily jammed the handle of a pin of a deadeye shackle into the steel loop on the boom without actually opening the shackle and properly screwing the post back in to hold the boom as it should be. This cockeyed kluge had only held up for a while because the wind had been a stable strain on it the whole time we were out there. A tiny let-up and the whole thing would have fallen apart, a dangerous thing with the boom swinging all over. Mr. Witgers suddenly saw it, and blanched. He didn't curse or yell, as a Marine would. Not everyone is a marine, I puzzled to myself. He calmly threw the boat into irons, grabbed the boom and hooked it up right. I apologized but he was very kind about it and blamed himself as much as me. Why tell this? Jump in. Do something, even if it's dumb. Learn from your mistakes. Repeat. I'd stumbled on a way to go forward in a confusing place, with no Mr. Witgers or Charles Kopp around. I especially suggest this to all the Sideline Sams who criticize someone trying to actually do something when our ship is so obviously sinking. Kind Mr. Witgers knew that.

In '68 when I was fourteen our family moved to Marin County up north. My grades jumped a full letter with the same studying, or less. I guess "good school district" in South Pas. meant hard grading, but Marin was reputed to have a good school too. It is impossible to overestimate the cultural difference between the two places. South Pas. was filled with World War II vets and widows; San Marino, just next door, was the first chapter of the John Birch Society. Marin was the home at one point or another of just about every 60's rock band you ever heard of. Santana's drummer even lived at the bottom of our hill on Eliseo, in Greenbrae. I'd hear him practicing at six-thirty every morning as I zipped past on my bike with my trumpet strapped to the back. There were no hippies in South Pas., not even a token one. In Marin everyone was a hippie most nearly, even a lot of my friends' parents. The teachers were kind of in the middle. Very cool.

## RALPH M. GABRIEL

My favorite science teacher was a man I didn't even know that well. He never drew on the chalkboard and I don't remember him lecturing. He'd sit on a stool and lean on the teaching bench and just talk all class time. He told lots of stories. I can't remember what they were about. This was something new for me. Mr. MacDonald, whatever he said, though, was a fascinating mix of knowledge on any subject, and an unspoken sadder-but-wiser mien he carried with him. I don't recall taking any notes but I do remember becoming very excited about biology. All of my life until then, biology was nature, or raccoons, but with Mr. MacDonald I started to see biology as a life's work, a calling. He had us do a research project. I counted gooseneck barnacles on a stone reef in Drake's Estero at the new National Seashore. Point Reyes is the most gorgeous piece of land in the world. Still is. It just sits there and no one knows. No one goes there. I loved it so much I volunteered to be the naturalist; later, when I got a semester off between high school and college. half the fun was riding out on my bike, 44 miles round trip each day; two hills.

Later that same semester of the Point Reyes job, I got a paying job deck handing for the boats that serviced Angel Island State Park. Angel Island is the land you're looking at as the backdrop to Alcatraz if you're looking from the San Francisco side, or, The City, as we called it. At night I'd go for walks around the island. Surrounded by nine million people, I had peace and quiet all to myself. By the time I'd stomped through the mudflats and surf at dawn with Mr. Molina, science, nature, outdoors and scholasticism all were coming together in one wonderful pathway. I loved it.

Everything Mr. McDonald taught and the sharpening nexus between the love of outdoors and scholasticism all came to a wonderful point at the humble Bolinas Marine Station, a tiny one-room lab out there run by the College of Marin. I took the Bolinas course while I was still at Redwood. The teacher was Al Molina, the most gifted naturalist and teacher in the world and the last in a dying breed in a biology field gone nuts over computers and DNA and CSI. Al could identify the species of a hawk from a half-mile by the angle of his wings alone. He knew marine stuff perfectly. He was the only biologist I know to happily operate right in the middle of the invertebrate/vertebrate divide. He unashamedly posted commercial fish taxonomy charts right there in a lab devoted to invertebrates, a mortal sin in any other teaching lab. "Marine biology" is a fake category, invented by Jacques Cousteau more than anyone else;

real biology was sharply divided between vert, and invert, and nobody messed with Mr. In-Between. We were terrible invert snobs. We studied half a dozen phyla and vert types that barely covered one class, and one with not many species, to boot. We even did plants, which is what plants were, so we were way on top. Bolinas Lagoon,..ahhh...go there, huh? Just a magic lagoon hidden away from the universe of cities, just north of Stinson Beach in Marin. I always believed it was like a little hobbit shire. Or the cover of Tea for the Tillerman by Cat Stevens, or where Maude wanted to carry her rescued tree to, in Harold and Maude. There, near Bolinas Lagoon, great blue herons have their babies. Nursery of heaven, for angels, there, in magic misty Bolinas.

Santa Cruz is located at the top of Monterey Bay, just over the hill from San Jose. If you come from that direction, you go by the old haunted house on the hill across from Santa's Village. Everyone said Hitchcock filmed Psycho there, or lived there. Or both. Santa Cruz was just about a three hour drive down from Marin past The City, and, if you're lucky, down the wonderful Pacific Coast Highway that keeps falling into the water. The Cal campus was up on the hill above the town, on the old Cowell Ranch, half in and half out of an old growth redwood forest, another hobbitshire-like location. The labs and lecture halls were built right in amongst the trees with tiny asphalt footpaths and a tiny pedestrian bridge connecting everything. A big fuss was made when it opened a few years earlier about that campus being a "cluster" college -- that meant a half-dozen sub-colleges, each of them with a community feel to them, and an area of specialty, but still the lab and physical plant advantages of a larger campus. After I saw it myself, I saw the wisdom of it: take Harvey Mudd, by comparison. A much pricier private school in the Pomona Valley down south, it had a cluster approach too, but no big labs that I ever heard of. The same with some small schools I've seen since then like Steubenville, Thomas Aquinas or Magdalene (New Hampshire). Fine for lit. majors, but Santa Cruz had it all while each college retained that homey feel of a small number, like Jesus or Magdalene at Oxford. The specializations were science, Western Civ., Soshe, performing arts and even a new one that had a lot of pop-psyche touchy-feely stuff going on, as if there weren't enough of that already in California to begin with.

I went to Cowell. To go to a Western Civ. sub school when I was a scientist was a kind of counterintuitive move, I suppose. I knew I'd already be getting a ton of science. A little high-tone wouldn't hurt me. It was also probably a little counterbalance to soothe my esthetic conscience, because even before I got to Cal, I had agonized over whether to go with science or music. You can't do both, they say, with all the labs and rehearsals, and this would be a little compensation, the old-school art and history at Cowell. High-tone started with the core course that all Cowell students had to take. We went to the biggest lecture hall on campus which had a massive screen and seats all canted up against it; perfect for looking at huge projections of Giotto or Caravaggio or ancient Roman or Greek stuff. We also all watched Harold and Maude in that hall on the weekends, and other flicks. If you want to get an idea of our attitude, Harold and Maude is probably a good place to start. Anti-war, for sure, but still fairly harmless politically. Butterfly chasers and tree rescuers. The two Cowell faculty who ran the course couldn't have been more different. You could actually see the difference in front of you between old and new. I should say, Old and New Worlds: Mary was a plain-speaking proletarian American art historian and Jasper Rose was, quite literally, a lecturer from Cambridge. He'd actually wear the Cambridge lecturer's gown during lectures, and at critical points in his speech he'd hitch it up, a little reminder of his authority, despite his humility.

"Giotto. [this, with a marvelous slide on the screen of some painting] Giotto was a curious figure," Jasper would intone, canting his eyes up to the lofty heights of the room, above any of the students, above the fray of earthly, non-art human concerns. "Not quite Rococo, not quite a Byzantine throwback, what? Mary! I say!" He'd hitch up his gown on the word "rococo" just in case we missed the operative word. The gown was a loose vestment, something like a vest with no buttons, that was very long. It seemed to need a lot of adjusting to keep it from falling off during Jasper's getting carried away waving his hands in emotion about the beauties of art. Mary was off to the side, arms crossed, musing. "Mary. I say, Mary, what's your take on our Giotto? Thoroughly pre-renaissance chap, or, what?" Mary would lean back against the teaching bench...this was Natural Sciences, after all...or sometimes she'd just sit on it and dandle her legs like a little girl on a railroad trestle in summer. "Giotto was a whore. Kicked out the stuff, some Roman patron, huh? Probably some fat, rich pope somewhere. Never really made it. A whore."

The elliptical European subtlety of a P.G. Wodehouse, [Il Promesso author] or Dorothy Sayers thought process would come up against the American directness of Amelia Earhart, Mark Twain or Robert Frost, right in front of me. I was a scientist. I'd never seen anything like this in the humanities. It was wonderful. And I like Giotto, the bum.

    First names to address professors? Pass/fail grading with a written evaluation, supposed to be an improvement on the Berkeley "machine" grade-grubbing? Small cluster colleges with a common dining hall for professors and students? Little hobbit pathways through the forest and a spectacular view of Monterey Bay, especially at night when the moon would shine over the water? Waltzes with live orchestras, fancy dress and ice sculptures? Everything clean and new with fancy, classy architecture where the buildings were nestled into existing forests and you couldn't study anywhere without lifting up your head and seeing a redwood tree? and all on the same "freight" as any other campus? Too good to be true, you're thinking. A ha. This is the perfect time to mention the UCSC Conspiracy Theory. But before I do that, let me mention that after a short visit to the campus only a few years later, I discovered that the hobbit/scientist/hippies of my years were totally replaced by a bunch of gum-popping bottle blond cheerleader type psyche/soshe types who'd never heard of Giotto or anyone like that, and who studied People magazine and National Enquirer to determine facts and history. The miracle hobbitshire in the redwoods of the mid-70's was gone, a Brigadoon that had floated off into the mists, a brief shining moment it was there and then disappeared in a swirl of Kardashians, never to be seen again. "Selah," as the psalmist would say.

    But back then when I was in school the conspiracy theory about the building of UCSC was quite the thing. It's a simple idea: the University Regents who ran the entire nine campus system from up in Berkeley had purposely invented UCSC as a hippie magnet to draw radical types away from UCB where they had caused so much trouble in the Free Speech Movement in the late 60's. That such radicals would walk away from the urban Berkeley campus and its access to forty thousand on-campus potential comrades, and a bunch more nearby off-campus, and go off to a hippy-trippy granola-yogurt spot in the woods in the middle of nowhere…could this have been a defect in the planning of the nefarious Regents? All I know is very few radicals made it down into the forest away from the city. Of course we were sympathetic to anti-war; we were kids. But radicals? I don't think so. We did march on downtown Santa Cruz's cutesy tourist giftshop main street, an unbelievably sleepy Ross MacDonald type surfing town. They were probably ready to call in the National Guard in the first five minutes of the "march," as they had never seen anything like it. Would all the fears of the older Santa Cruzan retirees about the new Cal campus be realized? In the next hour of our march, however, they probably noticed something about these radicals: no rocks. No broken windows. No shouts. On closer inspection, it really wasn't anything much else but a simple lark, a chance to cut classes, along with half of the liberal faculty. A little impromptu Caribbean Carnival, there, in sleepy downtown. Anyone hoping to hear bullhorn declamations of demands were more likely to hear madrigals, Shakespeare orations or The Love song of J. Albert Prufrock. Whatever that was, it wasn't Das Kapital or the Humanist Manifesto. Instead of Che Guevara t-shirts scrutinizing police were more likely to detect blue Levi worker shirts embroidered with figures from Wind In The Willows, Ursula LeGuin, or Dune. Tolkien. We didn't even litter. That would have been unecological.

Some radicals we turned out to be. If there were any Marxists there in Santa Cruz, they didn't get the memo. From Berkeley or Moscow, either one. The hippie paradise in the redwoods might just turn out to be...exactly that. Not long after the Big Radical March of Conspicuously Unbroken Glass, a tiny photo essay showed up on the door of my major advisor, the longsuffering, understated, incredibly brilliant and classy biologist Todd Newberry. I simply can't think of a better expression of his subtle wit and humor than that photo-essay. It was barely a dozen arty black & white shots of typical Cowell Ranch bucolic scenes, scenes familiar to any student since the Cowell family still ran cows in the pastures bordering the campus. All of the campus had been shoehorned into the existing forest and pastures; no one had bulldozed anything, really. Two or three cows grazing in a field. A dirt country lane no bigger than a hay wagon path. A bay tree on the edge of a redwood stand. An open meadow. A stream. All of the pictures were like this: nature shots of simple country scenes. What made the photo essay were the captions. The first picture -- a meadow with a stream running through it -- was captioned, "The morning started out peaceful on the university campus." The next picture was captioned: "By 9:30 AM a restless crowd had gathered on the commons." The picture showed two cows grazing. The next picture showed two crows sitting on a fence, the caption? "At 10:14 AM the campus police reported to the Governor that they had lost control of the mob." The next picture showed a sagging wooden hip-high gate as you'd see in an abandoned garden. Caption: "At one PM the Board of Regents ordered the main gates of the campus to be closed." The last picture? it was an exact copy of the first one, with a meadow and a tiny stream winding through it. The caption said, "By nightfall the full extent of the damage was plain to see." Call me a people person, but thinking back, I think of people, their shining personalities as much as events or even places, as many of those that I have seen or done.

By some Brownian Motion of energy, though, sooner or later the clueless Americans discovered a queue in front of a particular aged professor's office door. Inside wreaths of CS Lewis/Tolkien pipe smoke surrounded the old man sitting hour after hour in a comfortable armchair, furniture normally unknown in a lab. The man with the pipe and chair was in no hurry at all. He never shouted commands, as Yanks did. He didn't jump onto the gunnels of a departing research ship or do the Cousteau aqualung bit for the cameras. He just sat in the chair all day long quietly pondering piles of printout brought to him by the energetic but dumb-as-hunting-dogs American researchers. He couldn't care less if there was a queue; he was unaware of it. He'd get to his own research after the summer was over and these pesky Americans were gone.

After however long it took, the smiling old man, who'd gotten tenure before most of the American scientists' parents were born, would hand the stuff back. "Donque, ici, messieur, ouj?" He'd carefully lay his finger alongside a trend in a row of indecipherable numbers, or an anomaly, or a lacuna. This would be either the missing numerical portrait of a phenomenon any scientist looks for, or it would indicate a way forward to redesign the method in order to gather more conclusive data that would help narrow the spectrum of possible explanations. Todd was a scream telling this story.

"The Yanks would bound back out of his office, all excited to get to a typewriter," he would say with a philosophic tilt of his head as he gazed out of his office window, "without having thought of it themselves for one second. And the next guy in line would burst into L'Professeure's office with a new batch of stuff, and neither one of 'em could think for himself. Dumb as a box of rocks. Was this the first shot across the bow of my youthful anxious energy in the direction of quiet time? Well, color me dumb, because even after this marvelous story would you believe the exact same thing happened to me? Full disclosure: I did not play the part of the sage wise old professor with the pipe. I was the dumb researcher.

## RALPH M. GABRIEL

One summer I took the Berkeley Marine Biology course up at their station in Bodega, a town near Mendocino City, the place where they made Hitchcock's The Birds. Posted on a grad students office door was this: Ohm, ohm on the range,/Where the Cucumaria curata play/Where electrophoresis,/Will give me my thesis,/And the column's not turbid all day.

It hit me like a slap in the face with a wet sea cucumber. So, they're thesis-grubbers, over there at Berkeley, our little researcher friends are. Not quite the idealistic political activists we kept hearing about. Hmmm. Well, at Santa Cruz we were better than all that. We were not grubbing for a thesis. We were "excited" about this or that "direction of research," or we found your research "incredibly interesting." The central dogma of Santa Cruz science was that one followed one's passion, and the incredibly slim chance of anyone ever having a real job...anywhere, even in academia, would take care of itself. Just follow your passion. I mention Bodega because that's where I had my own Roscoff experience where I was the dummy. Yeah, it did take energy to get the numbers but I still couldn't figure them out. The younger of the two Berkeley profs told me to put it all on one graph in a log or semi-log printout, everything, side-by-side. It kicked out a fog-like cluster of tiny symbols: plus signs, asterisks or squares represented each mussel from each intertidal sampling horizon. The research was about mussel shell weight and shape relative to flesh weight. My excitement back then was about aquaculture for a hungry world: what was an optimum intertidal depth for that? Of course it's kind of a dumb question, looking back. The most flesh would be put on a mussel that is completely underwater. But there are sharks to consider, especially back when the use of subtidal cages was still in the future. So my study might have had some small application. I was thinking especially of the coastal beaches off India where everyone was so hungry.

The prof, took one look at the plot: Eureka! He trailed his finger along the clusters of x's and o's and stars and boxes. "This is a significant difference," he said, pointing to invisible lines running through the clumps of symbols. You see? Even after the great story from Todd, I had gone and done the exact same thing! I had walked into the trap. I had ripped the data off the machine without looking at it myself. I can just see Todd and the French emeritus prof both shaking their heads sadly to each other after a certain someone had left the room. "Les americaine...energetique, mais dumb as a bag of hammers, eh, Messur?" Makes you wonder. Will our dumb TV culture ever get to the point where we can't even find one pipe-smoking old guy in an easy chair, somewhere, that can help us out? And if we did, would we listen to him. Or are we already there.

    I stayed up all night charting all this onto big swatches of brown butcher paper I could hang up in front of the class. The next morning was the final presentation of everyone's stuff, and I had bumped into my Big Explanation just that afternoon. I used different colored chalks for each tidal level of sample, so you could tell them apart. All-nighters were too typical for me. I was a crammer, coasting though high school without ever learning how to study. But that next morning at the Bodega main teaching lab, the one facing the ocean, I was a wreck. Somehow I stumbled through it but I forgot that there was a question period after the presentation. Not good. Repeating what I knew from the study, zapped out from being up all night was one thing, but questions? Oh, no.

    Finally, I somehow came to the realization that I had been asked a question by the senior professor, a kind man. "Were you up all night cramming on this, Jim?" I was told later, was the question. I stared at him, blank-eyed, in front of the entire class in the middle of the most important stand-and-deliver moment of my entire college career. A tiny portion of my brain screamed: he asked a question, you dummy! Answer it! He's the Big Shot! The other students told me later that I had just stood there and stared at him and the class and never said a word, clueless as yesterday's road kill. Finally the old guy had smiled and deduced the answer for me despite my prima facie rudeness. He was a kind man despite his big status. I even got a good grade. Maybe they graded on energy and enthusiasm, not on thinking. Les americaines, eh, Pierre?

    Back at Santa Cruz I repeated the study with bigger samples and whiz-bang computers that proved a significant difference of the different strata levels of mussels on the reef. Not good enough, anymore, to just look at something and make an observation. Got to prove everything. Bigger samples meant more mussel shucking and cooking than I could handle so I cajoled a bunch of UG students into helping me out one day in that wonderful lab up on the hill in the forest with the south-facing windows, Nat. Sci. II. I enticed them with promises of beer and pizza, and then, in the crush and panic of trying to keep track of all the data, I forgot to deliver! Sorry, guys! I owe you! God bless 'em, no one grumbled. Beer and pizza was like a gold Cadillac, anyway. A dream, something people do on TV. We were all hobbits. To hell with fancy-ass beer and pizza.

That data led to a paper at the Western Society of Naturalists, though, a very loose and funky collection of leftover Cannery Row/Ed Ricketts/John Steinbeck types. Meaning, dreamy types who really did think marine biology was an actual science, and who tended to turn their noses up at anyone who talked about the money in, say, fisheries, pollution monitoring, aquaculture, etc. Practical stuff. We were old-fashioned British natural historians. We were snobs in two directions, come to think of it: we were superior to those hacks who stopped at popular lecture halls full of starry-eyed Bambi or Gorillas In The Mist types, and we were also "basic" scientists, superior to people who did applied research that might actually feed or protect someone. We were all that and a Steinbeck novel and a glass of beer. The others had their Jacques Cousteau media darlings, but a Cannery Row type biologist would kneel down in surf at the beach and come up with a tiny sea slug in a sandwich bag for all to see, an eye-popper of absolute electric colorful beauty in a tiny smudge; then we'd get knocked over by a wave.

A tiny thing with no fur, no warm blood, no legs, no economic impact, and very often, not even any proper eyes. What's to love about that? But we did. You see? We were very snobby about our eclectic tastes. An invertebrate world unto ourselves. Our own Middle Earth throve in a puddle at the beach. By the time I got to the WSN meeting in Santa Barbara, I had graduated from the pastel chalk markings on butcher paper. I now had fancy slides with computer generated white symbols on a cerulean diazo blue background, very cool in a dark room, like a reverse blueprint. It was a smash. Roger Seapy was there from Fullerton. He was enthusiastic. I still don't know if a thesis is required for the BA degree at Cal, but down in Santa Barbara it was a big hit.

I took a year off between Cal and grad. school. My first job in "the real world" was as a tech. at the Newport Marine Lab on the Oregon coast run by OSU. They weren't ashamed of Verts: they were their bread and butter. There they were, up on the wall in the labs: actual identifying charts of…fish, right out in front of God and everyone. Would I, the pure and basic scientist, become somehow corrupted by all this vertebrate activity? The blushing hippie violet, ruined by filthy vertebrate lucre? It was nervous-making, I can tell you. Not to worry. My boss Jeff Gonor was an invert type and my project was literature searching in support of an EPA-type white paper about pollution monitoring, especially relevant after the big Exxon Valdez crash and massive oil pollution in Alaska just a few years earlier. It was a hot topic among the Cannery row crowd, especially since lawyers could point to the little critters as quantitative markers to assess liability and payouts for future spills. A barnacle has nowhere to run or hide when the water gets dirty. We were setting things up for the next Erin Brokovich.

    I lived right there at the lab at first, in the dorms built for the summer course crowd, just like the Bodega dorms. But this was winter and I had the dorms all to myself, just me and a nice couple from Australia, a visiting fisheries professor and his wife. They took pity on the starving bachelor all alone with no cooking and decided also to infuse a little high culture into the life of this boorish Yank. I'm speaking of course, of a high tea. No, I'm not making this up. Every afternoon, in a corner of this cavernous empty dorm. This Ozzie couple was smiling, cheerful, funny, pleasant and hospitable to a fault, but this was all a front. A scam. It turns out underneath all this happy camouflage they were incredibly wicked. I've since learned on site that in England high tea is a pleasant ritual, with only a tiny nibble of a "bickee" to complement P.O. Wodehouse's "nourishing liquid that restored the membranes." The biscuit complemented the tea. Only. Not drowned in it. The Ozzies would have none of that. They sneaked in totally under the radar. "Like a biscuit?" they'd ask, innocently enough. Little did I know the biscuit in question was those weird cream crackers known to starving backpackers around the world. No salt on them, and big and strong enough to victual an aircraft carrier. And its wing. First it was a slice of pickle. If you go for a pickle, maybe you'd like a spot of relish, Jim? Same thing, right? What I didn't know and they didn't teach undergraduates in Santa Cruz is that relish is the gateway drug for chutney, a substance of dubious origin and dubiouser processing that could crack off half the plinth the Washington Monument is standing on.

    In a week I was huffing heavily spiced kippers as if they were Nabisco wafers. Smoking hot mustard, tartar sauce to make the Tartars run. Arid hide, mint jelly, real strawberry jam, something starving undergraduates could only dream of. Soon, there I was, sweating and exhausted, bloated and immersed in the fleshpots of Cairo, a hookah pipe dangling from my lips in between tea courses that could feed the US Cavalry. And its men. Ozzie and Harriet would daintily touch a napkin to their lips, smile and pack up all the leftovers for tomorrow. They had endless supplies, anyway. Only at the end of all this did I discover that Mr. Australian Fish

Biologist like frisson, specifically the friction that occurs between sweet and sour in one mouthful, like mint jelly and hydrochloric acid bitter chutney. At one point he loaded seventeen separate ingredients on one groaning, creaking cream cracker, dispatching all with a smile.

Before Oregon I was a phenomenologist, or Aristotelian. Purity of form was everything. Now, I can grope blindly in a refrigerator or some cheap dive of a dusty seven eleven in Waco and eat everything that comes to hand. Comes in handy when you're broke all the time. Or, as the Babs put it, "When you're living hand-to-mouth, it helps if you are ambidextrous." Another life lesson? Stored away there, CS Lewis-style, lo, those many moons before I had become a Christian, let alone a prolifer or an activist? Makes you wonder. And I love chutney. Now. By itself, please. With a little unpretentious Napa Cabernet to wash it down, thank you.

Jeff my boss had a great sense of humor. In his office was a stick figure with two aluminum foil discs strategically and anatomically correctly located. Gonar's Gonad Protectors, it announced. Something to do with x-ray analysis of something or other. The slumming with those nasty worldly vertebratologists didn't stop with high tea, either. One Saturday yet another fish type invited me out birding for the first time in my life. Yes, I was a biologist, but, not that kind of guy. Birds have backbones, or didn't you notice? They showed up in Disney movies with Bambi and all that. Ewwww… Anyway, my normal moral compass blunted, no doubt, with a chutney and kippers hangover, I got up early one Saturday and found out the birds started to look pretty good, too. I've been a birder ever since.

The vertebrate types had their anthropologist types who swooned over Goodall and monkeys and Cousteau. They had Bambi. Who wouldn't like Bambi? Stuff with fur and warm blood and little baby seals in Hudson Bay and right whales, which, let's face it, are quite cool. Us invertebrate types on the other hand would crouch down in leaky waders in the surf and squint at tiny slimy or prickly critters no one cared about. I remember a silver-collar size limpet mark on the dolomite under Chimney Rock out at the actual tip of Pt. Reyes itself. There's a cool football field-size cow pasture that floats a hundred feet in the air over the surf connected to the rest of the world by only a tiny land bridge you could barely drive a jeep over. "He's twenty years old. Or more," Al told me, measuring the spot worn down into the rock by the limpet, his little sleeping place he'd made for himself and kept clean to hang out at low tide. Al explained it: he's sat there all that time and never went farther than a foot away, grazing when the tide's in, hoping some hungry otter doesn't figure it out. He'd been there since before I was born. And are we so much better, with our e-travels of empty observation and experience or jet rides of thousands of miles with no arriving, just more partying?

Looking back, the unspoken but powerful idea slowly put itself into front and center of an unseen world of thought and feeling: I imagine a creature, a rock or a bug, helpless, stuck vulnerable, and…what? What is the meaning of this tiny helpless creature? It only took me forty more years to articulate it. No one can accuse me of being the fastest carrier in the fleet. The little snail says help me. Love me. I'm waiting. I'm waiting exactly here until you come and meet me. I can't move to come and find you. See me./Feel me./Touch me./Heal me. And some little limpets have little backbones, no?

After Newport Oregon and the high teas and birding and Dizzy Gillespie, the university of Texas at Austin was a step up. Oh, there were plenty of cowboys hanging around with hayseed in their boots, to be sure, but the main event at UT Austin was that geologists had struck oil, right there on the actual campus. They had so much dough that UT was the only school in the US with a permanent building fund. They had more money than they knew what to do with. But guess what costs more than buildings?

Professors. And not just any professors, but the best. UT, anxious to get past the hayseed image, grabbed all their oil cash and went on a little shopping spree for professorial flesh, up around the Ivy League. A kind of cash-for-snoots program. At first the snoots turned their noses up at it, but after a while comprehension dawned in their high-tone minds: maybe there is money in this business, after all. The first to roll were the humanities types -- I suspect because they have no labs and can just up and go. Also, even the gifted ones in Ivy League had to jump at a chance at tenure, a dicey thing for a history professor. But all this might explain why my uber-boss in Texas used to be a big gun at Merck. UT's fishing expedition went a little wider than just schools. Any grant rain-maker would do, in or out of academia. There. I said it, Bless me Father, I really screwed up this time. Yes, I was a tech whore for Big Pharma. Just before you rat me out to the Pope and tie me to the well-deserved telephone post and put faggots under my feet, I want first anxiously to abjure, abhor, denounce myself, and throw myself on the mercy of the People's Court.

Technically I was still not only not a Catholic at the time, I wasn't even an Evangelical yet, in the sense of knowing the Lord. At most I was a cultural Lutheran, lapsed for ten years. Does this get me a reprieve? No? Well, OK, but please put a crucifix on a pole then and hold it in front of my face at the end, OK? And get a priest. There. I had to get it off my chest. I feel better. Texas was a way station, waiting to hear back from grad schools about where or whether I got in. I had decided not just to jump straight in after Santa Cruz. I was also in Texas waiting to hear from Cheryl if we were off or maybe, just maybe, back on again. I was the last one to get the memo; we were going separate directions, but I sure had my fingers crossed, there, in Texas. But as for the Big Pharma research, even a pagan could see this research was a ghoulish 1984 drug and mind control disaster. Being pagan is no excuse.

Karl Folkers had his own division at Merck, I'm told, and he probably brought some of those money rainclouds with him to the campus. Once there, he got an endowed chair. A better patent break, too? It was called the Institute for Biomedical Research, and I've never seen or heard of such a huge abuse of oh-so intellectually free academic infrastructure and campus overhead in my life. An academic-industrial complex. Did the benefactors and Texas taxpayers know that on their campus they were funding mind altering drug research and genocide? The group was massive. Folker had at least a dozen post-docs and straight-up PhD's and MD-PhD's working for him in this group. A paper mill. "Publish-or-perish" is the academic mantra, but usually only for university faculty who have to teach. Thus, a conflict. There was no teaching at the IBR, Institute for Biomedical Research, as it was called. Just pure research. My immediate boss, Stephan Fuchs, was kicking out a paper every few months and Folker would get "second authorship" on every one, par for the course for the grant rainmaker, but it wasn't the process of the IBR that bugs me now, it was the content of the research.

Biologists call them micro-hormones but in our chem lab we always called them by their chemical name: oligopeptides. A short chain of amino acids that acted as a hormone, a bloodstream messenger. But then, ours was not the only lab where biology was more and more taken over by chemistry. Chem in its turn is taken over by physics, which is taken over by statistical models of electron disposition, so we're all victims of fate, it's all just some chemical, get it? No soul, no freedom, no free will, no responsibility to go with that. Blame it on CS1 Miami. I do. Women, mothers with daughters, and young women, and particularly feminists: please pay very close attention: I am about to describe your political future.

We're all familiar with a vanilla hormone like testosterone or progesterone that targets an organ like a gonad, or in the case of oxytocin, say, assists L & D. Microhormones are totally different. They are tiny messengers that only operate in between the hypothalamus, a part of the brain proper, and the pituitary gland, which kicks out the real hormones that go around the body and do whatever. None of us would have any sexual function from the classic hormones if those hormones themselves weren't signaled to be released from the pituitary by the microhormones, which come only from the brain. Sorry, feminists, but you have a female brain and guys got the other. This is why males with the "Y" chromosome always ask "Why?" when you ask them to take out the trash. A thoroughly sexist joke to help your students remember which is which, by the way, just in case you ever land a teaching gig!

But in that diabolic lab in Texas, we were doing research to manipulate, mimic and replace or otherwise block the little hormones from the brain. This in effect would convert female brains to neuter brains. "But, Jeem, zees is great zeeng!" my boss would say. 'Not zo many zide effectz az ze ozair contratzepteefs, yes?" And, yes, it's hard to keep a straight face when your boss sounds like Zsa Zsa Gabor. Again, as in the case of the weird alliance between feminists and Playboy, now, they are rushing to science to give them this new toy, not realizing they are being converted from female to neuter. Yes, neuter, not even male. In German a child is a neuter. Not male or female. Sterile. Like a mule which cannot reproduce. Mules are sterile slaves. They pull the load and then die and get out of the way, and no sick leave to foal. Get it? Do I need to draw you a picture?

In Blade Runner the dystopian political/scientific culture created a test-tube race of soldiers, but what to do with women? Cloned prostitutes, both the males and the females, were sterile and short-lived. I have never understood the Playboy/feminist alliance, but this is proof it's alive. If the feminists protested this garbage, it would be stopped under political pressure in a heartbeat. A world of disposable, sterile soldiers and hookers. Is this what we want? It also explains the other part of feminism I've never got: to be a feminist the price of admission is to sterilize yourself with the Pill or an abortion. Mothers need not apply. Not at the top. I have tons of feminists who are friends. But never got an answer on that one. Guess I've met too many women who are way more powerful than lazy men, beginning with Mother Teresa. Don't stand too close at that photo-op when she was alive! You'd be put to work. Now.

It bugs me a little to tell all this because among the enemies of life there are many who would happily shove the drug that results from this ghoulish research down the throats of 10-year-old girls worldwide, as they now do Plan B. Plan B started out as a desperation ex post facto measure, still bad; an endocrinological jackhammer with horrific side effects. Now its routine. Just the other day I heard a comedienne brag about how she did it, loved it, and now her Plan B has become her Plan A. Ha ha ha. It takes an old gray-haired prolife hand to remind us that this emergency approach was the original rationalization for all the formulae of the Pill, at their outsets. So now comedians joke about poisoning their own kids. They laughed at the Christians being torn up by the lions, too. Entertainment. No one was laughing when Rome fell the rest of the way. So I mention this in case a true feminist or a parent of a daughter wants to stop this before it comes online, or avoid it if it does. Without resistance it will go through simply because the culture of death is diabolic that way. Not just the devil horns symbol everyone makes at rock concerts and black masses, but overall. A push for death. And, a little perk for the elitists of the world, for whom you and I are just in the way. Useless eaters. "Nuclear war is the fruit of abortion," said mother Teresa. Couldn't say it any better myself. And, hey, it sure fixes that whole sex assault of female soldiers thing. If the whole world is just soldiers and hookers anyway, well, who cares? Anyway, Karl Folkers did discover B-17, the active ingredient in my sister's cancer-curing Laetrile, so, that's a good thing. He took injections of it himself all the time.

Another good things about the IBR was the weekly seminars which they let me, lowly tech, attend. It was a new experience for me to be the only non-PhD around the table and hear everyone reporting. I remember one guy in particular, a humbleTvID whose simple thesis was: "As we know, cancer was cured 20 years ago." He said this in 1978. Stop eating cold-cuts, smoking, etc. To him, it was all environmental triggers. True, those can trigger more likely in someone genetically inclined, but. they won't incline if there's no trigger. I believed him then, after my experience with Marty, and I believe him now

This doctor was a perfect example of a caring clinician, not a test-tube jock, who if he could have, would have been a brake, an attempt at getting the chemists to grow a conscience about the oligopeptide push.

One day one of the undergraduates who worked with me in the lab confided that he was interested in med school but didn't believe he could get in.

I don't know what my problem is. If I had to guess, i'd say it was growing up meeting presidents and other pals of my parents in their political efforts, but I have no shyness about writing letters of recommendation to big shots about anyone I've met. I flipped open the catalog of the Galveston med school, put it on the dartboard and let fly, sent the letter to I don't know who, and our boy got in. I only hope he never did an abortion because he told me he was interested in OB/GYN. But back then, it was a non-issue for me. Anyway, I believe in people, so there. God bless you, Hector.

I had a fish-tank next to my desk at IBR. Somehow, through neglect and attrition it got down to one fish that didn't look exotic at all, or even pretty. A miniature perch, our fish looked like. I had this weird compulsion to top off his tank so he'd get a little more room to swim around in. Einstein that I am, I never figured out the connection between this and the fact that every now and then I'd walk into my office and find him lying on the floor; the Great Escape, I suppose.

I thought he was dead! But I felt sorry for the little guy and I threw him back in the tank, just in case, hope springs eternal. What do you know, but a few minutes later he was swimming around in there, none the worse for wear and seeming to bear no grudge at all about the whole thing. This happened over and over before I figured out the waterline thing. I hope he's ok now, or happily flipping his tail with Flipper in perch heaven.

Well, all good things down here below must come to an end: one day I was brusquely summoned to Dr. Folker's office directly, a huge violation of chain-of-command in a very militant organization. I soon found out the cause of my über-boss's distress.

"What are your plans for the future, Jim?" It turns out Stefan had just suddenly given notice, a cardinal sin in academia but the Austrians are absolutely worldwide top dogs in the hormone-cooking business so they can write their own tickets. Folkers wanted me to promise right now to stay in the group to keep continuity of technique in the gel column isolation part of his Institute. Stefan's stuff. Did this guy even know I wasn't a chemist? That my undergraduate background was butterfly chasing, not even molecular biology? That the Fullerton shift to cellular biology was still in the future for me? That I was from California? That there's no surf in Texas, nothing like LA, anyway?

Somewhere in all that conversation he began to get a clue because he shifted from my job at the lab to A & M med school in Galveston. The grants this guy pulled into the system could probably buy his own school, so when he offered me the spot in Galveston that day, he meant it. Yes, I think he was a pure chemist, but he wasn't stupid. He knew all about the contribution that molecular biology post-grads and the MD-PhDs made to Big Pharma. Actually, chemists absolutely need them to do a little thing called "human trials."

Not to whine too much, but if it was up to the pure chemists of this world, we'd all just be pureed and dumped into test tubes so that they could adjust the pH and titrate – whatever -- without having to hear us complain about side effects. To a chemist, Big Pharm is just the Military-Industrial complex with a fig leaf of Marcus Welby clumsily pasted over it. 1 can tell you, as a prolifer, it most definitely is, when you get into the global culling thing. There, Big Pharma is just an adjunct of the other.

In fact, if the world knew how many MDs had been stolen from the clinical system to make Big Pharma labs run, they'd probably invent a new conspiracy theory. Not all docs are Marcus Welby, God bless 'em. Some of them just hang out in the basement and do posts, or even simple secretarial transcribing, like a couple of guys I bumped into even back in Anaheim. Cool on patient contact but still dweebs that could definitely make a contribution, just not into that whole liability thing. Heck, most radiologists never see a patient anymore at all, just hang out at night and read film, transcribe while eating (I know this for a fact!) and go home. I was reminded of all this at the weekly seminars in Austin when I'd bump into the pure, no-fooling, not-even-MD-PhD researcher there who'd been messing with test tubes so long it had been years since he had even seen a patient face-to-face. They kept him around to figure out "'protocols" for other docs to do when it came time for "human trials."

Anyway, in his office in the spring of 78, talking with Dr. Folkers and his full-court press, it was also a little harder to say no because there was a little esprits des corps that had built up, even over that small time I was there, barely a year. He invited me over to his house for a party one night and after the Europeans got into their cups -- you don't have to draw them a picture -- he went into the back of his house and came out with the exact tux he'd worn to accept the Nobel step-down that some scientific society in Sweden or somewhere had given him as the booby prize for the Nobel.

It turned out that the year that Dr. Folkers was shortlisted for the Nobel, he was cursed by his genes and country. The united states is a big dog in a small yard when it comes to the Nobel because of all our money. Big Pharma cash, military culling, whatever. This means that the Nobel Committee takes politics a little into consideration when they grant the prizes so that they don't offend or ignore the Flyover Countries, so to speak, the little countries that don't have the bucks or industry for the frantic American pace of science.

I remember very well when he appeared with his fancy tux, holding the same silk top hat he had gotten to receive the other prize, the one that he had gotten because he could not get the Noble for political reasons. The Nobel Committee wanted to mix it up in terms of how they handed out the prizes, and Europe or Asia was due in the informal cycle for consideration with small peptide chains. But Folkers will always go down in history as the discoverer of B-17, the compound that saved my sweetie pie and way cool sister Marty's life for so long, and also, even within the scientific community, to say that you isolated and identified a compound that was in the Krebs's Cycle itself was way more important than just some guy who found another peptide hormone. The Krebs's Cycle is basic, every cell has it, and we all use it every second of every day to live. With the impact of B-17 on Marty's cancer, I'm surprised no one has picked up on the research angle of that for cancer, but then, they can't. Laetrile is illegal as a cancer treatment, even if it is in the damn Kreb's cycle.

That party was bittersweet for another reason. In his experience as a researcher Folkers had to have known that Stefan and I, curmudgeonly old Austrians that we were, simply clicked for the lab work. Also, if I had stayed with the group, this would have been true for any other researcher that came in, because all micro hormones are monopolized by Swiss and Austrian Big Pharm, and, really, from that, everyone else. Pharm started in Switzerland, if I had to guess.

I remember that party. A bunch of hopeless nerds who could hardly explain their work to one out of a million people on the street, and yet we were all together having a good time. As with so many other things in life, if this horrible century weren't so cursed with death, it would have been a great life.

He can't have known how us invert types viewed med school, which dealt with vertebrates. Ewwwwwwwww…Bambi and Flipper: I don't think so.

Dutiful German son that I am, I still managed to make noncommittal noises. I may even have said I would have to get back to him after I had gone to Switzerland because I had been planning that trip for a while and I would need to see how I thought about things after that.

"Of course! Of course, Jim! Go to Switzerland! Have a nice trip! But…"

He begged me to come back and stay working for him and go to school in Galveston. It was embarrassing. I mean, it's not as if I were a Catholic yet and knew how wicked the human pesticide stuff was. I wouldn't be Catholic for another four years. If I didn't know that, you could hardly blame him for not knowing it.

Still, I wasn't a vertebratologist, and I sure as hell wasn't a chemist. I didn't even like chemistry in school. I only took it because you needed it to be a biologist. An invertebrate biologist, that is.

The campus of Cal State University at Fullerton is about as far away, in the feel of it, from the hobbit shire of UCSC as Hong Kong or Abidjan or Times Square is from the Gobi Desert. In the Gobi, all you have to do to hear the sound of your soul ticking over is shut off your cell. Actually, the cell tower situation in the Gobi would take care of that for you, like it or not, so even your own modern impulses wouldn't interfere with that soul-ticking thing. Contrast this with the Fullerton California campus situation: the instant you stepped outside any of the buildings there your ears are assaulted with one sound. Not rushing water, not the booming of surf like Manhattan Beach, not the whispering pines of Cedar Lake or the cooing mourning doves of South Pasadena. You hear a big-rig jake braking down the 57 incline bordering the campus. Freeway noise, something no one in SoCal is a stranger to. But still. In your face. Underlying the truck and traffic noise is that wearying and irritating tension between two things. On the one hand, the deeply embedded impulse somewhere in your head to convert the sound of traffic into the swish of a babbling brook. On the other hand, another part of your brain that says if you can hear freeway noise, at any second you could hear a crash. All

Greater Los Angeleans have seen and heard one. The thought of someone dying a few seconds from now, someone who is tootling down the Imperial Highway/big nasty redhead at my side/top down, crank up the beach boys/don't let the music stop one second, and the next is canned tuna, and perhaps going with them because we're too close, is just too scary to contemplate. This feeling, though subtle, is tiring after a time.

I only mention it because the Cal State campus is basically shoehorned into a freeway exchange between the 57 and the 22. The planning genius who first looked at a map and said, hey, look at this spot! No one cares about that place! Let's just dump that school in here! That guy needs a People's Heroic Civic Designer medal. The noise is completely overwhelming, crushing to the spirit and unavoidable in every nook and cranny of the campus. Other campuses, even an ugly Soviet apartment block style place, could still have a few students sitting on a lawn somewhere, talking or thinking, or smoking, or reading. Not Fullerton. Fullerton is like the freeway exchange itself. You come, you swoop through, you go. No love.

And what do you know? The buildings themselves at CSUF were as soulless as the freeway exchange. They were as ugly as the buildings in Santa Cruz were beautiful. At Fullerton, the library had no windows at all in it. Were they saving on AC or something? This is illegal even for a private residence, for humanitarian reasons, let alone a building designed to be used by thousands of people every day. If it weren't so, there's contractors who'd love to build houses from now 'till Christ returns with no windows just to save a buck, but they can't. It's illegal. But not for CSUF. To the blind mole who initialed the site purchase and library blueprints: I hope the IRS finds your Miami yacht someday. I hope it sinks. A guy can dream, huh? OK, so, rushing in and out of a commuter campus building is some kind of crime, especially in sunny Southern California, but, then again, it's what geeks tend to do even on a nicer campus, so what happens next?

Roger Seapy was my major advisor, a much bigger presence in a grad student's life than an undergrad. I'm not even sure U Cal required an advisor for undergrads, but in grad school you gotta have one, and he's everything in terms of getting done. Roger was the one, if you recall, who enthused when I gave the paper with the blue slides to the Western Society of Naturalists Conference in Santa Barbara a year or two before. He recruited me to Fullerton. Looking back, it's a little strange remembering the other grad schools that were interested, namely, Cal State San Francisco and Cal State San Luis Obispo. When it comes to grad school, and also a first teaching spot or whatever, you start to feel the pressure of competition for a small number of spots. You can't be picky, right? If you're passionate about science as I am, you certainly can't reject a school just because you don't like the campus. Still, looking back, it's a wistful thing. San Luis Obispo is much much closer to the remoteness and natural campus of a place like UCSC. Studying and research there, I could feel it from the interviews, would have been infinitely more laid back. I remember very clearly one lady biology professor in particular who started to actually sell the place to me at the end of our discussion. In the interview I had been forthright about the other offers I was looking at. She was painfully aware of the much superior science reputation of Fullerton, especially in molecular biology, whether it would be DNA or energetic metabolism. "Please come here," she said, "I know it's not Fullerton, but we have a great program and you would make a great contribution here."

The reason it catches at my memory now is not just that I had a lingering feeling of disappointing her and of missing out on a mellow cowboy campus. It goes beyond that. My dear and humble brother-in-law Rick had died suddenly at a young age only a year or two earlier, and San Luis Obispo would have been much closer to Anne and the kid's place in Thousand Oaks. Especially if you consider that if you drive from SLO you don't have to negotiate the Exchange From Hell, the 405/101 exchange above Hollywood, at commute time.

I have always believed that this difference would have meant a lot more time with Annie and the kids, and this haunts me now. On the other side of the coin however, I did still get to spend a lot of time with them and became something of an unofficial foster father for the kids, who turned out marvelous even with a daddy in heaven. Peace, Rick! It's all good, bro! But I wonder: if I had gone to SLO, would I have encountered the sad joy of third shift bedside terminal care at Anaheim Memorial? Would I have wound up in embryology because that embryologist guy was down the hall from the butterfly chasers? Would I even have slipped over to the prolife convention in Anaheim, which was just down the road from Fullerton?

No, no and no. So, even though I wound up at the noisy, smelly, intense molecular/cellular Fullerton Of The No Windows, it got all those three things too, things I wasn't looking for. As Donald Kennedy at the Farm never tired of telling his students, serendipity is underrated by today's kids in a hurry. I wonder if heaven can write blessedly crooked with our artificial and shortsighted damned straight compulsive lines, the straight line in this case being the "career" move to Fullerton.

    Back to Roger's lab. My desk looked out over a parking lot, but it had a few trees in it and it was second story with a window facing south, just like my room in the Oak Street house in South Pasadena when I was a kid. A great place for daydreaming. The desk on the other side of the door to Roger's office was another of his grad students, Karen. Karen was relaxed, good-looking and sharp as a tack. On top of all that, with the Irish lilt of laughter, wry humor and utter lack of whining -- something I appreciate the older I get. I wonder if she had a little Nordic log, there, tucked away in the woodpile, too. One day Karen, and I were just kicking back and gassing about everything and nothing. It was slowly dawning on us that an advanced degree just might involve 49 percent academics and 51 percent politics. Anyway, as we were talking, we also realized that we both shared an Awful Shameful Secret. What? You're thinking we both independently had a lost weekend in Bangkok? Our uncles taped the door at the Watergate apartment? We secretly liked (or hated) Alger Hiss? The truth of it was way worse than all these and a felony indictment. Somehow Karen and I had both managed to slog our way through not only high school science, but a BA degree as well, and good enough to get here without ever having actually dissected a frog. There. I said it. Bless me, Zoological Father, I have way sinned. Wait till you hear this one. (Point, point. Her first, the lightning thing, huh?) Oh, the shame. The horror. Because we both had teaching labs as part of our TA responsibilities, the Irish genes got kicked aside and the Kaiser Wilhelm stuff took control. There was another grad student there, a young woman, God bless her, whose chief academic qualification seemed to be sleeping with as many faculty as she could fit on her busy dance card. She being a big time Darwinist, I'd guess it was something to do with adaptation and natural selection. But who am I to judge? Anyway, I have nothing but admiration for her because Sadder But Wiser Girl had sympathy for our predicament and, perhaps with her heightened sensitivity to the idea of secrecy, she never ratted us out and got us into the lab at night when no one was around. She probably diddled the numbers on frog corpses to cover us, too. What a gal!

## RALPH M. GABRIEL

We started with frogs and frogmarched our way through rats, cats and sharks, looking at the lab guide and shrugging our shoulders at each other: whaddya think? Kidney? Good for kidney? OK, what's next? It was sad when the shark turned out to be a mommy shark, but the Miracle At Anaheim was still a year in the future for me, so, we plowed ahead. In this manner Karen and I initiated ourselves into what I would later discover to be a time-honored practice amongst all grad students, aka Keeping a Few Pages Ahead of the Students. Your tax dollars at work, what? But in defense of Karen and me, I must point out that frogs, rats, cats, etc., are all, you guessed it, vertebrates. So, as it was, the department should have been grateful to have two such ecumenical cutters as us. I still can't remember what the course load requirements were for grad students, as opposed to teaching or research, but for a reason I have no idea about, I signed up for Developmental Biology, there at Fullerton, Developmental Biology being the current buzzword for old school Embryology. My current political enemies who pull the heads off children for fun and profit can search and search for a conspiracy here, but I can't find it, and I was there. It's even funnier when you consider that my embryology teacher himself was a raging proabort. Not exactly the perfect soviet indoctrinator. And I can't even figure how I had the time for the class, slaving away teaching and at the hospital job to pay the rent. Also, I had absolutely no interest in embryology before this, strange as that may seem. I was the last of five kids and I had never even seen my own mother when she was pregnant. I never even saw little baby spiders sailing away on the wind like the clone in Blade Runner. How is this possible? That I would take this class that would set the course of my life ever after, ultimately, to Buffalo, NY? Sorry baby killers. Can't help you on that one.

In lab we "grew out" urchin, tunicate, chicken and maybe also feather duster worm embryos, the last one to fill out the AMA- EPC superphyla. I think that was the first time that I shot a light camera through a scope. I remember I shot a sequence catching a two-cell tunicate larva splitting into four and I loved pasting the sequence of pictures in my lab book. Snap, snap, snap, snap. Here was the first glimpse of something, I'm not sure what, something as normal and logical as an adult sea urchin, the thing we had to avoid stepping on when we were diving in Monterey Bay for fear it would pierce through our flippers. But here through the scope it was a tiny presence of two spheres of honey-colored material, not even as thick as a chicken egg yolk, and if it didn't make the handful-of-seconds move from two to four cells it would never grow up to be a big sea urchin and have fun running up and down the beach. When you look at The Rock, Dwayne Johnson, Schwarzenegger, Vin Diesel, Sly, Attila the Hun or Genghis Khan, it never occurs to you that these were all, and you and me too, once so tiny and fragile we could die from less pressure than it takes to crush a grape. A lot less pressure, a skinned grape. In the case of the urchin embryo in my scope, it would die if I simply let the slide dry out, the little drop of water on it. The veliger larva of the feather duster worm was like a stately floating planet from Dune with its own little girdle of undulating hairs to propel and guide it. A leaf floating on a pond goes where the water takes it. Here was a self-steering asteroid, blind, and most would say unthinking, but which had been give the capacity to move from here to where. And why?

An entire world of inchoate but nascent purpose, meaning even willfulness, was unfolding in front of my eyes in the space of a drop of water. You and I might travel across the world and meet interesting people and see wonderful things. Here was a blind embryo happy to spend her or his entire embryo life moving an eighth of an inch. I know. You'd say I'm nuts if I told you that when you watch these guys long enough, you find yourself wanting to ask, hey pal! what's so interesting, there, on the other side of that water droplet? Crazy, but you'd do it too, the way a million people look at live feeds of falcon nests in skyscrapers. We always want to know how the babies are coming along.

A humble sparrow flies from one side of Central Park in New York to another. What does he know that you don't? And here's the rest of it that any Greenpeacer or Earth First type can tell you: there comes a point, watching nature, when it finally dawns on you that a particular animal on a particular day, as you watch it, isn't doing anything. Not really. Biologically speaking. He's not reproducing. She's not searching for food. He's not building a nest. They're just hanging out. They're not in a rush to go see their hedge fund manager or their shrink or their divorce lawyer or cruise the web (well, OK. Some spiders do that) or anything like that. They're just living. I especially see this with dolphins and turkey vultures, the ones that soar all day in big lazy circles. You can see it in just about any creature if you look long enough. Even ants, those Type A's, if you get away from the slaves and look at the queens, say.

Just what are these guys up to? Darwinists have absolutely no answer for this Summer-and-the-livin'-is-easy kind of question, even if it's only part of the animal's time. Neither do I, outside of faith, but I ran across the answer in a dusty old power seminar book. It tells this story: the parents are about to close the door of their children's room for the night but at the last minute they hear the six-year-old ask the four-year-old: "Remind me what God looks like. I'm starting to forget." All animals are messengers from the invisible world. Embryos, including human embryos, are particularly laden with information for you and me, fresh from the other side as they are. I mean, why do they interview athletes before they leave the field? This is why.

Dr. Lambert, the embryology professor, was tall, thin, craggy, gray, intense -- very intense – smiley, and used to play the tuba in the navy, saluting incoming aircraft carriers down in San Diego from the bays hanging out from destroyers that would go out to meet them. I mean, what is not to like about a guy like this? Almost every single call to a microscope Lambert could you look at this? would produce a flush of excitement and shouts like "Cool!" and "That's really bitchin'!" I have always believed that biologists are the scientists most in love with their work and least interested in committees, money, politics or even too much publish or perish stuff. They just love inverts and they show it and they say it loud and say it proud. But even in this category of nature lovers, Lambert was head-and-shoulders above the rest. I've never met such a true believer in all my years of science anywhere. Never.

Parasitology was a mystery like embryology, as in, why did I take it? It was really a med school or nursing kind of class and very specialized without much connection to anything else, so, like with embryology, I can't figure why I took it. The professor was wide, short, quiet, and one of those silently brilliant people who doesn't say much. If he did talk, everything was a mild answer and a clever sense of humor. He was not a US PhD but a British DSc which is like a post-doc by comparison. The chalkboards and trays in his lecture lab were always perfectly clean, no chalk or erasers or dust anywhere. He never moved one inch from the lab stool that he'd draw up next to the teaching bench, also spic-and-span, which he leaned against. He showed up for the first fifteen minutes or so of every class, and then disappeared. Quite the mystery.

Only later, after that first class and the Harry LaRayne book and the Cheng and all that did I find out that that slow-moving parasitology professor did in fact move to someplace other than the lab and his office: lo and behold I was sidewalk-counselling in front of a mill in Fullerton one Saturday and there-he was! Sitting, as you'd imagine, in a beach chair, right up near the door of the mill. He was what we call in the business a "deathscort," there to make sure moms get in without a chance to change their minds. So, the proaborts weren't just on my own dissertation committee: they were all over the biology staff. Activists, too, not just theoreticians. On the first day of class he labored forth, broke a sweat and heaved a copy of the Cheng, the class textbook, up onto the teaching lab bench and then he sat down. No notes. No standing at a podium. No drawing on the chalkboard. The book was huge. Doorstop. Hell, it was a mortar round to make it all the way to Stalingrad. From Berlin. It was a little over a foot tall and all of eight inches wide. Two-and-a-half inches of coated paper, that size, and you got a really great door stop on your hands. If the Titanic had had a copy of Cheng on hand, it would have sailed into New York harbor, no problem. It was bright orange, as in, Danger! Danger! Danger! I should have got a clue and run out of the room right then. If anyone ever made a Charlie Chaplin move of Parasit. 501, the part where a Wile E. Coyote drops an Acme bank vault out of the sky on the sheriff's head would have been cast by a copy of the Cheng. It wouldn't just hit the poor student, either. It'd smash through all the way to China. Hopefully, landing on Dr. Cheng. At velocity.

We hated the Cheng. We hated Cheng, too, wherever he was counting up his money from selling his book to us poor students. But we especially hated what happened next. The professor sent around a several-pages handout, single space typed, both sides. "This is a list of the parasites you need to memorize for this class." Adrenaline and then serotonin flowed through our systems. Adrenalin, as we unbelievingly tentatively touched the pages of the instrument of our torture, afraid to even take possession of it. Serotonin, as we saw the extent of this list and passed through the thousand stage of shock, alarm, regret, why Can't I Be Surfing Right Now? I Hate You Forever, why Does God Allow Such Horrible Suffering When He Seems Like A Pretty Cool Dude? My Professor Is Pure Evil, My Momma Potty Trained Me Wrong, why couldn't I have signed up for the Marines so I could just get shot to death? and finally, Acceptance: we are so screwed. Just when we started into the post-adrenaline exhaustion and helplessness, we heard a slight buzzing in our ears. The professor dude wasn't done. He was still talking. We were barely breathing, holding our heads with our hands, in shock, mouths agape. Why are we still alive after this bomb blast? "I won't be doing any lecturing. At all.

This is a university. In order to get into here, you already have to have known how to study. Here is the text book, study it." There was more. The list in front of us listed only 300 parasites. We had to memorize not just their names, Latin too of course, but the entire life cycle of each species. And alternate life forms that the parasites shift into between hosts. So, intermediate vectors we also had to memorize.

There comes a point, oh, say, when the train is bearing down on you at a hundred mile an hour and your foot, say, is stuck in the switching rail a hundred yards down the track, when you realize that all your attempts to escape Just Won't Cut It. Maybe scenes from your life flash through your mind. Maybe you flip off your unjust aggressor in an ultimate gesture of defiance. Maybe you recall, just then, that you forgot to return a book to the library. When you were ten. And this is the just punishment for your sins. Karma. Kind of like when the good thief scolded the bad boy. Whatever. My stunned gaze drifted over to a smartass in the front row calmly taking notes as if this was some damn walk in the park. When I was young, I was you, I said to nobody. Now, at age 25, I was done. Washed up. Hanging rubber at Firestone and screaming air ratchets all day started to sound real good. More time for surfing, too. To make it worse I'd just gone to the prolife convention in Anaheim, so that sounded good, too. Anything other than parasite sounded good. Torture in an overseas prison? Pshah! No problemo.

The child of wonder about nature and love of tiny living things and microscopes was beginning to morph over into...whatever. I'm not sure what. But whatever it was, it did not involve an advanced degree. A last gasp from the prof, before he trundled home: a citation. A book that could help us with this galactically tiny task just dumped on us. Smartass in the front row wrote it down, and some little shred of working brain of mine said do that. Written by a magician, it turned out, who went on Carson and memorized the entire audience's names and addresses and phone numbers after hearing them only once. That's cute, Dr. Lazybones Who Doesn't Lecture. Pound us to smithereens and then go back to your office and donuts, but leave us a little joke in your wake. A magician's book? Who are you kidding?

"Someday" came the summer of the year between undergrad and grad school; in between the Newport Oregon marine lab job and the Austin Texas biomedical research job. I was up in Marin in between all those things and I happened to see a notice about the Evelyn Wood course,

$450 of my University of Oregon wages. I trusted Todd. I shelled it over. The course was held in the cramped meeting room in the back of a hotel in Terra Linda. My mom later rented a room in it from time to time, just so she could sit by a pool and invite all her RN friends over and party, like the old days in South Pas. Breezy loved it. But that was later. Now, here I was, paying lots of money to go to a class in a tacky hotel room. Quite a step down from the U Cal lecture halls. How I wish I'd found that dumb hotel conference room before I'd spent all that time in the Cal lecture halls. That silly speed-reading class was the beginning of learning how to actually study systematically, as opposed to just cram and pray. Once a chem prof at UCSC had pointed to his textbook and said, "Start with page one. Do not go to the next page until you've understood every single word that page, and so on." I was chuckleheaded enough to believe this guy. Lateral brains don't do straight lines. If you try to make them, you waste your time. Somewhere Evelyn Wood is laughing. That chem prof was a linear guy. I'll spare you the details of lateral brain thinking. Suffice it to say that an Evelyn Wood trained brain would get a huge stack of new textbooks in the fall, even for science, say, at a good school, and he wouldn't dream of doing what the chem prof said. Instead, you would see him casually flipping through the book as if it were a coffee table book or a tour guide. What's up with that?

After a few minutes, like an urchin larva in the surf or a leaf in a storm he would hone in on a particular factoid two thirds the way through the book and focus on it as if it were the benchmark for the Washington DC surveyor, which it is, according to Wood. Then, slowly he would draw a writing pad over and start to make a very few markings, in symbols, or hopscotch grid patterns and circles, but not lists or prose. Don't confuse this with web surfing, by the way, which, we know, creates stupidity, numbing, and finally, vacuity. The Wood trained brain channeling the veliger larva settles on one book, one course, one factoid, one exam pressure situation at a time. Also, a physical book enables a Wood-style browsing impossible on a computer screen. Impossible. A physical book enables the placer gold mining process of sifting the gold out of the confusing and endless sand that is useless- known to you already or peripheral.

For some reason (guilt over never having learned how to study properly and just getting by?) the parasite material started to intrigue me. This was despite mine and everyone's aversion to raw memorization, and also despite the lazy prof. The guy spent twenty minutes three times a week in the lab, not lecturing, and for this he gets a full salary? Not only would he not lecture, he wouldn't even answer a question if it turned out it was in the Cheng. "Look it up. You're a student. Students study." he said. He stuck around for those twenty minutes each day to see if we could think up a question that wasn't in the damned book. No rancor or opprobrium, just this is how it is. Then he'd smile a shy little smile, halfway between disarming self-deprecation, and a kid swinging his legs on a railway trestle in the summer. La-di-da. Then, back to his office, or even home, for all I know. Somewhere in all this I just took it as a challenge. I mean, why not? I had always wondered how the absolute top GRE scorers at Santa' Cruz had done it; I assumed it was just genius. But here, the magic book, was a little way, a small pathway no one would think of for a science student. Magic and science don't mix. Like Bill Walsh hiring Jerry Rice the ballet dancer for a wide receiver. Totally counterintuitive. Maybe it was Dad's Marine DNA or Mom's stubborn Irishness, I don't know; but whatever it was, some nights found me in the parasite lab, scratching out lists of things to memorize. I guess I figured if you just kept writing it down, you'd get it memorized, which is true, but not for 300 species, and all their other stuff about life cycle that went with them. And it's not like even one of them was a dog or cat that you could fake it on because you knew something about them. Each and every parasite was weird as hell. They all looked like space aliens on the scope.

 The Wood system taught me to mine large amounts of information and distill them into core principles without reading a whole book front to back, one word at a time. The LaRayne magic book had a massive universal mnemonic scheme which, once committed to your head, could be used for anything, like a row of a hundred coat hooks in your mud room. There was a way to connect any factoid phonetically to any number, one to a thousand. Somewhere in this I stopped rote rewriting of stuff and instead reduced each lifestyle to a string of five or fewer symbols. Each symbol was like what George Lucas would call a storyboard scene, but for me it was a critical part of a bug's lifecycle. Right off the top this saved time since instead of rote writing of words, in one or two seconds I could write out symbols representing a lifestyle. The classroom I went to at night was perfect: it had three walls of total chalkboard. The fourth wall was windows out to the south so I could feel the sun going down, great thing when you are working third shift.

    Guided by the coatrack thing that gave me the first element of each storyboard sequence, soon, all three chalkboards would be covered with strings of symbols that seemed to flow out like a sentence of Chinese characters. Then I'd take a break and sit in a chair and just look at it all. Then I'd get up and do it all again from bare slate and the coatrack. The first fifteen minutes of the exam time was spent writing out all this stuff on the backs of the exam questions. From that point onward, it might as well have been an open book exam. But even then, an open book exam doesn't do you much good if you have not already compressed the information, Wood-wise.

    Out of a class of 25 or so Mr. No Lecture gave one A, one B, half-a-dozen C's and all the rest D's or F's. No grade inflation here! He had an absolute point system developed from previous years, and he didn't care about curves. Get the points, get the grade. Rough, huh? But if you really think about it, the phrase "the class taught itself" had a different meaning in Parasite. This mild but stubborn prof was the one and only one of the all the professors who actually taught me how to study, and he did it without ever touching a piece of chalk, and his only help was a thin novelty book about magic tricks, for heaven's sake. Everything else sure looked like sloth, but it was inspired sloth; he threw us a rope. Peace, Dr. DSc. Sit-On-A-Stool. I know a lot of kids worked very hard for C's and D's in that class. I know it. I got the only B. Since I missed an A by four points out of 1500, all the other kids insisted I should go in and beg for the A, and, being that close, if I did, I'd get it. I never did. That dumb B was the first and last grade in my life I had ever really earned. I'm quite proud of it, actually. It may have been a B, but it was my B. Well, and I got my revenge, too, if that's the right word for it. We had to hunt parasites in the field for extra credit and after I got a bird louse from a chicken coop and a Remora-type gill clinger out of a dragnet I was out of ideas. One day I was lamenting all this to a fellow grad student. "See those lab dishes," he said, suppressing a little sly smile.

    The dishes in question had sawdust in them. In the dust were eighth-inch beetles that the principle investigator could care less about: he only kept them as hosts to some bug in their gut. Symbiont? Parasite? It was a close call. A quick squish between a cover glass and a slide; no priest, no blindfold, no cigarette and a dash off to Dr. Class-On-Autopilot got me the extra credit, reluctantly, but after I got it, he looked twice at the bug. "Huh. where'd you find this critter?" It turned out it was from his own research lab! I'd stolen one of his precious lab subjects! For all I knew that bug was carrying some retrovirus to cure cancer! He didn't flunk me, for all that. Very mellow, our Dr. DSc, London. But you see? I was happy to get the B. Way better than an F.'

Once in Fullerton I was enamored of CS Lewis's notion that a good thing done as a pagan could possibly still be a good thing eternally, once you come on board. This of course, is countered by the dramatic Franciscan notion of Throw it all out. now. Start over. I didn't know that then. But now? As I write? Hmmm. I wonder if the Lord didn't just send along Chuck Lambert right where I was, vacillation and all. Serendipity Miracle Numero Uno, right there. I think it was a grad. student of Lambert's who first pointed out to me that not all MA's take four years. You could go shorter than that. Four years? Many PhD's can be done in that time even at the big schools like Scripps in San Diego and "The Farm," Stanford, up on the Peninsula. Why take that long for a lowly MA? Welcome to the strange world of academic politics where the best interests of your grad students are not always up there on top. Part of the problem is that a grad student after a year or two can be a huge boon to his or her major advisor, especially if he gets good at running labs for Bio 101, say. Good grad students can lift a huge burden off the shoulders of their bosses, setting them free to give more time to research and the publish-or-perish tenure thing. A student can also help out with that even. He or she becomes a victim of her own success, her ability to help out, and the prof hates to let her go. This idea is big in academia. It's huge, it's so huge, it's even possible that a professor just might consider dragging his heels on signing off on your research project, precisely to keep you around another year or two. Especially if you start to become irreplaceable by helping out with the undergraduate teaching load. Or in the lab.

Some grad. students didn't mind this, but plenty of them did. They'd make snide remarks about "slave labor." Grad student wages couldn't support a hamster. A hamster fasting like Mahatma Gandhi. In my case, even with California resident tuition rates I still had to do bedpans and catheters at AMH nights and third shift to cover the bills, and that was sharing a house with four guys. In contrast to all this, another Lambert grad student told me: "Lambert's students all get out ASAP, as soon as they do the research. No fooling around. They want to get teaching jobs , get married, get out, get started with their own lives and not hang around here forever." This got me to thinking. I started looking around and observing other students and I saw that my friend was right. Not all the slave-grad. students hated it. The hardcore Darwinist population biology clique seemed to be happy with it. They also were demi-gods when it came to running the 101 labs. Then one day the story of a research field trip filtered back to me at my desk, which was still in Roger's lab. Maybe it was from Karen, my late-night frog dissection pal. The field trip was supposedly some kind of intertidal rocky plot counts or some net drags but as the story came out, it started to sound like ten percent research and 90 percent Annette Funicello and Frankie Avalon.

Now, here's where the serendipity of heaven kicks in. I was so busy at the hospital or EM labs or embryology or Parasit. classes, no one had even bothered to tell me about the beach "research." If he had, and I had gone, I can't imagine how I would not have just fallen into the fun of it -- my wild Irish genes. This is what grad. students do: they have fun at the beach! They don't just hang out for days in dark labs peering through microscopes. That's for chumps. Party! Beach Boys! Let's go! Even as an undergraduate I had definitely gotten the feeling of the Ricketts/Steinbeck enthusiasm of intertidal natural history at the beach, the oohs and aahs when a professor lifts a simple sandwich bag out of a mucky pool and suddenly you see it: the brilliant electric lavender or bright lemon yellow hues of a tiny humble slug, say, Hermissenda crassicorni ? with its feathery external lungs, or quiet Olivella biplicata, the shy and delicate snail with its carefully engraved shell. Or he'd drag out a shy hermit crab to see the subtle indigo iridescence of his normally invisible claws in the full sunlight. I could do that. I loved it. I could do that for a life, a career, a family, all of it. But those students? The ones at the beach party? Four years? No. I was in a hurry.

I felt very bad even asking Lambert about the possibility of switching over into his lab. I was a loyalty freak. "Bitchin," he shouted, the minute I suggested it. Sometimes I think Charley was arrested in some part of the 60's when he went off to the Navy. I hated breaking the news to Roger. He was the one after all who had brought me to Fullerton in the first place. He was the one who was so enthusiastic about my silly little paper at the Western Society of Naturalists in Monterey, the Rieketts-channeling crowd. But he went with it. All class, our Roger is. But did I know what I was doing? What if it didn't work out with Lambert? It was a massive shift, after all, from the simpler and let's admit it, less challenging area of population biology that we call "butterfly chasing" into an intense lab that amounted to a kind of cellular biology, much more intense, and even a big step closer to the DNA and metabolic biochemistry wonks, the ultimate nerds within the nerd population of biologists. It's kind of easy to spout off made-up theory on the spot when you are in the Darwinism wing, a very loose area intellectually, but the cellular guys got to know their stuff. I really didn't know what I was getting into.

Serendipity Number Dos, of God's great plan to get me out of Fullerton, pronto, takes a little explaining. It's about that new thing. I'll give you an example. Suppose you want to discover something new to report about, oh, say, Drosophila. If you do, you are in big trouble before you even start. Drosophila is a tiny fruit fly loved by DNA types because they already know all about its genes, which can be hijacked almost without extraction due to the way the fly is built, also, in terms of Mendelian genetics, meaning cross-breeding. Drosophila has a microscopic life span. You could do grandchildren phenotype cross-breeding in a week or two and still have time for lots of tennis. A geneticist's dream. The problem with Drosophila is everyone knows so much about the durn thing. It's just about impossible to find out anything new in the short timespan of an MA project. It would be like a graduate vet student picking a dog or cat for a research subject. In trouble from the start.

But here's the idea: suppose the same vet student said, hey, some people keep Komodo dragons for pets! I'll do a little something on them! See what I mean? Compared to dogs and cats, any dope with no budget and a few weeks can find out something new about the dragons. Nobody cares about them. And new is what publishes. In my case, fat chance of going down to Tasmania or wherever they have dragons. Hmmm. What to do? .

Phragmatopoma californiensis is barely a half inch long. You've seen something like it on Discovery channel when they show divers down in trenches and they swim by a "feather duster" worm. It hangs out looking like that, when no one's around, feeding with just a net sitting there in the water, catching tiny bits of stuff with slime on the net and reeling it in. About the same way mammals move an egg down the tube, come to think of it. When the diver comes by, it whoosh retracts the net thing in the blink of an eye. Feather duster worms are the humble hobbits of the Octopus Garden in the Shade. As baby worms floating around in the sea, they settle on rocks and start building their houses, one little sand grain at a time, set carefully in a wall better than the most skilled stonemason in the world. In the case of my worm, the little guy from Laguna Beach, if you take a part of the wall of this tiny house and set it on the dissecting scope just so, the light shines through and it looks like the most beautiful stained glass window in the world. All of this, from a tiny humble worm, eyes worse than Mr. McGoo, who lives in a house smaller than the fingernail of your little finger. And on top of it, the females when they came out of the tube had the most lovely pale lavender color to their eggs, which you could see plainly through the ventrum. Boys and girls are instantly distinguishable the minute you get them into the lab. Nice to know when you're doing reproductive biology, that.

The stained-glass windows weren't the only beauty that showed up in the funniest places. When we sliced the samples for the electron microscope (EM) we floated them out onto a tiny pond of water created on top of the knife. The sections were so thin and fragile they would just crumple up in the air alone. But as they floated out onto the little pond, we determined the thicknesses of the sections by their colors. Too-thick sections were a dull bronze, but as they got thinner, they shimmered out into bright silver, barely the thickness of the wavelength of light itself. There was color even in the thicker sections: wonderfully intense indigo, electric chartreuse, all mixed together like a tiffany lamp, everything you could hope to see in an infinite rainbow -- there's oil in the gutter in taffeta patterns/it runs down the lane/in colored arrangements that Michael will change/with a stick that he's found.

But thinking about the stained glass windows under your feet at the beach: you can crank it down until you're staring at a Boson-Higgs particle, or back until you can see a million galaxies at once. Nature is always beautiful, every little bit of it, the big picture too, and humble crawling little whelks and limpets at your feet, and birds and raccoons and rainbows in between. And all we can think of doing, when we get ahold of it, is cover it over with concrete, oil or smog or ticky-tacky boxes. I choose life, don't you? I love it, I love it to death, God help me, and I always have. I can't even remember how I stumbled on my earthly savior Phragmatopoma. I think Dr. Lambert knew I was in a hurry, and he knew it was understudied. Another angel thing. He let me go to the library to check it out, though. Sure enough, it only took a little while to find out that nobody cared about my little worm. It was open season, research-wise. Serendipity Miracle Number Two kicked in with a fierceness: Nothing.

International literature, Russian fishery journals, tropical aquaculture, Scandinavian genetics -- no one knew anything about P. californiensis. I could write a proposal about how I was surfing down at Laguna, where they hung out, and stumbled on a reef of them one day, and get the Nobel and grants and scopes and teaching jobs launching me into the academic ionoshpheric orbit forever. Throw in the EM angle, which was a bit of a newcomer itself, then, and Dr. Lambert's nine-nanoseconds-is-too-late approach to fertilizations experiments and I was home free.

I was so happy that day, fooling around in the library looking for the worm that wasn't there, that I indulged in a little random shelf-surfing, a luxury for a grad student working two jobs, but a little treat that day. What to my wandering eyes did appear but a copy of Aborted Women: Silent No More. Phragmatopoma, my ejection seat from school, and Silent No More, my parachute, had both shown up on the exact same godam day. God's timing is perfect, as they say. I can't even remember so much asking, and the time waiting vaporized into noting. I had a plan. A plan from heaven.

The library worm discovery wasn't just an ejection seat, it was a starter's pistol. I shot so fast out of there it was barely six months later that I left Fullerton for good. Enough data in only six months? For an advanced degree thesis at a not-too-bad science school? Part of the answer was that Dr. Lambert was chiefly interested in fertilization reactions, the process that takes place in the instant that the sperm hits the egg. If nine nanoseconds is too late to catch this thing...you can run a million experiments in an hour. It's not as if you're breeding elephants or something. Plus, the fertilization was external, right out there in the seawater column in front of God and everyone, so you didn't even have to keep the adult animals happy, just put sperm and eggs together in a test tube and wham. Nine nanoseconds and it's all over but the alimony hearing. So, how to get this on the 'scope? It was across the hall. It was huge. It looked like the result of a tragic accident between the periscope of a Tom Clancy submarine and the dashboard of a '69 Buick Electra 88. Not so easy to drag it across the hall to my fertilization lab, even with a tow truck. Also, you needed sections embedded in plastic, and polymerized, to be hard enough to slice into superskinny sections with an EM knife. It was Lambert who figured that out, also, but even so, to do it, you had to catch 'em at it real sneaky-like.

In a blink, what had started out as two sets of double membranes surrounding the egg and the sperm individually had changed over into one contiguous double membrane, like some Rube Goldberg gadget or an Escher print where everything runs in together; you know? The lizard flattens out into a drawing on one, that print? Biology-wise it was like the two cells were trying to form a temporary syncytium, the microscopic equivalent of a train vs. a train wreck with a Honda stuck in the middle there, somewhere. Or, it would have been a syncytium, if only the gametes were like two diploid cells. Which they weren't. Only haploid. Still. Until they weren't. Later, when in the new house, they get busy with recombination and all that. Involving soft lights and alcohol, 1 can only assume. Billy Ocean on the stereo. Like that. If you know what I mean. Got all that? So. How to catch 'em at it? By the time the contiguous membrane has formed, it was all over. Old hat. Old news. Just another zygote, folks. Keep moving. Nothing to see here.

Again, I think it was heaven's own angel, Dr. Lambert, who came up with the idea of combining the fertilization experiment with the EM prefixing and embedding process. It was his area, after all. Yes, any given reaction was fast, but if you found a way to play musical chairs, so to speak, you could catch 'em. In other words, get a whole high school prom worth of kids dancing on the same dance floor, and then if you stop the music and everyone stops in that instant, you can catch one reaction if you then go look at everything with time frozen. Some reactions are slow, like the kid who has to work up the nerve, so to speak, and some are lightning quick. So, we made sure the high school was big enough: lots of boys and girls. That way, even if it took entire seconds for you to dump in the fix (that's two or three whole billion nanoseconds) you could catch even a wallflower sperm in the act. Bam. If you're high school's big enough, there should be a spectrum of events, slow and fast and middle tempo. The slow ones like Perry Como, say, and the middle ones, more like Quincy Jones.

"Stopping the music" in a test tube means dumping the whole batch in fix, kaboom, all at once. Then, with each potential reaction frozen, you go ahead and complete the fixing and preserving process and then embed them in the plastic. Then you section the plastic blocks and carry the sections across the hall to the machine that can't be moved. Even then it is a slow process to search each section for the event you are looking for. Not exactly a needle in a haystack, but like that. A toothpick in a haystack, say. Plus, you had to look in three dimensions. Each successive slice in a string of them off the knife was a deeper layer in the same event. On a CAT scan or an MRI machine, flipping through tons of sections on one organ is as easy as turning a knob on your radio, but on the EM everything is frozen in time, so you had to search each little slice one at a time, moving each into and out of position. Impossible to look at the big picture. Everything is small. It's like looking at the Washington Monument with a Sherlock Holmes magnifying lens in the dark to see if it comes to a point. If you happen to start near the top, you're ok, but if not, you're in trouble. This all took time, a lot of time on the 'scope. A ton. And always with the press of teaching responsibilities and the night job. I loved it. If it wasn't for the new prolife thing, I would have fallen head over heels in love with my new toy the scope, and my hobbit worm in his little tunnel cottage. Even with all the pressure to get done and get on to the prolife work, I still loved it.

All good things here on earth must come to an end, and that started one day with a sudden discovery on the 'scope as I was racking the stage back and forth. In the literature, the scientific journals in the library with no windows, I had already seen pictures of what it was I was looking for: spermatozoa of similar invert species on an EM level. There was true nuclear DNA of the spermatozoon body, spherical mitochondrial "jet engine" clustered in the back, an acrosome nose-cone loaded with enzymes to dissolve the egg membrane, and finally a tail that went on forever. The front end of the sperm was about seven microns or so, just about the same size as a human red blood cell. Fullerton had an ancient EM. In fact it was called Model No. 1. No, I'm not making this up. I am still grateful for it because I bet not every state college system school even had one back then. But man, what a wheezing Model A! I could never get any focus or detail and I was so ignorant about it all that I could never be sure I was limited by ancient Japanese Godzilla era technology, operator error, or bad prep. Grid after grid I put on the machine and scanned day after day and night after night, the scalar equivalent of walking over Grand Canyon inch by inch with a Sherlock Holmes magnifying glass, looking for an inchworm. One day, bleary-eyed, I can't even remember if it was day or night because of my third shift schedule at the hospital and it's all the same in the EM room anyway, where you keep it dark all the time…I saw it!

Wow! Eureka! I saw what looked like it could have been an oblong tangential section of a sperm nucleus and in the same section, a nearby smaller sphere that could be a slice of the mitochondria behind the nucleus, barely a micron across. I reeled out of the dark closet and then out of the abandoned lab, bleary-eyed and exhausted, anxious to share my discovery with another human being. "Mary! You'll never believe it! I finally got my sperm on the "scope." Mary, a good-looking grad student instantly comprehended. We spend so much time on our projects, the subject of the research becomes my wombat, my bacterium, my egg cell, whatever. She gave me a hug. "Good for you Jim! I knew you could do it if you kept trying," and she wandered off. "Sam!" I said to the next grad student I could find, "I finally got my sperm on the "scope"! "Jim, Congratulations! What a guy! We've got to have a party and celebrate!" On down the hall I went until I'd told every grad student. We were all stoked. It's what researchers do. So few victories and so much slogging.

Only when I retraced my steps back to the dark, cramped tiny scope room did I realize I had also left in my wake a trail of horrified undergraduates, the women I recall most acutely, who were not at all privy to the notion that "my sperm" was an in-house researcher's reference to Phragmatopoma spermatozoa, the subject of "my" research. We always thought you grad students were weird, their shocked gaze indicated, but now we know. Ewwwww. "Uh, it's worm sperm. In the microscope. Wanna see?" were the words I never managed to get out. "Don't complain, don't explain," Marines and Henry Ford say. I put my head down and crawled back into my periscope closet. So much for coming out on the nucleus thing. Sheesh. Well, my cool surfer hobbit worms from Laguna would understand, anyway.

Buoyed by this thin sliver of success I was now doubly motivated to go back to the microtome and improve my sectioning technique. Later, at Stanford, I always cut with diamond knives, which cost a fortune and are fragile. But then, still at Fullerton, we were beggars. We made glass knives by ourselves, artfully cracking a square inch of quarter inch glass on a diagonal in just such a way on a fancy jig that a sharp edge would show up on one of the forty-five degree angles. All microtoming was done over that glass edge into a tiny Mylar moat glued onto the knife and grouted with wax. That way the ultrathin sections would float off onto the water and not crumple up at the knife edge, victim of massive static electrical forces. Gauging the thickness of the resin sections, with the specimen embedded, was crucial. You look for a tell-tale pale silver or bronze color in the section as it floated on the puddle, like oil on water. I can't recall but I think this thickness was as small as nanometers, close to the wavelength of light in that part of the spectrum. Not good sections came off into the puddle looking indigo, too thick for the delicate electronic beam to shine through inside the scope. We lifted the good sections off the puddle onto tiny copper grids to air dry and then load into the scope. The whole thing was a little like microsurgery, all done under a dissecting scope (2-7 power). Like old-school watch repair or diamond cutting. Delicate.

   I wonder what it is about the esthetics of science that is so appealing. Why should a weak silver-bronze color, with weak prismatic highlights, viewed through a dissecting scope, just cast resin, not natural, be so good-looking? For the rest of my life driving back and forth across this beloved wonderful country to commit "gypsy" crimes, whenever I saw a "sundog," also called a perihelion, I thought of EM sectioning. Sundogs are thumbprint-shaped little zero-dimensional rainbows that appear at dusk in high icy clouds. Why should this same pattern in the sky remind me of the hours spent looking for silver bronze in the dissecting scope? I love sundogs even to the present day. Keep an eye out. Beauty will out. In a lab in Orange County or driving feloniously across Flyover America, beauty will out. I just wish everyone could see it, not just us born people, you know? Life is damn worth living.

   As bad as it was, the Hitachi in Fullerton was good enough to give me an idea I was on the right track with the Phragmatopoma fertilization experiments, the ones that had been cast into plastic in the-middle of the crowded high school dance. Around about then I decided to make a big jump to get off campus, get a regular paying job, and start volunteering in the prolife activities I was hankering so bad to get started on. I could have done all that in SoCal, of course, but it was the Peninsula where I wound up. It was way providential, that. Up north I was farther away from school and less likely to be entangled in on-campus teaching for slave wages. But way more than that, Stanford had a way-sexy state-of-the-art 'scope up there, a brand new Siemens with all the bells and whistles you could ever hope for, a lowly tech's dream come true. When I got the job as the tech, I asked if I could use the 'scope at night. This was a win-win for the research grant and me, since they were desperate for someone on the spot to do that short bit of work, and I needed the 'scope for my own stuff.

## TO RECEIVE A CHILD

Getting time on a million-dollar piece of delicate equipment is a little bit like getting time on a 747. You don't just show up and say, "Let's take her for a spin, boys." Don't work like that.

The day job was research to try to re-connect the spinal cords of the Viet Nam vets who crowded into the day clinic at the Palo Alto VA Hospital, where Dr. Eng's lab was located. He was on staff at Stanford but his lab was at the VA across town. Our "model" was rat optic nerve, with uranium stain, looking for spinal fluid cell subpopulations that might act the same way that white blood cells do outside the spinal column. The theory was that CSF white cell equivalents could possibly come and lay down a scar tissue that would prematurely obstruct the nerve fibers from growing back by themselves. My sou-chef boss, Dr. Dixon, even hypothesized that in an ER or battlefield a medic could give a drug that would block that wound repair and let the fibers grow first. My job was to verify if there were such cells in the spinal fluid. I don't know where the research went after I left but I wish the vets the best, and the scientists, too. I clearly recall seeing with the naked eye, on a regular slide Richard showed me, a healed site with fibers growing across a gap. At one point he looked at some of my EM pics, pointing to cells he thought could be our elusive CSF "platelet" or "leukocyte" cells. "Clap your hands if you believe, Jim," he said, his cigarette smoke drifting over the pictures. No, he wasn't teasing me about church. He just had an extremely subtle and whimsical cynicism for TV evangelists. Or, overreaching scientists, for that matter. It would take a lot more pictures to catch our slinky jungle cat. I hope someone has pursued it because nerve fiber auto repair is way underappreciated in humans over five years old, where it stalls out. Richard was the smartest scientist I ever met. He had a quirky Tom Waits approach to life, too.

Back to my little worm from Laguna Beach. On the Palo Alto equipment the same material I had cast in Fullerton suddenly looked like someone had turned on the windshield wipers in the middle of a blizzard: it was gorgeous and clear and crisp and sharp with the new fancy stuff up north. I was in shock. Instead of vague blurry shapes to suggest mitochondria or a tail, I could now clearly count individual nerve fibers in the tail, and layers of membrane inside the mitochondria, like baffles inside a car radiator. It was amazing. I did a bunch of new cutting on the diamond knife and searched them all and shot them on the Siemens. Now I had a decent stack of photos of the worm fertilization reaction, when you catch the sperm hitting the egg in the crucial first instant. 1 kept up paying tuition down south even though I wasn't taking or teaching any classes there. Lambert defended me through thick and thin, another angel. He always had a clear notion that there was more to life than grad school, and he wanted all his students to get out there and get going. Even though I didn't want a PhD at this point, and I knew exactly why, if I did finish out, I could teach at a high school or maybe even a junior college like my earlier mentor Al Molina in Marin. But on a trip back down south I did find out that a meeting of my committee was coming up. It was during this time I wrapped up correcting galleys for the publication of the undergraduate thesis.

I was about to go back to Fullerton for that crucial meeting of my committee. What I didn't know is just before that, I wound up at the Anaheim Convention Center there in Orange County. It started out as the Committee Meeting From Hell but it didn't end that way. First of all, what do undergraduates know about committee meetings anyway? Committees imply dialogue, input, all that happy crap. Undergraduates don't have any of that; they just do what they're told and cross their fingers when the grades are posted. Secondly: if you had any one to blame, you could blame yourself. It was up to me to pick my own committee, beginning, of course, with Dr. Lambert, my thesis advisor with whom I clicked so well, especially after finding out how fast his students got out, and how slow everyone else's did. I started with him, and asked his advice, and one thing led to another, and the next thing you know, I had the minimum number of faculty on the committee, but what I did not fully realize is that I had picked all the molecular/genetic jocks on staff. Looking back, I understand clearly that there was a Great Divide in that department, and probably is in every department: the butterfly chasers on one side, who divided amongst themselves between the party animal hardcore Darwinists who leaned toward paleontology, and the party animal marine biology types.

On the other side were complete molecular jocks, who wouldn't recognize a metazoan, a multicelled animal, if it attacked them on the street or peed on their carpet. The biggest thing they saw were bacteria and viruses because that's where you could do your best molecular level stuff, whereas the bug was already in culture before you started and you didn't even have to do extraction Even that didn't last long, because the first thing they would do to a culture of bacteria or viruses would be to extract and sequence the DNA. They were really chemists trapped in the bodies of people who were paid by the biology department. I only mention it because, as much as I wanted to get out of there fast, I had jumped from the frying pan into the fire. At least Roger Seapy's crowd did things I could understand from my undergraduate emphasis on marine stuff. But in the name of hurrying up and getting out to do the prolife stuff I was hankering after so much, I now had thrown myself in with molecular types, totally over my head. My undergraduate background was completely different. I was unaware of this, walking into the committee. I was also unaware of another bombshell that was waiting for me, something worse than chemists.

At that committee meeting I don't recall saying so much as one word. Everyone did the talking the minute the door was closed so the secretary couldn't hear. They were not shy about it. It was a total ambush. Who the hell did I think I was? how could I have brought so much embarrassment to the department? how dare I infuse my personal beliefs into what was a scientific endeavor, meaning, research and getting a degree? Wha? I could hardly follow all the hate coming my way. They acted as if I had slept with each one of their wives, posted it on Facebook, and sold each of their children to some gypsies passing through. Also, I was the Guy On The Grassy Knoll, I Stole The Lindbergh Baby, and I was a terrible American. On the occasions when I even run into so much as one person who seems to be angry from out in left field, I slip into a kind of mode: watch and be quiet. Don't respond in anger. Don't complain, don't explain, as Henry Ford said. Still, I was reeling. I could feel my face blushing and I had a hard time breathing. Just when one guy would run out of steam, another would pick it up, and after a while I got to the point where I could see what they were talking about: they were all upset that I had sent a letter to the editor of the campus paper, when I got back from the Anaheim prolife conference with Drs. Jefferson, Koop and Schaeffer. The one where they screened "How Shall We Then Live?" and the same one where I became prolife, suddenly, overnight. You can definitely fault me for naiveté: no one had ever printed a letter to the editor that I wrote. I only wrote it because I felt I should do something about the new knowledge and heart feeling that I had, and a letter to the editor was something I could do.

The letter was barely 50 words. It just said, aren't we in the same era, morally, as Nazi Germany? Didn't the people back then deny the smokestacks? Aren't we now denying the bodies of the babies coming out of the mills? Like that. It was very short and simple. I had no way of knowing that the editors probably didn't get many letters from grad students. I certainly didn't know that in the eyes of the faculty being a grad student was a little like being faculty, or at least staff, and that my letter had reflected badly on the department, which was most definitely pro-abort. For 45 solid minutes these guys went around the table, worse than any communist struggle meeting in the sense that all were ganging up on one person. No one asked me to say a word, and they didn't give me the tiniest chance to defend myself. Not that I could have anyway, being so new to prolife. They finally got to the point where they left off shouting about their own politics, and instead got onto the topic of what a Christian would call prudence. Didn't I know I made the department look bad? didn't I know I was not allowed to speak for myself like that, if it would hurt the department? They really hammered on this point. No one said a single thing about my research. No one asked me a single thing about my grades, the design of my research, the topic, the species, or anything. Just, pure hate. From very powerful people. Who would never approve my thesis, by the way, and if I tried to go to the other staff, it was clear that they would be told in advance about me, and that would be that.

My dad used to tell me courtroom stories, beginning about when I was five. He'd get into his cups a little—I don't know if he was a real alky or not, but he definitely liked to drink, like most Marines, and he'd start in telling me stories about judges, trials, LA Bar Association gossip and whatever. He actually did this when he wasn't drinking, too; it's just that when he was drinking, he leaned toward things that were confidential and privileged material. If he wasn't drunk, he'd show me a nail in a board and say, "Watch this, Jim." Instead of trying to get at the head of the nail with the claw, he'd turn the board over and bang on the point of the nail as it stuck through the other side. This freed up the head on the other side so it pulled out easier with the claw; in fact, effortlessly." "An old carpenter's trick," he'd say, with a confidential wink. My Dad was full of little tricks he'd tell Walt and me. How bad I feel for kids with no Dad like that.

Anyway, sitting by the pool on a Saturday afternoon when all the chores were done but before the Saturday night neighborhood pool party had shown up, he'd impart Bar Association wisdom. "If you see the judge starting to make your point, Jim, Shut Up! This is very important!" I would take all this in, agog. I liked science and bugs and raccoons, so I couldn't imagine ever needing to know this bit of courtroom knowledge, but still, out of respect, I listened very carefully and realized that if my Dad were to lay such great emphasis on such an obscure possibility, I'd better remember it. It must be important.

Back in Fullerton, there, crammed into that tiny room just off the department boss's office, I saw a First-Class Charles Kopp Esq. miracle happen right in front of my eyes. I was just about to walk out of the room. I know when I'm licked. You don't have to paint me a picture. Here I was, hoping to get out soon, and now it looked like never. Even if I went crawling back to the butterfly chasers, cap-in-hand and full of apologies, they would be tipped off by these guys. It was no good. But I stayed my ground, a few more minutes. Might as well see what happens next. Finally, everyone in the room ran out of steam, the air was blue with the smoke of hatred. I wouldn't have dared to say a word in defense of myself, God or the babies, coward that I was. Even Lambert had joined in on the anger. A minute passed, and two. It turned out that this sound of silence was everyone waiting to hear what the department boss Dr. Rosenberg would say, and for a long moment, he didn't say a thing. This had the effect of a Grand Pause, since he was the boss and the committee would need to have his chop on it if they were to throw me out the door, which they so clearly wanted to do.

"I agree with everything that's been said," I heard. As if there were any hope otherwise, now I knew, it was over. All those boxes my Mom bought with her "pin money," all the science projects at school, all the show and tells in grade school -- forget it. Your son needs to find employment somewhere else, Mr. and Mrs. Kopp. "But I want to tell you all a story. It won't take a minute." Rosenberg proceeded to tell a story so common to prolifers; we've been telling them since we were kids, but no one listens. Shocked, in front of me, the department head was telling a typical prolife praise-the-Lord story. Dr. Rosenberg himself, was completely pro-"choice", and had been for as long as he could remember. He still was pro-choice, as of that moment in that committee meeting. But a year ago something funny had happened on his block. Halfway down the block lived another family, just like his. He had a couple kids, they had a couple kids, the kids all grew up together, and he watched his own and his neighbors kids run through everything kids run through, until one fine day his neighbors' daughter down the street had a problem. She was pregnant. To make it worse, she had come to Dr. Rosenberg to confide in him, since she knew he was a biologist and she wanted to confirm some medical details. He did, without really revealing his own feelings or giving much counseling on the subject, and he felt a little bad about it because he kept the confidence of the teenager and never told her parents.

Then began a kind of middle part of the story. Rosenberg was well aware that the daughter was really struggling with whether or not to carry to term. This is Orange County, California, in the late 70's, the height of the Charismatic movement and the tapering off or inclusion of the Jesus Movement before that, so it was a hotbed of evangelicalism either way. Rosenberg made it clear that the daughter's family background was Christian. He felt bad for the daughter, since he could see her droop in sadness under the weight of it all, a little more each day, and he also knew that the daughter dreaded her parents finding out. But he felt handicapped by the daughter's request to him to keep it a secret, and after a while the whole thing slipped out of his mind. They will find out sooner or later, her parents would, he told himself, and they will do whatever it is they will do. She was not his daughter.

One day a few months later there was a knock on the door. It was mother and child. The daughter had decided to come clean with her parents. They had gone back and forth about it, as so many Christians do when actually faced with reality, but in the end the daughter had come to the conclusion that she should give birth. There she was, in his house, beaming, holding her baby, cooing at her and having a ball. Rosenberg had talked with her about it, and the daughter had freely admitted that at several points in the last few months she had determined to get an abortion. But now she was extremely glad she hadn't, once she saw the baby, and was completely in love with her. The baby herself retroactively confirmed that she had absolutely done the right thing, and that the fear of coming so close to making the wrong decision was a horrible thought. She tried to put it out of her mind. This was not the end of the story as far as Rosenberg was concerned. I was hanging on every word and wondering how it all came into my thesis committee hearing room, no less than if a Stephen Spielberg monster had jumped up out of a hole in the floor. But it turned out that everyone else was listening to the story too, as if Rosenberg were recounting nothing more controversial than the atomic table or families of insects. Or nothing less definitive.

Rosenberg then began to tell a story of his own experience, meaning, how the whole thing had had an impact on his own life. If I was agog before, I was agoger now. What? A liberal Jew in my department was about "to testify about accepting Jesus Christ as His personal Lord and Savior? Oh, no. Even I had to put on my seatbelt. Well, OK, he didn't exactly do that, but he made it abundantly clear, by very slow and precise description, that the entire story of the neighborhood girl down the block had changed how he looked at the whole prolife thing. He directly implied that I might be right. (I hadn't said one word, so far. I was terrified. To me, the whole thing was like watching someone defuse an a-bomb in some movie. I was holding my breath. Did they really know what they were doing or was this going to just go boom in the end anyway?).

He wound up by reluctantly repeating what he had said in the beginning, that he still believed in "choice" in theory, but that now he was different, and he looked at the whole thing differently since the day he had seen the face of his neighbors' daughter light up when she had not had an abortion. He also stated that this had happened just about six months ago, and that he was still processing it all. He said that he didn't know how he would feel about it down the road. He could not predict, but he could imagine, that he would come around completely to the pro-life position. At the current moment, he wasn't sure, except that he was changed on a deep level.

"How's Jim's research going, Chuck?" he said, suddenly, looking at my major advisor. "Jim's research is bitchin!" Chuck shot back, with great emotion. Lambert was not one to hide his emotions. Oh, and he was one of those people whose development arrested in the 60's. Beach Boys, all that. "Good." Rosenberg looked at me. "Let me know how it goes, Jim," he said, and walked out of the room back into his office, ending the meeting.

A hint of a smurfy rainbow descended into the tiny cramped stuffy room. By asking Lambert that question, at that time, and in that way, Rosenberg had signaled without saying it that this was the last time he wanted to hear in my committee meetings anything about controversy. It was all science from here on out. Everyone accepted that, also. Outside in the Southern California sunshine after that meeting, I tried to catch up with God. Was that me, in there? And did I just witness, without saying a single word, that I had been fired, and then, by a miracle, re-hired into probably the best state college level science program in the state? A state that had given us the Manhattan Project, Livermore Labs and Linus Pauling, Kenneth Thiemann and a bunch of other Nobels, and Scripps

Institute of Oceanography, Cedars Sinai Hospital and Howard Hughes and the B1 bomber and a space shuttle landing pad at Edwards, and the SR-71 Lockheed Blackbird blueprints, and all of Silicon Valley, and the Moffett Field P-3 sub-snoopers, and tons of other science stuff? And when I was about to chuck it all anyway, if they felt that strongly about it? Sometimes you rail and weep and rage at the dying light and give it all your best and die trying, and die hard, and sweat and strain and all that… and sometimes, just sometimes, if you just sit there, you can feel a big huge humongous swoop as the knife just misses your head. This was like that.

And, looking back, for the second time my life had been impacted in a huge way, not just by some kindly professor who was doing what he thought was right, but by putting me back on my feet and firmly shoving me in the direction of prolife, specifically, and both times it had been by the much-scorned reform Jews. The first one was Symphony Sid, and his training of us in sensitivity at the Napa State Hospital. Now, here, the second time, a Jew again. And he was a liberal Jew, meaning a Reformed Jew, because I now know that if he had been a Lubavitcher or Hasidim or Orthodox or anything like that, he would have said or done something to indicate it. But he did not. He was just a regular modern liberal Jew, and he still went out of his way to save my bacon. Then there's me, the Jew. Even if my great grandmother was a Sephardic survivor from the Russian pale who wound up in Vienna, a haven for Jews then, in time to meet and marry my great grandfather Koppensteiner, our extended family at my generation hadn't darkened the door of a synagogue our entire lives. If Sid Gordon and Dr. Rosenberg were liberals, they were both at least true liberals in the sense that they were both open to the truth with regard to life. Christians, take note: God worked through the Jews, again. He sure as hell didn't work through the Christians that day, sad to say, even if it was Orange County.

But in the case of the committee meeting's sudden turn, it all started with a brave young woman whom I've never met, who stood up against her family and peers and did the right thing. And was happy, so happy. That's the big thing that caught Rosenberg's attention. And she sure as heck gave a shot in the arm to my nascent prolife career, even though I was a stranger to her. The bravery of that act ramified through her community and wound up being my salvation, on earth, in a stuffy committee room filled with Big Dogs who had it in for me. If you do the right thing, maybe it stands by itself as inherently good, even if you don't see all the good effects rippling out from this quiet, painful, brave act. And all this, through a channel she would never have expected, someone of a totally different faith and culture who happened to be a by standing witness. The influence of her soul and child were so strong it turned even a hard-core liberal into a soft prolifer, who was willing, in his turn, to jeopardize his own career. For me, to be prolife, what did I have to lose? I was a little grad. student. Dr. Rosenberg had a lot more to lose, and he risked it all. God bless ya, Mom, wherever you are, and your baby girl. You are my heroines on earth sent from heaven, no less.

I can't remember how that committee meeting ended. I was too stunned. Stunned at the department head's defense of me, someone he didn't even know, stunned he went up against his own faculty, who'd made it clear their knives were sharpened for this embarrassing prolifer, and stunned that Dr. Lambert came through with stellar personal integrity defending me at all costs even though he was vehemently pro-abort. Now, experienced or mature Christians reading this would say, "Oh, tut-tut. Ye of little faith," and they'd be right. Looking back, this was the first time in my life I had ever seen what I humbly consider to be the hand of God intervening in a wonderful way. Of course I can't prove that. Faith is like that. But I'll be damned if I won't point out the evidence and let you decide. It's not banging on the Bible. More like a quiet moment between you and the Lord and no one else.

Driving back up the coast to the Stanford day job, though, the whole thing weighed on my mind. Going through my daytime mammalian samples on the 'scope and my nighttime invert grids, I began to recall the feeling of that committee after the bombshell of Dr. Rosenberg's defending me. The feeling was not one of Oh, OK, Well, we'll just treat this Kopp guy like any other student, pass or fail his thesis on the merits. No. The feeling of the committee, except for Rosenberg and Lambert, was one of frustration, but only temporary frustration. Gnashing of teeth and re-sharpening of knives. You survived Round One, Kopp, but don't worry. We'll get you yet. You can't hide behind your little pals forever.

A pro-life call at the convention center, the counterattack from the pagan world, and then the defense from the invisible world had all come one, two, three in rapid sequence leaving me stunned and bewildered. But even then back at the beginning, it was the start of a tiny detente inside. All these scary forces were not meant to be fought full tilt on my own strength, even though that was definitely my Marine "devil pup" background. But a tiny bit deeper look into even that background reveals the better way: a team. Yes, the changes in my life would be a mess and a struggle from that day forward but it would also include standing aside as larger forces fought each other over my head. None of us can do it alone.

I don't recall how the name "Friend" inserted itself into this story but one night it popped into my head. I was yawning over the 'scope at Stanford and my worm samples, the sun long ago having set without my seeing it. I had only stepped outside into the parking lot for twenty minutes to gobble down my sack dinner in between my day job and night job sessions on the 'scope. But they have science libraries at Stanford, too, and one day I had ventured onto the main campus to continue searching the EM literature. In addition to the actual data, this is important. When you publish you have to answer the critical questions: where does your new data fit into the existing knowledge on your research topic? Does it confirm or deny other work? Does it suggest new paths of inquiry? Does it confirm an existing principal, but in a new species? You can't just throw data out there as Todd described les americaines in Roscoff. The burden is always on the researcher to offer the first explanation of how his or her data is positioned in the existing scientific landscape. Yawning and racking grids through the scope of the authors of these other papers I'd been looking at came into my mind along with the images of their EM research. I made a mental note when I was looking: go look again at these papers and start evaluating where my little hobbit worms fit in. Back and forth, library and scope, day and night. Somewhere in all this slog-commuting a dim bulb went on in the back of my head. Instead of waiting for the committee to chow down on my data as I sensed they would, why not try a little quiet end-around? Why not show the worm pics to someone else, first? Some expert? Some outside expert? Did I have anything to lose? The worst thing that could happen was the outside expert would hate my pics and I'd be back where I started anyway. But…hey. What if? You never know if you don't try.

Now this time when I went to the science library down on the main campus, it was with jets on. I still remember seeing the name "Friend" for the first time at the top of a scientific paper, but God help me if I remember it was at the "main stacks" across the courtyard from UGLI where the science journals were, or the smaller library that I think was over by Chem, between their building and the Rodin castings, and Grant's

Other Tomb. It was all a bit confusing because even though I was Stanford staff, I spent all my time at the Palo Alto VA Hospital, a few miles away up on the hill, where Dr. Eng's lab was. Either way, I spent a lot of time in the main stacks. That was where the George C. MacDonald first editions were, but that's a story for another chapter. So, I was "reviewing the scientific literature" but now I was looking for an independent expert. A scientific paper is a wonder of compression of information, filled with abbreviations, jargon, slang, and most especially, elliptical reference to other works. An entire complicated principle could be tossed around by simply citing, say, "Crick's idea"…followed by a hasty move on to some refinement.

But my attention was now devoted to two tiny portions of these ritualized data blocks: the authors of the papers, and the "Acknowledgement" sections, where an author might say where, physically, a lab was located. I scanned all these on the EM embryology papers with a view toward finding a possible outside expert who could help me. My dear Readers, what Serendipity Blessing Number are we up to, now? In what I suspect is the Lord's effort to pop me out of Fullerton with a degree, instead of just walking out? Is it Number Three? Four? Wait, gotta take my socks off. There was Phragmatopoma, the exotic newbie species no one had worked on, there was EM itself, which narrowed the field of competition for new stuff, and there were Dr. Rosenberg's heroic intervention and Dr. Lambert's backing me up, in committee, when I was toast. Ok. We'll call it Four. Well, the Anaheim convention itself, so, really, Five. Whatever! So. Serendipity Miracle Number Five: I looked at the locations of all the colleges that hosted the EM embryology research: U. Chicago, Sorbonne, NYU, Cold Spring Harbor, U. Mass., Mayo Clinic, Moscow, UCSF, Hong Kong, Seoul, Beijing, Sao Paulo, Cambridge. Huh? wait. What was that? I went back. Did I just read UCSF? As in, the University of California, San Francisco? Right around the corner from Stanford? I sat back in the chair and took a deep breath, a really deep breath, and looked out the windows at the sunny grass and trees outside. I was now, suddenly, Bertie Wooster, sallying forth with a cup of the supporting broth in me to revive the tissues and encourage fortitude for all that lay ahead. I was right with the world and all that was in it. The world, Suddenly Seymour, was not a teeming swamp of hostility and danger, but rather, my own personal Eden of frolic and joy. I now loved life and life, quite obviously, loved me back.

UCSF! It was barely fifty miles away! Even a starving lowly tech-day-job grad student like me could dash up there in a day and see if I could get an audience with his EM Holiness, our unknown Dr. Friend of the embryologic studies. I should probably explain that UCSF is the perfect example of an academic elephant that no one notices in the middle of the room. The best biological research in the world, let alone Cal, happens there, but everyone ignores it. Everyone who is an invertebrate type, I should say. In my world, anyone who works at a med school works with…ahem. How to put this nicely? You got it: vertebrates! Ignore them! They couldn't tell a copepod from a tunicate on their best day, so, pshaw! They were beneath our notice. Plus, UCSF had no undergrad courses there, so, they weren't as well-known as Berkeley and LA.

But if an EM embryology expert was just up the road from me, hey, I could go whoring and slumming in the fleshpots of. . . I tried to shrink into nothingness. I held my breath. Shuffle, Shuffle. Shuffle. No emotion. A tiny pause in the stack and a squint at my best picture, one of a spermatozoon reaction at the egg surface. "So. Where ya gonna publish these?" he said, as if talking to himself about whether he'd wash the car that afternoon or not. He set the stack back on his desk, blindly, but near the edge toward me. His eyes were already back at the pad he was writing on. I picked up the prints, desperately attempting to catch up with the ionospheric extra orbital speed of this conversation, where people casually talked about where to publish things, instead of spending all their time scrounging up a diamond knife, a few bucks for film and resin and stain, or wondering about whether they are even in the right business. That quality pre-owned car sale looks pretty good these days. I just couldn't escape the feeling that I was like a janitor pushing a broom in the Senate Building, but somebody had somehow sworn me in and now was peppering me with questions about Iran-Contra. Benghazi. Whatever.

I actually can't remember what happened next, I was so stunned. I was like the lady in the old bank ad who is told she's got the loan, and she's so stunned she can't believe it. "I'll come back later," she said, in the ad, in total disbelief. "I can see you're awfully busy." But back in real time, in the man's office, the man had asked me a question. I can't remember what I mumbled, and his mind obviously was on something else already. I'd had my two-and-a-half seconds and was glad for it, but it was now over. Still looking down at his writing -- he never looked in my eyes after the first one tenth of a second -- he whispered: "How about IJIR?" again, as if talking to himself. "Is this an invert?" How did he know that? Oh no! I'd be shot on the spot! Didn't I realize this was a med school, for heaven's sake? Guilty! an invertebratologist trespassing on the sacred vertebrate turf, about as sacred as it gets: Homo sapiens! Two seconds of silence deeper than an anechoic chamber later, I knew the interview was over, if only I could back out of the room without confessing to the Lindbergh kidnapping, or having a heart attack. A nice place to have one, come to think of it, if you were going to have one, but, still. I said thank you very quietly and backed out, ready to kowtow while retreating, tweak the forelock, make libations to the gods, and perform any other sign of respect necessary for having invaded the sancta sanctorum. The instant I got out of the office I could not contain my excitement. From the early hopeless struggles of the completely overwhelmed newbie out of his depth and sandbagged in committee, to the Light At The End Of The Tunnel, all in one swell foop! I couldn't believe it. All the way down the Peninsula back down to the Farm I was totally on Cloud 9. God's serendipity Numbers one to infinity had just kicked in.

This was not the end of it, by a long shot, but it was all downhill from that moment on, psychologically. Yes I would have to slog back down south to defend the work. Yes, the Stanford grant money ran out and I'd shift over to a non-science job with no microscope time: telephones, that paid twice as much and a hundredth of the stress. It would be another year or two before I got the degree, but all of that time was off campus. I had regular paying work, and the telephone job was part-time, so I could get more and more into prolife stuff, which was "the point of the exercise" as my Mayflower uncle never tired of saying. Two full years before I actually got the durn degree, I had made all the escape I cared about: I was started part-time into prolife work, and the crisis about whether to drop out of grad school or not had been resolved by a few powerful strokes by the Master. By the time I actually got the thesis and degree approved, I was half-way down the runway, prolife- wise, about to lift off. It was worse than cross-training, say from law to medicine, but it all worked out in the end, thank Almighty God.

At the next committee meeting I'm not even sure Dr. Rosenberg, my defender, was even present. Lambert was always susceptible to being run over by his much more aggressively pro-abort buddies on the committee. It was worse without Rosenberg to temper things. "You have to re-do all your blocks," Koch said, pointing to ruffled membranes near the egg reaction site. If I recall, he said it practically as my mouth had opened to tell the good news to the committee about Friend and the IJIR, the International Journal of Invertebrate Reproduction he had suggested as a place to publish the work. When I heard Koch's complaint about my prep, or technique, something clicked on real sharp on my intuition meter. On the one hand, this would be a disaster since the prolife work I had gotten into was all up in northern California. Also, my time on the state-of-the-art Stanford scope was over. I was a man with no lab, or, really, no lab except back in Fullerton down south. This was all worth mentioning, in the sense that you think your committee was Barney Fife, i.e., the friendly local public servant there to help you. If not, be careful.

 The intuition said: be quiet. Keep Friend in reserve. Silence helped me once, when Dr. Rosenberg came to my aid, and now Dr. Friend, in a way he was unaware of perhaps, was another figure coming to my aid, but you can't print a paper overnight. There is a peer review process that takes months. Lots of months. Play it cool. If I were to mention Friend now, it would directly contradict Koch's point and for all I know, premature mention of Friend, who wasn't on the committee, or even the faculty at Fullerton, could somehow jinx what was only an unofficial comment, however encouraging I had interpreted it to be. To even play with an EM was ambitious for any MA, for all I knew, also. To say the membranes were unhappy could involve anything electrolytic or osmotic happening in my little teaspoon of seawater universe. It could mean changing something that would make the entire reaction unhappy. As it was right then, with the blocks I had already set, the entire experiment was very close to a natural environment, and therefore realistic about natural fertilization in the species, which takes place externally, in the water column. A buffer to fix the membrane problem could do that, but also make the observation less authentic. As it was, even with the membrane problem, the results could still be useful because another researcher with more resources could use my prep as a starting point for something better, which is what most of science is anyway -- one worker building on the work of another.

 I don't doubt Koch was right about the membrane part of it; it's just that this was the kind of thing that would be done for a PhD. And, in a lab with money and a decent 'scope. Even buffering to help out the membranes could throw a wild card into what was already a successful experiment, and well-recorded. And all of this in "EM" time, where days were required to find out results from even a single block. I couldn't come back to Fullerton. Again, this looked like a good time to quit on the MA and go on to prolife. From that instant forward I decided to shut up about my off-campus "judge," Dr. Friend, who was an advocate for me, as far as I was concerned. I would go back up north, keep up with the transition to prolife, and let the degree take care of itself in the mail to Europe. In the committee when Koch said re-do, I nodded and smiled and kept my mouth shut.

That's exactly what I did. I kept up the prolife work up north, made happy happy noises to the committee, and meanwhile, just kept an eye on the mailbox. After the peer review process, the paper was accepted in Europe, and later, when I laid the acceptance letter on the table in the next committee meeting, I could almost hear the gas leak out of the let's re-do all your stuff idea. After all, it wasn't a PhD. Also, EM work is hard enough for an unfunded MA level lab. But mainly, I was at the point where I really didn't care anymore. The prolife work was the high priority. If I didn't get the MA, I'm not sure I would have cared that much. I don't know because it never came to that, but academia was fading and prolife was coming into the foreground. I nodded and smiled at Dr. Koch, bless his heart, and I bit my tongue. Those few years of holding back -- from '79 when I went to the Anaheim conference and got bitten on the spot by the prolife bug, and '81 or so when I left campus and still worked on the thesis -- did I learn anything useful for the immensely more difficult pro-life struggle that was ahead? No. I believe retroactively it was a waste of time. Later, I would find out that I would marry the movement anyway, so I didn't need a degree to support a family within the future. Also, even in prolife, it's not like some cop beating me on the head and handcuffing me would say, "so, master's degree, huh? I'm impressed," as he dragged me off to the hoosegow. It's not as if I were being groomed to be some public spokesman who could be introduced as a big wonk. The prolife movement already had a ton of those who were already being introduced all over the country and being ignored already, including their scientific credentials.

I wish I had dropped everything the minute I saw a single picture of a child dismembered and tortured to death, just like in Florida. Drop everything and follow the Lord. Don't waste any time. But there are levels of belief, ongoing deeper and deeper conversion. Then there was the SUMC incident in the morgue and the first glimpses of the faces of the young moms as they staggered out of the mills crying that I had yet to see on the Peninsula. Both of these were more deeply persuasive than the head knowledge and L'Abri feeling I had had in Anaheim. Both of these critical incidents happened during those intervening years, bringing the pot to a boil. I also learned from the experience in the committee to trust and be still when attacked by powerful forces. I had the chance to see a total stranger come to my rescue, someone who didn't even know me, but I believe angels sent him. I learned to trust prayers and gut as much as logic and reason. All of these things, however, are surmounted by the core principle: identify the substance of your calling, your purpose, and move steadily in that direction with God's help. Avoid or ignore irritations, obstacles, and distractions. Keep the extra can of gas (the European journal submission, say) on the side, like the wise virgins who kept guard over the oil for the lamps, and quietly await your opportunity.

## CHAPTER 3

# FROM ACADEMIA TO OPERATION RESCUE

The Plaster Cast Rescue in the San Jose area, about '85 or so, is an absolutely perfect rescue to learn from. We made every single mistake in the book. It's a wonder any kids got saved at all. If I had to guess, we might have gotten a handful. It was hard because of the way the mill was set up. The mill was a tenant on the second floor of a medical suite that had a kind of Frank Lloyd Wright type lightwell courtyard in the middle, which means that everyone could see every suite doorway from every other doorway. Think of a cheap two-story motel built around a common courtyard. This meant there was no sneaking up. Also, one of the rescuers had read a book by a prolifer which said when you rescue, you should call the cops the night before to let them know you are coming. This was the early days, on the West Coast, when naiveté like that could be excused I suppose, but I must add, that in addition to not being nearly the best thing for the babies, which are the highest priorities in the operation, and in addition to the simple cravenness of it, the idea that the police can't be wrong, poor hardworking civil servants that they are, it also has a self-serving component to it: I'm letting you know ahead of time, so therefore maybe you'll cut me some slack the next day when it's time to arrest me.

Whatever thinking this is, it's not thinking in terms of the babies. There is a certain large East Coast city which built an entire history of rescue on this simple idea of let's go ask daddy. What a disaster! As I say, naiveté alone is bad enough, but to add to it the selfishness of trying to make a softer nest for yourself is possibly even sinful. But we all love the guy who wrote the book, so, I won't go on and on. The rescue movement, obviously, got over this, so no need to dwell on it, but suffice to say, over my strong strong objections, they called the cops. Since I was the only one putting my ankles in the trap, I would never tolerate this now, but that was then. This forewarning, in addition to the approach to the mill, made it real rough. The bottom line is that there was no time for the plaster to set before the cops came. Instead of finding my leg cast attached to the understructure of the surgical table, they found wet plaster.

Now comes the really miserable part. The night before, as a last minute impulse, I had decided to imbed something hard in the plaster to defeat a plaster cutting saw, which I assume some doc could find from another doc. Pebbles or ball bearings would've been great, but I didn't think of that. I only thought of nails. The problem was that the only nails I could find that were small enough to embed in the plaster wrappings were sheetrock nails. The problem with old fashioned sheetrock nails is that they have a needle point on them, unlike just about every other nail i've ever seen. When the cop started to unwrap the wet plaster, he got a sharp stick from one of those nails, and he instantly went semi-hysterical. This was a few years after the isolation of the AIDS virus just up the peninsula in SF, and he basically took it real personal and got very angry, and never stopped being angry. He got so angry he decided to book both me, and my friend who helped me, with felony assault. When it's against a cop, it gets worse, of course.

We were at the mill less than 20 minutes after the landing and casting, I would guess. They were just right on top of it. Of course they were, we had called them the night before! There are only so many mills in San Jose, so they had a cop babysit each one. We walked in the door, they walked in the door right after. Boom! News about the felony charges made for a sweaty few hours; one minute we're thinking maybe just maybe a day in jail or whatever, and the next, just like up in SF, they're talking years and years in prison, for a simple rescue.

The RC moment, now I remember, came an hour or two after we were booked. The station house was so small I actually was capable of overhearing a heated discussion between the officer who got stuck and his watch captain. I didn't hear word for word, but I heard this rhythm over and over: "but...!" cop, complaining about being stuck."I understand, I understand," watch captain, trying to calm him down. Fortunately, the charges were unbooked before we left the station house. I don't recall doing a day in jail for this. Once the assault thing was off the table, after a week or two the whole thing started to retreat into insignificance. The mill almost certainly opened that day, only a half hour late. If we were lucky there were one or two turnaways, and since the news about East Coast arsons was starting to bubble over to the West Coast, I bet not a few types over there on the west said, well it could have been worse.

Don't call the cops, for God's sake. And for the babies' and moms' sake, too. If you really feel you have to, then just stay home and write a letter to your oh-so-concerned congressman instead. (Good luck with that.) I suppose the new epoxy fiberglass casting stuff sets faster? I don't know, I'm not into daytime stuff anymore, so I really can't advise. To me, your time in and out of jail and all that is worth something, something to God, to the babies, their moms, and everyone. Don't squander it. You owe it to all of them to try to make an effort that will mean something to the child himself or herself who is about to be toast. I'm not into symbolism, public awareness or "doing something." I know too much now. I want to be efficient. If we had a million people ready to go, that would be different, but we don't.

How to describe Craig? He looked like a weightlifter and plenty of tats but not quite as many as they have now. The bike was huge and yeah, it went a-CHUG-a-CHUG-a-CHUG-a-CHUG-a-CHUG-a-CHUG at idle and made your bones rattle. I am a people person. If you tell me you are the Pope or the President or the General Secretary all I want to know is who sent you? Who do you know? Who told you that? Why are you talking to me? To me there's no such thing as authority or money or power. All I want to know is, do you know someone I know? Even the pope is useless if he doesn't know Jesus, right? Back then I was not as cautious as I became later when I got into nighttime work, but before that, in San Francisco, the idea of some private eye or some creep from NOW or NARAL who would infiltrate us was pretty far out there. So, back then, in the Bay Area, everything I did was based on a very small community of prolifers who all knew one another. Everything was: we brave, we few, against the world, surrounded by Northern California liberals. How could some biker dude happen? He was not there one day, and the next day he was. Tommy the salesman didn't know him. Kathy or her family didn't know him. No one introduced me to him because no one knew him. I did not meet him in a church, or at a prolife meeting, the only places I would meet anyone in those days. Angels don't make a big splash, not the ones I know. One day I was sidewalk counseling in front of the Richmond District Planned Parenthood in San Francisco and there he was. No one said hi to him. No one acknowledged him. No one referred to him or vouched for him or said anything whatsoever about him. He walked straight up to me. He didn't speak to anyone else. "Have you ever done a blockade?" he asked. "No." He pointed at the mill, "We gotta do one. I did them in Phoenix." Everything I knew about Phoenix could be tattooed on the head of a pin. You'd think it's not so far away from California, but I did not know one single prolifer from there. But the idea of a chain rescue instantly got me going. It sounded a little bit like what the Coarsegold Seven had done, so I thought, hey, maybe I could do that. There was no planning or rehearsal or yakking about the rescue, unlike any other rescue I've ever done (about 150 or so). It was just, see ya there tomorrow. Oh, and he asked me to bring the chains.

A biker wants me to go get a chain. Hmmmmmm. In the hardware store buying the chain there in the Richmond District, my friend Bob and I got to thinking about fake assault raps that might be brought against us particularly by mill staff who could make up a story about what happened before the cops got there. We decided to get some handcuffs so we could cuff ourselves ahead of time and head off the fake assault charges. Did the nice helpful hardware store man happen to know where we might find some handcuffs, we whispered across the counter. It was only after I'd asked the question did I realize how stupid it was. I mean, I was an Eagle Scout, Bob was a med student, and yet here we were, two youngish, Irish-looking guys in a store in the Richmond District in the 80's asking for handcuffs. "Harry," the clerk shouted to the guy in the way-back of the shop, "Where do we keep the handcuffs?" Then he passed over the goods with a barely suppressed smile. Imagine that -- three heterosexual men still left in San Francisco, and this was 1985. I started to try to explain how Bob and I like girls but Bob kicked me in the shins. Don't. Pre-rescue security demanded preserving the element of surprise, and the mill was only half-a-mile away. You really need those magic first thirty seconds to get situated. Just when it looked like the embarrassment might be over…damn! We'd forgotten the chain! Bob and I left the handcuffs on the front counter and went back to where the chain was. Well, excuse me but there's only one way to buy chain. You gotta know how much? We were broke prolifers. We didn't have money to chain up Barnum and Bailey elephants, so we didn't know what else to do but loop the chain around our two waists to see how much we needed. I mean, hey, that's how they make suits, you know?

If this had been at a capacious Home Depot we might have gotten away with it until some precocious six-year-old chanced by and shouted, "Look, Mom! Cowboys and Indians!" As it was, the hardware store in the folksy artsy Richmond District isn't much bigger than your living room and when we were wiggling and squirming around back there in the chain department, the third man of the last three heteros in San Francisco was openly laughing, pointing, and calling his friends over. Hmm, this could be a sideline: popcorn sales. Uh, and there would have been a great market, there in The Richmond. We hurried up and cut the chain. At the counter, red faced, paying for a heap of chains and handcuffs, my Good Christian Boy Eagle Scout soul hated to leave the clerk with a False Impression, but Bob kept putting a lid on it. I settled for shouting, "Keep an eye on the papers tomorrow," over my shoulder as I left the store which as far as the clerk was concerned clinched the matter. Bob shoved me out the door.

There was a rescue or two before the stair rescue, so maybe a little background would help. The first time I went into that mill, if I recall correctly, I mini-krypted my ankles together while they were looped around a defibrillator cart or an ultrasound cart, I forget which. By the way, this is a chance to be a little peevish. I recall the mini-outrage when I told the Americans i'd clipped the wires on the defibrillator machine in Rome. "It's a life-saving machine," they said. "We're prolifers." Hello? Where to start with ignorance like this? This is as bad or worse than the hand-wringers who say all rescue is sinful because it invades private property. How will you feel when all rescues need to be done on public property, in the obamacare era? Good luck with that one. But it doesn't matter, since FACE "publicized" all private mills anyway, punishment-for-rescue-wise. Whiners like this are always looking for some excuse, and one is as good as another.

## RALPH M. GABRIEL

Note to whiners: defibrillators and US machines are required for mills to have. If you destroy one, they have to get another one to certify the operation. This adds to the cost of starting up again and it closes the mill longer. It's not like they'll do an abortion ten minutes after you rescue and oooooops! not have a defib. machine. The point is to shut them down as long as possible and make each arrest count as much as you can, not some ritual formula of rescue so you can brag about something that is actually ineffectual. It took them 30 days to tool up again the mill in Rome, just to re-order all the stuff we trashed, down to tiny bottles of anesthetic. Someone who would put forward a weak casuistry like this reminds me of the target of the ire of Dietrich Bonhoeffer (Ten Years After). He said the improperly conscientious man would and could always come up with an excuse to roll along with Adolf H., whereas the simple, straightforward man could see clearly that Jews and Poles were being burned, and he would hasten into the street, sweeping aside all obstacles, to get to a child about to be run over. This stuff makes me tired. Casuistry Excuses! To hell with all that. Get busy for heaven's sake. That casuistry and excuses will do you no good when the Master asks you painfully simple questions about how we spent our time while the babies were being shredded. Sorry. Old Man Rant over.

So, back to the pre-stair rescue. I looped my feet around one of the legs of a rolling ultrasound stand and connected with the mini-krypto lock, the kind you'd use to lock up your front wheel, which on a fancy bike can be removed with the quick-releases. I used it straight off the shelf, unmodified. The inside dimensions are perfect for two ankles, either from one person or two. Two, you can daisy-chain all day inside a mill, with stuff you can fit in your pocket. Anyhow, I was out of there with one little clip from a bolt cutter the firemen had on their truck. But that was only after they went through their protocol of running up and down the halls shutting all the doors, I gather to make sure the moms didn't see me. So, when I heard that, and when no one confronted me after about ten minutes, I started screaming at the absolute top of my lungs, Mommy Don't Kill Me! and like that, I was shouting so loud I was starting to see stars like I would black out. All in all they had me out of there in about 45 minutes -- nice work if you can get it for a one man rescue.

I'd take that, any day of the week, but I got to thinking about how quickly they clipped the leg on that cheap-o ultrasound stand. When In

Doubt, Reconsider. Some More. Upon reconsidering, I noticed an internal stairway snug to the outside wall of the building. I guess you could call it a back stairway, or maybe a fire escape. Imagine a glass wall as you see in so many malls, imagine a stairway inside that you see in so many cheap motels and apartment complexes, you know the kind? It has one tubular steel stringer down the middle, and each step is cast concrete that "floats" at its edges. There is no connection between the treads and the side rail. Think about this a minute: it means that if you wanted to, you could sit down on a tread, facing the upward direction of the staircase, and thread your legs in between the treads, and also, around the stringer. Now, your two ankles are approximate, on the far side of the stringer, and, with a little wiggling, it's not that terribly uncomfortable, especially if you can add maybe a little padding for sitting on the concrete for a long time (this could take a minute).

This whole rescue memory kind of breaks my heart because the mill was located just off Jack London Square in Alameda, CA., the city, not the county. The city of Alameda is one of those hidden gems that pop up in any big city -- a tiny backwater of peace, right in the middle of the square itself, Jack London Square. On recons in the a.m. it was so peaceful and nice, right on the water. Alameda is really a navy town. Hmmmm, a mill history connection? And this little nook of the woods is something even most bay area types might never have seen if they weren't in the navy, or vendors. During the war there must have been a ton of hellos and goodbyes on this dock, along with treasure island, etc. So many good memories of the Last Greatest Generation is what i'm trying to say, and all polluted now with killing. I wish I could show you a picture of the mill. It is one of the milliest mills of all the ones i've seen, esp. since it was built in the era before the pillboxes that are now being constructed to obstruct people like us. Even the sidewalk counseling aspect is diminished in these huge, regional new mills, but this was built before that. It was square, detached, two story, and it had an Eichler style flat roof with exposed beam tails coming out of the top. In other words, like the kind of pillbox you would make during a war with logs tossed on top and concrete on top of that. It was pale kelly green with white trim. It was a huge building to be devoted just to killing, and I recall little or no sidewalk presence from our side there, probably because Alameda is such a backwater for most bay area people. If you don't have business there, you just don't know about it. Other than the mill, the city of Alameda is a dusty tiny town, in the nicest way, right on the water, a gem, and they messed it up. The landing was smooth as glass. I don't recall a single problem, even though this was the same mill where i'd done the ultrasound cart rescue only a few weeks before. Don't ever forget that as you become familiar with the physical layout of each building and its environment, they are all available, all the time. To them, we are like whack-a-mole. No matter if your face is known, they can't keep looking all the time everywhere. However, later in life I stopped returning to mills i'd rescued at, and in fact, I quit day work almost entirely.

I can't remember if I got in the door at the bottom of that stairwell with the target staircase or if I walked through the building proper, from the one much more closely watched front door and stairs. In fact, now I think of it, it's possible Bob came through the front and opened the back door. This was all after I had already rescued coming through the front door. It was only on recon that Bob and I noticed this gorgeously vulnerable back staircase with its four by six stringer just begging to be attached to. The landing was perfectly smooth, and I had a chance to connect my ankles with all this stuff without anyone screaming at me or slamming doors or whatever.

The acoustics of the building as a whole was such that the back stairwell was still under the same soffit as the part of the building that was not in the stairwell, because it was all glass. There is the temptation to think of the back stairwell as being outside, the way a water heater closet is sort-of outside even if it's technically under the fingerprint of a building blueprint, and within its walls (ask me about water heaters later...oh my, my, my. Mm, mm, mm. Yes! yum.)

Anyhoo, acoustically that stairwell shared a common soffit with the entire building, which meant that sound form the stairwell could travel through the building via the soffit/roof interspace. Are there any construction guys left in the PL movement, at all, anymore? And if you aren't, just go to a site and watch, commercial or residential, sit on the street and watch. At night, walk on to the site and look closely at everything, especially things that changed since the day before when a tradesman put his hands on something. Again, I screamed my head off and the reaction of the staff clearly indicated that the sound travelled and interfered with their killing. Think about it, pilgrims: all that bang and no assault rap exposure: you're not even in the same room with anybody. I assume we're talking about Alameda, City of, FD that responded. I suppose it could have been, Alameda, County of, which is a much larger jurisdiction with tons of money. Whatever.

As in sf, there was an old skipper, the captain of that engine co., that first responded, and a younger turk who was anxious to help the boss in his dilemma. This skipper didn't make code RC noises like the other one, though. But you know how professionals talk past you in a situation? They completely ignore you and focus on the "problem"? Well it was that way here. I don't recall anything nice from them, but I don't recall anything hostile either, so, count your blessings. They got to the point where they could eyeball the ankle gemisch from below, a glance or two, and thinking about K2 saws, and they said, "naaaaaaaaaaah." Actually, come to think of it, that was code RC talk, but only between themselves, because without winking at me, they came to the correct conclusion (leave him be), although not as correct as it could be (quit your day job and pick up the night work, as the Vito Squad did in the 90's when Janet reno fired them.

Do you know this story? It's a rip. A bunch of disgruntled ex-feebs torched hundreds of mills (that's not a typo: ca. 450 mills) just for payback to the HRC dowager empress's lackey, who muscled them out at the same time she tasked the remaining feebs with chasing off after you and me and little old ladies with Bibles and rosaries in their hands in front of the mills. (WSJ, early 90's. Check it out.) So, ultimately the skipper decided to leave me be, but before he did that there was a lot of hemming and hawing and talking to staff and whatever, but I so well remember this part: there was the captain of the engine company. The boss, the guy in charge. Then there was this anxious lieutenant who was always at his side and making noises like, yeah boss, or no, boss, maybe we could try this and that. First it was about k2 saws, and in that case, unlike sf, they would have had good ventilation because the hydraulics on the power source are about 20 feet, and they could have put the engine outside and still had the tool on the bottom of the stairs, under where I was sitting. But for some reason they ruled that out. In the case of grinding with the k2 saw, there really wasn't much space to get the edge of the blade in, and as far as the shearing attachment ("jaws of life") for the hydraulics, there wasn't much space to get the edge of the shear in there. It is a steep angled jaw, designed for clipping door posts on cars, which it does very well, but only because there's tons of room all around the doorpost when you crack all the windows in a wreck. Not the same, when there's all this stuff crammed around one set of ankles. I think the overall overload of it was what discouraged them.

   Btw, somewhere in this algorithm they passed the train stop that had to do with forcing the ankles out of the clinch. I assure you it was tight, but in the future it would be nice to provide for a little something to loosen it a little after the police had come to this conclusion, and during the long haul, to help out with circulation. This reminds me of another story, in Levittown I think, where they pried the "Mahler" open just a little without frankly broaching it, and slipped the feet out. But this was after 10 hours of work, so even then, it's not as if it would be a quick fix at the scene of the rescue, which is what the FD is thinking about up front. So, the rig in Alameda was tighter than a "Mahler" but this presented circulation problems as the day wore on. Again, I used the free tail of the cobra to take some of the weight off. Then, they started to just brainstorm on the assumption that they couldn't open the clinch: how would we do that? Well, there's clipping through the stringer, isn't there? (I hope you can visualize these stairs, the cheap-o apartment stairs, because you need to see that 4 by 6 inch tubular stringer in your mind, the one that runs up the middle of the stairs? And each tread attaches to it? And there's no riser, or kicker, like on a wood staircase?) So, like good theoreticians, they then assumed they could get through the stringer one way or another, which they could, either with a torch or grinding. No problem, and they could have done it away from me, as much as six feet above or below me, since I had sat down in the middle of the staircase.

   What to do with him, still attached to the staircase, and the staircase loose from the building was the next question. They were being very logical and trying hard to rule out all possibilities. It makes sense that they got to where they got to. So, if I were still stuck onto the stairs, but they removed the stairs with me still stuck on them, how would they get the stairs outside, which was the point of the exercise, right? Especially since I was yelling and the customers didn't like that. First they started thinking about building jacks and "cribbing," something firemen think about because in some wrecks, like a car, you can't just snip your way out with the jaws of life. Sometimes, if a truck falls on you, for example, you need to think in terms of cribbing and house jacks, like when people lift a house to slide beams under it to move it. So logically they started in this direction of thought: Ok, we cut the stringer above and below him. Now the staircase is free, and we crib under it and jack it up. The next logical thought, to minimize damage to the customer, would be to try to get the staircase level so it would go out the bottom door. This meant more cribbing and jacking.

At one point the eager lieutenant burst into this part of the problem and said these words, and i'm not making this up: "OK, it's too much trouble to level and jack it and bring it out the door. Let's cut a hole in the roof and lift it out with a chopper." No, I am not making it up. Jesus and all the angels will testify. What made it even funnier is that the skipper, in a first reflex of trying to follow the ideas of the eager disciple, cast his eyes up to the second story roof (i saw him do this) and for one finite moment measured it to make the hole. Then, he realized how far this thinking had come, and the thought that he had just entertained, even if it was only for one minute, and slowly and sadly his eyes drifted back down to the face of the LT, who by now was embarrassed. Then the LT looked at the floor, but if you could put a cartoon balloon on the expression of the skipper, it would be: "I can't believe you got me thinking of that, for even one minute." That realization, that thought on the part of the skipper, was the denouement of the entire day. Once the skipper realized that they were seriously, even for one instant, thinking of the helocopter stairlift, it meant they really had a problem here, and there were no cheap quick solutions.

But for one magic moment, they really really were seriously thinking of demolishing the building and carrying away serious parts of it with a helo. I love it. There was a crowd and a fair amount of media on the north side of the building, the side which faced a street. The street was an east-west street that inserted into Jack London Square; I could see the square from the stairs I was stuck on. The FD and cops took the attitude that if they ignored me, maybe i'd go away by myself. Either way, the idea was, let's go away and see if he goes away. If I recall correctly, I stayed the whole day, screaming my head off maybe about once every 30 or 60 seconds. Especially towards the end of the day faintness and darkness would sometimes appear at the edge of my vision so I couldn't do it more frequently than that. Sidewalk counseling began once I got in place and they told us later that there were turnaways. I'm sad to say, though, that they still did some killing; a shame, because you always hope they wouldn't do any at all. There came a point in the early afternoon, maybe about 2 or 3 (it was a seven a.m. landing) when b. started really really strongly suggesting exeunt stage left. I hated to go when the mill was still going.

It's possible we waited till after five and the killers left, I can't remember for sure. Either way, there was the question of going to the bathroom (i NPO'd the previous night and I didn't seem need a bedpan, which was nearby). It was a dicey moment when I first stood on my feet, but b. was there and he helped me get in a car. Things were better when we got to wherever we went, up until two or three or five or whenever it was. B. and I had discussed the idea that maybe the other side is just pulling a trick; i.e., waiting around the corner to pounce on me once I got myself loose, but it turned out they didn't do that, and i'll bet they were relieved.

I still remember so well that first day we "landed" at a mill in Manhattan. Fifteen hundred! All in one place! All on one sidewalk! Where does a five-hundred-pound gorilla sit? The police were so helpless and behind, with all the to-and-fro on the subway system, that a tiny stream of little old ladies from the Midwest and Bible Belt had snuck up to the door past the vanguard of cops and made a beachhead. By the time the rest of the NYPD showed up with their pedestrian barricades and buses and cops and SWAT teams and what-not, we were already in place, a vanguard of LIPIVITS that couldn't quite be arrested fast enough to re-establish the blues at the door. We had the door. A thousand armed NYPD officers, who knew we were coming, and when we were coming, and even where we were coming within a half dozen targets…all outfoxed by a handful of little old ladies in no apparent distress. Power to the Gray Panthers! Power to the Silver Foxes! And if a peace officer were to let fly with a perfectly understandable cuss or crudity, he would be met with the gentle reproving gaze of a LIPIVIT, followed by: "Young man! Does your mother know you speak like this around elderly women?" but said with a twinkle. "Cookies and cocoa at my house, later, you little scamp! Now be a good boy…" This easygoingness lasted all that first day. For example, when Mark Bavaro, the NY Giants tight end No. 89, was arrested there was a complete swarm of blues around looking for autographs and shaking his hand. Bavaro wasn't even planning to rescue, but he was walking down the street and saw the little old ladies. "I can't let them do that and me not join them," he told us later. He wound up sitting right in front of me. I told him not to worry about reporting for Giants training camp; he'd be out in a day or two. He said he wasn't worried, but he sure had more to lose than we did.

Anyway, that morning in Manhattan was a funny day. For one, I never am quite comfortable over on the East Side. There, I said it. Lots of urban granola-eaters over there, south of Spanish Harlem and you never really know what to make of them. In their compulsive way you'd think they'd rise up and finish us off if they realized we were trying to shut down their precious mills. Those aging hippies didn't get the memo: you used to be counter-cultural; now you're just the establishment you hated so much when you were younger. The trick was carrying a hundred fifteen pounds of lock past the NYPD guard on duty at the front door of the mill, and still make it look like a little kid's backpack. We prayed, too. I honestly felt a little sorry for that cop who 90 seconds later was literally on his knees, upstairs, begging us to undo the locks again. "This is my first job, guarding this place. I'll get in a lot of trouble when the watch captain comes around." Once ESU finally got the locks open they were not so conciliatory. I remember egging on Fr. Norman, a fellow locker, to crawl with me toward the interior doors that led to the actual killing rooms. After seven grueling hours of being worked over by the power tools, we were exhausted, but it was still a rescue, and policy is always try to get as close to blocking the murder rooms as possible, if not in them to make sure. And always, before anything got started. Father was every bit of 65 or 70 back then but he, the career Lt. Col. Air Force officer and hardheaded Swede, got that glint in his eye. Let's go! We both Atlanta-crawled toward the hallway.

After standing around helpless for so long, that was all the blues needed to see. They pounced and tackled us and threw us on stretchers, "throw" being the operative word, even if we went limp after they grabbed us. Time for a little payback. One of them held my shoulders and another one held my ankles. They lifted me upside down, facing the ground. The shoulder guy let go but the ankle guy did not. The stretcher was canvas, with the material touching the floor in the sag in the middle. My forehead had an immediate and close encounter with the concrete floor and as it snapped back I felt and heard a nice loud pop in my neck. I had no idea it was coming. I'm not complaining. At least I could still breathe because somehow they managed not to break my nose. I don't have numbness in my arms but i've had a ferocious neck kink ever since. Some people play football, I guess, you know? When we finally got transported downtown, we found out that the NYPD had decided to process us all in their police academy. Even in the academy it was a problem though: where do fifteen hundred rescuers sit? They wound up putting us in a large lecture hall, the kind you see at UC Berkeley or Madison,

Wisconsin. Come to think of it, this rescue was a lot like Cherry Hill, a big party, even if it only lasted an afternoon: everyone all in one place, the pressure of the rescue off.

At one point my arresting officer shyly confessed that he was a cadet and that this was his very first arrest. A LIPIVIT clutched his arm and said "...and I'm sure your mother's very proud of you, young man. Just watch out for the babies next time." Yeah, it was that kind of a rescue. At one point in the height of the buzz of everyone being booked all at the same time and place, I was asked to stand up and turn around: Fr. Norm, myself, Joe Wall and the rest of the Kryptonite crowd. Randy introduced us to the entire group as the "A-Team." It turned out that was the name the NYPD had made up to describe the metal rescuers. There was enormous applause and I only found out later that as usual there was a method to Randy's sees-all knows-all madness: the good feeling and respect helped take the sting out of the bitter pill the police had to swallow, that it took so long to get through the locks. It turned out that behind the scenes, while all that embarrassment and delay was going on, Randy had been carrying out hard negotiations. He told them that if they didn't release the A-Team onto the street ahead of all the rest, he and they would go limp right there in the academy and rescue all over again. Right there in their nice clean lecture hall. All for one and one for all. What a guy our Randy is.

I need to explain "deathscort" to tell you the next part. A deathscort is our name for what the mills call a clinic escort and what the US Border Patrol calls a "coyote." Coyotes on the border, say at the Laredo Crossing, are hired to make sure their package, whether its drugs, guns, child sex slaves or immigrants, gets across the line. At a mill, the coyotes there, the deathscorts, make sure the mom gets past us and cannot change her mind at the last minute. If she did, they'd lose a sale. Pimps and aggressive controlling moms outside the mill would also use their own coyotes to make sure their prostitute or daughter would not change her mind at the last minute. Think about it: this is all on top of the schoolhouse monopoly Planned Parenthood has over brainwashing. Good luck trying to speak in a school if you are a prolifer. But the death culture is so obsessed with child killing they take away even that last little opportunity for choice in front of the mill. In the case of the Horse Rescue the deathscorts walked away from the mill, all the way through the DMZ to the end of the block, seeking women who wanted abortions. In a way, even this traversing of their own zone was a small victory for the Gray Panthers since no woman getting an abortion wants to walk down a red carpet with TV cameras and cops and a crowd all around. Impossible. So we might have saved some babies and moms that day anyway. And there's a good chance no real clients were willing to endure all the exposure, and that the handful of women who came over the barricades were actually shills who went in to deceive the press and conceal the fact that the DMZ had backfired, driving away any moms, especially with all those cameras there. But at the bottom of the DMZ, if a deathscort "found" a mom, real or otherwise, in the scrum outside the barricades at the end of the blocked-off street, she'd bring her over the barricade and traverse the DMZ with her. But first she'd put a Walkman on her head with loud heavy metal rock on it, to drown out us begging her to save her baby. Well, there's "choice" for ya. The deathscorts put the Walkman on them, like it or not. Wow. What oppression of real choice and thought women do in the name of women's liberation. It's even a little Big Brotherish, don't you think? To actually control what another person even hears? They use the Walkmans at the mill, too, for the woman whose conscience fires up at the very end. Why shouldn't it? Of course it does, happens every day. It's the overcoming of it, and the psychic price paid later, that makes my heart go out for these moms.

When we saw the set-up, I hopped inside the barricades on impulse and ran ahead of where the mom was walking. I threw myself down on the ground ahead of her on the path, ten feet ahead of her, with my legs and head on the ground, bent over like in the old nuclear alarm drills in the sixties, remember? This way, she would at least have to sidestep me. Kind of useless, but what else could we do? I called out "Mommy don't kill me!" the shortest Gospel I've ever heard, where the baby is Jesus proxy, I guess. Or messenger. The coyote manhandled the mom around me, and then I ran ahead of her again and repeated the process, like kids leapfrogging. I crouched down with my head down to the ground as we were taught in the A-bomb drills in the 50's.

"Stomp on his neck! Jump right on there!" the coyote shouted to her prisoner, the second time I kneeled down, but she wouldn't do it. I laced my fingers behind my neck just in case, just like in the nuclear drills. A bad neck is bad enough. I didn't need a bad back too. The Gray Panthers saw this and they didn't need someone to draw a picture for them. They hopped over the barricades too and did the same thing for each mom that was dragged up the phalanx, one at a time. We didn't have the manpower or panther power to rush the end of the open area and block the door to the mill. With only a dozen people, this was not an option; plus, once you sit down you invite arrest, unless you can scamper out of the way in time. This was not one of those blitz situations where the police give notice and count to ten. They were in a scooping-up mood. There were a lot more cops-down there at the mill end of the DMZ. When I leapfrogged my way up closer to the mill where they were jerking the first mom, I thought, oh heck, let's just bypass this whole arrest thing, and I scampered back to the crowd-end of the DMZ to try my luck with the next mom, as if I were a sidewalk counselor at that moment and not a rescuer. A rescuer will do whatever he or she can to stop that one actual killing. A sidewalk counselor tries to persuade, and if the mom won't listen, he or she cycles back for the next one. Strictly speaking, we weren't really rescuers that day. Also, we weren't even arrestable, since no cop ever bothered to order us to stop doing something. It was a weird day, half rescue and half sidewalk counseling.

It turned out that in addition to meter maids, cadets, and K9 cops up at the "Reuters" end of the DMZ, there were two groups I'd never seen before at a rescue: horse cops and a SWAT team. Full disclosure: I believe in SWAT teams. They are obviously necessary "As The Light Declines" in our death-saturated culture. They would achieve much more if they fixed the problem at its source and used their talents and energy to stop child killing, but they still have a crucial function, as long as they don't protect child murderers, which is exactly what they did that day, ESU also, in Manhattan. 1 don't think the horses actually galloped down the street, but they came. What exactly can horse cops do to effect the arrest of a dozen little old ladies who are scampering back and forth on an open street? Plus, what is going on? Legally speaking. It's not jaywalking: the street is blocked off from car traffic. It's not trespass because it's a public thoroughfare. It's not resisting arrest, since no cop had ordered us to…whatever. Martial law, then? Fine, the babies have had that since 1968 and 1973, but just don't bother me with a trial, OK? Give me a priest, a cigarette and a blindfold and I'll be fine.

The horses were a lovely russet color just a shade paler than the half-burnt sienna of a Tennessee Walker. And they were so dainty in close quarters. Once the Red Dogs got close, we all crouched down and didn't move, according to the "Atlanta Crawl" protocol. The minute the Red

Dogs saw that, they were temporarily flummoxed. How to manhandle a hundred pound soaking wet little old lady who's crouched down on the ground, unresisting? Maybe the cops were thinking of the Reuters cameras, just up the street, who by now had followed the horses?

It must have been the military genius who gave the next command: I distinctly remember the mounted cops commanding their horses to walk over us as we were on the ground, in a sideways dressage-kind-of move. It wasn't just to herd us. They definitely told the horses to walk on top of us. I distinctly remember the horses clearly understanding the command, and trying to comply, but refusing. God had sent us wonderful pro-life horsies! They were so prolife that they even recognized the sacredness of life in another species different from their own, a species even known for cruelty to them! Would that we homo sapiens could learn a trick or two from the noble and gentle dignified horses. Yes, the horses were also skittish, I think, about setting their hooves down on an uncertain surface such as an inert but squishy human body. I get that. But I strongly sensed that they just didn't want to do it anyway. We were no threat to them. It was a nervous moment, even so, down on the ground between the hooves as the poor horses were spurred to walk over us. But then they skitter away! The horses backed off, ineffectual, and we all poked our heads up and said let's go for it! back to the middle of the DMZ and that's when a Red Dog just got tired of it all, grabbed me from the back, and lifted me off my feet as if he were lifting weights. Which is what SWAT teams do all the time. That's the footage that made it to Berlin. One skinny white boy and a dozen little old ladies: Book 'Em, Danno! Horses, dogs, pirouetting synchronized meter maids, clowns (uh, that would be us rescuers, thank you very much), SWAT team Dudley Do-Rights, helpless children on the prairie, all in a weird Commander Cody's Wild West Show: Barnum and Bailey, I got your next act.

An hour later, lying on the floor of a microscopically tiny and cramped holding cell, the news filtered to me from radios turned on in the jail. First, a general disclaimer by OR leadership: this was not an officially OR authorized rescue. We don't know what these people were doing.

Well, fair enough; we were AWOL, but did they have to say this to the news? But, wait! In their usually annoying manner of trying to get both sides of an issue, the press had not only put on the killer's drone about women's rights, they also put on a pastor who made an interesting point: no one anytime, anywhere, can tell any human going not to follow her heart, and her own sense of human compassion, even if she does something desperate and ineffectual, if the life of a child is at risk. The Gray Panthers did the right thing, to even try.

At the first statement I had been hugely depressed and all the more on top of being exhausted since it had turned out to be a fairly physical rescue. But then, those other words came on the radio and it was music to my ears. I never heard such good news, the sound of someone making your point when you are incapable of doing that, and silent. God bless you, Pastor Joseph Forman! And it sure wasn't the "Dissension in the Prolife ranks" idea that the Saul Alinsky press was looking for and trying to create, either. I never got in trouble with Randy over the Horse Rescue. Also, if I had to guess, based on close inspection of the shill angle, I wouldn't be surprised if they didn't do a single real abortion that whole day. They just wanted to prove a point, that they could stay technically open. But somewhere, even if they're open, they're really closed.

I can't recall if it was from the Horse Rescue or not, but sooner or later DeKalb County ran out of barracks they could put us in but still keep us isolated from the General Population. There came the day that summer, though, when they had to mix us up. I suppose I've been in a hundred jails or so all over the world, but that massive puke green tank in Atlanta was one of the dingiest and filthiest spots I've ever been in. There were worse ones like the Stockport England bucket, or Murder Max. in Rome, but not many. Everything was the same puke green color, the walls, the bunks, the ceiling, everything. Also, there was no sunlight, not even a frosted window. I have never heard of a General Population inmate anywhere in the world who didn't have at least a grudging respect for prolifers, and for most of them, it's much more than that. "You're in here for a cause," "You really believe in what you're doing, not like me," "Abortion is terrible, I tol' my girlfriend not to do it, but she went on ahead anyway," "What are you doing here?" are all typical comments. Anyway, Atlanta's SWAT team at the time were all tricked out in their spiffy black ninja uniforms, which most SWAT teams guys around the country tailor to show off their muscles, which they get pumping iron at taxpayers' expense, since much of their time is spent waiting around for the next mall whackjob with an Uzi. These guys had brand-new black baseball caps with RED DOGS stitched on it in huge blood-red letters, like when you get a Mickey Mouse cap in Disneyland. Hmm.

When the Red Dogs saw the Gray Panthers running over the barricades of their precious DMZ, even with our pathetic blocking, they decided that this extreme violence had gone far enough. Time to swing into action. The problem was that there was only one or two Gray Panthers in the DMZ at a given moment, and the rest were blending in with the crowd that were ringing the barricades around the DMZ down at the rabble-rousers end of the street. They'd grab one and another would pop over, and some skittered back over the hustings if no mom was in sight. It was a great big Whack-A-Mole for the cops. This was the exact moment some military genius decided to send in the cavalry. I mean, if the infantry is having a bit of a sticky wicket and the issue is in question, why not send in the really big stuff, you know? I'm kind of surprised they didn't have tanks and artillery and dreadnoughts there, too.

There had to be at least one Old Confederate down there in Atlanta still smarting over Sherman's "Fustest With The Mostest" philosophy, and if there was one time in the history of APD and OR entanglement where the cops were supposed to be "Fustest," this had to be it, right? To lose with every overtime cop present (there must have been accountants and vending machine repairmen that day, too) would be really embarrassing. And expensive. All these obscure and rarely used police units would be in trouble if they couldn't make a show for the taxpayers in this circus. After we left town, I mean.

I can't remember why I was cutting three quarter inch rebar one day behind a house, no acetylene torch in sight, because I don't remember using it for anything. Instead, on the rescue we got going up there with some locks and blocks involved, off-the-shelf Kryptonite bike locks, but with a twist. The Vermont ones were embedded in a cast concrete block, the casting done inside a small plastic trash can. The only problem was that we'd cast the concrete the night before, and it was green as cheese the next morning! A few whacks from an enterprising BFD fireman got rid of the concrete and the rest of the assembly was exposed. They still had to cut the Kryptonite but now they had better access to do it. Next time we'd use chemicals that speed up the concrete curing, or just cast more in advance, but the problem with locks and blocks is the same as arson and sniping: how to tradeoff between propping a rescue or sabotage intervention with homework and design, and skill, sets, etc., when today's children keep dying today. Everyday. This is always a struggle and a puzzle. Quiet Time is the only answer, I believe, because a good case can be made for both sides of the dilemma: the warmhearted Godly impulse to jump in right now to save today's children, and the long view, which could be more effective in terms of an endgame. God must decide, but I could never condemn either approach. Both are Godly.

Connected to the green concrete block/lock mélange ménage were rescuers who also did the Pittsburgh McPherson strut thing: they kryptonite-locked their necks to the underside of cars that were brought to the mill and immobilized with the rescuers underneath. But unlike Pittsburgh, the car couldn't really block the door, it just got close. The police still had to deal with it though, and all the fuss and delay constituted opportunities for a mom to think twice, and many did just that. We know this because they tell us.

The first time in Vermont I was arrested with the green concrete block and the Macpherson strut crowd. It wasn't at the black mass mill, though; that came later. I recall one or two days in the Burlington County lockup but no more than that. Also, I think we "Baby Doe'd" there, too, as in Atlanta and NYC. Not only did we refuse to give our names but we also refused to walk anywhere. I seem to recall being carried from jail to van to jail until we were brought to Waterbury, Vermont where they had everyone else. Apparently, the early rescuers that responded to the call of help had already clogged up the jail in Burlington when they were put into the G.P. At some point the Burlington cops got tired of the smiling and singing suburbanite/farmer rescuers messing up their jail and some bureaucrat had a brainstorm: let's clear out a wing of a state mental hospital and stick 'em in there! This is exactly what they did and that's how I found myself dumped in the entranceway of a swanky modern building in a tiny Potemkin village North of Burlington in the middle of nowhere.

For reasons I've never understood, the mental hospital was located on the campus of a series of cute New England Cape Cod-looking cottages in Waterbury, which it turned out were also government buildings. It was as if the whole fake town was a campus of state buildings located away from Montpelier. When I got to Waterbury the party was already well underway. By the way, rescuers from outside Vermont call those rescues and jail time the "Vermont Rescue," but local Vermonters call it the "Waterbury" rescue. I guess it's like an outsider saying he went surfing in "California." I'd say, well, do you mean Huntington Beach? Why don't you say so? Then I'd ask him what lifeguard stand we're talking about. So, Waterbury mental institution it was, for us rescuers. I wish I could convey to you the difference between the Atlanta Green Hole and Waterbury. Waterbury was a very nice, well-built building and I was so convinced I was under arrest by the processing in Burlington that it took me weeks to come to the realization that the only thing holding us in that mental ward was window screen. No bars! No steel doors! No counts, not like any prison I was familiar with. The closest thing to a count was the C.O. strolling through the wing with a stack of Polaroids trying to match them to faces because we refused to stand still for a census count at the cell doors. They weren't even cells anyway. The counts were so predictable that "Thirsty Fenian" found a way to sneak out the back door for a quick one at O'Reilly's down the street and get back inside in time for count.

The Rome rescues are also referred to in RC circles as "Rome II" because it was preceded by another Rome rescue at the exact same mill a few years earlier. But when I think of the Rome rescue, I think of Rome II because it's the only one I was in. Thank God for Rome I, which paved the way, especially in terms of Intelligence, about the interior of the building, some of the political/legal climate, etc. so, a little backstory: If I had to guess, it was before '89. I can never remember which rescues happened in '89 and which ones happened in '93 because we did rescues in Italy both years. Wait, I remember now, some of it: '89 was the Joanie-out-of-jail tour that included a trip to Gdansk and Warsaw and Bologna, with rescues in each of those towns. Each one deserves a story, but for today all we need to remember is that Rome I was before '89 when Joan got out. Wait, I could be mixing, up Gdansk, etc., with the trip to Santiago de Compostela, northern Spain, and Fatima, and Lourdes. I can't remember now if they both happened on the same trip.

In Rome I, 126 and another dozen invaded the killing room itself, in what is a free-standing sub-division of a hospital so massive you'd think it was a university campus. Actually, it's larger than many, even US campuses, which can get big by European standards. St. Camillus de Lillis was founded by that guy as a place for pilgrims to heal up if they caught tropical diseases when they went to Palestine. Crossover to healing up crusaders? The crusades started as pilgrimages, (see, Characters of the Inquisition by Thomas Carroll, Black legends by John Rao, or Six Black 16 Legends by Dianne Mozcar if you'd like to know what actually happened during the crusades, as opposed to the disinformation in our history books.) Unfortunately, since the crusades, the hospital was ultimately taken over by the commie side of the (current) city of Rome, a side which is carefully shielded from tourists. The commies make a buck off pious tourists, so they stay on the down-low. Part of the down-low is that they paid for so much fixing up of tourist monuments that the RCs slowly became dependent on the commies in this matter (don't do this, it's wrong). One result of this is St. Camillus de Lillis started doing abortions, obviously against the will of the Church. (Write Frank, tell him to put a stop to it. I think he will.)

Lessons from Rome I: location and layout of killing rooms on a huge campus where you could get lost; likely killing days; political/legal situation gleaned from discovering that Rome, commie city of, let them go with little or no jail time (i forget exactly) and, perhaps most importantly: resolve to go "no fingerprints" next time. No fingerprints was an idea that generated from one of the OR NY follow-ups: one day I was being booked in my friendly local Tombs I (massive jail disguised as a modern skyscraper office building, in Manhattan). A cop pulled out a lower drawer, looking for an inkpad or something and I saw a rubber stamp there, marked with large letters: "REFUSES PRINTS." Well, heavens to Murgatroyd, if they've got the stamp, I bet they use it time to time. This became an obsession with me and 126, and ultimately to a rescue in NY with no prints, and released after a couple weeks with no record. We were just nameless smurf rescuers, kind of like babies that get tossed in the trash with no names or burial, but as far as Rome is concerned, it meant we were motivated to try the no-print thing over there.

I was about to go into Rome II, but I realized there's a little more backstory. I think Rome I was before '89; as I say it all kind of runs together. But it did not come before Fresno. Why invade a building at all? Where did this idea come from? ahhhhhhhhhhh, fellow rescuer, welcome to the story about Fresno, when men were men. Gee, our old LaSalle ran great. Those were the days. If I tell you 7 rescuers entered a mill in Fresno, California, in about '79 and disabled the whole place for weeks, barehanded, in broad daylight, you probably would be skeptical. But dear fellow PLer, it's true. It's true, it's true.

Catholics United For Life have re-morphed themselves so many times since then, I couldn't even begin to tell you what they call themselves now, but back then, that's what they called themselves. They did not start out Catholics, they started out as an atheist (culturally) Jewish hippie commune of free love. The free love involved children of uncertain parentage, no marriages, and, uh, limited clothing overall. The Jewish evangelist RC priest (yeah, he was all that, and supersize fries on the side) who visited the commune in the early 70's or earlier, once ended a doctrine/instruction/inquirers session by saying, oh, and next time, could you please put some clothes on? True story. By '78 they had found an old farm to live on, built a chapel, had a priest say Masses now and then, put clothes on, became very intense RCs/Messianic Jews/(insert your own oxymoron here) and had retreaded the purpose of the commune from free love to prolife.

In '78 they walked into the mill in Fresno, walked into the back office, declared themselves, and calmly announced to the baby killer proprietors that they needed to leave the building immediately. No, i'm not making this up. Some rescues have the Holy Spirit in them, and some rescues have THE HOLY SPIRIT IN THEM. Also, aiding the H.S a little that day could've been the fact that up until then no one had done this, and so they caught them a little off guard. Note: this is certainly true today, since rescue died, lo, these many moons ago. The staff bolted, aided and encouraged by the H.S., and then the Fresno Seven (as the press dubbed them, later) advised the patients/moms of the situation -- no staff, no abortions today.

The seven then proceeded to trash the mill, inside out, with their bare hands. No weapons, no arson, no chemicals, they just trashed it. Threw everything in a big pile, including medical records, files, medical supplies, anesthetic bottles, cannulae, etc. I suspect they tore open all the medical stuff also, to desterilize it. I can't remember how they got so much time in there alone. Again, the H.S. It took a minute for the cops to get a clue about what was going on. Also, the Seven barricaded the doors from the inside after everyone else had gone out. Sometimes when this happens the police tool up before they broach, because they are not sure what they will find vs. a quick and dirty broach where a "cowboy" cop just breaks a window in frustration and crawls in, early in the game ("cowboy" or "lone ranger" is what the cops themselves call such an impatient cop). Now of course, this means the tooling up could mean an HRT thing, and those guys tend to get offended when they get inside and find quiet peaceful types with no weapons, and it can become a little like the cop who answers a "domestic" by saying, well, someone's going to jail, I'm tired of these "nothing" calls, etc. But this was back then, way before 9/11 and all that. Yes, a favorable time could elapse without HRT, even now -- in a small town, with someone on the street telling the cops that the people inside are peaceful, if the cops believed that because they knew the representative, etc. etc. The bottom line is that CA was so embarrassed and afraid about the whole thing that they came up with a deal to avoid trial: we won't prosecute, but you have to leave CA and not come back. Interesting, huh? This was with supposed big time hanging over their heads, but actually CA was afraid of a show trial and 1979 was much closer to a time when everyone hated abortion. The take home is that the pattern of peaceful bare hands invasion was set in '79 in Ca., 10 years before Rome I.

Rome II began with a weird side trip. We made the mistake of going to the Vatican to ask for advice on what's the best mill to hit, and were sent to "Mater Dei" hospital in Milan, a big city up north. Think of New York, as opposed to WDC. Yours truly was so dumb, bullheaded, and weird I told everyone to empty out his and her pockets before we hit the train. I didn't want to give the government anything to ID us, not even money, not even Italian money (huge mistake). I don't know why I was so big on this, but maybe it was connected to the no-prints thing.

We took the overnight to Milan, hit the street early a.m., and couldn't find Mater Dei hospital, nowhere, a bust, also, due to the genius leadership, we had not a sou in our pockets even to get some food. Showing masterful leadership abilities, yours truly then proceeded to get a completely incapacitating migraine, which is what happens when I don't eat, and it's high stress. We didn't even have a coat and sat the whole night on the floor (cold marble) of the train station with the junkies there. If cooler more experienced heads had not prevailed the next day, we would never have hitched back to Rome, where there was food and a place to stay with friends. This was good so we could recoup. We also argued about whether to even take a day off to recoup, which was completely necessary. Again, Mr. leader said no, we gotta go hit the mill toute suite. Thank God again, cooler heads prevailed, and we went to see our Italian cousins. Thank God again again we did since they turned out to save the baby, (remember that part?).

A couple of days later we hit St. Camillus de Lillis, using the intelligence from the previous rescue. Our Intelligence was provided by someone who was used to hearing every little heavenly susurration of angel's wings, and ducking into churches to say hello to the Blessed Sacrament, so it was a little frustrating for German-type leader-types who had to stand around waiting for the spiritual enhanced to find the mill, but they did, even including a panic bathroom stop. It was spooky-good; the Lord's timing was perfect, even though we had argued about delaying, because the lady we met in town came to do sidewalk counselling at the rescue, and thank God she persuaded a young woman to keep her baby, and I think she's in contact to the present day. Better take a local when you go, because, I don't know how to put this, they don't speak English over there, you know what I mean? It's some other language, actually. After all the mish work my family has done over the years, we have concluded there is really only one human language, the language of love, and if you speak it, anyone can understand you, and if you don't, good luck with the Berlitz, or, these days, I should say, Rosetta Stone.

So we had a rescuer along who had done Rome 1, who knew the layout of the mill embedded within the huge campus hospits get up. I'm not sure how to put this. Yes, the Holy Spirit better be along if you try this trick, and thank God I don't remember one rescue that wasn't surrounded by prayer, but if I had to describe what happened, one way to put it is this: there were not a lot of women in the waiting room, and we kind of drifted past them into the corridor connecting the waiting room and the killing room. These were maybe 50 feet apart, with two doors and corridor turns in between them, so it's the kind of thing that never would have happened in a US mill, especially during the rescue era. Anyway, we kind of drifted back into the corridor, and it was not all instantly clear to the mill staff what our intentions were. After all, we were two couples, all of what you could call reproductive age, so at first glance as we kind of drifted up the corridor, any staff person who wasn't really thinking rescue could think, hey, maybe a boyfriend is coming into the back to sort of console (i.e. browbeat) his girlfriend past the last minute jitters (which all women have, as we know from the Silent No More website). At one point I do remember being challenged by a staff lady, about 25 years old or so, who was petite and not at all like the commanding type who run the US mills. The challenge was extremely mild, as in, can I help you vs. a body block and screaming which would be the US reaction, back in the day. I looked her straight in the eye with a really big smile as if to say, in heart language, don't worry, this is not what it looks like, as in, "This is not the droid you seek, move along," the part in Return of the Jedi, if i've got the right name. This is a trick you need to get decent at, short of Jedi mind control, in Rome. It had the effect of freezing the staff person for just a second while she processed this. After all, I suppose you can say that in the patient-friendly fake ethos of baby killing, you don't want to tick off patients or their boyfriends who are paying. You would think twice before doing that, and there are two good reasons to make them think twice: one, the Jedi mind trick; two, the customer's always right thing, and three; don't ever rescue without the Holy Spirit. This all reminds me of a Filipino rescue, but that's another story.

As I was effectively engaging her in silent conversation (I had to, one word out of my mouth and the gig was up) this traction made her focus on me for an instant to process what was going on, and during that time the other three really smoothly flowed past her. I mean, really smooth. Most rescuers might not know about this but in Atlanta we were taught to drop down and crawl, which of course was a brilliant technique for then, but this kind of betrays your intentions, n'est pas? In Rome the smooth gliding still left a few seconds to think, hey, maybe they really know what they are doing back there, or maybe someone else who works here did authorize them to be back here, even though they are not escorted, which would be the normal protocol.

Holy Spirit thank you, but the net effect of all this was that three people got past her and now they were in between her and the killing room, instead of the other way around. I was a rearguard blocking thing by continuing to look at her and pretending we're long lost friends from high school or whatever. At one point a few seconds after the droid thing, our intentions became clear to all and then it was just a footrace. Thank God one of our rescuers knew exactly where to go, and go there, fast, no opening and closing of many doors to search, etc., just one, two, three, yes. If you have a flighty super spiritual type who's always ducking in churches to say hi to the Blessed Sacrament, don't knock that gal off the crew. Even if she drives you to drink. She just might be your best spy, which is exactly what happened that day.

I can't remember if one of the staff came into the room with the four of us. If she did, she got out, but I think we beat her in there cleanly and shut the door. Before we got the door shut there was some yelling from a white coat babykiller who was hanging out in the area. How they didn't put it together quicker, considering that a dozen Americans had done the exact same thing in the exact same place only a year or two earlier, is beyond me, except of course that it's the Lord.

But I must say, this has to be one of the biggest miracles in the history of rescue. Then we barricaded ourselves into the room by shoving up against the door the heavy pedestal which supports the overhanging lights. Course this was not as good as Maurice Lewis's simply pushing up on the handle. A note about European hardware: You don't turn the knob as in the US; instead, there is a handle you push down, a little like a toilet handle, only bigger. It shows up in American construction here and there. In Europe, it's everywhere. The two handles, in and out, were linked without a release between them so that if you pushed up on the inner handle, it prevented someone from pushing down on the outside handle, and effectively you were locking the door by your own strength.

    Soon, of course, the mill got someone out there who was more footballish than the skinny fussy touchy feely receptionist we'd got past, who didn't hesitate to use a little more force, but Maurice is a tough English rugby player from way back, a scrapper from Liverpool or Paisley or wherever, one of those ghettoes, and he was tough. The neat thing is that the other side didn't push all the time, they just tried real hard for a moment, and then backed off to reconsider. During one of these miraculous interludes, we found something to kluge up from the floor to actually brace the handle so you quite possibly couldn't push it down from outside without breaking the handle spindle that went through the door, something the other side had to be at least a little worried about. We used the pedestal of the light stand plus something stacked on top of it and all held in position so the forces wouldn't make it slip off the kluge/stack. To open the door, you needed to rotate the handle/lever thing through at least forty-five degrees, so our stack had to be good.

    I don't think you can imagine how much stuff there was: a hundred of these little bottles, the one-dose disposable size, fit into a single box barely the size of a cigar box or a candy box, and there were stacks and stacks of these boxes in that tiny closet; then there were gloves, plastic 18 cannula, antibiotics, and stuff I can't remember. And all of it sterile. The others spent all their time ripping open hundreds of glove packages, the kind the gloves come in? After each desterilization, we'd throw the desterilized supplies into the center of the room, which was partly obscured by the top of the lamp as it extended into the room, as the pedestal part was shoved up against the door. Not that it was that small a room, every bit of 15x15, say.

    The heap of trash at the end of forty minutes was a circle about 8 feet around, and came up to about two feet in the middle. Knowing the purpose of all that expensive stuff, I don't think in my entire life was I more proud of a construction job I worked on. That heap was our Sistine Chapel. We ran through it all, and at the end I ran out of stuff to destroy, so I bent the hand tools of the abortionist into pretzels: the polyp forceps, the hemostats, the metal dilators, all that stuff. When you're doing prolife medical care, always treat your tools the proper way. The arrival of the judge, a slight woman about 50 or so, was heralded by the booming on the door of a fourteen pound sledge hammer. The door hardware was quite serious, the stainless heavy hinges you see in good hospitals, but it didn't take much, and the door came down slowly on top of me as I was behind it. It was not violent or scary, it just sort of fell down slowly onto me, and then onto the pile of debris.

Oh how I wish one day you could see the looks on the faces of those killer doctors. You would think Italians, especially after all that waiting, would wave their hands and yell a lot, as they do on the street, once they finally got a chance to speak to us, but it wasn't like that at all. It was never like that. The minute the door came down and they saw the pile of stuff on the floor, and the destroyed equipment and machines, they were stunned, and I really mean it. They didn't say one word. The judge was behind them, kind of like a general issuing orders from behind the lines, and no one felt empowered to do anything while she was there. She tended to say nothing, like the image of Joseph II put forward in Amadeus, where he consciously lets underlings argue in front of him until they come to some kind of conclusion of how to go forward, and then he quietly says, "There it is." Like that, she was like that, and this impacted the arrest, in its own way, kind of quiet and friendly. Now, rescuers, from here on out the story has to do with what happened after we were arrested.

Normally you might have a tendency to yawn or skip over to the good part of another story, or whatever, but i'd like you to stick with this one. Before it's over, this story has (yet another) Vatican representative, a Scotch priest rescuer, a family tragedy, a tricolor revolving lighthouse (you really want to stick around for that), torture, mayhem, Murder Max, prison rioting (well, a tiny riot), Judy Garland, (yeah, Dorothy), wild cats, The Wall where all the Jew smuggler priests got shot, drinking wine in custody. I mean, this story's got just about everything. Oh, I almost forgot. There was an attempt to overthrow the Italian government. And Mother Teresa showed up at the very end. It wasn't over till the skinny lady sang. I mention all this because rescue is one of those things that irritates the modern technocracy. It is one of the last activities that cannot be done by a machine, and as such it is very suspect. Since it involves human beings, those human beings just might be thrown in jail, especially if they do the equivalent of blowing up or bringing down a mill, without fire or explosives, just with their bare hands, kind of low tech. If human beings can be thrown in jail, things can happen to them that you might find interesting, from a reductionist, materialistic perspective. You might say that the rest of this story is about the care and feeding of the rescue "machine," and since it has a happy ending in terms of the humans, and it also has a happy ending in terms of our best efforts to save the tiny humans, it's all still part of the story.

Once, when we had just finished a particularly unsuccessful rescue which got us a lot of jail time, I asked a fellow rescuer why we rescue. He said, we have to. If we don't, babies are killed without any witness at all, and rescue (or nighttime work) is a witness which is commensurate with the emergency, just as if you'd run across the street if your kid wandered into it. Rescue, even if it doesn't "work," is still required witness to a quite obviously dying culture. Now, in 2013, we tend to design our lives around whatever-won't-send-us-to-jail, but I assure you most solemnly, in fact I promise you, and I'm sad to have to say it, we're headed for jail in the near future, like it or not, and not just for serious Thomistic force like those listed on the skypl.blogspot.com blog. For saying homosexuality is a sin, from the pulpit, like the Canadian pastor. For refusing to pay taxes specifically because o'care pays for abortions, like the other Canadian guy. For simply holding a sign on public property, like the two Canadian gals. Hmm, do I detect a trend here?

I was asked to give a few more details about jail by a good Christian sister, ok, my own sister squared (blood and spirit) who said she thought all Christians are headed there. As Mel Gibson once said (ignore his lifestyle for a second, ahem) "everybody dies. Not everybody lives." It was the character of "Willie Walla" William Wallace, a Scotch freedom fighter who first Raised the Standard against the English, just about the same time Joan of Arc did the same thing in Bretagne. Willie did it on the shores of a loch up north. If you were in a horrible wreck today, heaven forbid, you might realize you are mortally wounded, before the firemen come. When that happens, a certain detente comes over you, and you realize that this exact time and place is the time to make it right with God. Right now, and right here, no matter how inconvenient or painful. All thoughts about anyone or anything else go from your mind, and you face squarely that thing which we run from all our lives.

Please, I beg you: consider the possibility that that time for you can come earlier than you think, and not because of a car wreck; instead, because you realize for once in your life that it is wrong to sit and watch children get their heads torn off in front of your eyes, and do nothing for them as you would do for your own children. When the fireman comes and you are in the wreck, he doesn't look at his watch and say, well, i've got that MacDonald's in the truck that I just happened to buy. I'll eat that first. He doesn't say, can we drag this thing over to the side of the road? All these cars whizzing by are bothering me. No. He kneels down on the tarmac right there, exactly where you are, and begins talking to you in the most endearing and personal way, and then proceeds to risk his life for yours.

Godammit, be the fireman. I beg you. Today. Somehow, rescue isn't dead-witness Canada -- it just has no Americans doing it anymore. Nighttime work is just waiting like ripe plums to pick. If you'd like to make a better use of your time and save more babies, my crew had a 14 year run -- hundreds of successful belligera contra edificium, before it got all rolled up, and during those 14 years we had jobs and saw our families, a lot. They're coming for you anyway (unless you roll with o'care premiums, God forbid) so why not make it count? Why not "Give it everything you've got, or you won't have anything to talk about in the locker room," as Ruth Gordon once said.

How many Jurisdictions are there in Washington DC? Quite a few. There is a DC government, which is like a city government, and there are various departments within it, and within the fed, and each of them has a say in dealing with a public event that happens inside the magic square mile. This is the way it was in Rome. After we were arrested, we spent the first night in a City of Rome lockup which was bare brick, no toilets, like Stockport for the Manchester rescue. One rescuer had a jaw injury from resisting prints. Remember resisting prints? Part of the idea of Rome II. At one point a cop put a choke hold on her and we saw that it was an amateur chokehold. I did not want a martyr on the spot, and, plus, the babies needed that rescuer, so I begged her to go ahead and give the prints. I know, it was a departure from policy, but I could see plainly that that cop did not know how to apply a choke hold, which is illegal in the US and for all I know, in Italy also. But we are rescuers and laws like that don't apply. Later, she couldn't eat an apple they gave us to eat, the only thing they could come up with at the time in the little lockup, which really was just a drunk tank. So another rescuer munched on an apple, made a kind of applesauce out of it, and gave it to her. I know, but, hey, when you've been in enough jails together on normal rescues, what are a few germs between friends? Our immune systems have already survived everything the junkies can bring in.

The next morning they brought us coffee and asked us to walk. We had refused to walk at all up to that point, and they were forced to carry us out of the mill, into cruisers (tiny fiats, a joke, those tiny cars wouldn't have lasted a minute in a race with Burt Reynolds) and into the lockups. When they carried us, after they had picked us up, the cops went through this absolutely laughable ritual of carefully dusting off and straightening their uniforms, the ones with the snazzy white leather slanting cross part? Turns out they were caribinieri, a kind of federal police, and boy were they into their uniforms. After two days we wound up in the Italian equivalent of a federal court, and guess who was on the bench? None other than the same judge lady who had given the order not to break down the doors till she got there (and saved a dozen babies in the process). What your enemy plans for evil, God can make into good, and btw, he's the only God who can do that. The other gods only know how to throw fits and destroy.

In English felony courtrooms there is a thing called a dock, a small square palisade of balusters in the middle of the room where the suspect stands. It has a stairway down to the lockup below, and if you are found guilty, you are "sent down," back to the lockup. If you are found not guilty, they open a wicket in the balustrade and you walk into the well of the court where everyone else is standing. In the federal courtroom in Italy it was like that. Thank God, we still had the energy to non-cooperate, and the caribinieri with all their fancy uniforms had to find a way to carry us all the way up and down the stairs that led into the dock, only those stairs were extremely narrow and cast concrete, with sharp edges on the treads! Come to think of it if we didn't have females on this rescue, I don't think the caribinieri would have been so slow to use the more serious compliance holds. You can say we men hid behind the skirts of the lady rescuers. Selah. Do you remember the Rowan and Martin Laugh-In skit with Henry Gibson where he wore a Nazi helmut and held a cigarette, continental style? He'd slowly turn his eyes to the side and say, "vedy interesting" as if he were a spy checking something out and waiting to report it to his masters.

And that wasn't even the biggest miracle! We only found out later what happened next -- (wait'll you hear this!) Someone at the mill (I can't believe i'm writing this) actually called the judge of what amounted to the District of Columbia federal court (this is Rome, remember, capital of Italy) and told her what was going on, and for whatever reasons known only to the H.S. (are we detecting a theme, here?) she instantly ordered them not to broach the room until she got there to personally witness what was going on. Sports fans: this is so bizarre you just really can't imagine. I mean, what the heck? Sometimes the Lord is just waiting to do all kinds of stuff, and all you have to do is roll out of bed -- and more than sometimes, I believe, if you get into nighttime work where you don't stand around waiting for the police to arrest you, but instead, pull an elvis (off, to help others.). I really really think we should all examine the idea that there are only so many people in this benighted era willing to try new things that really give kids a chance and are not purely symbolic. It was Flannery O'Connor who said, If it's just a symbol, to hell with it. She was talking about the Real Presence, but I wonder if that same thinking could apply to PL work. If it's just a symbol, to hell with it.

To give yourselves up to the cops and long dockets and stupid trials where you can't speak anyway. This has to be justified in the current era, given the symbolism failure of many decades now. I mean, not justified to lame stream prolifers, but to the Lord. Back to Rome, a US cop would never call a judge from the crime scene, right? This is just too bizarre. In the US, there is the infinitesimally small fig leaf remaining of impartiality whereby a judge can't be a witness to a crime. He would then have to be recused, right? Well, no problem in Rome! (I'm sure the US will catch up. Quickly.) Miracle on top of miracle, the judge then jumped in her car to make it to the mill, which was across town. St. Camillus de Lillis Hospital is in Trastevere, the part of Rome on the other side of the river from the communists, the part of Rome where the Vatican is. In fact, St. Camillus de Lillis is barely a 1000 yards from the Vatican. Shame on the RCs (mention that when you write the pope, eh?). "Across town" in Rome is like saying from Manhattan to Philly, almost, or, from Dallas to Houston, or from Hollywood to Sin Diego in terms of all the traffic you have to fight. Rome is a perpetual traffic jam because the core of it is an ancient city, and kept that way for tourist purposes or whatever, and all the new cars can't fit on all the tiny old roads.

    I found this out later when we were being driven in cop cars through Rome to get from one jurisdiction to another. The cops would wave a little sign out the window because the legislators got tired of hearing sirens all day from cop cars that were stuck in traffic anyway, so they waved this little sign that's supposed to mean, hey, pull over or you're really in trouble because I'm a cop. The problem is, there is no "over" to pull over to. Everybody's jammed up. All this was taking place while we were barricaded in the mill. We had no idea why, but due to the judge's order, and the traffic angel's order, they left us in there a full forty minutes before they broached the door. The longer we got in there, the more scared we were about what they must be planning outside. They must be really pissed, went the thinking. They are calling a swat team, they are constructing a gallows for a shortened legal process. Whatever, we decided to make use of the time. Oh, pilgrims, how I wish, just once, you could know the heaven of just for once, even with all your fake gandhian scruples, what it's like to do what God wants when He wants it, no excuses. That's the gift of what we got that day. For forty wonderful minutes we got to destroy all the contents of that room with our bare hands, so extensively that it took them 30 days to restock everything and get it back operating. Do you realize what this means? At one point in the middle of the low tech holy sabotage, Maurice and I looked at each other, as the pile of useless debris accumulated in the middle of the room. "We'll get a long patch of time for this, huh, Maurice?" " No, Jim, how about a couple years, ten." Then we both smiled a little, nervously. What the hell, this was new territory for us. Both of us had spent years being hauled off to the clink, but we'd never had the opportunity to do a Fresno. Carpe diem, as they say.

    Next to the killing room was a closet maybe 6'x15'. It had an outside window, so nighttime wise, this would be the place to start. The closet was stuffed top to bottom with supplies totally specialized to abortion. This was in contrast to the hospital in Gdansk we rescued in once, where a doctor came into the room, upset with me, and proceeded to show me every instrument in the place and explain that none of it had to do with baby killing. I think he was right and I was finally persuaded. It's the kind of thing Dr. Nathanson or Dr. Wilkie could help you on, or really, any nurse, too. This closet, though, was packed with disposable cannula, tiny bottles of anesthetic, one-dose, I assume to anesthetize the cervix, antibiotics, needles, gloves, Chux, it went on and on, and all of it related to baby killing. Even in a general OB/GYN exam room or surgery there would be a few other medications and instruments, but this place had none. It would have been totally impossible to deliver a baby or even treat polyps or endometriosis in this room. The vacuum pump and defibrillator gave it away, too. Your usual OB/GYN exam room doesn't have a defibrillator. We pumped water through the air intake pipe on the pumps until oil/water mousse came out the bottom, a sure sign of blowing the seals. I cut all the wires on the defibrillator I could get. If I had had more time, I would have just picked the thing up and bashed it on the ground (see earlier discussion on this). Most of my time in that 40 minutes was spent bending over one tiny corner of the aluminum cap on the top of anesthetic bottles, you know the tiny kind, barely 100 cc., say, a third of a fluid ounce, that are clear glass with a label and the little rubber whats-a-ma-jigger on top? The thing you put the needle in? I figured if I just bent that cap up enough to exposes the top lip of the glass bottle, this would desterilize the contents and make it all a must for disposal. I know we were right because they had to replace it all. So, for me, most of that 40 minutes was my wrist getting tired using a hemostat to grab the lower edge of one of these aluminum bottle tops and flipping it up.

 I just can't find a better way to describe that judge's courtroom behavior. She held the cigarette the exact same way, pointing straight up next to her face, and only rarely smoked it, or never, just wanted it smoking near her. That's what I mean by continental style, but the effect could be as if it were a tiny bowl of incense. Well, you get the picture, and let there be no doubt about the deity involved here. But also, she was quiet, as in, scary quiet. We are used to American judges who barge in and are bluff and interrupt all the time, but this was different. Here's how her courtroom operated: she was the king, the deity, and all her little minions would scurry over to her and whisper in her ear. No, i'm not kidding at all, and I can't imagine i'd have something nice to say about an American courtroom except that i've never seen this in one of them except in rare cases, where there is essentially a private hearing, and the whispering off record would be done by a confidential clerk. The Rome courtroom didn't have a raised bench for the judge to sit at; she just sat at a kind of big table, to make it easier for the minions to run back and chat with her off-record. The entire floor of the courtroom was all on one level. As I was saying before, she had this Joseph II (in Amadeus) feel to how she did things. She mainly just listened to people suggesting things, debating quietly, and after a while she'd make the tiniest inclination of her head, yea, or nay, and they'd go on. Good luck trying to find out what was happening to you and the babies. You could almost feel what they were saying and how they were saying it: so. what'll we do with these crazy backpackers? oh, I don't know, how about... no, I don't think so. if we did that, well... yeah, yeah, I see what you mean, well, we could always do, hmmm. that's interesting, we could try that, and if, exactly, if x, then y. And of-course, all of it with the presupposition that the killing must continue and any trueblue RCs left in Modernist Italy would have to be kept in the dark and the whole thing swept under the rug as soon as possible, so any other backpackers, or for that matter, anyone in Italy left who hadn't bent the knee to baal, wouldn't get any ideas.

The feel of the courtroom was calm. With the suppositions firmly in place, there was never any perceived threat, only, how to do this? While we were clueless. How to put this? people solidly in power, who perceive no threat, don't need to raise their voices. They just discover the coalition of legal mechanics from their fawning underlings who do the details of how it will be put down officially, and then, when she hears the denouement, nods her head. It reminds me of my theory of supe cert, petition (habe) handling: the supe clerk gets in a case, sees it's from a prolifer, and hands it to a lower clerk. lower clerk: What do you want me to do with this? upper clerk: Well, it's a prolifer. Do you want me to draw you a picture? lower clerk: So, it's denied? upper clerk: You have potential. That's what I pay you for. you figure it out. I'm bored already, now, here's the next one.

And the part about the Rome courtroom that frosted me the most is that one of the terrified pantywaist minions that rushed up to her and whispered into her ear off record was my own assigned lawyer! Another thing that would be totally unacceptable in a US courtroom, but we can't hold up the American system as anything great, due to the substance of what they do, regardless of their appearance of "fairness" or "parity." Once in Buffalo the prosecutor stepped into chambers while the judge was in there and I was in court, waiting for a hearing. I told one of my lawyers, the one who was on duty for that day, to go in there to find out what they were gossiping about. He refused, he was scared to death, (this was not Bruce Barket, who isn't scared of anything). I asked him repeatedly and repeatedly he refused, terrified, for some reason (the "dungeon" there in Buffalo comes up through the judge's secretary's office... go figure). I caught the convicted child molester judge (oh, that's another story!) again talking to the prosecutor without me or my counsel present, and I confronted him. (This is an ex parte conversation, totally unethical according to their own stupid standards, which it isn't even worth discussing because of their substantial, iterating error.) He replied, oh, we were talking about something else. He knew he was dirty.

    I wouldn't go on about this except to say that the Italians were ex parting all over the place and didn't think it was wrong at all. They were total ex parte animals. They were, those Italians, and it had a creepy European economic community (EEC) feel to it. We are the future; shut up and obey; soft communism; endless regulations that make you give up and go away; unrepresented decisions, running roughshod over the Irish Constitution which is pro-life, etc.) If American jurisprudence, many of them, most of them, especially at the Supes level, didn't have a running dog mentality about EEC apparatchik groupthink, I wouldn't make a point of it, but they do, and you can see it on several critical issues, kid-issues only one of them. For example, no matter what you think about the death penalty, the Pope respects both sides. The morphing of it into a universal global constitutional idea, with European post-enlightenment (really, endarkenment) eggheads leading the way, is something you can see plainly. Other people than I have already talked a lot about this, the idea of American courtrooms sheepishly following liberal European ideas on critical areas, so i'll stop, but I wanted point it out. I saw the future of American, and I daresay "global" jurisprudence in that Roman courtroom that day, and it creeps me out in an infowars.com kind of way. Once I realized what was going on (we were all lying on the floor in front of the bench, basically still being like babies and not walking, and not talking and refusing to ID ourselves) I went so far as to tell my translator to get up there at the bench and listen to the whispered conversation between my lawyer and the judge, but again, just as in Buffalo, he refused, and, exactly as in Buffalo, he was terrified of the major domo.

    I'm trying to put across a feeling of what the future is like. You will not speak. Other people will speak for you. Even in a trial things will be compressed, and most of the time the people will be strangers, even if they are supposed jury members, discussing what they think you are thinking, without ever even consulting you. It all has the feeling of a reality show where they show a little footage of a real event (something as dumb as the jackass movies, let's say) and then, since that footage doesn't fill up the mindless hour, they cut away to one of the principals in the action, after the action, neatly dressed and dreamily lighted in a studio, discussing what it felt like at the time, right? I don't watch TV (exception: old movies) but i've seen enough of hits to know how it goes. Say a wreck happens on a cop show, and the fireman did X heroic act to get someone out of a burning car. Most of the show is him talking about it later. They rarely or never show footage of the person in the car. OK, sometimes, but i'm trying to explain that the feel of it all is, well, talking about this is more important than substance. A real fireman I don't see giving an interview. It's just another day's work, and where is the interview with the FBI agents who burned down 450 mills in the 90's? Why don't we see that?

The translator told me in the most general terms what was happening. Imagine someone talking about your case for an hour in another language, and during the hour the translator nods and laughs the whole time, listening, and after that he returns to you, realizes what he's paid for, and says, "Oh, they were talking about your case." It was like that. I wouldn't care to explain this at length unless I believed strongly. It's coming to a courtroom in your town soon, and from the babies' perspective, this train pulled into the station a long time ago. This jail, Regina Coeli, was like a massive star with radiating blocks in a circle, a little like Stockport. All of it was inside a huge wall, urban, and with a tower in the middle. I really don't think Americans have any idea how tall the gun towers in an old European dungeon can get. We're talking, in the case of Stockport, every inch of a hundred feet, or ten stories, over a jail maybe three stories tall.

Regina Coeli was maybe five stories, all radiating star blocks. A huge number of people in a small place, all of it shoehorned into Trastevere, the same part of town where the mill was and the Vatican is. All of it crowded and urban, that area. I struggled for years deciding whether to tell the part of the story i'm about to tell, but I think it's time. No, it's not terrible, but it is a little, and I worried that if I tell the story, it will discourage rescuers. But on the other hand, if I don't, that's really not right, because it did happen. It really is true, by the way, that it looks scarier from the telling. In the moment, there was always the knowledge that the Lord would not abandon us. We suffered a little, yes, but, "not to the point of blood" as the Bible says. And of course, nowhere near how babies suffer all the time. So, please, don't be scared. It's not as scary when you are in it as when you read about it. And gently I add, the scariest thing out there I see is under response, iterated through day after day of cultural acceptance, even, functionally, by Christians.

The beginning of the story is really the whole issue of how far to take non-cooperation in custody. The theory of it I get real good: we rescue more people than Dr. Mlk did, bless his heart, and you don't listen to us as you listened to him. So, we refuse to cooperate to paint a picture of a helpless child. We treat you the way you require us to treat you: as someone who is deaf. We must use sign-language, and since the matter and situation is grave, we must do the best we can in an even crude way, by miming how babies would act just before they are killed: they have no name, they can't speak, they can't walk. So, the question is, how far do we take this? Once you are arrested? I have been in rescues where we walked the minute we were carried over to a bus (Manhattan, 1988). I have been in rescues where we didn't walk, until we were actually told in a hearing in the jail that we were released forthwith ("disciples" rescue, Manhattan, 1990). We are all aware of Joanie's incredible sacrifice where she went the whole nine yards.

I believe this whole thing is elective, between each rescuer and the Lord. Obviously, in a given rescue, there is the tendency to want all to keep one standard. However, some rescuers will want to follow one standard, and others another. Also, there's the problem of aging rescuers, or rescuers with medical problems. Sometimes the young turks don't realize how much being dragged around is harder on an older person than on them. It's one of those things that's up to you and the Lord. In Rome, we had all pretty much agreed that we were going to try to "go hard" as they say. There were four of us, and we were all fairly young and in good health, and determined.Hanoi Hilton the book by Jeremiah Denton, about his struggles in the tiger cages and prisons of North Vietnam after he was shot down and captured. Not to endorse the war, or attack it right now, or make my usual John Bircher points, I only bring up Denton because when he was in the clink, he and his soldiers often broke under torture and did what they were told to do. I think this included giving some info to the bad guys, etc. But Denton made a policy with his men: if you do break, don't feel like that's the end of the game. Just pick yourself up the next day and start over in the process of resistance. Don't assume that if you cooperated once, you will only continue to cooperate. The next day you could get a second wind and decide to resist them again.

When we first got dumped on the lobby floor of the prison by the carabinieri, we sat there for a while. Every now and then, a guard would come over to tell us to get up and walk, and we'd refuse. Actually, since we didn't say a word, one could claim we never even got the message. We hadn't i'd ourselves so they couldn't have known what language we understood. To get over this communication problem, every now and then the guard permitted a trustee to come over and persuade us, by tapping us with an "orange stick." Oh, gentle reader, how these two words "trustee" and "orange stick" need to be explained! An orange stick is the limb of an orange or lemon tree. Since you might not be from California or Texas or Florida, you might know that the wood of a citrus tree is very dense, denser than rock maple or black walnut. It's like solid steel, and the orange stick this trustee was using was two inches in diameter and three feet long.

Also, "trustees" are inmates who are given many special privileges by the jail in return for doing nasty work the guards don't want to do. The trustees are extremely zealous at maintaining their special privileges by doing whatever is asked very enthusiastically and without hesitation. For those of you familiar with Shoah literature, these are the capos of the system, betrayers of their own kind. Maurice Lewis, the other male rescuer, and I were scrunched up in a kind of fetal position on the floor, facing each other, and the trustee kept tapping on Maurice's back with the stick. I felt bad about this but Maurice also knew I had a bad back.

The guard would come over now and then and play "good cop," telling the trustee, hey, there's no need for that, but only after he'd done some tapping for a while. I've always wondered what would happen if i'd tried to carry out non-cooperation to the level that Joanie did. Do they whip the tar out of you all day long? How does it end? Do you wind up in a cell? Also, I had always wondered if Joan's sister was right, that a woman can get away with some stuff that a man cannot, i.e., a guard has no hesitation with beating the tar out of a guy, whereas with a woman, he hesitates. But I know Joan was beaten up a lot. We were about to find out. In the lobby, with lots of possible trustee witnesses around, they decided to "move this discussion to a remote location."

They lifted us up onto a hospital gurney, both of us on one gurney, and again, like in Levittown, we had to decided whether totally limp meant actively hanging on to a rolling stretcher. We hung on! They got the gurney outside and were rolling it across a courtyard when one of the wheels hit a pothole in the tarmac. Now I need to tell a tiny backstory. Before that point I had already seen the movie "The Scarlet and the Black" with Gregory peck, the story of an Irish priest who smuggled Jews out of Rome under the Nazi occupation there. It's a great story and a great movie. You should see it. That priest was quite a character, and very clever, and, like Bonhoeffer, he didn't waste any time publicly denouncing the Nazis, which would have resulted in instant death for the Jews he was smuggling. Instead, he played it cool on the outside, like the Lavender Hill Mob did successfully in the u.s. for 14 years. The Vito squad also, for about 8 years. In the flick there is a scene where they show the execution of priests who did openly denounce the Nazis. They were stood up in front of a wall and shot.

When the gurney almost tipped over, we were less than 20 feet from a dark purple wall, the inside of the prison perimeter wall, and, brothers and sisters, as the Lord is my witness, when my head hung over upside down off that gurney, I saw the wall, and I was completely convinced that that wasn't any wall, it was the scarlet and the black wall, and further, that we were being dumped onto the ground in front of that wall, and they were going to do to us what they did to the Jew smuggler priests in the movie, and in reality in '43. When we were finally pushed on the gurney into the central hub of the star of the main jail in Regina Coeli -- no, they didn't shoot us at the wall, but I sure thought they were for a moment, and I sure felt sorry for all those priests, and the Jews they would have smuggled if they hadn't been shot.

It was really something. Just before we got pushed into the hub, I saw a bunch of mangy cats at the bars on the side. These cats were all jail cats, permanently hanging out near the jail, and at their feet were old fish bones they had already eaten. The prisoners fed the cats through the bars. The cats were so skinny they could walk through the bars anytime they wanted, but they didn't want. They're not dumb. In the center of the hub part is a big statue of Mary as Queen of Heaven, with a big crown of stars around her head. (My dear evangelical fellow rescuers: feel free to insert your favorite comment about icons here. Just don't worship a statue! Bad!) The stars were actually individual light bulbs, like Christmas lights. Little did I know how soon Maurice and I were to seeing some other stars, ourselves!

"Murder Max" is what they call the bucket, the shu, or solitary, in Italy. Every prison in the world has a jail within a jail for the tough guys who can't stop fighting, for snitch witnesses who wouldn't survive on the yard, and for general troublemakers. In Italy Murder Max was it. It was located in one of the radiating arms of the star. It had a two story Plexiglas wall covering the bars so no one could throw anything in or out of it. We were wheeled still on the gurney into Murder Max, and then to a strip cell on the bottom level. Strip cells are used to search incoming inmates, even inmates coming into murder max from some other part of the jail due to a fight, check-in, or whatever. I should have known once we got through the plexiglass wall what was coming next. Plexiglass stops sound in addition to trash, so the rest of the jail couldn't hear what was going on inside. I also should have known what was coming next when they slammed the door on the strip cell in Murder Max after they dragged Maurice and me in there. The guard had to turn the key on the outside of that door to lock us in, but he did not open the "beanhole" wicket hatch in the door through which prisoners are fed in a "marion rules" (24 hour lockdown) prison. The sound of the door lock locking and the sound of the wicket hatch opening were simultaneous. That means that the same time the guard locked the door, a Murder Max trustee whipped open the wicket hatch without asking permission. He is a trustee after all. The reason he whipped it open so fast was so that he could watch what was happening inside. This is because he knew what was about to happen, and it would be the high point of his day.

You know how, on the street, when rubberneckers pass a wreck on the road, they say they don't want to look, but they do? In prison, this fascination with violence takes a form totally unknown to non-prisoners. I also should have known what was going to happen next because, oooops! Locked up in the cell with Maurice and me were four guards! Uh oh! I bet that never happened to you in an American rescue, right? Completely violates every principle of prison operation in the history of prisons, unless…Guards would never allow themselves to be in the same room with a prisoner, for fear of their own safety, unless…persuasion by other means. They were going to make us walk. Maurice and I should be grateful they didn't use batons. The first kick from the steel-toed boot of the four guards caught me in the right chest. Let's just say it was a short discussion, ok? and it's embarrassing, because any man hates to admit another man got the better of him, without him giving something back.

But we were in fake-gandhi mode (a mode gandhi himself repudiated when life is at stake, not just salt taxes).

They got us up and cooperating with the body search required by any prison in the world. Ok, you win that one, guards. By the way, if I may speak for Maurice, of course we hold no grudge against these guys. Yes, they were enabling baby killing, and in that sense of course they were our enemies, but one could also imagine how frustrating it was for them to drag us into and out of court for three long days. Italy: if you don't want non-coop rescuers clogging up your jails, stop ripping the heads off children. And most especially, stop stealing Catholic hospitals to do that in. We walked, forced, against our will, up to the third level of the murder max and celled up. Once I got there I discovered that I could not lie down on my right side since all the ribs were broken or dislocated there. We had no doctor, no priest, no lawyer, no translator, no ambassador, no nothing. Just stuck in a cell. Jesus makes three, though, I must add.

I mentioned the Hanoi Hilton story a minute ago to explain what happened next: despite the cowing effect the beating produced in us, two days later on Sunday morning, Maurice discovered that he had regained his courage. Beginning at dawn, he began kicking the solid wood door of the cell, otherwise a big no-no in prison, due, you guessed it, to more beatings from the guards if you don't stop. They came by and told us so, but Maurice told them he had a right to go to Mass.

You know, in his own way, Maurice was an incredibly stubborn guy, in a very holy way. Most British Catholics can still remember the centuries where not only priests but the lay people who hid them were drawn and quartered and then dragged through London so everyone had a chance to spit on you while you were dying without having to inconvenience themselves to walk over to the gallows. This has got to have a chilling effect on ecumenism, you know? But Maurice also had that British sense of rights and entitlement and he was going to get his Mass that morning.

I am much more of a go along get along kind of guy, especially in custody where there are no abortion mills, but Maurice wouldn't stop beating on the door, and finally they let us go down to the bottom floor of the unit, and we received communion through the door of Murder Max, which was opened just a tad for us to do that, a huge violation of the Murder Max protocols. Judy Garland shows up in the funniest places.

We were there six weeks. It was a strange jail, and the funniest things happened. At one point they got prints off us even though we had tried to resist earlier in the process. Even with the prints, where to send them? What country? There are 257 countries. At one point they wanted to interrogate me further, not so much with beating, but just with the Chef D'Gard. I refused to talk to him and played dumb. At one point, though, I said a few words in German. In the future don't say anything. Once you say anything in any language, it's a giveaway you're not mentally ill or a mute, and they pounce. It surely stopped our attempt to be released and I thought we could have been, but i'm not complaining. Life is a journey, not a finished product. So, the chef d'gard whistles down the corridor and finds a Dutch drug dealer trustee, yet another guy who cooperates with the jail in return for little favors. This happens in every jail in the world. Guards do not mop floors, right? I actually feel a little guilty for what happened next, but even so I admire that Dutch drug dealer a lot for all he did for me, a total stranger! The chef d'gard brought him into the office and told him in Italian to tell me to tell my name. The drug dealer dutifully translated into German, but now I suppose I could still have played dumb and said to him, sorry, I don't understand German so well, but now, there was another problem. Even if I only spoke a few words to the drug dealer in German, he could tell by my accent that I was not only an English speaker, but also that I was an American. I mean: think about it: a Dutch drug dealer? This guy has to have every heavy metal rock album ever made in America on his shelf. (Survivors: they didn't have mps's back then.)

 I spun the drug dealer a little story about how we were camping out in the forest on the way to Rome. This was also what the guard was interested in, how did we get in the country. But I wouldn't tell my name or nation. To his credit, the drug dealer tucked his chin in and held his ground even though the chef d'gard yelled at him to tell me to say my name. The drug dealer didn't volunteer the obvious, that my accent was American. There was a kind of peace of Westphalia that happened for a few weeks after they got the prints and sent them out to wherever. This was also in the days before an Interpol Prints or DNA analysis metadata bank was in place for multiple nations.

 One day Maurice and I were hanging out in the cell and we heard the strangest sound come up out of the light well in between the star arms of the prison: singing. I love singing, I come from a singing family, and at first I thought: how nice. Some nice Arabic folk songs are being sung by the nice Tunisian drug dealers who are tossed in the Roman clinks faster than Julio in America. But after a while, I noticed something funny about this "authentic" Arabic folk song. Wait, could it possibly be? I listened again: there it was, for certain this time! The drunk Tunisian drug dealers were singing Somewhere Over the Rrainbow, in Arabic, at the top of their lungs. So, when Muslims fall off the wagon, they not only get into drugs, strictly forbidden in Islam, but they also sing popular western songs, also forbidden! These guys were having a good time. Maurice and I couldn't stop laughing. When I flew back to America and imitated the singing to my mom, she never stopped laughing either. Till the day she died, she'd laugh like that every time I did it. Irving Berlin in drunken Arabic. You just had to be there.

One day they brought us each a tiny drink box of (my dear Baptist brothers and sisters, skip this paragraph) wine! The Italian youth day was such a great fest, they had to give everybody some wine, even us criminals. So that explained the artillery sound I had heard the night before! fireworks! And I had thought it was "i" corps, coming to liberate us from the foreign baby killers.

This next part is also painful to tell, even more painful than busted ribs. One night about six weeks into this, with us holding fast on noncooperation and refusing to give our names, Maurice was called downstairs for a visit. "I am a Vatican official, but I am not here on official Vatican business." Try translating that into any one of a half dozen European languages, without misunderstanding. It can't be done. But try he did, that official, to Maurice, that night. It seems someone had tipped off the opera set that we were being badly treated in the gunk. I don't know how that happened, how that information got out, because neither of us had had any visitors. It turned out the brave and holy Scotch priest, Fr. Morrow, had come to Rome after the rescue started. He bicycled all the way from Balmoral, no doubt to save money. He's scotch, get it? And somehow he had found out from sources, which he had a few of in Rome since he had gone to the seminary in Rome.

Father Morrow it turns out had also confronted the archbishop who was the chaplain at the prison and who, to his everlasting shame, had thrown him out of his office. Late that night in our cell, Maurice was telling me all about this information, about Fr. Ryan, about the mysterious Vatican visitor, about all sorts of things. But then he hit his head, like "duh"! Like Fred Simpson and was very upset with himself. He had forgotten in all this flood of information (after six weeks of nothing to do, read, or anything) the most important part of the message: Fr. Morrow, the Scotch priest who'd bicycled down from Scotland, had also desperately in a rush talked his way into the prison (remember, he spoke Italian from when he was in seminary at "the Scotia", the Scotch seminary in Rome, years earlier). It turns out my own mom had somehow gotten ahold of father's support group in Balmoral up north near Aberdeen Shire (it's not the name of the village he was in but it's nearby). Father wanted Maurice to relay to me an emergency message: that my dear sister Marty was having an unremission of her cancer of 20 years ago and my mom wanted me to come home to see Marty.

This is the beginning of a weird controversy that continues to the present day, not to me so much, but to others. I suppose you could call them "sideline sams," the guys who yell at sports events about the incompetence of the players, but who can't themselves throw a ball to save their lives, or, as one dear lawyer put it to me in the height of press mess up in Buffalo: "The view must be pretty good from the cheap seats." I have always loved that expression. Or, a quote from Winnie Churchill I found only lately: "Criticism is easy. Achievement requires more effort." Going at the controversy from the back end of it, the most recent part, there is a high ranking rescue leader out there who says to this day, he is convinced that I committed a sin in coming out of prison to go see Marty. Then, there are some other rescuers who say, not at all, it was right for me to go see my sister before she died.

One thing we could ponder is to ask the critic how many sisters he had who died of cancer while he was in prison, and where is he coming from? Well, this debate could go on forever. You could imagine people arguing both sides, and saying a lot of bad things. My final take on it, for what it's worth -- and I mean that, because rescue is bigger than any one of us -- is that the decision whether or not to come out of prison because of a family emergency is something that falls into the category of what Dr. Schaeffer used to call "the freedom of Christ." We are not free, obviously, in Christ, to open an abortion mill, or vote for one, or do anything to protect one. We are not free to open a brothel. We are not free to commit a frank sin.

But in the course of our human attempts to hew as close to the will of the Lord as best we can, and walk with him, there are decisions that are not as clear cut. The Bible talks about this, for example, in the matter of celibacy in ii cor. 6 or so. We are used to declamations or commands from

Paul, elsewhere, but in this matter he suddenly gets all delicate about it, and hems and haws, and basically says it's up to us and the Lord. Rescuers have a natural aversion to language like this, even when it's legitimate, because we spend so darn much of our time opposing it when it shows up in discussing abortion. See what I mean? It is a very important task we have: we must resist the atheist's constant attempts to conflate the decision surrounding sin, vs. a truly free act, on the one hand, and we must also stick to our guns when it comes to apodictically certain matters such as abortion.

To tell the story in brief, my dear sister, 20 years earlier, had said take a hike to the white coats, the modern md's who told her she had to do all kinds of awful surgery and take all kinds of poison drugs to fix the cancer. Instead, she ran down to Mexico, Tijuana, and took a bunch of laetrile, illegal in the u.s., under the care of Dr. Hector Contrarrez, a great doc. If you ever hear of others with cancer, be sure to send them down to him. While she was down there Marty saw a ton of people get carried in on a stretcher and walk back out in a day or two. And this says nothing about laetrile's preventative effect. Marty's dying words were that laetrile is illegal precisely because it works and would put a ton of cancer people out of work. I agree wholeheartedly. See, infowars.com for more. At first that night talking to Maurice, as this story came out late at night, my tendency was against returning to the states. The whole Roman rescue had been pretty much my idea, and I hated to leave everyone in the lurch over there without my being there to suffer along with them. There is the scripture about leaving your own family, etc. There is my Irish German usmc determination. Yes, it sounds heartless, but that was my position.

Maurice and I went back and forth all night long about this, in that cell on the third floor of Murder Max, where the window faced the south and the stone steps had smooth hollows worn in them by the feet of centuries of prisoners. It turned out that Maurice had been in a similar situation once before, where a family emergency had occurred while he was in the clink. In that case, he had decided to stay with the rescue, and then he bitterly regretted it later on and realized that he had made a mistake. "Family comes first," he kept saying to me over and over.

Oh, I almost forgot to mention. Part of the message was from Fr. Morrow, and it was that he was scheduled to return to Balmoral the next day unless we asked him to try to secure my release to go to see Marty. So, the pressure was on, on Maurice and me that night, and we had to have an answer for Father by the next morning, or he would go. Through the course of the night Maurice finally wore me down. I finally said, ok, i'll get out and go back to see Marty in California. It was a real heart breaker. It's not like prolifers are jet setters or anything. To arrange and save up and scrimp and save and hitchhike and everything to make this rescue happen would all go down the drain. On the other hand, if you do the right thing, the Lord will fill in the blanks since we can't do everything. Actually, we can do precious little in the face of an evil so huge as this one.

I deprived the chef d'gard of the satisfaction of telling him my name to his face, and instead we authorized Fr. Morrow to tell the prison authorities on our behalf. Linked with the decision of whether or not I would go was what would happen to the rest of the rescue? We were four, two women and two men, and both pairs were housed in separate prisons across town from each other. The women were held in a prison I forgot the name of but it sounds like babbio. If only one guy got out, the other one would be alone. Same with the women. What to do? This is the kind of thing that rarely or never showed up in large rescues in the states where the government would usually just clear out a gym and house us all together. And there were lawyers and priests everywhere going in and out and communicating with everyone, including family. I will say this, though, that in the beginning of rescue it wasn't like that. There were lots of times where you could be the only rescuer in stir at one time, and you had to go it alone. Also, if there was only one, that usually meant general population, something a lot of rescuers might have had a hard time with. Well, let me be more specific. Most rescuers are simply suburban, culturally speaking. For them, this is a big step. Myself, I have led a kind of charmed existence, I suspect, but I can't just say, well, go ahead, if someone has a problem. If the question is, well, how do you actually stop abortion, as opposed to making symbolic gestures only, even including "chocolate shake" rescues, then I say, well, talk to the Lord. I just work here.

The next part of the story is quite unbelievable. One of the women got out 1,2,3, as soon as she found out about my sister and gave her name. Then she switched roles and now was one of those tireless people who support rescuers from the outside. She went to the courts, the police, the Vatican, all over the place to try to get us out. Add to this the confusion that Maurice and the other woman were thinking seriously about sticking around, which would be a great thing, of course, and maybe even I could come back once i'd seen Marty. All of this was bandied about. During those intense hours of negotiation, Fran (the woman now on the outside) was walking to or from court and she saw Mother Teresa at some public function. Well, it could happen. That woman was a fast moving target, and she had a habit of showing up anywhere. Fran rushed up to her and filled her in on the problem. I had been a seminarian in Mother's order of mc priests for a while a few years earlier, in the late 80's. Mother told Fran, "Why are you talking to me? Go to the blessed sacrament and tell Jesus what you want." Fran did so. Then, Mirabile Dictu, Fran ran into the judge coming off the bench. She could see Fran was upset – "so what's the problem?" Fran told her.

The next day Fran ran into Mother Teresa again and again asked her to pray for us, and Mother turned to Fran and said clearly, "He'll be out at nine am tomorrow morning." That's exactly when I did get out, to the minute, walking past the wall where they shot the priests, and through the vestibule where they tapped us with the orange log. They dumped me straight out onto the streets of Trastevere, no paperwork, no probation, no more prints, no nothing. Just go. Part of the thinking of the "disciples" rescue in Manhattan, which happened about the same time, was that if they say they're letting you go, we walk out, so I did. Also, at that point, they were trying to do what my family wanted, so I walked.

Marty died about a year after that. She had stopped taking the laetrile. Please read this part carefully because it was working. She had been in remission for 20 years and during that time she had a lovely daughter. She even found time in the last year of her life to visit a monastery and a church, to light a candle and to say some office prayers. Marty was a stubborn agnostic much of her life, but she softened a little right at the end. She didn't weep and throw herself down at the mercy seat, which us Evan's are inclined to prefer, but she did stop resisting God so much at the end, and her precious daughter, also, at the very end, most definitely. Bree even was visited by an angel four hours before she died. I have always been hopeful of the mercy of God, even though Bree and Marty both spent most of their lives wandering away from Christianity, even though both of them knew about Jesus when they were young. I believe it is possible that all's well that ends well. But I still get chatter from certain quarters about leaving the rescue.

Maurice and the other woman rescuer hung around in the jails in Rome there for another six weeks, giving a brave witness. As to the critics, I say: the airspace between here and Rome is quite open, thank you very much. Tell the pope I sent you. "Send us news of our victory" as that king in Braveheart said, played so well by Patrick McGeehan. None of us regret it. We had a great rescue, we pushed the no prints thing, the mill was shut for a month due to the destruction of all the supplies and equipment, so who knows how many children and moms could have been saved at that time? This is a tool that needs to be pried out of the hands of cads and bullies and pimps and embarrassed parents who don't pay the price. Even an unwanted pregnancy carried to term is so much better than the nightmares, drug addictions and suicides. And in the south in the old days, the embarrassment thing for the parents was resolved by hidden away homes they could go to. In their own way, they had great bonding experiences there, the moms. What an experience to share. And due to the work of a local Roman, there is the "one child born" from this rescue, saved that morning, -- "to carry on, to carry on." Thanks be to God almighty.

## RALPH M. GABRIEL

*Walter Leonard, MD, Jim's grandfather. Also, John Wayne's third shift on-call trauma doc in Hollywood. Hated, hated, hated abortion, like all his colleagues then. Listen carefully to Baby's dad, Jerry Orbach, in* Dirty Dancing.

*James Kopp, USN, Pacific Fleet; their mom Katherine Zirwes Koppensteiner; and Charles Kopp, USMC, 4th Div. 7MB, Saipan, Tinian, Ryukyus, Home Islands. Picture just after Pearl Harbor. She had already lost her husband to injuries from WWI, and now her only two boys were shipping out.*

# TO RECEIVE A CHILD

*Jim's Grandmother Leonard, nee Katherine Marie Murphy. Everybody needs an Irish-Choctaw Gramma.*

*J.J., the dog who swam the Golden Gate to find Jim's family and then laid down and died. That's Surgeon General Dr. Steinfeldt's house in the background, across Fletcher Ave.*

*Jim planted the cypress peeking over the Justin Morgan ridgepole barn. He planted it in March, 1872, just after Lady Bird Johnson dedicated the Point Reyes National Seashore. The mule deer are all Republicans. This being Marin County, they are nervous Republicans.*

*Al Molina's off-campus man-cave. He and Gordie Chan did it all: vertebrates and invertebrates, marine and terrestrial, plants and animals. Along with Todd Newbury they were the best all-around naturalists Jim ever knew.*

*M.A., Fullerton, mid-1980s. Laguna Beach feather duster reef worm embryology.*

*Wycliffe tech support, Ivory Coast, mid-1980, with a French mish. couple. That's a Thompson switch behind Jim, his responsibility.*

*Nancy Kopp, RN. Felt the same way as her dad, Dr. Leonard, about life.*

*CPC councilor training, Panhandle District, mid-1980's. Everybody got Jim's three central dogmas about postabortion harms: permanent* Chlamydia *mesenteric infections, massively increased risk of miscarriage and infection from a permanently incompetent cervix, and guaranteed jacked up risk of ectopics from endometrial scarring that partially occludes the oviduct ostia. That's the top of Jim's head at the bottom of the picture.*

## TO RECEIVE A CHILD

> "How can we expect righteousness to prevail when there is hardly anyone willing to give himself up individually to a righteous cause?"
>
> **Sophie Scholl**

*Sophie Scholl. Co-founder of White Rose. Executed by Hitler for pamphleting against Nazism and genocide.*

*John Six in Atlanta, 1988. That's Fr. Arentsen towards the left, a saintly rescue priest from St. Louis.*

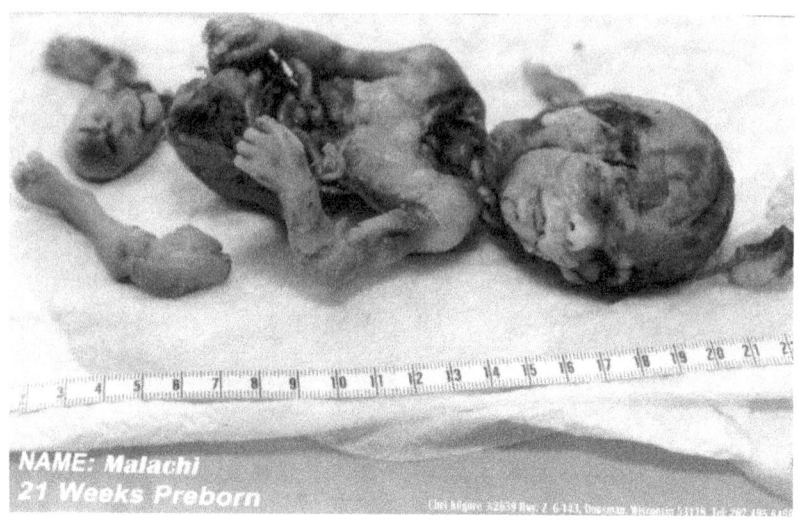

*Baby Malachi. What mom never sees, but every RN and pathologist must. We found these babies and shot these pictures in the 1980's. See* Abandoned.

*John Salvi, Boston baby saver. He "committed suicide" like Jeffrey Epstein, Vince Foster, and Ron Brown "committed suicide."*

Fr. Norm Weslin, Lt. Col., USAF (ret'd). Waterbury survivor. Put a shelter in his own home, did 12 Step and went to seminary at age 60. Great civilian rescue leader.

The swag's in the bag. The take from a raid on an illegal mill in Quezon City, late 1990's. Horse-doses of mifepristone and polyp forceps stamped "UNICEF." Your US tax dollars at work. The abortionist fled the country that night, Asian family-shamed when her face showed up on TV.

RALPH M. GABRIEL

*Fresne Prison booking picture, Paris, 2002. Biggest prison, maybe, outside of China.*

*Where do the Malachis go when we find them? Here. Then moms come out at night to leave toys for their children. This collage of toys should be enlarged and cast in bronze – like the Central Park Lewis Carroll figures – and put in every cemetery in the world, so all the moms can grieve. In the Buddhist cemeteries in Japan, the moms offer rice and water for the baby stones that represent their aborted babies.*

## Chapter 4

## Keith Green, Rome, Catholicism

In between starting grad school in Fullerton and entering the Catholic Church five years later was a time of many different small activities. A jumble. A "dog's breakfast" as we say on the Auld Sod. I was "going through a phase" as we say in California. I'll spare you each little stop along the way. But one way to describe the phase might be to try to characterize what the beginning of it looked like, and what the end of it looked like. The changes that happened over the five years, in other words. At the beginning of the phase, I was fulltime on campus at Fullerton, a grad student doing my own research, teaching an Intro. Bio. lab section, taking grad courses and floating as an Assistant Nurse at Anaheim Memorial on weekend third shifts. I lived in Placentia with the house full of hulking, wise-cracking, born-again, charismatic, Bible studying, youth group leading Polish Roman Catholic engineers. I know, it's exhausting just thinking about it. I went to church with the Quakers and night-time surfed at Corona now and then. I was still depressed about the breakup with Cheryl. I spent a ton of time staring out the back window at the cricket pumps and the eucalyptus trees and listening to Linda Ronstadt's' dark phase, but, as the Depression survivors say, I was also trying to "keep busy and stay out of trouble." At the end of the five years, in 1985, a million things had happened to mark a sharp closure to the "phase," and a different direction.

    No more moping, way less uncertainty about how to spend a day, a year, or a life. The research paper had been published, the thesis accepted and the "masters" granted. In 1985 I was 99 percent certain I was called into prolife work fulltime even though such a thing didn't pay a dime, and more likely, an arrest record that played havoc with the day job. I was much more directed and focused in 1985. In 1980 I was mopey, unsure, and half in and half out of grad school. So, a big difference. Almost all of this difference was due to events that took place on what Californians call "The Peninsula," and what the rest of the U.S. might call the "San Francisco Peninsula," because technically it includes that city. The California name, the Peninsula, is not merely Great Lebowski brevity, either. Someone living on the Peninsula would never admit that it was the San Francisco Peninsula because to us it was not. We had nothing to do with San Francisco, the same way people in Marin say the same thing about San Francisco. If you want cable cars and the Golden Gate, have at it. Go up there. This is the Peninsula. Horses and sleepy Ross Macdonald satellite towns. We are our own place. Since MacDonald, of course, Silicon Valley has made serious effort to shanghai the identity of the Peninsula, but the old school types reject that, also.

    Avoiding both of these imposters, namely, the Tourist Trap/Sodom and Gomorrah up north, and the nouveau riche geeks in our midst, in 1980 Palo Alto, square in the middle of the Peninsula, was a nice sleepy college town even if it did grow a mean silicon chip in its Material Sciences Department on the down-low. To this day I can't recall exactly how I wound up in Palo Alto with an unfinished M.A. thesis, and all mopey. Maybe it was desire to get off-campus and avoid the perpetual grad student/slave wages Teaching Assistant trap back in Fullerton. But another explanation might be that Stanford is on the way between Marin and Fullerton. On a trip home I probably stopped by Palo Alto to say a brief hello to old high school friends who were in the med school there. In the process I bumped into a dream job on campus. I would be able to support myself with this day job and at the same time the day job, by agreement, granted me access to a state-of-the-art Siemens electron microscope at night so I could wrap up my thesis work. If you're halfway through a thesis that requires an electron microscope, it's not quite the same thing as if your thesis is lying on your belly in some Sierras meadow counting bugs in a hand lens, you know? Running a big 'scope like that is a little bit like flying a 747. You don't just walk up, a stranger, and say, hey boys, how about a spin around the block? I'll drive.

This job was really a Godsend, a chance to finish the thesis work and still be away from the perpetual TA trap in Fullerton. And, pay the bills and come out of school debt-free. The mechanics and miracles surrounding the thesis wrap-up -- I hate unfinished things, don't you? -- were crucial at the time, but something else happened in Palo Alto that I was completely unprepared for. It transformed me from the running sadness and dubiousness of 1980 into the confidence and forward-looking of 1985. In 1980 I was still like an undifferentiated stem cell; I could go in any direction. Some people enjoy a perpetual state like this, but it has dead-end problems. In 1985 I was a focused specialist with little doubt in my mind about my life's work.

Someone could say Switzerland was a cultural event. That is to say, it could have happened simply as a natural result of my upbringing, a mother's milk, cradle Catholic thing. But the older I get the less I worry about what atheists think about us Christians. There's no end to the stories and excuses they will come up with to deny Someone whom they have yet to encounter. If you search for heaven, and then are fortunate enough to encounter it, it must be due to this or that reductionist force, or brain chemicals, or you need a crutch, or it's the opiate of the masses, goes the secular thinking. Atheists are so certain about how God allows this and that, and He's cruel, etc., and yet it's obviously someone they have never met. Then, God dispensed with, they will be happy to weigh in on us Christians. We're too arrogant. We think we're better than others. No wait! We're too damn humble! We can't assert ourselves a la Sartre's freedom from the shackles of religious frictions. No, no, that's not it. Here I've got it: we hate ourselves, our bodies and our lives, so sin terrifies us. But no, wait: we love sin. We talk about it all the time and as hypocrites we sure as heck have fun when we think no one's looking. We love it so much we need some religious crutch as a kind of oil change to keep us going another 15 thousand miles.

Sex? Way too hung up on that; we talk about it all the time. No, that's not it! We're not quite hung up enough about it; God knows we breed like rabbits. But wait, we've got monks and nuns, so we must be hung up about it! Money? Way too much! Look at the Pope flaunting all that stuff, running around, or the obsessive prosperity doctrine of the Protestants, like Mr. T explaining all the gold around his neck: My God is a rich God. No. Wait. We put up St. Francis as a model, or Mother Teresa, and they obviously had a real problem with having a "good time," right? Running around in rags and never partying. Every which way, no matter what you look at, why is it Christians are always wrong? Why is that? The older I get the less I try to respond to all this nonsense. The short answer is that for a perpetual partying culture, the Catholics have got to be wrong, because if they're not, the party's over. Uh, never mind the fact that Catholics can have a good time with little things like marriages and kids, thanks very much. But in the trenches, under a challenge, I just take a deep breath and smile a Big Smile. I make a "time-out" sign with my hands, in front of the face of the TV-compulsively-repeating guy I'm talking to, and if he pauses, I look at him and say, you haven't met the Lord yet, have you? This usually makes a Deer in The Headlights look, if you say it softly enough. Then I pat him on the shoulder. When you do, come on back. We'll talk about it. Then I walk away, because I've got some asphalt somewhere that urgently needs watching. Acres of paint, somewhere, drying all by itself.

I mention all this because at this point, there in Fullerton in the fall of 1978, my life was about to take a turn, from what we could call the cultural background of my Lutheran upbringing and even its reinforcement in Switzerland, to a totally different direction. Up until Fullerton, California, 1978, my life was all Protestant. Once I got to Fullerton, a sojourn began in the direction of Catholicism, or what I call cosmopolitan Christianity, for lack of a better word. There are evangelicals all over the world, now, but their theology is strictly limited to what did and did not come out of the German and English reforms of the early 1500's, and their religious sequelae in the New World. On the other hand, Catholicism speaks for all Christians all over world, and they never cease looking at it from that perspective. Protestants claim the same thing, but the history just isn't there. If a Protestant missionary goes into the Amazon jungle, he's got a lot of American suburban head stuff to bring. Catholics are thinking more like Francis or Mother Teresa did. Don't get me wrong: In my case l could never have had one without the other. If I had not been born-again in Switzerland, I can't imagine how a more cosmopolitan Christianity would've had any appeal whatsoever. But the journey of a thousand cultures, so to speak, has to begin with one, or it hasn't begun.

In my case I started out in 1500's Germany and wound up in a group that cannot take a single step without thinking about how that step will affect one-and-a-half billion other people, and actually, more than that. And I found out that the Road to Rome Leads Through Placentia and I soon discovered in my new digs that not only were the Scholar-Athletes big, and Polish, and the smart-alecks that always had their hands raised in math class, they were Catholics. Not to put too fine a point on it. I mean, I don't know how else to describe it. Catholics. The guy with the white dress who speaks Italian and waves. Mother Teresa. Inquisition. Crusades. All that and a lighted candle. Only, these Catholics in Placentia were different from any Catholics I'd ever known. Not that I knew a lot, being from the Catholics-are-all-going-to-hell-on-a-guided-rail branch of the Lutheran church. So, I suppose it makes sense that before the Placentia StaPrest experience, I'd only known a few Catholics, and those, dimly.

My own best friend in high school in Marin was Catholic, but I never saw the inside of his church. I think his Mom and Dad were from the last generation that remembered the "Irish Need Not Apply" Help Wanted signs era, and worse, so they maybe kept it on the down-low? I don't know. Despite her own virulent anti-Catholicism -- "Those damn Catholics! All that damn money!" -- my mom did have one Catholic friend, to whom I think my mom was attracted to in the way white people would Take The A-Train. Let's go slumming up in Harlem and hear some hot jazz, you know? Her Catholic friend smoked like a chimney and cussed like a sailor and did everything else she hated, and Mom loved it. Her Catholic friend seemed to enjoy life just a little bit more than the Missouri Synod/Lake Woebegone types. It seems my mom, the jokester for so many, needed her own little jokester on the side

Back in Placentia, these hulking Polish Texas Instruments types were a new slice of life for me, also, but they weren't shy about it like the Marin Catholics. The Placentia Poles were happy and open about their faith. No, they didn't push like the TV evangelist Big Hair/Put Your Hands On TV types, but they weren't embarrassed about it either. They even ran a youth group at the local parish, St. Joseph's. So much has been said about the abuse of kids in Catholic churches. The truth of it is so far in the other direction it's hard for someone who gets all his information from major media to imagine. Much more could be said but suffice it to say that it's a wonderful thing to see any institution where children are a hundred times safer than they would be in a secular public school. I didn't think of the Catholics at first as people I wanted to join with but just their bright spirits alone had a calming and healing effect on me. How to describe those times, there in Placentia? It's not like there was a lot of time at home, with all the teaching, research and the part-time nursing work at a local hospital to help pay the rent. But I clearly remember the hours I did have as a refuge from all the rest of it. There was an open field just behind the house, with towering eucalyptus that swished in the slightest breeze, something that non- Californians and non-Ozzies have never heard. It's a wonderfully subtle sound and smell. Menthol cough drops don't do it justice. There was also a grasshopper style oil pump that ran constantly, a cradle rocking motion that was also calming. I needed healing because the news from Texas was that Cheryl had gotten engaged to someone else. It was over. We were through. I think even before I left Austin for Switzerland, I'd heard a rumor that she had a new boyfriend, chaste, of course, since they were both Christians, but the denial side of me still hoped for a reprieve.

By the time I got to Placentia, I'd sit at the windowsill of a second-floor room that overlooked the field behind the house and listen to music. Bless me, Father, for I have sinned: it was 1979, not quite the 80's, and I was already committing the cardinal sin of listening to Linda Ronstadt. There. Isn't confession good for the soul? I feel so much better. But wait! It's not what you think? I don't mean mainstream Ronstadt, all those pop standards. By 1979 she'd left the Stone Ponies days and kicked out a dark album, with a black cover, all unusual cuts. "Someone to Lay Down Beside Me" conveys the overall feel of desperation. In only a few years I would find out how well it explained so much of the abortion horror in this country. No doubt abortion is a direct attack on children and mothers, but it is also the sequel of general societal desperation in a country that abandoned God and His ways long ago. History professors love saying how horrible history was, but they are wrong. Any culture that followed God was happy, in the home. Fact -- Joni Mitchell also hit that theme of quiet desperation but in a Franciscan movie of zero budgeting. I sold all those records I used to listen to in Santa Cruz to a store down at the beach. I even threw away my stereo. That's how I wound up listening to Ronstadt, I guess. Children: beware.

Listening to someone else's stereo was not confined to slumming with Ronstadt, however. I also heard John Michael Talbot and Second Chapter of Acts, and these could be the earthly explanation for how I wound up at a Christian music festival at Knott's Berry Farm that Fall, the Fall of 1978. That year wasn't the first time a Kopp had set foot on Knott's Berry Farm. When he first returned from the Pacific Theater my Dad's first job after the war was driving an armored car, a natural fit for a Marine. One of his accounts was Knott's Berry Farm. Mrs. Knott would always give my Dad a slice of warm blueberry pie. "I carried a fork on the dashboard of the truck," he said, when he told the story. Apparently, the drivers had to eat on the run. This was when it was just a berry farm and a restaurant, not like it is now, like a Six Flags. But 1 still don't know how I wound up at the Christian music festival at Knott's Berry Farm that fall. I'm not into Christian music. I even did backup on a small distribution record once, but it just doesn't do much for me.

At the festival the bands played at different places around the park instead of just one concert in one place, which I would have expected. I went to see Pat Boone sing; I knew that name anyway, and I remember him singing "Why does the devil get all the good music?" A good question, actually. Too bad Pat's never heard ancient Byzantine chant. Some unpredictable impulses I will never understand but by now maybe you can see this trend. When you let go and let God, you'd be surprised what happens, the people you wind up meeting. So, that fall evening in '78 at Knott's Berry Farm in Anaheim, I left the Boone act and wandered past an outdoor theatre. It looked a little like the Greek theatre in Berkeley, or the Red Rock place near Denver, but in miniature. I had absolutely no reason to stop to listen at that venue. I had no idea who was singing, but if I hadn't stopped there, I really doubt you and I would be talking now, because of what happened next. What is it with you, God? So mysterious, so coincidental, so accidental, massive events hanging on the tiniest "chance" occurrence? When you work, it's like an aircraft carrier being pulled by a single strand of silk, and yet the chanciness of it all never seems to bother you. If a child's tricycle were being pulled by a ship's anchor chain, the chain will break, and the mighty and powerful will fall, but with your little thread you lead where you will, and we can break the thread anytime we want. A boxer sliding around in a ring coated with ice, a surgeon trying to do his best in the open in a hurricane, a diamond cutter desperately trying to cut the largest stone, sitting on a thoroughbred rounding a corner -- these are the ecstatic miseries we operate under and yet it all seems to work.

I had absolutely no reason to stop to listen to the man singing and playing the piano at that festival. There were a dozen other groups there at other spots, each of them easier to listen to and understand. For reasons known only to heaven's little helpers I paused on the upper deck of that bowl theatre long enough to hear a song. Then some preaching. But the guy in that bowl place didn't preach like other preachers, the last few centuries, who preach mostly hearts and flowers and teddy bears and candygrams, hugs and kisses, and only occasionally, like a pinch of salt in a cake, a tiny weak reminder of the possible bad consequences of sin. Sins of other people, usually. "I'm not impressed with Orange County Christians," he said, by contrast. "I keep hearing such great things about the faith in Orange County, but if it was so, I would have seen an orange glow on the horizon when I came into town. But I didn't see any orange glow tonight."

Now, this was interesting. I was captivated by this preaching which was what the fundie Reform Presbyterian Switzerland crowd would've instantly labeled too "works" oriented. What Catholic theologians would call Pelagianism. What charismatics would call "in the flesh," a kind of anger that was not "the righteousness of God." But here was this kid with Borneo wild hair, sandals, T-shirt and blue jeans and shouting, and he was preaching just that. Hell is real and you can go there, even if you think you're born again. He was breaking all the rules with this preaching. Wow! this was a switch from Switzerland! I was so offended by this "works" orientation type of preaching that I think I only stayed so that I could learn enough to combat it, kind of like the prolifer who infiltrates an AGOG or a NARAL meeting. There's more to it than even that. My German mind may have been working on the theology of this preaching, but my Marine/Irish heart was hearing a sound it hadn't heard for a long time, not since Pastor Mees, anyway. It was the sound of someone who really believed what he was saying. Was this what the scribes in the Temple meant when they said the child Jesus spoke "'with authority'"? Keith Green, the preacher in the Greek-type outdoor theatre, was not repeating something he'd heard in any church I knew, and by then I'd been in a few churches. He was speaking straight from the heart, against what he'd heard in church. Not against God Himself, but against the human invented weaselly-ness that we humans had invented in God's Name. "'Man-pleasing," as the epistles say.

It was just like Schaeffer on the original Romans tapes: a jeremiad against the American self-serving soft lifestyle which had invaded the churches and was turning them into something invented by man, not God. Something comfortable, like you'd make a couch easy to sit on. Not rocky-crag God made. New Agers, on the other hand, love to say how the real God is Smurfy and touchy-feely, and the "angry god" of the Old Testament was invented by fire and brimstone preachers, or, at least, is out-of-date. Both sides miss. I humbly suggest the reality: God is angry, yes, at sin -- especially child decapitation -- but he tenderly loves us, and wants to draw us away from sin to the only place we'll be happy anyway, a place without sin. For example, right now the world has more abortions and other wickedness than there ever has been, by far, but people are not happy. You'd think they would be, they have what they think they want. But they go to shrinks, believe any damn thing on the TV, and suck down Prozac and cocaine and meth like they're water. Just look at everyone at the market or the bank, when there's no kids around. Tense, sour grumpy.

We got rid of the angry God and substituted one much worse: ourselves. Unlike with the real God, however, we never get happy. Keith Green was on top of all this Schaeffer stuff, challenging the Soft-Serve fake church, but he was even more direct than those '50s Roman tapes I'd heard in Switzerland. Green started by establishing the category of counterfeit Christians, those who thought they believed but really didn't. This could include someone who made a heartfelt commitment to Christ, years ago, but since then had fallen away and stopped following Him, even if he did go to church on Sunday and talk the lingo. Then there were backsliders who may once have been Christians but turned away. Then there were those who had accepted god in some form, but it was counterfeit, not the true God. How about the lukewarm pseudo Christians, neither hot nor cold? One by one, Green identified each variety -- once-was, wannabee, never-was, confused, weak, backslider, et al.

At one point he came to himself in the middle of a rant and went to the keyboard and started singing, almost as if he remembered it was supposed to be a music festival after all. Part of the way through the song he became emotional, he started to cry and couldn't sing. In a swirl of emotion, he jumped up from the piano and went back to preaching, roving back and forth across the front edge of the stage, confronting, challenging, pointing, pleading, crying out.

## TO RECEIVE A CHILD

One by one, quietly, without being asked, we got down on our knees on the rough concrete deck of the outdoor theatre, about three thousand of us. I was twenty-four that year, a brand-new Christian in terms of an adult and more conscious faith, but no stranger to churches before that, and I had never heard preaching like this, nothing even close, and I most certainly had never seen a reaction like this. When I went back up to Placentia that night I was very troubled. Over the next few days I came to the conclusion that even though I was a brand-new Christian and had no business doing it, that I should cult-hunt Green, meaning, turn him in to Walter Martin, a famous cult-hunter of the day who regularly knocked out newsletter screeds and books against all the dingbats cults at that time who'd panhandle at the airports or knock on your door.

Looking back, I'm quite ashamed of this and repent of it heartily. Fortunately, I had a chance to apologize to Green personally, but that came a little later. Fortunately, also, the damage I did was slight, I believe, since it began and ended pretty much with one letter to Martin. One of his assistants answered the letter to the effect that they didn't think Green was heterodox, even if he was a little bit intense on the obedience side of the Gospel. Little did I know then how much I would appreciate Green's intensity and agree heartily with him that in the balance between grace and obedience most Southern California preachers went too far to pure pew-sitting. The Calvinist would argue that it's impossible to over-emphasize grace. Green and I would say, it's definitely possible, especially when you corrupt the meaning of grace to exclude simple obedience, an emphasis Jesus put there from the start. Much has been written on this tired subject, but I like J. Vernon McGee's take the best: "A life saved by grace has good works in it." The misunderstanding of this, and the separating out of "churchy-stuff" from simple charity is the root cause of the self-destruction of this country, witness child-killing as Exhibit One. The so-called Prosperity Doctrine and what Green called "greasy grace and sloppy agape" doesn't fly in the Third World; it only works in the overdeveloped world's cushy suburbs.

The letter back from Martin slowed me down but I still worried about it a little bit, enough to send a letter to Green. Surprisingly, he answered, and invited me over to his house to talk about it if I wanted to. Reason No. 5,736 why Green was not just another rock star. You're probably wondering why a chance encounter with a not-so-famous musician could get so much attention in a book about prolife. I wonder if the answer is that Green, for all his hippie out-there mannerism, underneath represented a continuation of the headiness of the conversations in Europe. Schaeffer was all Old World class, but the two of them agreed in their righteous anger against the lazy u.s. church. How strange and wonderful that immediately upon my arrival back in the States, I would "bump into" another prophetic man who picked up the exact same cudgels, not only against the too-rich, arrogant church, but also, to follow Jesus into the tough places.

Green's house it turned out was exactly on the way from my school to my sister Annie's house where I spent a lot of weekends trying desperately to be a good uncle and foster father to my niece and nephew. Their father, my brother-in-law Rick, had died two years earlier when he was only 28 and his kids were only four and one. Looking back, I was the one "'being fed" as my evangelical brothers and sisters say, by contact with both Annie and Green at that crucial time when I was a baby Christian. A mighty oak may from the little acorn grow, but it takes a helluva lot of watering.

What to my wondering eyes did appear when I got to Woodland Hills: not a quiet, nice house of a successful musician who'd sold a lot of records and could buy a little privacy and class, no, but a ramshackle decrepit two houses next to each other, typical tawdry "Valley" post-World War II stucco construction crammed with dozens of Jesus Movement sad sacks, all needful and clamoring for help or attention. Recovering drug addicts, I mean. Well, suhprahs, suhprahs! Schaeffer wasn't the only one with a ministry that included a place where inquiring sorts could just drop in, personal life get out of the way. True, when I was there the general tone of the Switzerland students was classier than the Rodeo Drive dropouts at Green's house. But the overlap was unmistakable: both ministries were open to the spin-offs, the wandering souls who had been cut off. Freud's "Discontents." All the people bypassed by tsunamis of technology and TV-think that had left them adrift. People who would've done fine in a medieval rural economy were now clueless and helpless. Some could be movie star wannabees from flyover countries who didn't make it, but many were just wandering souls from LA suburbs, lost in the cosmos.

The Jesus Movement swept through all this modern confusion only a year or two after the "Summer of Love" in 1969 in Haight Ashbury up north in San Francisco. The Jesus Movement involved a lot of sacrifice from churches trying to pick up some of the pieces from all the mess, to their everlasting credit. In California we have the task of picking up a lot of other people's broken pieces because so many want to come out West to do whatever. Try something new. Start over. Schaeffer had maybe ten percent druggie burnouts but the crowd at Green's house in the Valley seemed to run to eighty percent. There they were, all jittery and twitchy and word-salad, trying to balance Bibles in their hands and read them, bless their hearts.

There it was again, that personal touch including sacrifice by his own family and with unsavory guests in his own house, just like Switzerland. A mark of the real stuff. Before during and after the Bible studies on Friday nights in Woodland Hills the few times I went there, I bumped into a capable aide of Green's, Martin Bennet. Bennet was intelligent and soft-spoken, a Radar O'Reilly type who followed in his master's tempestuous footsteps and offered explanations and soothing suggestions if Keith couldn't talk to everyone. I was one of those. At one point in our conversations, Bennet said: "Keith is like a guy who sees a red shirt and likes it. He goes to the store, buys a dozen, and goes home and throws out all his other shirts." Now, Keith and all his survivors would make the General Disclaimer at the front of this book, and if they don't, I make it now for them provisionally. But do you see why I was drawn to this thinking? Green and Schaeffer, unlike so many evangelicals who talk about it, were like The Whale – he go all in.. In a world of soft compromise and endless waffling about Jesus' shocking claim, Schaeffer and Green went all in. They were shining beacons in a murky world. Up until then I was most definitely a smoother of ruffled feathers, an explainer, a compromiser.

I started out denouncing Keith. Fortunately, by the time he came by one of the Friday night Bible studies at the Woodland Hills house, I had a chance to buttonhole him to personally apologize to him for doing that. He was in a big hurry, and used to being buttonholed, but he was very gracious about it and forgiving, even though he hadn't even really heard the story. He took it all in in a second and didn't even ask for details. Instantly a scripture came to his mind, about building up the brethren. As I say, I make the Standard Disclaimer for both Schaeffer and Green and their survivors but I also must acknowledge the impact on me, the new Christian, of two souls out of seven billion who had not "bent the knee to Baal" or "touched the plow and turned back." No, they never joined me in jail or at the sporting goods store or the Home Depot or at Pep Boys for road flares but in their own way I think I picked up a little bit of "all in" from them. God knows best the answer to all these things. Ask Him. How I wish the feebs and the liberal press and NOW would do that instead of their usual witch hunting. But then, without that, they'd all be out of work, wouldn't they?

After those weekends visiting Anne and the kids, I still had to come back to Placentia and school. Green wasn't the only one running Bible studies. The hulking energetic Polish engineers of the Placentia house ran one too, but oddly, based on the writings of a Quaker, not Thomas Aquinas or Augustine. They coordinated ski weekends, bowling nights and all sorts of similar outings for the youth program at St. Joseph's. It all had such a healthy feel to it, this Catholic stuff, as if they really did have a better way to go about dealing with a generation headed into raves, drunken orgies, etc. The Poles were intense in their faith, but self-deprecating too, though never at the expense of God Himself. They were fun, casual, easy to be around, and they didn't pound on your head the way the typical Orange County evangelicals did. The sum of it all seemed to be that they were not only not defensive about their faith, or its alleged shortcomings, but rather they were just too busy having fun, and doing whatever God and man required of them, to stop to argue fine points. They knew Jesus and that was enough. More than enough! And this, not in an intellectually sloppy way, either; it was more of a feeling of, well, you're welcome to join us if you'd like, and if you don't, that's fine too. See ya, hopefully, at the finish line. The result of all this is that I did indeed want to join them, and at that time I'm not sure I could have said why, other than the vague emotional draw of their confidence and fun and absence of the Protestant hang-ups about everyone else going to hell. I don't recall any point of doctrinal draw but one day after two years in Placentia I called the pastor of their church to tell him I wanted to join the Catholic church and how do I do that? Boy, was I was in for a shock!

I can still feel the sting when I called the pastor of St. Joseph's church: "Being Catholic is an entire lifestyle. It's not something you just jump into," he said. He then proceeded to grudgingly say, yes, it's possible to join the church, but I would need to take a two-year Catechism class for adults. Two years! After I had been raised and catechized and confirmed a Lutheran, spent all that time studying Luther's Catechism, and then self-studied a year-and-a-half before I got to Switzerland? The thought of two more years was disheartening. But that was not nearly as disheartening as the overall sound of the pastor. My mind registered the technical "yes" of his answer, but my Irish Cherokee heart read only the feeling of what he was saying: go away. You are not welcome here. When I hung up the phone joining the Catholic church was at that instant the furthest thing from my mind even though my making the call itself was the result of two years of hope and enthusiasm I'd picked up from the Polish guys.

One of them, Tad, explained it to me later in his patient, Longview way. "Oh yeah. That's Fr. X. He's a canon lawyer, you know. He's like that with everyone." It only took another couple of decades but I now have a very good idea of where Fr. X was coming from, and strangely enough, I agree with his approach wholeheartedly. He didn't shut the door, he just added a legitimate hurdle to make sure you really knew what you were getting into. The background for that attitude on his part at the time is easy to see now: at that time in the late 70's, the push for annulments and even some priest laicizations was only just getting underway in the US. For each of these, the canon lawyer was the one caught in the middle. If he was not in fact a flower-child liberal type priest, it would break his heart to have to have anything to do with annulling a sacrament, as a canon lawyer might in those cases. So, when he ran into some bubbly enthusiastic wannabee on the phone, I suspect it could have crossed his mind: is this a future annulment or laicization waiting to happen? From someone who just doesn't get it about the ethical rigors of Catholicism? That marriage and the priesthood are permanent? No divorce? I think this might have been on his mind, and now I see why. I agree wholeheartedly with the go-slowly approach. My head was still in Protestant land, where every inquirer is gleefully accepted in a swirl of emotion and baptized on the spot. Praise the Lord! Another lost soul saved from hell! (applause, tears, music). Then, off to help others, but no growth. That old u.s. Protestant curse. *Selah* I get ya, Fr. X. More power to ya.

The slow train coming to the cosmopolitan faith, meaning, the international Catholic faith as opposed to the more provincial and culturally bound Protestant tradition, came after I'd left Southern California and had moved to what we Californians call "The Peninsula." The Peninsula is the stretch in between San Francisco and San Jose. The Pacific Ocean is on the western side and San Francisco Bay is on the eastern side. Right in the middle of it is what the world now calls Silicon Valley, not a valley at all as much as a slope from the mountains down to the Bay. In the

Peninsula I lived in a house of Christians, like in Placentia, only these Christians were Protestants. Come to think of it, they were also all brainiacs engineer computer wizards, just like the Placentia Poles. Instead of being students, however, the Peninsula kids were all working engineers, most of them at PARC, a Xerox R and D place that was all hot about digitization of video images. The spirituality of the Palo Alto house of guys was a sort of continuation of the Swiss theology, minus, of course, Schaeffer's diatribes against the failings of American Protestant Christianity. A typical Peninsula Protestant would be more inclined to defend his church against such attacks, or simply ignore them in the midst of the piety so common at the time. A nice exception, in its own little way, was the "Body Life" theology of Ray Stedman's church, right down the street from our house, one of the very few Protestant fellowships that seemed to be sincere about growth and sanctification of your walk. This approach, based on a deep analysis of the early chapters of I Corinthians would seem to hold out hope for outreach one day, but sadly I never got a prolife vibe from that church or any other Protestant church on the Peninsula. It's a suburban thing, and it's worse in the wealthier 'burbs. But I went to the Stedman spinoff Bible study on campus in the chem. building just across from the UGL1, the undergraduate library.

There were Bible studies at home, too, those led by the thinking of MPPC, Menlo Park Presbyterian Church. The young women of that church came to refer to the house the bachelors lived in as "The Home for Unwed Fathers." The biggest news spiritually on The Peninsula did not come from any of these Protestant circles. They maintained the Reform Evangelical charism and spirituality I got in Switzerland. The big increase in faith came from shy, quiet Catholics who crept into my life on little cat's feet, despite the rejection I'd felt from the Orange County church. All of these new Catholic faces that I would meet I did not meet in Bible studies or churches or churchy activities. I met them on the street. Specifically, the patch of street located in front of abortion mills. With one exception.

Let me tell about the exception first because I think it came first in time. Yes, when I arrived in Palo Alto for mainly professional reasons -- the advanced 'scope at Stanford -- my prolife interest continued up north there also, after hours. But not at first. When I first arrived in Palo Alto, right in the middle of the Peninsula, even though the science was doing well, my personal life was a mess. I'd just learned that Cheryl was engaged to another guy in Texas, for one. We're talking 1979 or '80, by now. Yes, I knew Cheryl and I were almost certainly over, even back in Texas, but I still hoped. When I got to Palo Alto and got the neuropath tech job, I didn't have a place to stay so I wound up on the living room couch of a friend of a friend who was just going through a divorce. After a 17 hour day, doing the day work for Stanford and the moonlighting on my own research, I'd come home wiped out and my generous host would want to talk all about his divorce, bless his heart, and he had every right to. Sadness is a funny thing, isn't it? Something that will absolutely waylay a quiet sheltered child, say, is just another day in the 'hood for someone from "Southie" or the Bronx.

Being of a background somewhere in the middle with my Irish poet Gramma Murphy Leonard and my "bullet-catcher" Marine dad, all the sadness of my Palo Alto host's divorce, my own seemingly interminable breakup with Cheryl, and the stress of the two technical jobs and the struggle against a non-prolife thesis committee back in Fullerton were all quite a load on my plate. This was before I had found my way into the Middlefield Manor Home for Unwed Fathers yet, so it was all quite crushing. One day the emotional load of all this was so bad that I couldn't even get out of bed. I can't remember how I kept the Stanford job with all that but I do remember confiding in my sou-chef boss at work, Dr. Richard Dixon, about the breakup. "Too bad for her!" was his instant and hearty reply. Hmmm I thought to myself. This was a different take on it all, as opposed to beating up on myself. Richard's casual but quick response didn't quite cut the mustard, however. I still remained sad about it all and thank Goodness one day I was talking with some on-campus Christians who tended to be a little high church., as they say in England. Mainstream. Formal. Episcopalians, old school Presbyterians, Methodist, like that. These, in turn, as part of their ecumenism, had contacts with Catholics. Specifically, a priest whom one of the on-campus crowd thought would be great for me to talk to about my situations. The wisdom of the on-campus crowd was that this might be a little more useful to me than the usual low-church "let's pray" approach. Nothing wrong with that, it's just, sometimes you need a little more, I guess. Come to think of it, it was just like in the old, old days before I started reading Schaeffer.

Reluctantly I made the appointment to see the priest, and I'm awfully glad I did. He opened the door for an entire mental lifestyle shift that's been with me every day, ever since. But when I first met him I had no idea. All I knew was that I was some kind of subfunctional. Germans are slow to cotton to stuff like this. The first thing I noticed about the priest was that he didn't always have a parish secretary running in the room saying "Sorry to interrupt, Father, but it's the Vicar General on the phone." It turned out that this priest was not a parish priest, and he didn't have a parish always clamoring to talk to him. He was some kind of monk. We could talk more at length. Father was also an intense listener. In my own case, I have a hard time listening to anyone's troubles without jumping in with "Grow up…Get over it…Get a job…Are you nuts?" and other such sensitive offerings. I can't stand whiners. If it weren't for the mercy of God, I'm sure I'd merit hell for this reason alone. I guess I save it up for helpless children. The rest of us need to put it in gear. Not only was Fr. Malachi an intense listener, he'd get curious about some detail in such a way that I sensed he enjoyed listening to my complicated life, almost as if he didn't get out much. We got together quite often. Hard to imagine that happening now, things are so hectic. Even after I had gotten back to a better efficiency and found a better place to live, I still went to see Fr. Malachi. Looking back, it was as if God wasn't just interested in a new spark plug or a gap tweak. He wanted to do a very careful tune-up or even rebuild an engine in areas I had no clue about and didn't think were relevant. You and I, if a friend brings in a rough-idle car, we'd look at the plugs and wires and dwell and lean, and the minute it smoothed out, we'd quick-like give it back to our friend and hope it made it down the block before it died again, and if it did we'd tell him to go junk it and leave us alone, right? This is America! I got places to go, things to do. And if you're not that lazy, I am.

But what the Lord did with talking with Fr. Malachi seems more like what we see in National Geographic now and then, pictures of a ton of technicians swarming over a satellite being prepped for a launch. They've all got Tyvek suits on and little OR booties and shower caps. The satellite parts are all gold. They aren't just getting something up and running, they are taking the time to get it perfect because it only has one chance to deploy perfectly in space. How I wish that you could have that feeling just once, that you are being carefully prepared for…something. One day I hope you will be a very small part of something very big, or, I will prepare and await my time and educate myself, and one day I will achieve something great, or, if I were told I must cut down a tree, and I had six hours to do it, I would spend four hours sharpening the ax. Come to think of it, I think it was Fr. Malachi who introduced me to a micro-library, along these lines: Imitation of Christ, Cloud of Unknowing, Ascent of Mt. Carmel. Later on after I bumped into the Missionaries of Charity crowd, I would add: Interior Castle, He and I, Science of the Cross.

Of all these and by far, Cloud of Unknowing opened a new world, a world of silence as theological lifestyle. Later on I would hear from the MC's that silence has many levels, only beginning with merely not talking and taking yourself off to the side for a little time each day from electronics, books, and even people who want to talk.

It wasn't until several years after this, probably the 90's, until I remembered what I'd like to tell you next, but it's relevant to the time in Palo Alto and the meetings I had with Fr. Malachi: When I was about eight years old, about 1962, I was standing in the middle of the South Pasadena Junior High School baseball field, the one on the east side of the railroad tracks there. The football field and track are on the other side. I was standing in right field next to the half-tennis courts there which had a wall you could practice tennis or handball against. As I recall it was maybe nine AM or so and no one was in either field. I remember a pair of Keds, the old canvas kind. I remember nothing but blue skies, bright sunshine, equable climate, and that Saturday morning feeling of no school and no church. Singing in the choir or being an acolyte could make Sunday mornings a little bit like school, you know? Also, despite my Dad's stern idea of chores around the house and his Semper Fi desire to teach us kids teamwork about sweeping up leaves and cleaning up the place, for some reason he never seemed to mind if I got up early and snuck out with my bike and went all over the place on Saturday morning. It's not as if I were going to Cairo or something and he knew I'd get hungry before long, but Saturday morning I'd seem to get a pass on Kopp family solidarity, keeping up what was a fairly big property with lots of trees and shrubs. Also, in the summers often there'd be a party Saturday night, and we kids were on duty with all that. Getting back to Palo Alto, it was when I was talking with Fr. Malachi about books like Cloud of Unknowing or Dark Night of the Soul that I remembered that incident in the field when I was a boy, and between us we deduced that it was of great importance, as if perhaps it might be some natural contemplative event.

That serenely joyous moment wasn't the only childhood thing Father got me to remember. I also told him about the hours I spent trolling encyclopedias when I was little and staring out windows at sunsets. My brother Walt and I would tinker with models and spend hours digging funny little canals and flooding them, in the side yard there in South Pasadena. All these events became of great significance to Fr. Malachi. All good things must come to an end, even in Palo Alto, and one day Fr. Malachi told me that he believed I didn't need the meetings any more. But at that last meeting he said something that changed my life permanently, from that day, to the present day, and every day since. "Think about a time set aside every day, to 'stare out the window,' as you did when you were small." I knew enough by then from Cloud of Unknowing and a Kempis and John of the Cross to know that Father was not talking about transcendental meditation, or any other Hindu or Buddhist-based practice.

"Huh," I said. "How much time?" "Think about one-and-a-half hours. Each day. Minimum." The answer came back calmly without either hesitation or forcefulness. Like a satellite technician giving a reading from some measuring instrument. Without the trust and the back-story with this man, and those books, if anyone else had said I needed one-and-a-half hours a day to do anything other than eat or sleep, and most certainly something "self-helpy," I would've said he was nuts. That year I was still wrapping up the master's research, I still was commuting to LA to keep up the part time nursing job, I still forked for Stanford during the day and did moonlighting research at night on the thesis, and I was working part-time on call as a temp nurse for the Stanford hospital. I was also still getting over Cheryl, which seemed to take forever. I had started the prolife volunteer work, and I was also tuning microwave radios part-time for a Peninsula electronics plant. Not only that, but the competition of all these concerns in itself added to the stress of it all.

But when Father said those words, one-and-a-half hours, the feeling I got was not of resistance at all. Instead, it was surprisingly like a tiny stone falling down a very deep well. It was going in, and not coming out. It would go in once and for all. I wonder if this isn't the reason: You and I, we race here and there, doing and seeing many things, but I wonder how often we miss one central simplifying idea that will smooth everything out in a celestial or universal way. Like the welders I met when I started to make locks for rescues. The professional welder doesn't scurry here and there or work fast. He starts his day with a long coffee break and talks about old, complicated jobs. When he's done with hours of careful prep-grinding and finally picks up the stinger, his movements are slow, careful and thoughtful. When he sets it down, he has created something that will last a century or more, and he's well-paid, more than the people who hustle and sweat. The idea of one-and-a-half hours a day of silence, from Father Malachi, hit me like that: of course. This is the unifying principle of my life that had been missing, even though by then I had already been an adult Christian for three years. Do you see what I mean about sanctification as opposed to the obsession with in-or-out? Travelling halfway around the world, anxiously, to make a convert twice as fit for hell as yourself?

I bid adieu to Fr. Malachi with much gratitude, and that day I started what I call quiet quiet time, in the late afternoon as the sun is going down. I call it "quiet, quiet" to distinguish it from what evangelicals call "quiet time," meaning, devotional Bible reading and journaling and praying, great activities, but not long and deep quiet. It started in a room at the Middlefield Manor, a.k.a. the Home for Unwed Fathers, but quickly morphed into neighborhood strolls when my roommates didn't know how to deal with phone calls during quiet quiet time. Evening strolls around the block quickly morphed into strolls around someone else's neighborhood so I wouldn't run into someone I knew. When I started the evening quiet time as a discipline, I was clueless and scrupulous. I would start the time clock over just because someone smiled and said hello and I said hello back. But after a while I found out a way to smile and say hello but keep walking to keep the silence going. Within a year I was up to an hour or so from the start of half-an-hour at first and then forty-five minutes. Slowly I found the time. It seems that after quiet quiet time, for mysterious reasons, I had been given the capacity to really say no to many requests for my time doing this or that. Up until I started quiet quiet time, I was a sucker for any heart wrenching volunteer plan, and I wanted them all to go, especially startup ones. Due to this and other things like it, I discovered that the more time I spent-in quiet quiet time the more time I had available overall. As if, the more you make God first priority with time, the more He makes you a priority, but especially in the area of smoothing things out and simplifying life twenty-four hours a day in a hectic world. Less activities, and more thoughtfulness or quality to each one that remains.

God was slowly making me into a journeyman welder despite all my impulses to the contrary, especially impulses to be scattered all over in a million things. I mention this because a few years later the idea of a conscious prayerful letting go of distractions and focusing on one task would become critical in the prolife calling.

    Just about when quiet quiet time kicked in, I first started Crisis Pregnancy Center work. The MA research was finally tapering down and the spine re-connect contract ran out at Neuropath at the med school. I finally had time to begin the prolife work I had been hankering after so deeply all through grad school. This volunteer prolife work took the form of CPC training, sidewalk counseling and PAG work. Other than Fr. Malachi, whom I met through on-campus contacts, this was the other area where I met a whole new slice of people, in all three of these prolife activities. They were all a kick. If you want to find a bunch of really rough-and-ready, can-do people, just scratch the surface of all us "religious nuts" who shout and wave signs at the killing centers. And hurry up! We're a dying breed. Mrs. Williams was black urban Baptist of the old school. If I had to guess, she might hate Pentecostals as much as she hated Catholics, but she was class all the way, a very loving soul for all that. Mrs. Williams was the director of the Crisis Pregnancy Center in Sunnyvale and she was my first CPC teacher. Her patient and loving character would come in handy running the CPC where love for the mother is the focus. Just as it is in all CPCs, and in all prolife work, much as our enemies say it is not! For all their hot air, none of them ever took teen moms into their houses and ran the risk of interfering with their precious devotion to NPR , MSLSD, and other forms of self-worship. I was the only male in that class of counselors but just as in the North Richmond Tutoring Center only a few years before, I was welcomed all the same. Of course, before it was over, Mrs. Williams and her fellow counselors pulled me over the hump, from being a baby-focused baby saver to being a mother-focused mother-and-child saver. This is an important distinction since before I went up to the Peninsula, I had been more of an intellectual prolifer, thinking about test tubes and microscopes more than moms. Not good.

    But another thing I remember about Mrs. Williams was that she took the time to talk with me about Catholicism, how bad it was. By then, we're talking '82 and '83, I had started to bump into a ton of Catholics up on the Peninsula in the course of my expanding prolife work. I had mentioned to Mrs. Williams my on-again/off-again passing interest in their faith. I couldn't help noticing it since they were "the fustest with the mustest" in every prolife area. Suddenly, the loving counselor charm of Mrs. Williams evaporated in the flurry of emotion against all things Catholic. Looking back, it's almost charming to contemplate this feisty anti-Catholicism in a world of New Age/All-roads-lead-to-heaven Smurfiness. Still, this was my first contact with red-blooded anti-Catholicism. Mrs. Williams was not at all like Pastor Mees with his slow-burn Missouri Synod Reformation approach. The difference was that this time around I was able to evaluate it all as an inquiring adult. In addition to the usual ill-informed attacks about idolatry, Mariolatry, saintolatry, works, papalotry, etc., Mrs. Williams brought an anti-Catholic book for me to read. The book is in a well-established genre of shoddy, bigoted, and simplistic books which attempt to connect this or that symbol or practice to ancient Gnostic or pagan Egyptian sources. Every Catholic apologist is tediously familiar with this junk literature.

It only took a few decades but I finally stumbled across the answer. It's in the form of a question: If you knew Jesus were hanging out at a 7-11 or a Piggy-Wiggly down the block, or at the post office right now, would you go there? I would. I'll tell you in plain English. To make the point clearer, I would go to a whorehouse or a rave or inside an abortion mill if I thought He was there. Do you see? Protestants are like people who say they would not go to such-and-such a place on the principle that they have constructed, namely, that it is impossible for Him to be there. To make the point clearer, it is impossible for Him to be inside a building which also has this or that ancient marking on it that they have decided is God. Not only does the building have some pagan mark on it, it is lacking the peculiar Jesus-My-Teddy bear markings that they have decided are correct, in their trendy feeling of the moment about stuff like that. For this exact reason, they will flock to any TV or Cash Now preacher, if he also shouts "Praise the Lord!" while he's handing out the money (or, collecting it), a.k.a. Prosperity Doctrine.

They are still my brothers and sisters in the Lord, and fellow prolife workers, and more than that, my heritage, but this is exactly what the Protestants do when they also neglect the substance of the Real Presence and spend all their time dickering about their weird take on superficialities and irrelevant old stuff about symbols that were pointed out to them by those ingenious historical scholars, the Big Hair crowd and Hank the Eighth who led to all that, who're always trying to shill for a few more bucks on the TV by setting themselves apart from…somebody. It doesn't matter who, as long as they are better than you and the working stiff standing next to you. Slowly it dawned on me that Protestantism is a culture-bound racial movement whereby each pastor has to please his individual congregation, not the living God. Not Jesus, as much as they say they are. Starting out, building his money-makers, beating up on Catholics is only the start of the profit. He still wants to grow his dynamic, new ministry and to do that he also must beat up, subtly or otherwise, on every other Christian church, even including other Protestants. This endless repeating pickiness and argumentativeness is only one reason why there are 28 thousand Protestant denominations for about a half billion Protestants worldwide, and one denomination for the one billion Catholics.

Catholics try to stay together even if they fight amongst themselves, just as a natural family would. They don't wander away and keep splitting into other groups. I pray that they would all be one. This divisiveness is just one reason why there is a killing center on every street corner in the US, and a fake church on every other corner. I also slowly became aware that the most man-pleasing churches are also soft on what let's call The Big Four: abortion, divorce, The Pill, and sodomy and the child molesting that seems to accompany it, even if not in every case. All of these came through the one door opened by Henry VIII in 1535. Strong opposition to these is not a Big Box church builder! And I include weak US Catholic churches when I say Big Box. They are offering the new thing. Any sincere Christians need only ask themselves one question: is this higher standard of classic Catholicism from God, or not? If so, go, no matter what the price. "Cafeteria Christianity" must be avoided at all costs. Protestant or "liberal" Catholic, it's no good.

C.S. Lewis brought this out in an answer about circumcision or the OT ban on eating pork. He said that any religion that makes perfect human sense and doesn't have at least one quirk in it that boggles the mind most likely is of human origin -- it's too good to be true. Jesus calls us to a higher level of good than we can conceive of with our own finite minds and certainly with our self-serving desires. An unexplainable quirk is not an irritation; it's a signpost to a different direction than "pure logic would dictate. As far as the back-and-forth about faith and works this has already been covered by others. You know what? Peace to all my dearest evangelical Protestant brothers and sisters! Peace, peace, rivers of peace and warm feeling. If it weren't for my evangelical mom and sister praying me into the faith, and the sacrifice of the Swiss crowd, I would never have bumped into real Catholicism buried away overseas safely away from the horrible corruption of US money power and arrogance. Or buried away in dusty Byzantine liturgies. And peace to my fellow prolifers who get their heads knocked in at rescues with me, all of us together. Those are the Protestants I will die with, and gladly. It's an honor.

To get back to Mrs. Williams and the Peninsula, I must say she did get the ball rolling by giving me that book. It had never occurred to me that anyone would think so much of that little beef that they would write an entire book on it, even a sleazy one. How skanky? At one point it was waxing on and on about works, legalism, and what Catholics themselves identified as a problem for all Christians seventeen centuries ago, namely, Pelagianism, and for some reason the book brought up the Stations of the Cross, the reminder to Catholics of what Jesus did for us because we forget all the time. Especially in this soft suburban era. The only problem was that in this book there were only seven stations, and there are really fourteen! This author hadn't even bothered to walk around an entire church in his investigation of things Catholic. He could only bear to walk up one aisle! That would be as silly as me saying, "What does being born again have to do with it?" if I wrote a book about Protestants. I stopped reading the yellow tabloids after that and moved to encyclicals and patristics.

Some of the events that happened in these strange intermediate years on the Peninsula are related to my prolife journey, and so I'll cover them in a different chapter, but as far as spiritual things are concerned, suffice it to say that when I was on the Peninsula, I started to bump into a lot of prolifers who were Catholic. I became aware of their quiet and sustained approach to faith and prolife. Take the Kochanskis for example. They ran a political action committee in Sunnyvale. I ultimately was lovingly dragooned into being VP at one point if I recall correctly. We got together once a month to put voter information newsletters about the Hyde and Hatch amendments that were swirling at the time, and things like that. One day standing outside their house after another issue was put to bed, we were talking. "The debate on abortion is over," Mrs. Kochanski told me. How so? I wanted to know. "Every woman who's had an abortion knows it's a disaster. They're just not telling the younger women who don't know. They're too embarrassed or whatever, but they are selling their own sisters short." There it is was again, that theme I ran into in the stacks in the library at Fullerton when I bumped into Aborted Women

Silent No More. Post-abortive women were the key to it all. This was a spiritual moment to me; that the Kochanskis had the heart and objectivity to stand back and at the same time delve into something, an area that even profilers have a hard time seeing. It's about the moms.

Another of the Catholics I'd run into when I started the volunteer prolife work on the Peninsula was Tommy. I hope some of my readers have met a Tommy at one point in their lives. I didn't know it yet but in a completely different style Tommy would be the angel sent by heaven to escort me into a knowledge of the cosmopolitan width and breadth of Christianity just as surely as He sent Schaeffer to show me the first step, albeit into the more local church, the culture-bound one. In fairness to Schaeffer however you can't look at all the wonderful rooms inside the palace until you step off the porch into the entry hall; i.e., into some denomination or other.

Tommy drinks rocket fuel for breakfast, eats galactic satanic attacks against humans, such as international abortion and "population control" for lunch and dinner. In between meals he nibbles on nuclear reactor rods for a snack. Tommy cannot get into his head, for longer than two or three milliseconds at a time, why you and Ii aren't already where he is.

In a word, Tommy is Irish. In his 40's and 50's he was carted off to the E.R. and O.R. a half a dozen times for injuries received making field tackles in touch football. Yes, he's that kind of guy, all that, and a pint of Bulmer's. I met Tommy in front of an abortion mill. I suppose that's not saying much: I met every interesting person I ever met since 1979 in front of a mill, including the only woman I ever asked to marry me. Tommy was different from many, however. It was in Tommy's nature to wonder why the world isn't on the ship he's sailing, isn't wearing the shirt he's wearing, isn't…like that. A Keith green type. It was a divine set up that I met Tommy in front of a mill in Sunnyvale, just down the road from Palo Alto, because if I had not, I don't think I would have stuck with it. I first met Tommy before I met Father Xavier, back when I was still sad about Cheryl, and what I saw at the mill made me even more depressed. Tommy fixed that with the whole Irish manic joy approach to life.

The first time I had even gone to a mill was in Fullerton, and the feeling of the sidewalk counselors was the cheerful upbeat emotion of Orange County Evangelical Charismatic Pentecostals: God is in control, joy about Jesus, etc. this is all good. But up north, at the first mill I went to, in Sunnyvale, it was a different feeling even amongst the counselors. It was

Catholics, and they say the rosary and have a slightly more dour approach to the whole thing, a kind of weary longsuffering, probably a penal times, great famine, "Irish need not apply" leftover, that. Both approaches are good and needful: the Prots get you pumped up, and the Catholics keep you going, right into the firing squad. Prots are in sales, shall we say? Or the building fund. Catholics are in payroll. Either one approach, without the other, is a disaster. Before Luther, both ideas were combined in one place, in one spirituality. Now, you have to go searching around to find parts here and there to build a coalition and to put all the pieces of the puzzle together to make a complete picture of what Mother Teresa called the Body of Christ.

When it came to spiritual matters, it was Tommy who was the one who kept calling me at night, when I was exhausted from phone work that i'd gotten into, and bug me about becoming a Catholic. I was in a phase back then where I kept asking the same questions to every Catholic I could find. In a Catholic way, it was kind of similar thing to the run-up to l'abri, when I asked every Protestant I could find a set of basic questions over and over, and compared what they said, one thing to another.

The Catholic list of questions was shorter, however. Fr. Lawrence Goode, a living saint, put in succinctly to me one day while I was an altar boy for him at a teen conference up in Marina.

"Jim, it's a simple matter, really. The Catholics and the Protestants both believe in the same thing, really, except for three things. Doncha love it when someone comes along and takes a complicated mess and makes it very simple? Especially without doing violence to the intrinsic complexity of a matter? You can be deep without being complicated, seeking like this.

It's as if a high energy physicist were to say a cyclotron target is really like a big leaf blower, and most leaves blow away but some pebbles knock into each other and fall to the side. According to Father, the three things were: 1 real presence, 2 Mary's status, 3 the pope. This was a huge consolation to me because up until then Catholicism had appeared to me to be hopelessly extensive complex and even arbitrary. For a couple years before that, I had gone up to every Catholic I could find to ask him one question: what is the Immaculate Conception? I only know now that I was going about things completely backwards and Tommy and Fr. Goode set me straight. But if I could play back all the answers to my one pathetic question, you wouldn't believe it. i'll summarize: 1 no one had the slightest idea of what he was talking about, 2 no one could refer me to a single source that I could go to and "'look it up," 3 most of them lamely retired from my request by simply saying, this is what we believe. (This reminded me of the Protestant fideists i'd run into before Switzerland who said, to believe, you need faith, you obviously don't have it, so…) 4 most could not provide a single reason why anyone should believe it, other than the fact that Catholics believe it. They were all cradle Catholics; in other words, they had never analyzed the question as an adult, 5 those who evaded the question would then go on to describe why they loved the church, invariably some obscure point about an inaccessible saint or Mary or a pope.

In fairness to the dim-bulb Catholics, there's a point to fideism, when it's in balance with reason, meaning, the brain and logic and conscious thinking. As C. S. Lewis said, not everything of God is explainable or even understandable by human logic alone. But still -- nothing? no dice on the Immaculate Conception? More on the Immaculate Conception later, but at this point, the main thing Fr. Goode and Tommy got me doing was reading encyclicals. Without them, I cannot imagine a single way that I could or would or should have got the skinny. Anyone who has the slightest interest in Catholicism, even if only that you are an academic, or a new ager, or a NPR open-minded type, or even an enemy of the Church -- whatever you perceive it to be, or wherever you find yourself in regard to the Catholic Church, stop talking to people and start reading encyclicals. Welcome to the big wide wonderful world of encyclicals.

For one, they are accessible. All of them ever published can fit into one book smaller than Huckleberry Finn. Another thing about encyclicals is that they are to the point. The most controversial encyclical ever written is 12 words long, in essence. [That's what Jim said but what does it mean? Why didn't I ask him?] I'm not talking about commentary about encyclicals, only the encyclical itself. Encyclicals originally were literally one letter on one parchment page, in the days when paper as we know it didn't exist. There were no printing presses, no Xerox back then. The letter had to be carried, often in secret to avoid robbers or counterfeiters. The popes had to get to the point fast. This went against every stereotype i'd ever heard about a pope, which would have pegged him as a kind of a gasbag. Intimately connected to the necessary efficiency of this parchment letter carried on pony express riders is the notion of an ex cathedra pronouncement, meaning, "I really mean it. no fooling." The two ideas go together. My favorite part of Brideshead Revisited, both the book and the BBC series, is the part where the erstwhile suitor of a young Catholic woman must receive instruction from a Jesuit in order to get married. "Do you understand the concept of papal infallibility?" the priest asks. "Whatever you say, father. I'll go with that." She's a cute girl, this bride-to-be. Our man is quite anxious to-do whatever it takes. "I'm afraid we need a little bit more than that, young man," the priest says, "suppose the pope says it's raining?" "Well, it'd be raining, now, wouldn't it? He's the pope after all!" "Yes, but suppose it isn't raining," the priest persisted. "Well…I suppose it would be that it really is raining, I'm just not spiritual enough to see it." The priest groans and rests his head in his hands. This is going to be a lot tougher than he thought.

 I only found out years later that it's an old well-worn trick of enemies of the Church to inflate or misstate a doctrine and then tout the false one as true, appealing to bystanders to join them in derision of the alleged false teaching, which is actually only a chimera that swims in their heads. At this moment, I can't think of a single evangelical out of 500 million of them, who even remotely understands the severe limitations placed on the concept of infallibility. Those who do understand, we call Catholics. It is also true, sadly, that I can't think of a single Protestant who understands the need for a humble referee here on earth to be, grace of the Holy Spirit, the final arbiter of what would otherwise be hopelessly endless arguments over everything. Sinful, self-interested arguing, not some noble concept of helping God clean up shop. This latter idea takes place all the time within the Catholic Church, and it even happened when Luther and Henry split off. They just weren't around to see it. They'd gone off to do their own thing, for perfectly selfish reasons. The absence of a solid teaching on such a humble referee is precisely why we have 25,000 Protestant sects, each with its own de facto pope. Let's not kid ourselves. And one Catholic community, of near-infinite legitimate diversity. I mean we have everything from dour fundies to Pentecostal charismaniacs, all under one loud roof, like a very extended family. It's easy to present a false stepford wife uniformity when you spend all your time kicking out people who aren't in your tiny me-me clique.

 Fr. Goode had explained how it boils down to three ideas. Once I stopped talking to lay Catholics and instead only read encyclicals, and once I bumped into the true infallibility teaching, not the fake one, then, right on the heels of these two ideas came a third one -- the idea was that it was an absolutely crucial distinction between a core belief of the Catholics, as opposed to stuff you can take or leave. Marian apparitions, the rosary, all the saint stories, and a million billion other things, as interesting or even sometimes as helpful as they can be, all fall into this latter category.

At this time I bumped into an Orange County monk who explained this crucial distinction, and also, that the core Catholic teachings essential to faith, called de fide teachings, are not that extensive. You can find all of them in a booklet no bigger than the DMV study pamphlet to get a driver's license. The Baltimore penny catechism is smaller than that, actually. In very short order, there, in those in-between years on the peninsula, I began to see how something that looked enormously complicated and extensive was boiling down to something simple and approachable, and that actually hung together more coherently than even the Protestant teachings I had known as a child. Those Protestant teachings, for example, had never explained John 6. Jesus himself is simple and approachable, isn't he? But there are also depths to him as you know him better, like john 17. In heaven, DV, we'll find so many other ways to embrace and encounter the infinite him and his friendship for us, won't we?

George Macdonald talks about this when he describes a fantasy where a tiny neglected rusty door to a hut in the woods opens out, once you step through it, into a wonderful castle of infinite joys and beauties and riches, but only if you step through the little rusty door. I began to see then that the Catholic Church is that rusty door. In my case, the Evangelical church was the legitimate pathway to that door, but only a pathway and still, an earthbound pathway, lovely as it is. The Catholic Church is the door to heavenly infinitude and a much closer and more complete physical/realtime encounter with the infinite personal God Schaeffer had kept talking about. All those years that my dear evangelical brothers and sisters cried about how you can't have heaven on earth, and this is no insult to the Protestants, they cheerfully agree that they have no real presence and no apostolic succession. But if you knew Jesus was sitting on a bench in a local park, now, wouldn't you go there? Right away? Rather than sit and listen to someone talking about him? That's what the Catholic Church does – she presents Jesus. It's all in John 6, Revelations 5, 6, et al.

Now, my friend, suppose like me, you come to the conclusion that this whole pope thing has a certain logic to it? Counties, states, symphonies, trade unions, operating room teams, airplanes, armies, navies, air forces, scientific research teams, universities, football teams…all these wonderful human endeavors and a million more we could name, are not run by committee. There is one boss, like it or not, male or female, good or not so good, in charge. There are certain good things that a committee just can't do. There are also a million good things you cannot do without a team. You just can't.

Jesus is not a stranger in all this structure talk. He invented even the idea of a personality, a truly unique individual personality. Try getting a real honest pantheist to even admit that such a thing exists. Good luck with that. The history of the U.S. is such that it covets rugged individualism. Fine, fine fine. But, as my dad used to say, there are some things really really big that we can only hope to be a part of. Jesus will keep track of our individuality, no matter what: don't be afraid of that. He will, that is, unless we immerse it in the fake individual impulse toward sin. There, I said it. Sue me. Drug addicts, celebrity creative types, and who knows who in between love to trumpet how individual they are, when really the pathetic rivulets of sin all tend to run along the same tired furrows. No freedom in that. There are certain good things that a committee just can't do, and certain bad things that committees, or even unbridled individuals, always do. Committees are famous for always obfuscating, stalling, and complicating the obvious. Unbridled individuals always seems to wind up operating from self-interest, to the detriment of everyone else. Sometimes a humble or charitable top-down situation is a good thing, even allowing right individualism and community to flourish. A good team player not only does not rankle at the idea of one boss, who knows what he's doing, say, and is not a tyrant; he even loves it. Nothing is more pathetic than a wavering, unsure leader; the uncertain trumpet assuming you agreed with the German side of me, about this one-boss thing, ok? Just for a second? Suppose also, you can't get a straight answer yay or nay, without endless confabs. It drives you nuts! Even in this situation, you and I could never invent a papacy on our own.

Look at all the endeavors that agreed with the one-boss idea. Even with that idea in place, none of them have ever created a country or even a city-state that has survived twenty centuries. On a trip to Rome once, a nun on the plane pointed this exact point out to me. She was an adult convert also. Her former profession? History professor. Her own studies of organizations or politics down through the ages drove her to convert at the de facto success of the papacy over time. I believe that the durability of the papacy and the magisterium behind it are proofs of a divine origin and maintenance. The u.s.is barely two centuries old, and sadly, obviously in its death throes, morally speaking. The technology will follow the humans down the hole. Wait and see. Also, even the concept of democracy itself, as much as we've been trained to love it, has inherent flaws. For these and a million other reasons, it's easy to see that the Catholics did not invent the pope. You or I or the man on the moon could not sit down now and make a pope or a papacy to survive from now until the year 4000, or even the year 2400. Impossible, and we know it. Catholics did not invent the pope. They were given a pope. This is an important difference.

Oh, and the first pope? The minute he was appointed, he denied his boss, ran for cover and hid like a coward, and became one of a group that called crucial eyewitness Mary Magdalene a liar. God has a great sense of humor, ya think? You can almost hear the angel gossiping on the first Easter: "hmmmm...this whole papacy thing...I just don't know...people are stiff-necked." But in twenty centuries, no pope has since denied the lord.

During this time on the peninsula I was starting to spend more and more time with the Catholics I'd met in the prolife movement, but this did not mean my time with Protestants was over, not by a long shot. I met Tommy and and a lot of other Catholics in a kind of transition, in-between time that lasted all of four years or so, and during that time I still had plenty of contact with Protestant Evangelicals. To this day I am comfortable with both crowds; i'm only uncomfortable with their disjunction. Like a family, where you love everyone, but they won't stop fighting. Five centuries is enough, guys! Sheesh. So, at that time, I was still going to a Protestant church on Sundays but sneaking off to weekday Latin masses at St, Anne's, on the sly. And I still lived in the home for un-wed fathers on Middlefield Avenue, also called Middlefield manor, with its houseful of evangelical electronic engineer video pixilation software geeks, most of whom worked at "park" xerox there in Palo Alto.

Here's where it gets weird: one day I was invited to a party of the Protestant crowd. It was at a very nice house on the peninsula, hostessed by the sort-of fiancée of one of the unwed fathers, my housemate. It was definitely not an intensely prolife crowd, even if all the people there would have readily called themselves that. In other words, they were prolife but not activists. But it was still a party of great Christians. After a while, the hostess, an intense intelligent woman ever alert to the well-being of her guests, noticed a disturbing trend. Every time I joined a conversational group, a pattern would emerge. I would listen to all that was being said politely for a few minutes. Then, I would interject something. There would be an intermediate phase a few minutes long, with back-and-forth. Then inevitably, the terminal phase came. I would drone on quietly for a few minutes while the group became utterly silent and still and frowning. Then I would quietly stand up, go to another group and repeat the process. Some of her guests had reported back to the hostess about my disturbing "downer" stuff.

Beware the born-again! I mean, the brand-new one, the guy who's just stumbled across Jesus, or the Bible, or titleist number three hi-flite golf balls, or titanium tennis rackets, or omega-3 oils, or e-cigs, or the juice downtown, or some dot.com stock shares, or the obamacare waiver, or Canadian shale sand shares! These people will drive you nuts because our culture worships what is new and despises what is old. We're wrong in both cases but so what. It's what we do; it's how we sell everything. No one made a pile selling rice or wheat or a good condition used bike. At that party I was driving everyone nuts with my new found prolife emotion. They'd timidly agree; in fact, no one could think of a single argument against my position. But they were put out of the party mood by my intensity, or the fact that I would even bring abortion up at all at a party. This led to an argument, on the spot, with my housemate's fiancée, a woman i'd known a while, but perhaps not this side of her, the grizzly mama perfect hostess protecting her party guest cubs.

When I say argument, I mean, she yelled at me a good ten minutes that I shouldn't rain on her parade, while I was silent. I can't remember everything she said but I perfectly remember her final accusation: "Jim, you've put prolife above Jesus. That's wrong. Jesus is above everything. You need to give everything up." So beware, also, the sophomore zealot! The jaws that bite, the teeth that clash! Beware the Bandersnatch! Who heard one, even a legitimate biblical principle, and instead of weaving that in with the organic whole of the personality of the living God, uses it as a stick to beat the other principles to pieces especially if it helps make their nice dinner party go a little smoother. Peace, housemate's fiancée! Guess what? In the give-and-take of a true working relationship with Jesus, she could be right, even if she did it wrongly, and for the wrong reason. That doesn't mean the Lord isn't trying to tell you something through a vessel of clay. Full disclosure: I am a vessel of clay, too, all day long, you betcha, all that and a glass of cold Cinzano.

Ahhhh…where were we? Ooh, yeah. God can write straight with crooked lines, and when she said that line, that i'd put prolife over Jesus, it was like stone falling down a deep well. It dawned on me: she could be absolutely right even if all this charismatic, evangelical, liberal Catholic theology leans a little bit suburbanish at times. Lots of times. So. Could my soul be dying? Hitched to the prolife star? In my own walk with the Lord? Is it possible that even if prolife is a great good, I still could put it above God, just as surely as the "greasy grace/sloppy agape crowd" contorts passive virtues and puts them over him, also? Could this be God talking to me? Even through this possibly suburban whitebread false peace, false superficial tranquility in the middle of the child slaughter channel? I'll never know for sure if it was all a cheap trick because from that moment onward I acted as if in fact that's exactly what was happening. For that reason, I basically abandoned all prolife effort, on the spot. I stopped going to the mills, I stopped reading about prolife, I stopped following the case of the Coarsegold Seven, and I even stopped studying about the Catholic Church.

Well, what do you do with yourself, when you're doing nothing? By that time, I had gotten a job in the telephone business, a job i'd picked up as soon as I wrote up the M.A. thesis and shipped it off to Europe. While I was waiting to hear back from Holland, i'd gotten the telephone job. It paid better than nursing or teaching, and it was less physically demanding than the stonework electrical or carpentry and truck driving i'd done in the Caribbean and elsewhere to pay for school. A funny thing happened: on a fluke, and with an old friendship from Santa Cruz, I got a job in a tiny company. I was one of only three employees, total, that covered all the microwave links, key equipment and pbx work for a largish silicon valley dot.com engineering firm. I got a lot of experience with a lot of different kinds of equipment in a tiny amount of time, experience that normally might only happen with a long career. I can't remember how it came about, what happened next, but somehow I found out that Wycliffe Bible Translators was looking for Telco people to help maintain their overseas missionary equipment.

Uh, why does a missionary need telephone equipment, anyway? Aren't they more into reading smoke signals or listening to drumbeats in

## TO RECEIVE A CHILD

the jungle at night? And how the heck did I make such a sudden switch from prolife to overseas missions? What's up with that? One short way to answer that would be simply to say that every good Christian -- I believe this, and i'm not the only one -- should be flexible, and anxious to do what the lord wants, and when he wants it, not just what you want to do. The subject of discernment, meaning, how do we know in particular what God wants, is a subject of many books. I'm not sure i'm the best one to tell about it. But I wonder, though, if it's part objective and part subjective.

The objective part is: we know it grieves Jesus if we sin, especially frank sins like lying, stealing and murder and idolatry. For the more delicate questions that involve borderline cases, I get the impression that a life steeped in regular restfulness in the presence of God helps us avoid the tendency to want to skate past God's perfect will for us, i.e., that we be perfect. But even with quiet time, it still leaves the question of what to do when faced with two options, both of which are good possibilities? So, assuming for the moment we've got an idea how God nudges us in subtle areas of guidance, when I heard about the need in a missionary group for phone workers, I got interested. I am, after all, a fourth generation missionary. My great aunt Ethyl was a medical mish to China in the early 1900's just after the fall of the Manchus. There were also other missionaries in my family. Wycliffe Bible Translators, the missionary group needing the phone work, is an absolutely unbelievable ministry. Talk about faith and courage! The typical Wycliffe mish is a middle aged suburban widow or spinster, or a couple, clinging to a cliff in the Andes, or getting shot at with bow and arrow in he Amazon Basin, or quietly reading the Bible in the middle of a revolution counter-fuselage in Africa. Oh, and dodging militant commies everywhere, and drug dealers who like to plink at Americans on sight, any time they find them. Or, kidnap them for ransom. Nothing personal. Wait -- this is all just what they do before their morning coffee. There's more. There's all their kids who have died from icky tropical diseases, and there's every other third world country trying to throw them out because some global elitist didn't want them there as a witness.

And all of this they do with absolutely zero political or economic agenda. They have no political agenda; once they've translated the New Testament into the obscure unwritten language of the locals, if they're still alive, they either go on to another tribe, or go home. No economic agenda, either, since all this suffering they do they pay for themselves! The Wycliffe agency doesn't pay them a dime. It requires them to raise support entirely from their own friends. Wow! This is like buying handcuffs to give to guards to lock them up with. I could say a lot more about Wycliffe but when I went to work for them, I was drawn to this humble no-frills ministry. A part of my thinking was this, however: if the Lord wanted me to actually do prolife work, he'd find a way to get me back there. But meanwhile a stint in the mish field would be a good way of discerning whether or not I was in fact placing prolife above Jesus. The phone work I did for Wycliffe Associates, not Wycliffe Bible Translators itself. Wycliffe Associates was a group of stateside tradesmen who assisted the translators with their infrastructural needs, like the cb's construction battalion helped the marines in the Pacific in World War II. For this reason, I never actually made it to a tribal location when I was overseas, but instead made short trips to mission bases which supported the missions in the tribes. I saw these mission bases and headquarters in South America and Central Africa.

    The interesting thing about a mish base is how practical it is. Yes, the little old ladies and young married couples from the U.S. suburbs did in fact approach and hang out in the tribes that had nothing of what we take for granted in terms of creature comforts. The tribes had fewer amenities, by far, than a u.s. boy scout troop camping out in a wilderness. How to do this? How to take u.s. suburbanites and put them in hostile jungles? Suppose, even if they would meet with some bows and arrows as some have? Part of the answer, in addition to heroic jungle survival training and radios and hacked-out landing strips, is the mission base, a place to keep planes, computers for the translations, hospitals, etc. My job was to keep the phone systems going on the bases, which were like a small u.s. town plopped down in the middle of a jungle with creepy crawlies, bullets whizzing by between the commies and the drug runners, and a whole lot of nothing. While I was working for Wycliffe, subtle spiritual things took place that I didn't expect. For one, I caught a glimpse of how hard people would work, completely out of the limelight and out of their own comfort zone, to achieve something no one would know or care about except God. Also, the mishes were content and pleased with their task. They didn't complain about the horrible conditions or whine that no one appreciated their work. Could u.s. prolifers be glory hogs by contrast? Some, perhaps, but to see this lesson so clearly played out in steamy jungles was a great eye-opener.

The whole Wycliffe experience reminds me of the World War II Gallipoli battle portrayed so well in Chariots of Fire. A watch being off by a crucial thirty seconds is crucial. An entire company was ordered to certain death by a fat lazy C.O. behind the lines who couldn't be bothered to double check his watch for coordination of the artillery attack, or even so much as to watch the battle. The men in the trenches saw the Turkish machine guns being brought back into the opposing trenches in the gap of time after the artillery attack and before the now-delayed infantry attack. They were victims of an officer who wasn't even watching. The men didn't complain in the slightest, but they knew it was over. They took off their wedding rings and hastily scribbled a last note to their wives telling them how much they loved them. Not do or die, it was do and die. And without complaint. and looking all the while at the Lord for rescue. All that, and a broiled python for lunch, I learned from the mishes, and they were funny. One day we did nothing but try to remember the entire section of Jeeves and Prufrock to keep up our spirits when we were all getting bit by malarial skeeters in Nairobi.

Once we road overnight from Santiago Chile south to Temuco to do some phone work. The sun started going down and I looked out the window of the train at the passing mud houses. I thought: this is great. Man, before lights and TV, has a much better chance at a natural quiet time at the end of his day. As the light left the sky, however, I saw spilling out of the doorway of each mud house the dull grey glow of a TV. This saddened me. I had always believed the third world had a natural buffer against modern technomania. In Santiago I got into a casual conversation with a Chilean. "What is America like?" he asked me. I knew they were filled with images of Hollywood movies, wealth, etc., but I felt an impulse toward honesty. "They do abortions there," I said. He didn't know what an abortion was. When I explained it, he said, completely without rancor, "This must be why they say the Americans are barbarians."

In Lima Peru I looked out of the window of the Wycliffe headquarters and saw a communist parade down in the street, with huge red banners, and in the interior, in Pucallpa, I heard the blare throughout the entire town of the open-air loudspeakers playing tacky marching music to announce public "struggle" meetings. Communism is a huge, understandable draw in the third world. Socialism, without the atheism, totalitarianism, stalinist and maoist cruelty, and without the elitism of the party strata, is right there in Acts. In Lome, Togo I met a blind mish with a guide dog named Brandy. This dear and gentle man agreed with me about the high and subtle irony of teetotlar Baptists paying for food for a dog named Brandy. He was also proof: if a blind man can be a mish, what's my excuse? It turned out that there was a large local colony of blind people who took to Brandy's master well. Brandy too, for that matter.

By far the strangest thing that ever happened to me in Wycliffe was my less-than-dignified exit from the Ivory Coast. Minirevolutions seemed to happen there about as regularly as u.s. elections, or Italian government changes. But the locals were quite concerned. If a white guy were to catch a bullet by accident, this could be an embarrassment, perhaps even to the rebels. This was the summer of '84 or '85. My boss wanted me on the next plane out of town; it didn't matter where to, as long as it was out of the Ivory Coast. So, my boss and I went down to the microscopically small airport, smaller even than the old Burbank airport. It was about the size of a decent-size bowling alley, one with a bar and some video games. I've never seen anything, before or since, like what happened at that airport that morning: the airport building crammed with everyone who had to get out of town, now. It turned out -- I had no idea -- every country in the world, no matter how small, has a government airline 747 in national livery, on tap, all the time, just for situations like this.

One man with a rolling staircase was in position halfway down the runway. A 747 from, say, U.A.E would short land, slam the brakes, and shudder to a halt. And everyone from that country would clamber on board. No taxiing, no gate, no jet way, no baggage handling, no food, no fuel, no nothing. Just, jump on and let's go! He pulled the stairs away and the skipper gunned it into a one-eighty and hit the gas. Just like that. A minute later another landed and it all repeated. For reasons known only to heaven's quirky sense of humor, my fundamentalist Protestant boss tucked a ticket into my hand for Al Italia. One minute I was in an airport crammed with mishes and diplomats and business people from all over the world. The next minute I was stuffed into absolutely the last seat on a 747 crammed with priests, monks and nuns, all dressed in their Sunday-do-to-dressed stuff, all of it perfectly clean, as if it had been hanging in a closet with plastic over it, waiting for emergencies.

The announcements on the plane were in Italian, and everyone on the plane was speaking Italian. I didn't speak a word of the stuff and I was terrified in case someone were to ask me a question. I began to think about all those thousands of times I had heard and repeated in my fundie Lutheran upbringing that all Catholics were going straight to hell. Was this God's chance for a little payback? I mean, these were real Catholics on this plane. I bet they knew what the Immaculate Conception was about, with all their fancy clothes. If somehow I revealed something Missouri Synodish, would they seize me and burn me at the stake? Did the Catholic God accept microwave burnt offerings if they were to improvise on the plane? Did they know that the most intensely Protestant fundamentalist mish agency in the world had snuck one of their own onto their nice Catholic plane?

I kept my head down, didn't make a peep, and tried to make sure I wasn't chanting Luther's small catechism as a mantra under my breath. If there's nothing to read, nothing to watch, and no one to talk to, planes have a rhythm all their own. Takeoff, ascension, leveling, and descension are all like invisible brackets to one big quiet time, with puffy clouds, too. Soon we landed…in Rome. The instant we got to the gate I got a funny feeling. Wow, here I am, an ultra-fundie-Protestant missionary…in Rome. Also, I'd been interested in people places and things Roman Catholic these past few years, and now here I was, in Romeo roam, smack dab in the middle of all those Eyetalians. I looked out the window. That was Roman tarmac. I looked at the sunlight. Roman light.

The jolt of a sudden escape from an invitation-only third world revolution flummoxed me. One minute bullets were almost whizzing by my head, and then I was surrounded by daily routine, and peace. Hmmm. All tourist service workers or civil servants in Italy spend their entire workday yelling at their coworkers, or lawyers over the phone about their divorces. It's like a massive soap opera, cast of thousands, with no camera. So, at the head of the plane, at the ticket counter, and at the taxi stand I had to stand and wait while these weightier matters were hashed out, but after a while I gleaned this information: yes, the emergency ticket thrust into my hand in war-torn Abidjan went through all the way to California; yes, I could hang out in Rome a couple days and catch the rest of the flight later; yes, there were cheap hostels in Rome; yes, I can take you there.

God is just so damn funny sometimes, dontcha think? I mean, one minute I was a Protestant fundie preaching the good news to tribals on the Ivory Coast, and in a matter of a few hours I was sitting in St. Peter's Basilica, courtesy of a Protestant plane ticket, staring up, up and up, all agog, at the depth and beauty of it. TU ES PETRUS in letters ten feet tall. Ok, ok, Catholics! I get the message! Sheesh. Would the ghost of Father Martin Luther break up through the floor of the Vatican and drag me back to Germany where I belonged? Umm, I didn't feel that. Did I have PTSD from the narrow escape in Africa? Ah, a negativo on that one, too. Was my soul in peril form salvation-by-works theology, while I was working there, sitting quietly, and staring up at the ceiling of that huge cathedral? Jet-lag? Guilt about abandoning my evangelical pals and their white man's burden to tell the world about Jesus?

If someone had bumped me, I would have reflexively shouted out in self defense, "Hail Caesar! Hail Mary! Love what you've done to St. Peter's! Very chic!" No, no, no, no and no. How I wish I could assure my Evangelical brothers and sisters that I was thinking about them in my Catholic reverie, but the truth of it was, my mind was a pleasant blank and I had a more solid and palpable and sweet peace, there, in that apparently empty stone box, than I had had since, well, since the time I was paralyzed by peace in the schoolyard when I was eight.

In the case of Rome, it lasted three days. During that time I don't recall eating, sleeping, or walking or talking, or doing anything at all. Now I recall that I peeked into the tiny medieval gospel side sacristy in the transept, the place where Leo XIII had the vision of catastrophe a century into the future, and the same place, I suspect, where the Satanic Masons snuck in in disguise and did their thing in '63. But most of the time I just sat, in the one place, gospel side, near the back. There was a tiny plaque there to Mary Queen of Scots. Not even a saint but the Romans made room for a humble servant who tried to protect the priests from slaughter when Hank went nuts. Of all the millions of martyrs in the world, they found room for a tiny plaque for a British Catholic. This idea, the idea that someone not welcomed in their own anti-Catholic homeland would be honored in Rome, was somehow consoling to me.

American Protestants, all, to a man, children of British Christianity of that time, have no place in their world for celibacy and for what I called then the theology of sadness. I call it the Way of the Cross, now. These things and anti-divorce, anti-abortion, and the positive, life-affirming things behind them, such as happy holy marriage and childbirth and love of children, and a hundred other perceived pebbles in the path of a Christian walk, just don't exist in happy-happy-joy-joy suburban white bread developed world Protestant smurfland, and yet here 1 was, feeling perfectly at home in a big empty stone box, knowing that for the first time in my life, if I were to mention any one of these things to a card-carrying Catholic, he'd reply, "Of course. That's our faith." Everything. Everything, everything, everything changed, that week in Rome as magically as the magic carpet that got me there.

In the end, it's like standing in the kitchen in Oregon, or kneeling by my bed in Switzerland. God just does things, by grace, in his time, and as he wills, because lots of people do these things, and nothing happens, or i'd be running all over the world preaching: stand here, do this.

He found me, if I had to guess. Even the tiniest initial impulse away from the world and toward the infinite-personal God…that's grace too, isn't it? Grab it, it comes 'round, is my advice. Don't ever let go.

Once back in California, everything was different now. What was once sweatily pushing a ball uphill now was a ball rolling downhill so fast I could barely keep up, in terms of my feelings about Catholicism. My friend's boss at work, a publishing house, was a priest, and he quickly sent me to another Jesuit for an answer to my remaining questions. The Jesuits have a little more freedom than the parish priest, who is probably required to run you through the two-year course of adult catechism. I would always recommend a religious priest, meaning, one in an order, to anyone with questions. Monks and nuns might have a little more time available than a busy parish priest, too. Fr. Monaghan simply put a small book on the desk and said to let him know if I had a problem with anything in there. Gone was the two-year study of things, most of which i'd learned as a child already. Gone, I was to find out later, also, were the liberals who often taught those parish courses, and could twist the shorts of possible conservative converts into knots, to say nothing of misrepresenting essential teaching and even driving the conservatives away. Reading the book, it all came back to Fr. Goode's big three: the real presence, Mary, and the pope.

By then -- this is '84 or '85, by now -- the idea of the real presence was a comfort to me, but probably by the intuition of sitting through all those Latin Masses in Palo Alto at St. Anne's, more than reason or logic, which came later. It was the nearness of Jesus himself in the tabernacle that did it, something, or someone, that you sense is near, much nearer than Palestine twenty centuries ago, great as that was. The idea of a pope to solve arguments and prevent constant bickering and splits had appealed to my German heart even before I saw proof of it, by its absence, in the endless Protestant divisiveness and fissiparousness as a way of ecclesiastical life.

This Left Mary. Was she a deity or idol? I knew too much by that time to be taken in by this anti-Catholic slur. Impossible, and the Church said so in plain language, but that still left the teensy matter of the Immaculate Conception, a de fide teaching. Not peripheral or elective. I can still hear my dear evangelical brothers and sisters of the time, if I were to mention it, say, see? See? We told you the Catholics went too far with the Immaculate Conception! Of course we accept the virgin birth, but … It was a good two decades later that I intellectually and scientifically settled the matter of the Immaculate Conception in my mind but back then in '85 my rapprochement happened by an indirect and intuitive process. What a shame that modern reductionist scientists have lost intuition and indirection! All great science happened that way. The indirection was weird. How about this: I heard there was a book that explained Mary stuff real well. I found it and sat down to read it. It was a tiny book.

I opened it in the middle to just begin browsing a little, an old speed reading trick, and my eye fell on a single sentence. I can't remember the sentence, now, but the effect of it on me was this: I instantly shut the book and put it back on the shelf. Here was someone who actually knew what he was talking about. That one sentence was so filled with knowledge and wisdom and explanation and faith about the role of Mary, a simple b-girl but also the mother of Jesus, the Man-God, that I came away from that abrupt experience with an intense conviction: even if I didn't get all this Mary stuff, somebody did. It was almost as if I didn't need to know the details. I believed. Lo and behold, I also discovered that the author of the book was teaching at that same school, USF. I caught him after a lecture one day, just as I had buttonholed the Oxford don James Houston in Texas 6 years before.

Fr. Buyer was kindly, happy to talk to me, and spoke with a strong French accent. We only spoke for a couple of minutes, but, again, I was completely filled with a feeling that finally I had encountered someone who knew all about the Immaculate Conception, but once I had found him, it was an epiphany more than a college lecture. Just the contact alone pushed me toward belief. I didn't need to know the details. Also, I already had found many of them from Newman, another convert from

Protestantism. So, it wasn't pure intuition, I guess, but it felt like it. Believe it or not, as much as these happy events nudged me in a comforting way toward understanding the Immaculate Conception better, the doctrine still stuck in my craw. Again, the Protestants would say there's a reason for that, brother! But I couldn't leave Catholicism alone, either. They were plainly correct in too darn many other areas, especially the love and charity and joyful god-centeredness and respect for the holiness of God in the big four push to unity and the real presence.

Around about this same time in the whole process, I had come to the realization that, as near as you or I can tell anything about things like this, St. Francis and Mother Teresa and JP II were born again in the Protestant sense, even if it was in a form unusual to my evangelical eyes, and even if they were also card-carrying Catholics in the bargain. Prots would love to say this or that person isn't born again, but I wonder if they really hold the keys in that matter? At this time I also had come to realize that the invisible part of any endeavor, the quiet time part, was as important as the visible, or, let's say, the purely logical or rational part of it. Doctrine, discussion, history, all that, even Bible study, as wonderful as that is, is still a rational process. We need prayer to absorb it and live it.

I was doing medical transcription as a part time job in SF by this time, and I remember standing by the typesetter machine one day and just deciding to pray and put it all into God's hands. I asked him to please show me the truth about the Immaculate Conception, but also, did I have his permission to join this wild and woolly Catholic Church with all their out-there teachings, their history of saints and sinners, their incredible diversity, and their simple hugeness, in space and time. Of all the times the Protestants had cautioned me: you can't be Catholic and born-again, now it was time to put that exact question to the master himself.

Well, my gentle atheist or agnostic, or evangelical brothers and sisters, if you do not like change, do not ask God direct questions. He just might answer them! In this case, the answer came in invisible ways, and in two parts. The first part, I was standing next to the typesetter again and the answer was a feeling but it was as clear as if i'd heard words, which I did not. The feeling was this: yes, you can become a Catholic and still walk with me if you wish. There's just one catch: if you do, you can't hate the Protestants. Play nice. You can take or leave feelings like this, of course. Who can prove anything about how God actually operates or communicates? We can't presume. We can sense the will of God for sure, all the time. We each blunder forward as best as we can according to the lights we are given. But even if it only had subjective validity, this condition was asking a lot. By this time I had become aware of all I had been missing outside the more replete truth of Catholicism -- i'm especially thinking of John 6 -- and harboring some resentment against the Protestants for suppressing this and other truths would be understandable. Like Mary Magdalene, though, the Lord invites us forward, I believe, and at the same times gives us a corresponding invitation to a task, and now I had one. To love the Protestants even as I left their day-to-day fellowship. Even that's not accurate because I never left them. In this sense: once you've come to know the Lord as a person how can you go back from that? From Him? It would be like saying I don't know my own brother or sister or mom or dad. Wothout trying, I had stumbled backwards into the best of both worlds: born again and Eucharistic, both together, exactly how it was in 1516 for everyone, all Christians.

In the science and spiritual parts of this book I've tried to explain how these areas could lead to rescue, Europe, Asia, or even night-time work or Buffalo. But even if you know that, it still leaves other experiences that were prolife, or that happened after I became a prolifer, that specifically pointed toward the incredibly high value of each life, no matter how disfigured or seemingly inconsequential. I'd like to tell you about those specifically prolife events now. How to explain, though, the start of a prolife life, a prolife lifestyle, especially one that resulted in activism. The answer might be that from the perspective of earlier inhabitants of our planet, what we now call prolife would just be part of normal life. Any man or woman or child would dash into the street to grab a toddler who's wandered into the path of a truck and she would smartly knock over anyone slow enough to stand in the way. In our modern world however, a Modernist person would stare as the child was crushed, as if were a 3-D TV show, with really great sound effects! Then -- pay close attention now -- they'd tweet all their friends that they were OK. The prolife attitude is rare nowadays, isn't it? So why me? For that matter, why not you? Why the Lavender Hill Mob? Let me give it a try, but some things are mysteries even so. I don't know.

Much of it had to have come from my parents and they didn't roll out from under a cabbage leaf. Great Aunt Ethyl on my Mom's side was a medical missionary to China in the Sun Yat Sen days, just after the last Manchu Emperor. Her brother, Granddad Walter Leonard was a Hollywood MD with a reputation for high success rate and fast recovery of his patients from surgery. He was so fastidious about cauterizing bleeders on the way in. But also, he was very conservative about operating at all. Never risk a surgery if it wasn't life-saving was his philosophy, an obviously out-of-date idea. "When there's life, there's hope" he'd always say to the gravely ill and their families. I got all this from my Mom, who understudied him and became an RN.

When I was small I'd play hooky in the early mornings when I was supposed to be doing my homework on the heater vent downstairs. I'd lay all my school books out, so it looked as if I was working, but then I'd sneak off under the piano to the bottom of a bookshelf there. All the big heavy books were on that shelf. Usually I'd grab a volume of the Encyclopedia Britannica and flip through it and look at the captions. One day I found a book that looked like a high school yearbook, and in a way it was, but for a weird "school." It was the year book for the Fourth Division, LJSMC, my Dad's division. It was a late 40's book, just after the war.

My sister Mary and I had already come to the conclusion, about life, that the division of suffering was thus: women suffered having babies, and men suffered too, because they had to get shots to get in the army. To us two kids this was perfectly straightforward. Modernists scoff at this because modern techno-man doesn't have to do either activity. From test tube babies, surrogate moms for hire for the Beautiful People, or in the case of soldiering, push-button wars, drones, M-25's, missiles, aerial bombardment. We can't be bothered getting our hands dirty. Babies and carrying a rifle are for the little people, the suckers. But think about it. Do you believe this technology will always be here? And, overall, should it be? No limit to the dehumanization of labor, war, childbirth, food-growing, etc.?

I think Mary was pretty smart. The main reason she believed war involved real suffering for men was a picture we'd found in a book showing a man grimacing as he got a shot from an air gun that pushed vaccine thorough the skin. Mary was convinced. Men suffer too. But in the Fourth Division yearbook, something else happened. In the back were pages filled with pictures of all the Division marines who'd ever gotten the Congressional Medal of Honor. There were dozens of pictures but after a while I noticed something: some of the men's pictures showed the medal around their necks and the pictures were clearly focused, in color. But other pictures didn't show the man wearing the medal, and the pictures were grainy and in black and white. Now, here was a mystery to a 6-year-old. What's up? What's going on here? I went to my Dad while he was upstairs shaving, the place I always took the big questions of life. I asked him about the pictures.

Marine officers don't cry, I suppose, not in front of enlisted men anyway, but he came close that morning. Very slowly he told me about posthumous awards of the medals. It wasn't the only time he got misty-eyed over the war. "If it wasn't for the Bomb, you would've never been born," he used to say on Saturday nights into his cups, a little bit sometimes, by the poor near the fire. He'd ask over and over, portentously: "Do you know how many enlisted men died in the first ten minutes at Tarawa?" It was only years later I realized my Dad had a Hiroshima complex, not only due to his having survived the war, but also because he was called upon by MacArthur to be among those who pacified Japan after the surrender. He saw the effect of the Bomb close up. He found clean water and food for all the survivors. All this, by the year he turned twenty-three.

I only mention this because I think the impact on me was that life is worth dying for, right now, hurry, hurry! An innocent life at risk is not something you picket about or write your congressman. There were no congressmen or media cameras on Saipan and Tinian, just a fight to live. Most of the Medals of Honor in the Pacific Campaign were grenades thrown into trenches. The men who jumped on them had about one second to decide what to do, and they made the right decision and saved a half dozen other lives that were at risk. In the process, by the way, they saved their own lives, but that's a subtle point we could talk about later.

Back on my Mom's side of things, in terms of her influence. I knew she was a nurse but the heart of good nursing didn't hit me until the day we went to see her mother, my Irish-Cherokee Gramma, in the hospital when Gramma had a stroke. Down on the steps of the hospital Mom asked another relative if she would like to come up and see Gramma. The relative said, "Oh, no, I want to remember her the way she was before she got sick."

I had no idea at the time, the impact of this simple statement would have on me upon reflection. At the time I just thought huh. My Mom didn't miss a beat. She turned to me, "Jim, do you want to come?" This was a switch up for me. In our family, no one asked you anything, especially if you are the baby. You're told what the program is! But here I was, being asked. I said yes, and that single trip up the stairs made all the difference in the world. I assure you, I would not be here now and you would not be reading this if my Mom had not invited me upstairs to that med/surg. floor. Upstairs, Gramma wasn't even in a hospital room. They had wheeled her bed into a corner at the end of a corridor to make room somewhere else. An old lady with red skin in a coma doesn't rank much, I guess. The most amazing thing about it was my mom's reaction. She normally was the kind of person to rent a sound truck and castigate the world if she gets a glass with a spot on it in a restaurant, and yet here she was, not batting an eyelash about Gramma being shoved to the side.

I had never seen anyone put so much Love into someone who couldn't even talk, and here it was my own Mom and Gramma, so it was kind of a double shock. Mom was completely filled with joy and love for Gramma and she let it out like I'd never seen before. She bubbled all over the place, talking as if Gramma could hear her, and talking about just everything. "She was awake yesterday," Mom told me, "She told me she dreamt she went fishing with Mary." That would be my dear sister who died only a year before Gramma Leonard. Mom took this as a confirmation that Mary was in heaven already. Looking back, I see it as a sign that my Cherokee-Irish Gramma, who'd had a problem with drinking when she was younger, was headed in the same direction, grace of God.

At that time I was still an agnostic going to liberal Cal., but it definitely got me thinking. Gramma herself was not one to darken the door of a church, but the thief on the cross slid in under the wire, too, right? Ever since this bedside experience I have kept an open mind about it all; even when I worked in cancer, even if it's also true that "today is the day of salvation." You can't really chance it, on purpose, and delay like that, especially not once you have a good idea in your heart that He is there and He is not silent. He loves us all, in the now. Mom bustled all around the bed caring for Gramma. She didn't care that the bed was shoved into a corridor with no privacy. She went at it the way a good fireman doesn't care if his patient is crumpled up in a tin can in the hammer lane of the Nimitz Freeway during rush hour. He gets out the Hurst tool and goes to work right there, no hesitation, no complaining. Let's go! Right now! That's the feeling I got from Mom. Mom undid Gramma's hair which she always kept in a kind of Swedish housekeeper bun around her head. It was a huge braid and Mom undid it all and combed out her hair. I had never seen her hair like this before but even at 72 Gram's hair was still almost all glossy blue-black Asian/Native American hair.

It went even beyond loving care for another human being, though. My Mom's approach was so intense that for me it actually transformed the act of death into an act of life. The same thing had happened when my brother-in-law died and my sister was so devastated, so young, still 25, and with two little babies. Her kinda goofy charismaniac church showed so much love for her it shone so bright it even lightened up my little agnostic corner of the world. The beginning of my life, my salvation in earthly terms was the death of my brother-in-law and my sister and Gramma. Agnostics who only whine all the time about the hypocrisy of Christians give me a pain now. But I wish they could have what I had.

Whether it was Gramma dying -- or, living for the first time in her life, perhaps? -- or Annie's widowhood -- or Mary's death at such a terribly young age, 19, my family was showing me that life is a beautiful thing, and it's worth living, every second of it. The disabled, the hurt, the broke, the poor, the starving, the cold, the ones with bullets flying over their heads tonight...all these people in the world, and that's most of us, get this. No problem. The beautiful people, the ones who think a perfect suburb is typical life, they will never get it. By the time they find out that broken air conditioning isn't that important, it will be too late, sad to say, unless they repent before then. I believe this approach, that life is worth living under any circumstances; when it's so over the top like this, as in my family, it set the stage for seeing all life in that way, even the silent life of a child the size of your fist and the bond he or she has with his or her mother no matter how distraught or bullied she is.

And the same death-reveals-life showed up on the beaches of Tarawa and in Hiroshima as I heard about these sad places from the Old Man. Within even their own generation my mom and dad had found that dearness of life, also, simply in being survivors of the Depression and World War II. All the people I met from that generation seemed to me to have none of the whining, someone-rescue-me attitude so common later and now. If life was at risk, there was something you could do about it, yourself, now, was the spirit. Back then there was no Great Society to become dependent on. Do it yourself was the word of the day. Get it done. Don't complain. My coming into the prolife movement was accompanied by going to week day Masses, and I ran into the Last Greatest Generation there.

But back to some more early childhood prolife events that heightened my awareness of the value of life. When I was nine I injured my eye in a gruesome accident while doing the kind of foolish things little boys will do. Thank God I didn't go blind, but it was a near thing. When I got out of the hospital the surgeon wanted to remove a scar from the injury which he said would make for trouble later on when I grew up. Citing the extreme conservatism of my grandfather Dr. Leonard, my Mom said no. But when she told me, she said this: "Jim, if it cost a million dollars to save your eyes, we would find the money and do it in a heartbeat. It's not about the money." She went on to talk about the risk/benefits analysis that her own father would have applied. But all I heard was the million dollar thing. Even just a part of your life, like an eye, is worth a million bucks! And that was back when a million bucks could get you a cup of coffee and a phone call, both.

The training we had as kids said life was valuable and to be treated with care even outside of life and death matters. What about kindness to strangers, helpfulness, cheerfulness as much as possible, in a tight spot? And always stick up for the little guy, or your home team, your school, your family. Loyalty. This was part of it also. Mary, Gram and my quiet and thoughtful brother-in-law Rick all died within a short time in the early 70's. The year I became prolife, 1979, wasn't that far away. But in-between was a decade of turning away from the faith. I didn't give prolife or abortion a single thought. If asked I would've simply repeated the notions of any college crowd about "choice," but no one asked. It was all taken for granted. Abortion wasn't even legalized outside New York until 1973. This all changed in 1979; only one year after I had been baptized in Switzerland. Dr. Schaeffer came to the US and did a tour with Dr. Everet Koop and Dr. Mildred Jefferson. They spoke and showed a prolife film.

Even though I had been an adult Christian for a year, and studied Christianity for years before that, and studied embryology, the fact is that when I walked into the Anaheim Convention Center that fall weekend I was not prolife at all; when I walked out, I was. At an interval during the convention I overheard Dr. Koop speaking to another surgeon. "What do you think the percent chance of success of that same surgery would be under my hand?" he said to someone he was talking to. The context was a surgery to correct a birth defect. Dr. Koop's point was that many children were doomed to abortion simply because they needed a surgery at birth to correct a congenital defect and that if surgeons were more diligent in their duty the whole idea of "birth defect" as a rationale for abortion would disappear. In fact, in the movie that they showed that weekend, there's a scene in which dozens of Dr. Koop's adult former patients are in his office, all of whom had birth defects and all of whom had wonderful lives, after he repaired them. Without the surgery all of them would have been doomed and many such babies now are in fact doomed without an advocate like Dr. Koop to believe in them, just as my mom believed in Gramma even when she was sick.

How many times have we heard the mantra: rape, incest, birth defect, as if this were some medical dogma? Millions of kids are alive today, their moms happy to have ignored this sick lockstep. According to Koop, the simple sloth and lack of faith of current surgeons help make the if-it's-not-perfect-throw-it-away mindset, an idea that has obviously outgrown even the evil of child murdering. There are levels to things, I discovered. Gramma's death, Tower Five, the Schaeffer/Jefferson/Koop tour, and what I saw through the microscope at school all brought me closer to an intellectual understanding of how children should never be ground into hamburger. But the incident up on the Peninsula in 1981 transformed all that head knowledge into something more, with more heart in it. Before the incident at Stanford, I had started to join in the rosary in front of abortion mills. I worked on a PAC on the Peninsula that did voter awareness newsletters, and I wrote a letter to my school paper and to Sam Hayakawa. But after the incident at Stanford I cut straight to CPCs and rescue. No more fooling around with the lobbying or writing a letter to the editor stuff. Here is the incident at Stanford:

Everything changed in that morgue: Before then, I was a write-your-congressman prolifer. Afterward, I was a CPC builder and a rescuer. To those who want to blame something like the Anaheim Schaeffer convention, alone, for my subsequent activism -- a friendly media KGB thing to do, to use as a weapon to go after the Schaeffers and Koops and Jeffersons of this world -- here's something to consider: 20,000 people went to the Anaheim convention and fewer than a half dozen shooters are locked up now (not counting the Vito Squad, who evaded arrest, thank God). So, what's the difference? Why didn't twenty thousand people jump up, stream out of the Center and belly up to the hustings? Could it possibly be they didn't see the poor kid in the morgue? We don't know. But if the whining pro-abort witch hunters want to look for a culprit for the more serious stuff, they should put the blame exactly where it belongs: themselves. In this case if they didn't want a shooter, they should never have set a hand on that poor girl who had absolutely not one substantial thing wrong with her and was helpless to defend herself from wicked murderers. How dare they blame a gentle helpful intelligent soul like Schaeffer when they are the ones with kids' blood on their hands? They can start with the man in the mirror if they're torn up about shooters.

The second event of the two huge turbo-charged changes from intellectual-only prolifer to activist took place only one or two years later, in the sleepy central California town of Fresno. How did I get over there? To answer that, I must explain a little bit about a prolife group that formed back then. I found out about them when I saw a tiny article in a peninsula newspaper while I was living in the Palo Alto House for Unwed Fathers on Middlefield Avenue. The article talked about the "Coarsegold Seven." Coarsegold is a village next to Fresno, which is tiny also, even if they do have a great high school football team. The "Coarsegold Seven" turned out to be seven prolifers who had barricaded themselves in a mill in Fresno one bright sunny California morning, tossed out the staff and patients and proceeded to non-violently trash the place. "Non-violent" in this story means no bombs or guns or arson. They tossed the furniture all over the place and threw all the medical files on the ground. Like in the movies when some mob guy tosses your apartment, I suppose.

Well, the fine political fathers of Fresno wouldn't have any of this, even if Fresno was still part of the crowd of conservative Republican farmers at that time in the Central Valley. Tax relief was one thing, I suppose, but their conservatism did not extend far enough to kicking a mill out of their town, for which this incident provided a perfect opportunity. I guess they didn't want their daughters to have to make the trek all the way into Sacramento or Oakland for an abortion. As we know, the rest of California conservatism, which used to be vibrant and powerful, is now history. After the incident in the morgue at Stanford, I was on the lookout for something more than a PAC to "stop abortion now." I contacted the Coarsegold Seven crowd and they invited me right over.

I was there a week, I think, and I was quite impressed with their can-do Franciscanism, even including families, even though they considered themselves Dominicans. Every Saturday all these converted hippie Brooklyn Jews and all their commune-raised fun and unaffected kids would pile into ancient Suburbans and sidewalk counsel at a mill in Fresno. It was a morning of bright sunshine and blue skies, as usual in the summer in the Valley. I wound up with a sub-group of counselors on the edge of a parking lot on the south side of the mill. The main counselling was happening around the corner of the building on the northeastern corner of the property where the front driveway came onto the property. That driveway was where most of the moms drove in, off the main street. I was on the western side of the building where there was a second entrance into the same parking lot, but off of a side street. The parking lot was in the back. This second entrance is where the incident happened.

The first thing I remember is the sound of a Volkswagen Bug door being snapped open so forcefully it bounced against the stops of its hinges and slammed itself shut again. Think about this, for starters: This is something quite dangerous to the person sitting in the car, isn't it? In that moment when the car door is momentarily open, if the person sitting in the car had put her hand on the doorframe, all her fingers would have been broken when the door slammed shut again so forcefully as it did. This was the first clue that the man whipping the door open was a steroid meat puppet. If you don't know what I'm talking about, just look up YouTube footage of the jackass Number 25, Christian Stewart, a corner for the Seattle Seahawks, raving at the end of the last game just before the Superbowl, 2014, the NFC Championship game vs. the San Francisco 49ers. By the way: normal citizens? This is your future. People behaving like this will flood your world, mess with your kids and break into your house at three AM. Hey, maybe three PM; what's the difference? Get used to it. Mr. Stewart? My name is spelled K-O-P-P. Please go quietly to the end of the queue if you want to sue me. I can hardly wait. I might move you up. Oh, and just in case you don't actually do 'roids or raves or meth, stop acting as if you do.

Getting back to the parking lot, it turns out that the best thing that could have happened to that young mother -- she will vehemently agree -- would have been if her fingers had indeed been broken. She might have been at least temporarily ineligible for the forced murder of her child. Heartless of me to say this, you'll say. Read on. Public bullies sooner or later get attention. That's the point. Who was this guy opening the door like that? He had a Gold's Gym wife-beater-shirt on, yellow with red letters. Death's Head narcissism Clue Number Two after the door-whippin' thing.

The mother in the car refused even to get out, so he jerked her to her feet as if she were some barbell. A light one. Once tottering on her feet by the side of the car the rest of the story was plain to see: she was 95 pounds soaking wet, and was a polio victim with braces on her feet and arm calipers. In the context she was completely helpless with 'Roid Rage Boyfriend around. If he clean-jerked her out of the car like that in the presence of a dozen men standing fifteen feet away, what do you think he did to get her into the car, back home when no one was looking? Uh, attention, feminists! Thumbing through your revisionist PhD theses, do you even know if there was any real consent to the original act that made her a mom? Gentle Pilgrim, Do you see how the diabolic mantra "rape, incest, birth defect" takes on a different meaning when you see the real truth like this? Better believe Mr. Charm School Dropout believes in abortion for rape, right? Of course he does! It's his salvation from five years in the clink! All that's left is slapping around the gimpy skinny girl. This guy is your soul mate, feminists, just as you adopted Hugh Hefner back in the beginning. Did you put that part in your textbooks?

But let's suppose there was some form of consent from the mom. I say "some form" because there most definitely is not consent to the holistic natural sense of sex which includes children and the meaning of sex in her mind. Not to say a standard biology textbook, and, oh, sixty-five centuries of recorded human experience. There's that. But suppose there was some consent, even lopsided consent. If you can love a pet hamster, or a whale about to get whacked with a harpoon, or a baby seal, I bet you can understand the pathos of this young mother, her heart. She knew the child was helpless, just as she was. Out of seven billion people heaven had ordained that she and her tiny child would be in a do-or-die club of two, the magic number required for human love, or the love of a family, a village, a nation, or from heaven to earth.

But in the years since that day in Fresno another thought has occurred to me, from something in an old prolife film. A kindly doctor said in reference to a woman who was sterilized from her first and only abortion: "She'd live the rest of her life knowing that she'd killed the only child she ever conceived." Would this young woman in Fresno ever have another chance to have a baby? Ever? Had she, in her suffering, telescoped into the moment all the wisdom that the rest of us usually only acquire after fifty years? What life really means? Her life and her baby's? What is really most important? I'm the kind of guy who normally likes two words to remember: Next Time, and two words to forget: if Only. As young prolifers came to me in the following decades with new versions of this same tragic story of sidewalk bullying, I would always be the one to cut them off and say live and learn. Try to do better next time. Get over it. Put it behind you.

Full disclosure: I never put Fresno behind me. It eats away at me all the time. It motivates everything I do, and most definitely was the absolutely necessary intermediate step to Buffalo. Before Fresno if someone said the word "choice" I would run and hide. After Fresno if he said that word, I'd laugh in his face. With scorn. A lot of scorn. Big-rig truckloads of scorn. "So. You like being a bully?" His face would either take on the clueless stunned look of someone for whom the word "choice" is a political slogan about something he is completely ignorant of, or the look of someone in shamed retreat.

To the proabort politicians, press, liberals and other Sideline Sams who want to blame this or that Christian leader in their own self-styled inquisitions, or this or that earthy rhetoric, I say to you: Grow up. Blame your own damn self. Take responsibility. Shame on you, that you have resisted all the costly effort prolifers have put out over the years trying to stop something as obvious as Mr. Dream Date Gold's Gym boyfriend, such as twenty-four hour waits, parental consent, required ultrasound (really just part of true informed consent), and all the rest of it. Don't be putting it off on us. We are simply responding to your foolishness. If you don't want doctors shot, they can stop pulling the heads off children any day they want, and thousands have already done so.

On Judgment Day it'll be a hot seat for you and all the child-decapitating lames who rolled with you. Whether they are the Fake US Catholic or Fake US Protestant flavor, it doesn't matter. We're all in trouble that day, me too. Until then, good luck with the booze, bimbos on the side, divorce lawyers, Prozac and all the rest of it you need to get through your wretched day once you've seen what I have seen with my own tired eyes. "Choice" was also gone for me, forever, once I saw what I saw in the morgue at Stanford. I am not afraid of your power on earth but if I do not warn you, you will die in sin and the Lord will ask me to account for your life. Repent. Turn away from this horrible evil and hurry up. I assure you, you literally will not have forever to figure it out. If you deceive yourself about that, you're an even bigger fool.

The Fresno Polio Mom forced abortion was 1983. Shortly after that I moved from the Peninsula to San Francisco itself and I was doing a little typesetting and medical transcription work and hanging out with Kathy now and then. I was studying Catholic encyclicals, doing sidewalk counseling and rescuing at some mills in the Bay Area with a miniscule but loyal, brave and intense San Francisco prolife crowd. I also did Wycliffe Bible Translators support work on the side; Nairobi, Lome and Abidjan, all Sub-Saharan, that year, if I recall correctly. I was asked to help open a Crisis Pregnancy Center in San Francisco but I told them no. The reason is…Wow. This is where it gets real weird.

Have you ever had a guardian angel show up in unusual circumstances? I better give you an example. Suppose you were some KKK grand knight poo-bah broke down in a storm a million miles from nowhere and the only guy that stopped to help was black? Your stereotype hater would've said over and over: never in a million years would I accept help, even in a tornado, but I have heard tell of some who in fact just came down to the level where the rest of us live and accepted the help. Or, in my case, say, the time when the black Shore Patrol Marine guy in Daly City jail stuck up for me, the skinny white suburban kid. Before then I had no contact with blacks at all. After that I looked at blacks in a different light. For one thing, they're much funnier than stuck-up white people and they take life a little easier. Well, I mention this seemingly strange KKK scenario because before 1984 I wouldn't have known anything at all about bikers. Not many bikers in chi-chi, sushi-eating pansy Marin County. But in that year, 1984, a biker came into my life and he was a guardian angel sent from above, just like the black who stopped for the redneck, there is absolutely no doubt in my mind. A biker! To me, the geeky clueless stumbles over his own feet kid in the lame 'burbs. I tell you, if you happen to tune into it, God's sense of humor gets you through just about everything. You're too busy laughing to care about the slings and arrows. It's a scratchy channel at first, but once you're used to hearing it, it comes in real clear. This biker was all that and a big-ass nasty flathead, no pipes. In your face, pal. Get off the street. Sigh…if only he'd been there in Fresno.

I never caught Mr. Testosterone Boyfriend actually slapping his girlfriend but I didn't need to. He was in a completely steroid rage and she was constantly flinching at the promise of violence. The history of abuse was plain to see. Don't go against me b or you will get it right now was the program. He was a MTV/BET rapper/ meth video dream date. Any moron can recognize this kind of ultraviolent bullying misogyny. It's on the TV all the time. There, I said it. Sue me, Rev. Sharpton, Eminem, you other white spinoff wannabees, and all the rest of you with your TV women-hating thing. On this one I side with Dr. Huxtable.

There were three people there that day, not two, and now it's time to talk about my sins. She never never took one single step toward the mill. He jerked her off her balance each step of the way and it was all she could do with her braces and arm calipers to keep from falling over. At this point I found myself about fifteen feet onto the precious private property of the killing center as Boyfriend bitch-slapped his slave concubine closer and closer to the door. Geeky skinny white boys from the lame/burbs are slow to intervene, even in situations like this. We invented cowardice. I mean, even the Minnesota Vikings beat us up. Ninety pound Weaklings beat us up, to impress their girlfriends. So, reluctantly, I found myself slowly traipsing my way up to within ten feet of the couple and closing in for a confrontation. Even at that early stage of my prolife experience I knew the drill: engage the boyfriend in a faced abortion situation; try to get him to swing on you. Then, because of the nice bloody nose, another sidewalk counselor calls the police. When they bring boyfriend from the mill, out comes the bullied girlfriend seizing the opportunity to slide between the various yelling males.

I wasn't exactly "running toward the sound of the guns" but I was definitely slow walking. If I hadn't been interrupted, I would have simply got in between Mr. Dream Date and the building and then I would have turned to confront him, all ninety-seven and-a-half pounds of me. I was definitely a coward, don't get me wrong, but I was moving into position. This is where something already tragic enough became a sin that cries out to God. A fellow prolifer chased after me and ordered me off private property and back onto the sidewalk. Didn't he see the story here? Absolutely. But he, in turn, had already been ordered never ever ever ever step onto the parking lot property, no matter what.

It's the "no matter what" inculcation that made us all proaborts that day. Each and every abortion is a flat-out emergency demanding immediate effective action to save a life in danger, just as you would if your own child were in danger, but this one screamed it. What followed was ninety-nine percent my fault because I listened to him. Damn the Corps and their obey-first training they gave this devil-pup, you know? Let's see… my fellow prolifers…the Corps…is there anyone else I can blame for my own cowardice? The boyfriend? No, they're always lame anyway. Hmmmm…hey, wait! There's the fact that I was a new prolifer and the other sidewalk counselors were effectively my hosts and trainers. It was their party. It turned out that the lawyer working with the Fresno prolifers had previously negotiated a temporary restraining order with the owners of the mill and the judge: we'll allow you one counselor to talk to women on private property on the front driveway, but you have to keep all the rest of the prolifers off the rest of the property. The guy who restrained me in the Polio Mom drama told me this, in a hurry. Oh. One more thing. The guy who restrained me, who ultimately became a close friend, was himself a Green Card immigrant and, with his family, was terrified of so-called "police contact," which in his case could have resulted in the deportation for him and his huge family. Did I mention that? Sunspot activity? Magnetic flux? Cats in Zanzibar? Global warming? Global cooling? Help me out here. There isn't enough paper and ink for me to give all the lame excuses I've tried and rejected over the years.

Polio Mom, I'm so sorry I didn't step up that day. The same day your child died, another Fresno couple turned around and went home, needing only mild rhetoric and a siphoned gallon of gas to get back home. How I wish you could be Godmother to that child, the child which should have been born to you. She never took one step of her own will toward the mill. She pulled back as much as her ninety-five pounds and leg braces and arm calipers would allow. He jerked her off her feet, stumbling, to the building every inch of the way. What a tough guy you are, Mr. Gold's Gym! To hell with you, absent the Mercy of Jesus. I wish the prolife bikers were there that day. When he'd finally, literally dragged her sobbing the entire time to within about ten feet of the back door, the door opened up and a white coated RN's arm reached out, grabbed her off her feet and yanked her the rest of the way in. To hell with you, too, traitor RN, same conditions. Last but not least, to hell with me. We prolifers know better. All of us, also, because the chattering sheep masses rolled with all of this all along the way.

Up until now, I've split this story into categories like science or music. But in 1985 many things came together and made it all one. That year seems to need its own little chapter, and from then on, after this chapter, I'll just tell the story in one line without subdivisions anymore. After 1985 everything seemed to flow together into one thing only, and that was prolife. When I had arrived on the Peninsula in '79, I still wasn't quite sure if I might go to med school back in Texas, or do basic science research, or teach. I was still checking out overseas missionary work and

CPC training, and maybe a family of course. Any one of these could have been a ministry for me for the rest of my life, before '85 came along.

How about the priesthood? Not unusual for a new convert to get interested in that. Why not? Lots of converts have done exactly that, and a good thing they did. During 1985 a million things happened, pulling me in a million directions, but by the end of that year I was interested in exactly and only one thing and I pursued that exclusively for the rest of my life with absolutely no regrets. How did this happen? What happened in '85 that was so unusual? I honestly don't know how to answer that question. The sun rose and set three hundred and sixty-five times that year on nine million people in San Francisco, but when it was done with me, I bugged out. As with the kitchen sink at the beach house in Oregon, and the tiny chalet on the mountainside in Switzerland, and the convention center in Anaheim, I really don't know what was going on in those places either. The Lord works in mysterious ways, maybe. I don't know what else to do, however, except to try to do my best to recount these things so you can judge for yourself. If you come to any great conclusions, let me know. It's a poser to me, my own self.

I don't know if you remember, but in '84 or so I got out of starting up a Crisis Pregnancy Center by telling my sincere promoters that they shouldn't hire a director who's about to go to jail. I think I also told them, to keep them at bay, that if I was exonerated from the fake assault rap that I would be their director for their center. At the time I told myself, hey, this is a win-win: if I go to jail, I won't have to run the CPC. And if I run the CPC, I won't be in jail! What a sucker I was! Who could've guessed SFPD would let me off the hook! I was a known prolifer and this was San Francisco! No one sticks up for us, so, they had nothing to lose by smashing us, even on a false conviction. But hey, one fine day we heard from the police: they filed a nolle prosequi after an equivocal lineup. This was unusual, because they had nothing politically to lose by leaving me or any other prolifer on the hook forever waiting to find out how it would come out, interfering with your ability to act or make plans. This is what they do all the time, all over the country.

It was what Fr. Norm would call a "divine set-up," this release from prosecution. God was working to make something happen against all odds. There were people already lined up to help with fundraising, incorporation paperwork, etc., but they needed someone fairly judgment-proof to actually hold the bag, legally speaking. To be on the hook in terms of liability for the new center. I was unmarried with no house or career, so you're It, pal! Musical chairs and no chair for you! Short straw!

About the same time I got off the hook with SFPD, I got on the hook somewhere else even in addition to the CPC. Those days I would run down to the Mission District once a week or so to hear Mass with some nuns. I caught a ride with a priest, Fr. Frank. "Some nuns in the Mission" turned out to be Mother Teresa's sisters. If you ever need to find a Missionary of Charity nun, and I mean, you are really in trouble and don't know where to turn, just go to the deepest grimiest darkest corner of the worst ghetto in any large city, and look around. They tend to walk in pairs, like the Mormon mishes. But you can always tell the "MC's" by their "blue par," a white sari with blue racing stripes on the edges. No one else in the world has anything even remotely like it. And good luck trying to catch up with them, either. NASCAR is a turtle race by comparison.

One day Fr. Frank was about to drop me off after the Mission Mass. We were just off-campus near USF in the Richmond district near the Carmelite Monastery. Father said, "Would you like to meet Mother Teresa?" Wow! You don't get too many invitations like that! "Sure!" I told him. We walked over to the steps in front of the convent and in a few minutes a beat-up Suburban rolled up and there she was with a few other MCs and friends who were ferrying her around. It turned out that Mother Teresa liked to go check out the "Carmel," the OCD Foundation in every town where she had one of her own cells. I believe she trusted the Carmelites to pray for her new foundations, especially since each one consisted of no more than four naive, rural Kerala, very young women thrown into a foreign and urban and rough environment with junkies, vice, and fifty three kinds of street foolishness and violence. Father introduced me to Mother. "Mother, Jim just spent last night in jail for a prolife rescue."

Quick as lightning Mother turned to me with those eyes piercing out from under the little half-way baseball cap visor thing that they wear. She was tiny. "And did you have a nice sleep?" Total deadpan delivery, better than Rodney Dangerfield. It turned out that the night before was the night I'd been tossed into a tank with 200 drunks and it was so crowded the only place to lie down in was immediately in front of the toilet. I had to wake up, get up and move every single time any one of the two hundred wanted to go to the bathroom, which was often, since they were sleeping it off. But how could she know that? And zoom in so intensely on the only thing that mattered to me at that moment, which was the fact that I was wrecked on my feet? It was almost creepy, but a nice creepy. While Father was laughing at my expense -- he's a priest, so he certainly knew what Mother was getting at, about jails -- Mother moved on to the next topic at hand.

"How many brothers and sisters?" "Five, counting me," I said, "And one in heaven." She reached in the pocket of her worn out sweater and pulled out a raggedy plastic sandwich bag. She carefully counted out five tiny Miraculous Medals into my hand, kissing each one, and said, "Holy priests, holy nuns." It turned out she did that with everyone she met. It was her little campaign to bring some holiness back to an obviously un-holy-and-proud-of-it world. Shortly after that meeting Fr. Frank got an urgent phone call. Real priests and monks and nuns are always getting urgent phone calls, and they get so many, they delegate. It turns out rainwater was flooding into one of the Missionary of Charity (MC) buildings in the Mission from a broken roof drain. Father asked me if I knew anything about home repairs. I told him I'd look at it. I re-routed the roof drain which was built through a wall and had gotten clogged and then broken and had splashed out into the house. This became the start of a lot of handyman work down in the Mission.

Shortly after the roof pipe repair the MCs were given a three-story apartment building in the Mission and Mother decided to turn it into what would be one of three homes for single moms in the U.S. On the day the place was due to be vacated, my mom and my sister Anne showed up to pitch in. I can't forget what turned out to be the toughest part of the day: throwing out a stunningly ugly piece of furniture left over from the previous occupants. Try to visualize; then, grab your Prozac: it was a plush velvet electric chartreuse overstuffed love seat in the free form random shape of a teardrop, in a hurricane. Sort of. I mean, these have just got to be flying out the door down at Target, know what I mean? But the worst thing about this esthetic abomination was that it was so damn heavy. And huge. You could hardly get it over the banisters on a turn in the stairs. It took a dozen people an hour just to get it to the street. Once we did, we all laughed. It was as if this damn couch represented everything wicked and self-indulgent in San Francisco and we were trying to carve out a tiny nook of clean and simplicity for the moms about to move in, in most cases to find shelter from boyfriends or husbands who wanted to kill their babies. And I like chartreuse. Usually.

After evicting the Couch From Hell, I had a chance to look around the job. I promptly had a heart attack when I saw the nuns tearing out a bed of ivy in the backyard. The ivy was holding back a small hillside there, and the muddy, clayey hillside was holding up the near side of another three story apartment building just behind the shelter, but on higher ground. This is San Francisco. If an earthquake hit on a monsoon day I had visions of that hillside going to quicksand and the higher building tumbling into the backyard of the new shelter. Sure enough, there was a fresh hairline crack in the downhill side of the tiny unfooted property line wall above the steep backyard slope. God provided a volunteer bricklayer to get the new retaining wall, and an engineer to design it. But what about concrete for the footing and grouting? The concrete plant dispatcher was pleased to donate a truck drum remnant from a paying customer to Mother, but we would have to hang out "on-call." When he came the actual driver refused to believe Mother T's nuns were actually going to pour a third of a truckload with a Chinese fire drill bucket brigade, two gallons at a time. When he saw the truth of it, he couldn't stop laughing. MC people power! For the next two weeks the nuns were chipping concrete out of their racing stripe saris and out of their buckets, two almost-sacred things to an MC. "Jeemsab! Are you making any more concrete things any time soon?" "No, Sister." (Big Smile) "Good! I hope not!" After this, they called the level space above the new retaining wall "Jeemsab's Garden." Little did they know John Smalley designed it, a helluva guy.

At the same time the remodel in the Mission was going on, we had another one to do also: the new CPC Board had found a rental medical office suite on 19th Ave., not too far from the old Hippoburger and the Olympic Club, down toward the Marina. It's the same part of town where Steve McQueen and Dirty Harry and Michael Douglas liked to bounce their cars up and over the bumps on the steep hills in chase scenes, with Alcatraz in the background. The medical suite was incredibly cramped and we had to divide it up to get two counseling rooms. Plus it was dingy. It was a lot of work.

The number and intensity of things that all happened in 1985 I couldn't describe in a hundred books. One highlight, though, was that I entered the Catholic Church finally, that year, after seven years of study. I had been a Catholic already in my heart for years, but that's not the same as Catholic Communion. There you get spiritual food and medicine unavailable anywhere else. I know this sounds politically incorrect to say, but the Real Presence is not as controversial as you might think. The main reason is that my dear evangelical brothers and sisters freely admit that what they eat and drink at their Communion time is not the Real Body and Blood of Jesus. Instead, it is symbolic only. This is a deep subject. I mention it because maybe that First Communion at age thirty-one could explain the sudden changes and decisiveness of 1985. I don't know.

When I was received into the Church, Sister Martha threw a little party at a friend's house across the street from the USF Chapel. I invited my evangelical friends from down the Peninsula and Switzerland but I was late getting there. I had to sign the registry in the chapel. As I was walking from the chapel to the party, I was thinking: Great! Now all my Protestant friends can meet my new Catholic friends! What a shock when I walked in the room: The Protestants and the Catholics were standing on opposite sides of the room and wouldn't say a word to each other. This was doubly surprising to me since they had a lot in common: all of them were prolife, and some on both sides were grad students in philosophy. The sadness I felt back then about this coolness has never left me. The godammed schism of selfish Henry VIII and needs-a-date Fr. Marty Luther had iterated down the centuries to wreck even that little party. I'm still sad about it. I always will be, until it goes away. The Greeks took eight centuries, and counting, to get over it. I wish the Protestants would hurry up, at least in terms of liaison and coalition. Operation Rescue was a start, but not near enough.

When I entered the Catholic Church an interesting mix of prolife contacts and influences came into my life. Bob Pearson was not the only national prolife figure I met then. One day Cardinal Sin from Manila came to give a speech on campus at USF. He was a total crackup. He has a Chinese name, but he knows exactly what it means in English, too. "Tell the Pope that Sin has come to San Francisco!" he started out his speech, to a huge laugh. Cardinals don't do much stand-up, you've got to understand. He proceeded to keep all of us on the edge of our seats telling the story about how he and his fellow Filipinos kicked Marcos and his wife and her shoes out of the Philippines only weeks before. Not with revolution or violence, but with legitimate force, "People Power." Sin even told the Carmelites to pray during the entire time of the "EDTA" uprising, just as Mother Teresa had enlisted them for her shelter down in the Mission District. This was a window into Asia, the place I've loved ever since I saw pictures of my Great Aunt Ethyl when I was little. Ethyl was a medical missionary in China. At the end of the speech an enthusiastic student asked Cardinal Sin how he could contact him. "Send a letter to the House of Sin, Manila. It will get there." Everybody loved this guy. He was very prolife.

That same year Fr. Paul Marx gave a speech at USF also. What a different speaking style! The beginning of every Fr. Marx speech I ever heard, public or private, was a droning list of replacement birth rates in every European country, recounted from memory in rapid desultory fashion. This was worse than organic chemistry! Father knew how boring it was. "I know these statistics are tedious," he said, "but Our Lord said, 'If you do not do penance, you shall likewise also perish'."

I did not meet all the new people I met that year in person. The most important one was by mail. One day at work -- l had a part-time job fixing up antique stoves -- a friend handed me a letter. It was typed, not typeset, and kind of blurry from being rexeroxed a million times. It was the first "samizdat" I'd ever seen. But that tattered, faded, single spaced, legal-sized piece of paper, hastily typed on both sides, would change my life. Of all the many diverse and competing things that influenced me in 1985 and before that, during the Peninsula years leading up to it, this newsletter I held in my hands would reach into my life and pick up the tiny thread that had started with the first time I had read about the "Coursegold Seven" in a tiny newspaper article in Palo Alto years earlier. The same tiny thread that continued with Craig, the mysterious biker-dude rescuer who said we've got to barricade that San Francisco mill. Here in my hands was the shocking and heartbreaking story of how a judge in Florida had given a five-year sentence to a young woman whose only crime was to walk into a room to try to unplug a vacuum pump that was used to suck the heads off helpless babies.

The sentence was bad enough, but the samizdat went on to say that that young woman had been so distraught at the idea of being unable to try to rescue babies and their moms for five whole years, that she had decided to non-cooperate with her own jailing, and with the entire killing machine system, by not even walking into jail on her own feet. She sat down right in the courtroom floor when she heard the sentence. In theory you could imagine some medieval saint holding her head high as she walked to the gallows and Miguel Pro standing up to be shot. But Joan Andrews, a soft-spoken, sweet southern farm girl from Tennessee believed that even the simple act of walking into jail made it easy on the overall system that killed babies.

When you count jailing rescuers as part of the cost the system must pay to keep the killing going, Joan did not want to do anything to lower that cost. And it was not whim, caprice, or peevishness on her part. She had come to this conclusion after much prayer and thought. We're all glad she did, because that single act of sitting down changed the flavor of rescues from that time forward. Children were still being killed even after our arrests, and this was a move closer to the Gandhian thing about sacrifice connected to active resistance, even if it was also non-violent. In Gandhi's terms, satyagraha did not mean passiveness; it was simply a different form of force. And it was a desperate attempt to jam the gears of the juggernaut with her own body, the last act of a powerless person. I was stunned. Standing there in my repair shop I stopped working -- tough to make a German do that -- and I sat down and stared at that piece of paper samizdat.

In our modern world, especially with the computer enthroned as Mr. Smartypants-Know-it-All, sometimes it's hard to tell the forest from the trees with the flood of TMI, Too Much Information. But that day, sitting in that stove shop, I felt as if, with a simple piece of paper, I had stumbled across the Holy Grail, the Rosetta Stone, and the two Tablets, Gandalf's staff, Merlin's sword, and the Oracle at Delphi. In my short prolife career up to that point, I had followed others who knew better than I. But in the last couple of years before 1985, I was beginning to bump into a problem: I wanted to do a rescue or open a new CPC, and I couldn't find enough people to help. And those are team activities, to be sure. But here I was, reading the newsletter, looking at evidence of a young woman who had simply stepped out in faith in a bold fearlessness that set a completely different standard for all of us for how to approach a huge and tough problem. Suddenly I felt like two cents waiting for change.

But the samizdat said even more: it said there was a whole rescue movement back East, way beyond the handful of pathetic rescues and marches we had done on the liberal, non-Catholic Left Coast. That idea, that shortcoming, started to work away at me. Looking back, I suppose you can say, "Well, I've been kicked out of better places than this," but it still hurts to be thrown out of the state of your birth, the state that produced Reagan and Nixon and George Patton, and by a handful of lesbian lawyers who've taken over the place. It hurts a little, you know? But the lesbians actually did me a favor. Without their thuggery, I might never have gone East and found out how to play hardball with the big boys.

All of this to say that the next event of '85 was a shocker. The two lesbians sued our tiny, starving, always broke CPC. They did it with money from a slush fund raised out East by Katy Hepburn, the movie star.

Let me back up a little. When we opened our San Francisco CPC, we decided to nudge the envelope a little in terms of public image. Down on the Peninsula I had seen an openly prolife CPC with all sorts of manpower. Then they wait all day for the phone to ring. The few women who did come in weren't really being shoved into an abortion anyway. In San Francisco we decided to call ourselves the Free Pregnancy Center with no mention of our religious faith. After all, Planned Parenthood wasn't required to put a sign on their door "Atheists For Hire To Decapitate Your Child," right? Right.

When the moms came in, we'd do a pregnancy test. We asked them if they'd like to watch a slide show while they were waiting for the test results. They always said, sure. On the phone, when they called, if they asked "Do you do abortions?" we answered by saying, "Come on down and we'll talk about it." This is not one iota worse than the car salesman who knows for a fact that the last green Volt just rolled off the lot, but he tells the Greenpeacers to come on down, we'll talk about it. In the context of babies, not only is this not a lie, it's actually a nudge in the direction of a much bigger truth.

There is nothing truthful, good or beautiful about pulling the head off a child, and every single woman in the world knows this, even in our benighted culture. If I say Come on down, my soul is actually saying to your soul, there is something better than abortion out there to answer your problem. Suppose a man crawls across the desert dying of thirst. He sees somebody. "I beg you, do you have a spoonful of water?" he croaks out. It turns out, this is all he had dreamed of in his delirium. What a cruel human being who would say, "Yes!" and then proceed to give him only that, and watch the poor man die of thirst, with gallons of water nearby. "But he only asked for a spoonful," the inhuman one would say. It is due to foolishness like this and infantile mislogic like this that child decapitation has been sold to young kids in public school brainwashing, as something good.

When I say, "come on down," my soul is saying to your soul if you come down, we have gallons and gallons of water to offer you. You will never thirst again. In this manner in the CPCs, the lies and horse manure of pop culture are sidestepped, and a tiny ray of light shines through in the darkness. Darkness so obvious nowadays that everyone can see it, even the ones who don't want to. The liberals who sued us in San Francisco didn't see it that way. Theirs was the only truth, and not only had they kicked prolifers and normal people, people who might want to be married and have kids, out of the public schools so that they could brainwash the kids without any interruptions, we weren't even allowed free speech in a shelter where we paid the rent and didn't use any government money. The much-vaunted liberalness of San Francisco doesn't extend to first amendment rights for prolifers -- only child killers. The little people lose.

The lawsuit against us is a long story but the bottom line is that the San Francisco liberals got a ruling: we were no longer allowed to list in the Yellow Pages in the same category as abortion mills. Let me restate that. In addition to telling public schools who can and can't speak in them, the anti-baby power cartel in San Francisco was now turning its attention to the private sector, the Yellow Pages, and telling them what to do, also. "Well, you don't do abortions, do you?" goes the logic of spoonful-of-water baby killers.

No, thank God, but we do help women to resolve unwanted pregnancies, exactly what the abortion people claim to do. And if you want to get technical about it, baby killers don't even provide abortions, which are, strictly speaking, spontaneous biological events, not induced ones. It's wrong for them to advertise even that. But who cares about the truth? And even with a popular misunderstanding of the word, it's not as if the abortionists are hanging out a shingle that says literally "Child Murder For Hire," are they? No, they sell resolution of pregnancy. So do we. Ours is free, too. Actually, abortion never resolves a single pregnancy. The mother-child bond is there, like it or not, from the beginning; the rupture of it, without childbirth, is a permanent scar. Ask any mom who's had an abortion. Ask her, don't take my word for it.

The upshot of the lawsuit for CPCs nationwide was the Yellow Pages ruling which was a devastating totalitarian power play. We were cutting into their revenue by intercepting their "market" before it got to them. We were also stepping on the toes of bully pimps, too, the paid kind and the nightclub kind. At one point the lawyers advised me that my record of a handful of rescues was harming the center in the courtroom. It helped the bad guys to paint a picture of all the CPC workers as "criminals'" or associates of "criminals." The lawyers wanted to be able to tell the judge that "criminals" were no longer associated with the CPC. As grieving as it is, there is actually a logic to this, when the goal is to keep the doors of the place open, and by that time, I was one among many. Something can be said for the idea that if you start out as chief cook and bottle washer, there's a point where someone says, I got the chief cook part, you can relax. There are a thousand ways to stop child killing. This could be a good time to move on to some of the other ones. Thanks, Ailie Marie Victoire and your ex parte girlfriends! You launched my career into other things. Al of of these things pushed me East: the news about East coast rescue and Joan Andrews' in-custody protest, the legal team nudging me away from the CPC work, the other lawyers in town refusing to help after the Juvie incident; phone calls to the East coast rescuers; the increasing difficulty in finding prolifers who would rescue; the bogging down effect of the lawsuit. It all seemed to push me in the direction of going East. San Francisco and Wycliffe Bible Translators will always be wonderful growing experiences, but the main energy of the new rescue movement seemed to be out East.

RALPH M. GABRIEL

CHAPTER 5

THE LIFE AND DEATH OF RESCUE

In 1986 I drove from Marina County to New York City. If you turn the radio off even some of the time, driving across this absolutely wonderful country, you will have an amazing quiet time -- sand dunes, coral bluffs, big red moons, flat desert waste, West Texas, prairie, small towns, small forest glens embedded in dry land, and then farms and then rivers and then forests and then cat-cracking plants and cities and places with the older more crowded feel of immigrant waves. All of these will unfold. It's all a backdrop to a reverse-hegira of how my Irish and Cherokee great grandmothers and great grandfathers had been driven out west, along with the famine, and other waves that followed. But for the most part, the wide spaces are quiet time, especially if you turn the radio off all the time and wait for the subtle buzz of quiet, quiet, very quiet, to start. It all becomes one massive quiet time and in '86 I think it was a time of trying to leave behind the West Coast expectations for how to deal with massive child massacre, and opening up the mind and heart to the East Coast way. In the east, the other way took the form of numbers, numbers of rescuers undreamt of out in the liberal let's-go-surfing West.

The first East Coast rescue I went to was in Chamblee, Georgia. The afternoon before the rescue I attended a rescue conference. There were rescuers from all over the country, with even a smattering of other West Coasters. Could it possibly be that I had finally stumbled into the endeavor my dad had prophesied for me my entire life: "I hope someday you'll know what it's like to be a very small part of something very very big." I now am convinced that he was talking about his involvement in the Pacific campaign against Hirohito, and more specifically, the rape of Nanjing in 1936, five long years before U.S. involvement in the war. In Nanjing, the Japanese murdered, slaughtered, raped, and cut to pieces with swords and Mitsubishi plane strafing a million women and children and old men. When the people tried to run out of the city, a city the size of Los Angeles at the time, the Japanese strafed the people who were fleeing. This all happened when China had no navy, army or air force. This chapter of history is much better known on the West Coast.

For my dad, it meant he was taken from his Echo Park ghetto where he was something of a big fish in a little pond, to being part of a team where each man knew without any question that he was part of something bigger than himself, and that he was doing something so big, fighting an evil so immense, that it was utterly impossible for him to fight it alone. This is an alien concept in our current atomistic, individualistic and narcissistic world of today. In the South Pacific a marine couldn't even preserve so much as his own life or his own strength, let alone achieve the goal of driving back the tyrants who'd steamrolled over the helpless Chinese people.

All of this I had heard about at my father's knee, especially on Saturday nights, late, when most of the guests had gone home from the pool parties we had in summer in South Pasadena. The partiers would dwindle to a few old-before-their-time South Pacific vets who surrounded my father, in a circle there by the fire, drank, and cried over strange-sounding names like Peleliu, Tarawa, Saipan, Tinian, Iwo and the Rykus. They cried over the winddrifts of bodies on the beaches, bodies of 17, 18 and 19-year-old boys who were scythed down by machine guns on the cliffs.

Sitting in the parish hall that day in '86 in Chamblee Georgia, the sun shining through the windows, one speaker after another going to the podium, a couple hundred people in attendance, I began to get a sense of something bigger than myself, like Dad was always talking about.

At last. Think of it: a rescue with fifty people in it, some of whom had been arrested dozens of times already. By contrast, in the San Francisco Bay area I had become the old man of rescue when I had only just started myself, and where I was lucky to find one or two others to padlock myself to in liberal Northern California. One rescuer, it was either John Cavanaugh-O'keefe, a Vietnam war conscientious objector and a brother of a man who'd died in Vietnam, or John Ryan from St. Louis, had put two clipboards at the side of the hall. One said at the top I will commit to rescue if a hundred people sign this list and also commit. In other words, you didn't have to commit to a rescue of fewer than a hundred people. The more people the less punishment went the logic. The other clipboard, with many hopeful numbered blank spaces and pages attached, said the same thing but required a thousand people signing up. A hundred people! A thousand people? What was this all about?

The Protestants shouted praise the lord! and hallelujah! and the Catholics talked about protests against the Vietnam war, and rosary crusades and the Polish solitariness theory. It was a heady atmosphere. In the space of a few minutes any doubts I had had about leaving the state of my birth and childhood had flown away. I had finally found my lost battalion of South Pacific vets. Now all I needed was a division. The Chamblee police station never know what hit them. They let us go by two p.m. the same day we rescued. Why? At noon they wiped out their entire annual budget for feeding prisoners simply by going across the street to buy "burgers and coffee for sixty." And they seriously dinged the paper clip budget, too, to boot. And once we told them we'd love to come back and do it all over again when they brought us to trial, they said, thanks, but no thanks. They dropped all the charges on the spot.

Someone out east had done her homework and prayed about this exact scenario: a half-decent number of rescuers and a small town, what would they do? How would they cope? This was early days in the movement, the movement of trying for ever larger rescues. We responded to cracks by the Chamblee police about "carpetbaggers" with our own comments: "Stop killing babies in Chamblee and we'll leave you alone!" "You should know better anyway!" "Does your mother know you are arresting grandmothers?" Stuff like that. It was early days in terms of how the police felt. They were still capable of embarrassment. A comeback like ours was received with blushes, embarrassed and awkward silence, or even a quiet acknowledgement. This was the Bible Belt. These are responses police normally just don't do.

That all changed later, but back then it was so. Even as late as 1986 there was still a moral sense among most police, and also in the big Catholic towns farther north like New York, Boston, Philly and Chicago, which still showed the effect of the Great Irish Famine immigrants within their ranks. That is all gone now, along with discussions we used to have with the police about the Philly P.O. conscience clause for cops. But back then, cops still had a conscience. They hated abortion as much as we did. Why? because of their job, cops just know murder when they see it. They know. One cop simply handed his gun and badge to his boss and walked over and sat down with us one day, ending his career as a cop. Chet Gallagher will always go down in history as proof that there was at least one cop left in America who knew murder when he saw it, and would not play along with it, and acted to stop it. He had more to lose than any of us, so it was a double heroism.

Fresh from the victory in Chamblee, the same crowd rolled south and did another rescue in Pensacola, Florida, in solidarity with Joan Andrews, the Tennessee farm girl who was protesting in custody and whom I had read about in California. When a dozen of us got clinked, all the rest, friends and family maybe a hundred, came to protest at the local jail. I remember the cops put snipers on the roof. What, like we were going to storm the jail? I wonder if they ever pulled those snipers out for Dr. King, God bless him.

On the Pensacola charges I did wind up going to trial a couple of months later. The potential jurors cried and whined to the judge that it would be impossible for fine Christian ladies of the south such as themselves to be impartial in such a weighty matter as abortion, which was strictly forbidden by their nice churches. After excusing a couple dozen of them, the judge saw the writing on the wall. He started to persuade and plead with them. He was a fine Christian gentleman himself, after all. Are you ladies absolutely certain you couldn't even try to be impartial? Even granting your fine Christian upbringing? They preened their feathers just a bit and coyly demurred that, perhaps they could try, since the judge, being such a fine Christian gentleman himself, put it so nicely. Once in chambers, however, the jury convicted me faster than it takes to mix milk and sugar into coffee. Filing back into the box not one of them would look into the eyes of the Yankee interloper with his strange notion of rescuing babies, and I knew then what it's like for a clam to be eaten by a walrus that can't stop crying. Or eating, too, come to think of it.

The South! You have let us all down! We expect the North to be corrupt with all their factory money, and Wall Street money, their citified ways, and even, according to you, hanging out with those nasty popish antichrist types. But you were supposed to be the Bible Belt! You have the slower lifestyle, and nature and the country and farms to reinforce the natural truth to you, and God's truth. You were the ones who preach over and over, there are 800 men who have not bent the knee to Baal. You preach it practically every Sunday. Well, where are they? Wake up, South! I'll make you a deal. It's late in the day. I'd settle for eighty. How about eight? Send 'em, or shut up. Your Bible reading is doing you no good. I got a fine in Pensacola. I told the judge I wouldn't pay. He said, "Well, do your best." I never paid and Florida never came to pick me up.

After the Pensacola trial I hung out again up north in New York. The East Coast has a completely different feel to it, everywhere, in and out of jail, the people, all of it. Before 1986 I and my family were no strangers to travel but this was the first time I'd lived day after day in the East, and the strangeness of it every day was a reminder that I was there for work, not for fun. I bet you could say the same for the East Coasters themselves, who had by definition resisted the siren song of California, Phoenix, Vegas, Texas and Florida and the rest of the Sun Belt. I had grown up surfing on the beaches of Southern California, the most beautiful beaches in the world. Nearby were high deserts and higher snowy mountains, skiing, piney forests and lakes, and Bluewater fishing. In the California Central Valley we grow every kind of crop in the world from dates to rice, and fruits and vegetables. The East Coast hit me as muggy in summer, by contrast, freezing in winter, and very cramped and dirty and tired and bitter. It was only years later that I discovered that one of the places I lived in in New York at first was a notorious slum called "Alphabet City," in the Lower East Side of Manhattan. It's called Alphabet City because it's in a bulge in Manhattan that sticks out into the East River. Since it bulges east of First Avenue, and there are no numbers below "First," they called the streets A, B and C and so forth.

Every night for centuries, the residents of Alphabet City would make their way north at dusk to the unendingly dumb suburbanites who would dress up and come to "diamond alley" for the Broadway shows, always wearing their finest jewelry and Rolexes in plain view. After relieving the sheep of their cash and other luxuries, my fellow Alphabet City citizens would retire to their slum to put the needle in, burn the rock and blow the pipe. It seems that Republicans never learn, whether they're catching a show on Broadway or sending a congressman to DC. Either way, they get fleeced. I could feel all of this, around me. It was a jolt, a second jolt, after leaving sunny green and blue California, and also, the wonderful recent successes down south. The East Coast was old and cold and settled in its ways.

Ah, but California, California…

Almost any cop in California would joke or sympathize with you, a little, as they were loading you into the cruiser. But the East Coast was a much bigger problem. It was all the more entrenched by virtue of the fact that most of the rescuers in those first southern rescuers came from huge "Catholic" towns up north: New York, Boston, Philly, Chicago.

I was happy to meet my new Catholic brothers and sisters, and my Evangelical and Pentecostal brother and sister rescuers too, but it was a bittersweet feeling when I discovered how thoroughly rotten stubborn and close-minded their cities were. Cities don't like babies, the country does.

Shortly after I came north and had hung out for a month or two in Alphabet City and at Co-Op City in the Bronx, I received an urgent request for help to go west again, but this time, not as far as California. St. Louis is a perfect example of a town not quite as bitter as the East Coast cities, but stubborn enough in the end to resist rescue and keep killing. Back then we actually believed that the rescue movement could grow quickly, like the street part of Dr King's movement or the anti-Vietnam War movement, and that we could, grace of God, garner success against abortion in perhaps a handful of years, just like those movements had done. The flavor of each town was different and interesting, but we were still surprised to discover the actual extent to which every region of the U.S. would, in the need, abandon its own particular faith and cultural traditions. No, thank you very much, but we must continue killing children.

The flavor of a happy mix of papists and fundie prots in St. Louis was different from the East Coast towns. St. Louis was imbued with more of a farming and settlers feel. But they caved in, too, just the same. It's a shame because the prophetic witness in the case of St. Louis was enormous. Most of it came from one man, John Ryan, and the judge who made him. No one can have his own judge, of course. Well, unless you happen to have a million dollars cash in your pocket. John Ryan did not own that St. Louis judge because God provided him and God doesn't charge. His help is for free. John Ryan was arrested, almost always alone, no less than four hundred times between the late 70's and 1986. If you do a little higher math that means he was arrested every weekend for eight years. During much of that time he had a house, a job, and a family. How could this be? Especially since any small time crook in America can tell you that long before there was ever a "Three Strikes" law in any federal or state law, there was a similar application of "bench law" with misdemeanors, in every court of the land. Once or twice, sure, you can go, but each time the judge would warn you: on the third offense, he would give you the statutory max, usually six months but it could be a year. I can't remember a judge not telling me this in all of the 150 or so times I've been arrested for rescues. But here John Ryan was getting off, effectively, over and over. Apparently, that judge had made it clear that he would be happy to see all the Ryan dockets himself, no assistance needed from the rest of the bench. That in itself was another miracle. Docketing a case to a particular judge is tricky stuff, it involves politics.

When I arrived in St. Louis in '86 in response to the emergency call for help, I was told that for the first time in eight years, John had finally gotten some county jail time.

For John, it meant jail had finally affected his employment situation and he'd lost his day job. John had decided to accept help from some of county jail supporters in St. Louis and elsewhere who had always said they would like to help. This intrigued me. Here was someone trying to mix family and rescue. Was this possible? If it could work for John, maybe it could for me, too? In my case I had assumed that the incredibly durable push in my life to keep rescuing no matter what would get me a big patch of jail time sooner or later and that this was no good for a family. I hoped John would prove me wrong. St. Louis was probably the best rescue town I'd ever seen. We'd rescue the whole weekend and I don't recall ever doing a stretch in jail. We always seemed to get out by dinnertime. Once on the way to a rescue, though, I was talking to one of my fellow rescuers about it all. I was getting tired of being arrested. "Why do we do rescues?" I asked, "It doesn't seem to be getting anywhere." "It doesn't matter if it catches or not, Jim," he said, "We still need to do it. It's a witness. Plus, if we don't at least try, we'll never know if it would've worked." "But it isn't working. Most people don't care." "We save babies, too, though. On a given day, I mean." My fellow rescuer was a Marine. Can you tell? "And on some days we don't." I said, "Everyone just goes on in." "It's still important to try. It's a witness and an offer of help to these moms." "But what if they don't listen?" "We still need to do it." "Why?" "If we don't, it could be said that God himself doesn't care. And we know he does. It's about God, too. Atheists are saying all the time, how could a loving God allow this or that evil? Well, if we all did our part, it wouldn't happen. Just like with the Jews and the Poles and Germany. Evil must be resisted. I'd heard these words before, but for some reason, they sunk down deep when I heard them this time.

I was asked to be the interim head of the St. Louis organization John had built up, but it was a short tenure, maybe six months. After jail John was unable to keep the job due to a personal problem, and this also affected me deeply. It was the first of many times that I had seen at close quarters the effect of what I would call a spiritual attack against anyone who tries to actually stop abortion, instead of just talk about it. The problem is that if you turn down the volume on the TV, so to speak, the actions of prolifers start to look awfully similar to the actions of the abortionists. If you look at actions alone, I mean, instead of words. Prolifers are voting for death with their feet in a way they would not if it were their own children dying, right now. I know this is a bitter pill for the "let's talk" majority of prolifers and I grieve for their grieving. But the Children of Israel, by contrast, learned to "swallow their tears in haste" and then do what The Boss says, skedaddle the heck out of Egypt toute suite.

The next year or so, parts of '86, '87 and '88 was a gemish of running from one rescue to another and being a perennial houseguest in a lot of places where I was welcomed by heroic hosts. I had yet to learn the trick of finding enough part time work in between rescues and there were some patches of rescue so intense I couldn't even have done that. At different points I stayed in Alphabet City on the Lower East Side of Manhattan, or Newark Delaware, or in the Bronx. Sometimes I'd wind up at the house of what I called a LIPV2R: A Long Island Pre-Vatican Two Rescuer. Some of them invited me in after they gave me a ride home from jail or a court appearance. LIPV2R were the true Gray Panthers of rescue. It's so sad that most of them are gone now. I miss them a lot. We tended to get out of jail pretty soon back then, if the number of rescuers was over twenty or so, if for no other reason than that the jurisdictions didn't want to mess up their jails by trying to put us into the general population.

One way around this I recall was Cherry Hill which was yet another attempt at getting "numbers." We had about a hundred and fifty there, a lot of men and women together and even some pastors and priests. Cherry Hill, New Jersey, in the middle of the state, and across from Philly, dealt with the whole mess by putting us all together in the gym. They gave each of us a "boat," a funny plastic thing a little bit like a toboggan with sides that we'd sleep in and fed us cafeteria style from a chow line. If I had to guess, the reason they did this was to diminish some of the problems they might have had by simply putting all us suburbanites in with what's called the "general population" of the jail -- honest criminals, bless their hearts. Also, isolating us neophytes didn't help the rest of the jail when we clogged up the gym. Inmates need rec., I can assure you.

I suppose some conflicted law-and-order type in the county government had insisted on giving us at least some jail time up front to discourage future rescues in that town, but this isn't always a smart thing. True, it put enormous pressure on the rescuers who had a nine-to-five job and a house and kids and bills to pay, for sure. And, sure enough, Cherry Hill was the start of a sub-movement among those family men to try to shift into freelance or general contractor or farming jobs so they'd have more independence, or at least could miss some work and still have it. It was a huge shift for them, riskier, and heroic, but many men did this. That fact and the married women rescuers, who often incurred criticism from their more lukewarm spouses, were among the many efforts made by early rescuers to try to really make a go of it; to turn rescue from being a one-time lark like scooping soup out in an inner city mission on Christmas Eve, into a growing movement that would win for all babies and moms, not just some. At the time, there was a lot of talk about stopping abortion within one or two years, about a big push and then going back home.

All of these concerns came into play on the personal level of all the rescuers to be sure, but absolutely no one did so much for the movement as whatever county bureaucrat it was in Camden who said "Lock 'em up! They broke the law!" Why? We had a ball in that jail. Cherry Hill was the first time I ever remember a large group of rescuers all in one room together, for several days. We ate and slept and sung and prayed and worshipped together, all in one room. It was the intense fellowship of finally being in a crowd of like-minded prolifers for the first time in our lives.

Everyone in the room was committed. Unlike the times when we had found ourselves arguing with friends and family and even fellow church members, here, at last, was a meeting of the minds and hearts. There was also the added effect of no work or home responsibilities. It was one big treehouse lark, a sleepover for adults who had passed their treehouse/sleepover days decades before. The fundie evans pounded their Bibles and got red in the face about Calvinism or whatever, but they still smiled. The LIPV2R quietly sought each other out and said their rosaries. But after a couple of days both groups discovered much to their delight that the other side didn't bite. We had more in common than in disagreement.

I have always carried the personal belief that abortion will never stop, at least in the U.S. and the rest of the English-speaking world, until Christians find a way to at least work together, if not pray together. Cherry Hill was the first time I saw that start to happen. Dr. Schaeffer had made the suggestion back in 78 in Switzerland: "If the sewer is broken on my street, I can join forces with a Hindu or a Buddhist neighbor of mine to get it fixed without jeopardizing my own faith. "Broken sewer" meant abortion, and "Hindu and Buddhist" were code words for Catholics. There, in Cherry Hill in 1986 I started to see this for-the-task ecumenism play out in front of my eyes. It was especially wonderful to me, since I have always grieved over this split. Protestants and Catholics are both members of my spiritual family and background, and even of my heritage. This was still years before Randy Terry and Atlanta and New York, but Cherry Hill was the first national convention of rescuers, all on the taxpayers' nickel. Thanks to that one law-and-order nameless bureaucrat in Camden New Jersey in 1986. God bless him! Gotta love those Republicans.

Randy Terry hired me to work for Operation Rescue in Atlanta in the Summer of 1988. You've probably only heard bad things about Randall. He's an ex-used car salesman, for example, with no mention of his theological training. You hear all this if you only listen to the lamestream media and you believe them too. Bet you also believe everything you've been told about the Spanish Inquisition. I bless, bless, bless the day I first ever hear the name Randy Terry. I bless the day his dear and gentle parents gave birth to him, Bozo hair, caffeinated central nervous system, Toscanini channeling and Ernest Goes to Jail, included. All that, and he loves everyone and everyone loves him.

Any prolifer in the world feels the same, who met him. We learned to discount mainstream media/Saul Alinsky/Chicago Community Organizer playbook horse manure long ago. Randy had to be attacked by the other side and mischaracterized, from the very get-go, because he was hot as a pistol in front of a camera and was the first national prolife leader I ever met who was completely heartbroken over child dismemberment, and would get right up in your face and tell you so. He is completely sincere, and he holds nothing back, and still loves you. It was all the more amazing and blessed because many old rescuers get tired of the ignorance and stubbornness, and they lose patience in the public debate. Not so, with Randy. He always had that kindness for anyone he talked to, always there like a roaring flame and easy to see.

For this reason, NOW and FWHO and NARAL and all the other paid-to-be-there murderers had to focus on stopping him. He was that good. Before Randy, and before rescue, we were the ones who would try to contact the media. We would issue press releases and newsletters which the mainstream media routinely ignored.

Randy changed all that. In New York City once he simply said, "Pencil press, over here!" and he pointed to a thin spot in the wall of people, and they came running. He never had faux pas or "brain farts" on camera, and he always had a twinkling sense of humor where appropriate, and the press could sense that he was completely sincere. They loved him at first, before they realized how dangerous he was to them, and they flocked to him. He loved Jesus, too, and never ran ahead of Him. It was obvious. If I had to guess, the most critical task of the murderers-for-hire money crowd of that era was to stop him or demonize him or try very hard to make him look dumb. They never succeeded with us little people who pay the taxes. But they hated Randy the way the Pharisees hated Jesus The Rebel. All of us rescuers, tired of being beaten down and sued and attacked and over indicted and hassled and threatened by the cops, even on free speech stuff like simple signs knew Randy was a huge breath of fresh air just when we needed it.

I think it was the winter of '86/'87 when I first wound up in Binghamton, Terry's hometown. At first it wasn't much more than a place to stay between rescues, something we jailbirds really appreciated. We'd had so many arrests and jail stints by then, a regular job was nigh impossible. First, I stayed with an acquaintance of Randy's. In the winter, up there, people cast about for something to do at night. Randy's friend had a strange videotape that in some ways changed my life.

Jim Varney is the man who made half dozen movies with a big dopey guy in it named Ernest. Ernest Goes To Jail, Ernest Goes to Camp, Scared Stupid, and Ernest Saves Christmas are all familiar to anyone who raised kids in the 80's. But the even funnier and stranger video was the one that was a splicing together of all the commercials Jim Varney had ever made in the years before he was able to make his own films. That winter we watched it over and over. It's the funniest stuff I've ever seen, and no one knows about it. The desperate broken battlefield scramble of life and death to try to save a child and mom and then get up and do it again tomorrow, has a sadness all its own, no less for all that, in that it is a struggle against essential evil, in addition to the knocks and jail. But I still laugh when I run into anyone who's seen the Varney commercials tape. All of this gets us moving in the direction of the spring of '88 when the huge rescues started, when the dream back in Chamblee Georgia in '86 of a thousand man rescue finally came true. It was dreamed of even before that, chiefly in New York and St. Louis, but Chamblee was an important stop on the way.

In my own case however there was one more curious stop before New York City, 1988, and the large Operation Rescues there. In case you're not sufficiently confused already by all this to-ing and fro-ing, it also took place in New York City, just not in Manhattan. My detour was to the Bronx. hmmm. The story of the Bronx you could say is part of a spiritual sojourn and should be in that chapter, but i'll tell it now since everything after 1985 in my life all runs together. Just because I had decided that prolife would be my entire future doesn't mean God says it that way, right? We plan and God laughs, as they say in Regio Calabria. But the trip to the Bronx was a continuation of the exact same process of discernment that was in play earlier, in '84, when I went overseas with Wycliffe even though I already had such a strong calling to prolife.

It was in about '86 or so, to back up a little, when I first showed up in the Bronx. It turned out that in the middle 80's Mother Teresa and John Paul II had formed up a new order, an order of priests who would live the missionaries of charity "charism," or spiritual lifestyle. The lifestyle was physically rigorous, also, because Mother Teresa had decided, along with her sisters, to go back to the joyful, but extreme poverty of St. Francis. John Paul II and Mother had come to the conclusions that when it came to sacraments, confessions and spiritual direction of the sisters, it would be good if the priests were living the same rigorous lifestyle as the sisters. Otherwise, a visiting priest at confession might not be inclined to take the rule of the sisters too seriously. A story about the San Francisco foundation of the Missionary of Charity (mc) Sisters is revealing about all this.

In the early 80's before the mc sisters and Mother came to San Francisco, there was great excitement among the lay people there. They loved Mother, loved her sisters, and loved her mission to the poorest of the poor. Like big-city Christians all over the world, they had begged Mother and the pope to start a cell of sisters in their own town. Mother was always slow to do this, not for lack of charity or will, but because mother was always very picky about who would become a sister. Even in Goa, India, a town which has been Christian for twenty centuries straight, there are only so many big smiles from the heart and available to be nuns. Mother got most of her first sisters from Goa.

When the news finally came that there were enough professed sisters to open the San Francisco cell, there was great excitement among the lay people who had invited them there. These lay people got together and arranged for an old convent in the mission district for the nuns to live in, cleaned it up, and spent their own money for new carpentry, plumbing, electric fans and potted plants to spruce the place up a little bit, a kind of home-warming thing. The sisters flew in, mother came, everything was smiles all day. The next morning the laypeople went down to the convent to see if the sisters needed anything in their new home. They were shocked to see the new carpet, the plants and the fans all dumped in the dumpster behind the convent. We all remember the smiling Mother Teresa and many of us are familiar with the cheerful tireless sacrifice of the sisters. What we might not know is that the sweetness doesn't come from sensitivity training sessions. It comes from hours of silence in front of the blessed sacrament, and from an austere lifestyle of no distractions from contemplation, and also, long hours sweating away trying to help out the poorest of the poor.

Doing construction and repair work, I've seen the inside of a convent or two, and I still remember how my heart fell when I saw one with a roomful of Barcalounger recliners in front of a TV. The mc's don't have TVs, or recliners. They don't even have chairs with backs on them except maybe for visitors. You sit on a stool to eat, or you sit on concrete. A shower is water from a bucket splashed over your head. The happiness we all feel from the sisters does not come from clown seminars and self-help motivational seminars. It comes from a hard life. This is a paradox all happy and broke farmers or cheaper-by-the-dozen parents are well familiar with. In fact, when I was in MC seminary, I recall an explanation from one of the priests for all the fasting and early wakeups and long hours. "Think of all the mothers who get up at two a.m. to nurse their babies. Think of all the farmers who get up at four a.m. to milk their cows. If we did not have a life like this, a monastery could just become a carefree bachelor life, and escape from real life, on someone else's nickel. The calling of holy monks and nuns and priests is to pray and work for the same spiritual and charitable goals Jesus worked for, including reaching out to the poorest of the poor, or the fasting and prayer required to expel demons (which is so obviously lacking nowadays). All of us should at least try this in some way, no matter how small.

Back in '86 one of the Goa Kerala sisters in San Francisco asked me if I wanted to be in the new MC order of priests. Watch out single men! They smile and will crack you up, but all these sisters had been put on alert by Mother to keep an eye out for stray sheep on the edge of the flock that could be picked off! I never saw it coming.

Some friends at the time said the only reason I went to the MC seminary in the Bronx was because I was a new convert, and they tend to try to go into religious life or the priesthood out of zeal for their new-found faith. Cradle Catholics got over that long ago, or got a vocation long ago, goes the theory. The simple answer is that I found it very hard to say no to Mother and her Kerala gal-pals. They were the ones who roped me into helping remodel the messy home for single moms' property in the mission district in San Francisco, after all. Also, I knew I wasn't the only one who had a hard time refusing Mother. Besides, once the idea was floated, I thought maybe it was God's way of either moving me in another direction, if he wanted, or re-verifying the prolife calling. Either way, you never know till you try.

So, in '86 I went to an old convent near Jerome and 279th in the South Bronx that had been given over to the MC fathers by Cardinal O'Connor, a helluva guy and a great prolifer. I first went for what the mc's call a "come-and-see," a ten-day visit. I was very surprised to find out that the father superior of this new order, the order which was the great hope of Mother Teresa and John Paul II, was none other than a fellow Californian surfer from San Diego, barely a hundred miles from where I grew up surfing on Huntington and Manhattan (California) beaches. Surprise

-- Fr. Joseph was the first non-east Indian, non-European I'd ever seen in the mc's. There were three dozen or so guys there at the start, a half dozen of them priests already and in the process of switching orders, and another half dozen seminarians. The rest were young, and the greatest diversity of people I've ever seen in one place, in one effort. Mother Theresa's little munchkins had been busy all over the world looking for priest candidates, and now here they were, collecting in the Bronx. Fr. Joseph, the surfer dude, cajoled me into singing Randy Newman's "political science" with the guitar for everyone at dinner. That was quite a feat, considering I had no idea what the chords were -- I still don't -- and I can't remember lyrics to save my life. I also have no clue why I introduced the song by saying very somberly that "Mother shared with me a little bit about her vision of how all of us can live together in the world in peace and harmony, and now i'd like to share that vision with you." I mean, here was a roomful of idealistic young men from South America, the Caribbean, Asia, Central Europe and Africa, and all over. Fr. Joseph and I had a hard time keeping straight faces as the song progressed. The guys were expecting something you'd hear at World Youth Day, but here's what they got: boom, goes London,/boom, Paris,/more room for you and more room for me,/south America stole our name,/let's drop the big one,/there'll be no one left to blame us. . .

It was a California thing, the sense of humor, I suppose. Not the dreary pious type, Our Father Joseph. The ten days of silence before the blessed sacrament and scooping out soup in the Harlem 125th St. MC soup kitchen zoomed by, but at the end of it I was pulled aside by one of the priests. "You have no vocation here," he said, "you don't need to worry about coming back. "Well, I'm just a grunt. I know how to take orders. I thanked them all and said goodbye and took the A train back down to Alphabet City. Two years later after a ton of bicoastal rescues, I happened to be visiting the Max Kolbe shrine in Libertyville near Chicago. I don't remember why. Some kind of Franciscan t.o.r. conference, maybe. While I was there a priest overheard someone talking to me. "Are you Jim Kopp?" he asked, "I have a message for you from Mother." It turned out that Mother had heard about some seminary candidate turnaways. She had appointed the priest who was there talking to me in Chicago to run around the world to find every guy who'd been bounced out of the Bronx and invite him to come back again. Hmm. Here it was, 1988, two years after, and I was way deeper into rescues. We had done big crowd rescues in Chamblee, St. Louis, Boston, Cherry Hill, Dobbs Ferry, New York City, and some more in northern California. My spirit was once again totally back into prolife, just as it had been when I'd gone from Wycliffe in Africa to Rome in '84. The problem is that it was real hard to say no to Mother. We all have the image on the TV of her smiling and talking as she scurried from the airport to the local MC foundation, or to conspire with the OCD's, but she had a way about her when it came to the order. She had a strong notion of how it should go. She never bossed anyone around but you'd know what she wanted and it's hard to say no to someone who has a clue, especially in such a clueless world. Also, aside from Mother, there was the simple idea: how do you know the Lord himself doesn't want you to shift gears in this or that situation? It is good to be single minded in any pursuit, especially in a world of tmi, too much information, so many distractions and possibilities. I can't help but wonder if life in a medieval village wasn't better, if not also simpler. In any event, I guess I believe part of walking with God is to try to be open to anything he wants, even if you're already all caught up in one ministry, such as prolife. When I finally made it back to the Bronx there was a loud standing ovation as I walked into the dining room at the first common meal. It turned out mother had made a little prediction about the number of guys who would show up for seminary at that current moment of recruitment. She had asked the lord for fifteen, one for each mystery of the rosary. She didn't usually talk about stuff like that, but I guess in this case she had told Fr. Joseph. Before I arrived there had been a sense of doom rolling around the place because guys had been assembling for weeks from all over the world and the number just wasn't quite right. It turned out I was number fifteen!

It was a shock to me, anyway, to be welcomed anywhere, being an underemployed phone repairman/carpenter/jailbird. Well, I wasn't late for dinner, anyway. The minute I sat down Fr. Joe popped up and got a guitar. "You're late, and you gotta sing for your supper, surfer boy!" Well, you know, a failed vocation. What can I say? There's a little sadness to it, akin, I suppose, to that of a failed courtship, since both are sacraments. Everyone loves to see a happy wedding or a happy ordination. They are happy events that are little bulwarks against sadness and evil, all the more now that the world is so in love with evil and selfishness and everyone doing what he thinks is right in his own eyes, and the rejection of any permanent commitment at all.

Part of it is you sure don't want to be in a serious vocation like either of those if it isn't right, and yet there is always the USMC or counter-cultural notion part that things get right by holy compromise, and more, holy sacrifice. It is that to live in a world where these things are is so rare as to be nonexistent. Everyone has to have it his own way or forget it. Teamwork, to achieve the good goals that only teams can do; the body politic; the social contract; a really priestly vocation; a real family, a real village, nation or tribe, a clan…call it what you will, they are all gone, lost in a world of smart phone boopings and beepings and everyone staring at a square inch of isinglass to find out what somebody did since five minutes ago. For this reason, the marine in me gave the MC's a real good college second try, especially since this second time around Mother had intervened to get the vocation back on track. Still, the news in the Bronx was a shocker: "You have to give up prolife work, as you know it," Fr. Joe told me one day not long after I got there. Of course Mother and the order were prolife, but the charism of the order did not include "political activity," which was how rescue was viewed.

This made me recall the time Mother had told a rescuer she might show up at a recue in New York, but it didn't turn out that way. There had been much excitement. I recall an extensive debrief on the subject with Jack, an intense East Coast rescuer of the finial school who had introduced me to Irish fight songs like "come on out ye black and tans." Back then, after much to and fro, we'd reluctantly concluded that the reason Mother hadn't come to the rescue was due to our country's definition of abortion as politics, which is nonsense. Define rescue as politics, goes the anti-logic, and then presto-chango, hocus-pocus, you silly Catholics can't do it, right? Because of the separation of church and state, another smokescreen. When in reality, saving a child is no more political than dialing 911 when you hear glass shattering at three am. In the suburbs, anyway.

Anyway, back in the Bronx, in the order, I had a heavy heart as I was instructed to give up my notion of rescue. So was a heartbreaker to finally leave the MC's for the second and last time. From time to time I recall wistfully the advice of a visiting monk at the time. "Give it a year," he'd said, there, in the Bronx. "to be sure. Then, go, if you must." Just about this time a funny thing happened. A quiet storm behind the scenes broke out into the open after I'd been there a couple of months. It came in the form of a phone call. Those of us who are not monks must understand that in a convent or a monastery in the old school there's no such thing as a phone call. In the monastery you are supposed to be given the space to carry out prayer, untroubled by events outside. Fr. Joseph would make rare exceptions at his discretion, such as one last call to the girlfriend back home when it became apparent that a young man had clearly decided for the order. In my case, when 1 was summoned with much suppressed excitement to the phone in the kitchen used for this purpose, it wasn't an old girlfriend.

When I picked up the phone -- such a strange thing to do -- the voice at the other end said: "This is Monsignor Woolsey." Oh criminy! Msgr. Woolsey did not need to introduce himself to me! He was not only the respect life commission chaplain for the entire archdiocese of New York, but he also, it turned out, was the vocations director up at St. John's College in Yonkers, the archdiocesan seminary. These two responsibilities alone could make him almost numero dos or tres in a shop run by the likes of Cardinal O'Connor who had actually visited rescuers in the clink and publicly permitted Bishop Austin Vaughn to rescue. What a guy! It turned out that Woolsey had been pestered to death by Randy over several days or weeks. There was a big rescue coming up and Randy wanted me to come out to play! It might embarrass him just a microscopic smidge to think about it now, now that he's a Catholic too, but back then he was a Pentecostal preacher. I doubt he realized quite what was involved in interrupting a discernment process of a vocation, and with such an incompatible demand as that. Like all good prolifers however, Randy doesn't get embarrassed too easily. Still, it wasn't as if he was inviting me to some ecumenical prayer meeting when he told Woolsey he wanted me to come to the NYC rescues. People who are unfamiliar with the cheerful badgering capability of Randy, such as Msgr. Woolsey, often don't know what hit them. It's like Return of the Jedi stormtroopers doing exactly what Obi Wan Kenobi tells 'em to do. They just do it. This is not the droid we seek. Move along. On the phone, though, Monsignor started to come to his senses. "I'm not exactly sure why I'm calling you." He told me about Randy and the upcoming rescues in New York that spring. I'd heard about them already, of course. The old Chamblee diehard crowd with the clipboards, remember them? They had finally fixed a date for what we all hoped would be the first thousand-man rescue in history.

On the other hand, Monsignor made it clear that he was also a vocations director, and far be it from him to do anything to dissuade anyone from a calling. After talking a while, Monsignor came to the point of simply admitting that he had only called because Randy had pestered him to death, but that I should not let outside influences interfere with such an important decision, and Operation Rescue would be fine without me if 1 wanted to stay in seminary. He needn't have worried, really and I felt sorry for his predicament and grateful for his honesty and the trouble he went to. The decision to leave when I did wasn't hastened by the spring rescue. It grew organically out of many years of quiet times and discernment, when you hope and pray you are walking with the Lord.

While I was still in the order, I met Fr. Norman Weslin. At that point in his life, he had just been ordained, in his early 60's. Fr. Norm was an extremely colorful and interesting character about whom much has been written, but back then he was interested in joining the MC's. Once we discovered we were similar prolifers, we'd gossip about rescue and all the risks, talking under the stairs between "bells" for prayer times, there, in the Bronx. Little did Mother know that two chicks were about the fly the coop! When I did leave the MC's that spring for the second and last time, it was with a very heavy heart. I hated to go, but I knew deep down it was fish-or-cut-bait time with prolife. You could always say I could have known before I went back to the Bronx that I would have to give up rescue to be a priest. For that matter, you could say I was a mindless wimp buffeted back and forth between stronger more charismatic personalities such as Mother and Randy. You can say what you want, actually! We live in a carping, armchair general culture that way. Lots of vicarious TV living.

In the end however there is no substitute for a walk with the Lord and quietly putting all these things before him on the altar and quiet time. Then, go forward, working out your own salvation with fear and trembling. We can't do everything even if we'd like to, but we also can't do nothing. To focus is to exclude and before I had quiet times and the blessed sacrament in my life, I had a hard time with that. Also, in Wycliffe, harking back to another discernment phase, I realized that there were at least two ministries very close to the heart of God: missions, such as the MC's, and prolife. I couldn't do both. I absolutely had to trust and believe that the Lord would watch over the bigger picture.

After the intensity of the back-and-forth from holy hours to the Harlem soup kitchen and the Greenwich Village aids hospice, it was a shock to be a civilian again. Father Norm strongly suggested I do a mini retreat of silence to calm down and get over all this. Boy was he right. He arranged for two weeks all by myself, a huge luxury, in an empty beach house owned by a prolife friend of his. I spent the entire time reading Pat Conroy and walking on the beach in Asbury Park. I'd need it for what was about to happen: the world's biggest rescue, ever.

The A-Ream rescue was the last thing I remember before the horror of my life, the worst horror after Fresno and Stanford, which happened in Philly. Prolifers use words like horror, slaughter, holocaust, child murder and the words lose effect. If it's so horrible, how come it's still around? I'll tell you what: Let me try to describe Philly, the Spring of '88, and then you can decide for yourself what words to use. Fresh from being popped out of seminary, and from a little vacation in Asbury Park, it was a jolt to be back in the saddle, prepping for Atlanta, due up just a few days later. The New York City area rescues were all done and considered by all to be a resounding success. The "numbers" strategy of jamming up the jails had worked. We had been arrested, or not, after committing a half dozen prima facie misdemeanors, and no one spent a night in jail, as I recall, and a lot of us weren't even arrested. The NOW big shot silk-stocking lawyers had not yet devised their Cruella Deville counterattack of pulling a few sheep out of the flock. Now, it was all good, the whole group all together.

But why Atlanta? Randy had got it in his head that we had to go there to save babies, stop Dukakis by what amounted to counterdemonstration, keep the NY wave of energy going, and also, as a distinctively second priority, capitalize on the international press that would be in town for the Democratic Convention that summer. It turned out to be inspired and genius, but it was a huge leap of faith. It's not as if he'd schmoozed a ton of pastors or consulted them beforehand and stroked their egos. He was in touch with them, but most of his decisions were carried out praying with his wife, his microscopically tiny charismatic church in Binghamton New York, and one or two trusted friends. With all that, the entire Atlanta project began with a single step side vanload of rescuers and pastors driving from Binghamton to Atlanta, Randy in the middle of it thinking, in the Lord: if you go there, they will come. I wasn't the only one who couldn't yawn wide enough when I heard about messing with the twin evil sister witches: politicians and press. But we decided on teamwork anyway. Semper Gumby, as the grunts say.

## RALPH M. GABRIEL

How I wish I could convey to you the joy of Atlanta, Reader! The New York City series of rescues lasted a week and were spread out over two or three boroughs with fifteen hundred rescuers. This was the beginning of what my Dad had always talked about -- something bigger than yourself. If New York was something bigger than myself, Atlanta was New York on steroids. All that and Tara and Jean Simmons. The difference in time between New York and Atlanta was barely a couple of months, but during that short time many people around the country had got bitten by the rescue bug. To my enemies -- God bless you, I forgive you, but you need to check in with The Boss. These following names are names of derision and scorn and mockery, but I'm proud they came on board, each and every one of them:

Jerry Farwell, Dr. James Dobson, Pat Robertson, Dr. D. James Kennedy (Coral Gables), Rabbi Yehudi Levin (New York). Then there were the smaller names but giant presences: there was a Greek Orthodox lay community from somewhere else in Georgia, there were the quiet stalwart Last Greatest Generation LIPIVITS, and there were innumerable Evangelical Protestant Bible-based pastors. There were even a whole bunch of Hang-Out-Your-Shingle good ole boy preachers from the hollers of Caintuck and Raccoon Piss, Tennessee, who shut the church up, threw the dawgs out the pickup, and piled all thirteen of their parishioners in the back and jes' came a-huntin' Revenooers, Praise the Lowerd! Salt of the earth, I tell ya. Where would we be without 'em?

I never saw such an across-the-board turnout for anything in my life. I suspect Americans have let their obsession with specialization -- bad as it is for babies and moms, since the defense of the helpless is hardly a specialization -- drift on over into how we live. The Evangelicals, the Papists, the Mainlines, the suburbanites, the tea-sipping lace curtain Irish (but crusty World War I I vets underneath), the LIPIVITS, the Parish of the Perpetually Peeved (uh, that would be South Boston, there, for you uninitiated west of the Mississippi), the oh-so-genteel St. Louis crowd, the Let's Go Surfing Now, Everybody's Surfing Now crowd, the Quiet But Thoughtful Portland Gore Tex and granola crowd, the dark-haired Motown/Chicago/Twin Cities/Ditka crowd, the tall skinny poetical but dark Yankees from Vermont and even some New World French Norman friends from there, too, and the First Church of the Holy Ghost and You Damn Well Better Believe It! All of these and more showed up. Everyone was there, I'm telling you. We even had a few Missouri Synod,

Swedish Reformed, and High Church American Presbyterian or Episcopalian types there who wandered from group to group like lost puppies, not exactly sure where to fit in in all that mess. It's hard to do that when you're already perfect in every way, but at least they made the effort and we took 'em in anyway. And to think that all of this glorious Christianity was welded into one song-singing, worshipping Praise the Lord crowd by the one simple experience of jail together, thanks to the stubbornness of law and order Atlanta -- Be a hero save a whale,/Save a baby go to jail./Keep your eyes on the prize, hold on. We would sing that in the clink, and lots of other songs -- Be not afraid/I go before you always/Come follow Me, and I will give you rest; Alabare, alabare, alabare a mi Senyor Juan cuentaron/el numero los remidios y todos alababan al Senyor.

Before it was all over I'm not sure if the Sheriff of DeKalb County knew if he was incarcerating criminals or presiding over some ecumenical First World Peace Congress. All we were missing was the Dalai Lama. We would've had space for him too.

Come to think of it, I think Atlanta, and OR in general, was the first time any prolife leader had ever tried to form a coalition of Protestants and Catholics. Up until then the German Reformation was still strongly in effect -- pretty durable, that, from 1517 to 1988 -- and the two groups wouldn't talk to each other.

It's worth taking a second to stop to realize what really happened that summer in Atlanta. Have you ever heard of anyone say to three hundred million people, "Let's Go"? Now? Especially when the entire last three centuries of history of those people was and is solidly predicated upon the self-sacred principle of You Can't Tell Me What to Do? Well, I've never heard of that, or anything remotely like it. Have you ever heard of anyone saying to even thirty million people, everyone in Southern California as an example, Come Here? Now? Everyone? 'Cuz I say so? I've never heard of that. Have you? Have you ever heard of someone telling three million people to Meet Me in St. Louis? A group the size of the city of St. Louis? Or the Bronx? In a country where getting two people to agree about anything, even the status of the weather, is more difficult that worm-herding? I've never even heard of a priest at Mass telling three thousand people to come to the parish hall and having more than thirty show up. Unless it's free beer.

To pull the heads off four thousand helpless children a day, and get away with it, and do it all over again tomorrow, takes a lot of passive cooperation, just like burning a million Jews and Poles. Randy was directly attacking the magnitude of that problem by confessing publicly: I've got a problem bigger than myself. Help me. Now. In the Name of Jesus. Three hundred million heard the call. We got ten thousand. And they were the highest quality for being the tiny fraction of those who should have come.

 I can't remember if it was in a Catholic or a Presbyterian church where I first saw the "Atlanta Crawl" demonstrated. Whoever dreamed it up that summer was genius, a definite refinement of Gandhi/Dr. King street people power, especially in the presence of cops. Lots of cops. I think Joseph Foreman was God's little angel on earth, inventing this crawl. The goal in a large rescue is always to take the door of a mill. Get there "fustest with the mustest," with enough people that the cops can't arrest all of the vanguard quickly, and then the rest just kind of accumulate like autumn leaves; unstoppable. But what if the cops are there first, actually ringing the mill? The Atlanta crawl was an inspired way to beat that. We'd rush toward the mill on foot as fast as we could, dodging cops as we went. But if a cop actually put his hand on you, you'd drop down onto hands and knees. As long as he had his hand on you, you'd stay there, but the minute he let go to try to stop someone who'd crawled past you, you'd start crawling. The on-all-fours thing beat any kind of assault rap. The problem from the cops' perspective is that unless you have one-on-one cop numbers, you can't stop the flow of crawling humanity, and once we got a couple dozen to the door, you're not able to arrest them together. And a crowd would accumulate. Thus in Atlanta we found a way to gain the door even with a ring of guards there ahead of time, a trick we didn't know about up North in the Big Apple.

 We had a ball in that tank. Once, in the middle of the night, a huge BANG! rang out. It seems that one of the P's was cooking pruno in a commode with a slow-burn roll of toilet paper, and it cracked the commode clean in half. We all, prolifers and the general population, scampered back to bed giggling like kids at summer camp puling a prank, hoping not to get busted. The Smell Museum is a venerable civic institution, kind of like a bank or an opera or the Oldest Established Crap Game in New York. It got its start right there in the Green Hole in DeKalb Co. jail in Atlanta. It began with the simple act of an inmate handing me an opened but unused fancy organic raspberry hippie teabag, which came in a foil wrapper. How that got in there I couldn't guess. "You can still smell it. See?" He held it out to me like it was ambrosia, nectar of the gods, or frankincense. You could fold the wrapper closed and keep it fresh. The museum grew rapidly from such a humble start. Tiny pine twigs or magnolia blossom leaves and acorns were added, and one day we were forced to seek funding to open a new wing. The Hall of Rocks: a bit of seeming like obsidian or amber-and Paleontology ,.. a bird wing bone.

For some reason I was made curator, on tap, day and night, to conduct tours of the collections which were on display in a three by five inch museum, which was housed on top of the tiny steel table between bunks where you set your milk carton down. On-the-spot tours were requested for visiting dignitaries -- just-arrived inmates -- especially. My job responsibilities extended to accepting and classifying new donations from explorers returning from expeditions to the yard, a dismal square of asphalt ringed with wire and guard towers, but nevertheless filled with tiny treasures. Mothers! Don't ever let your sons gamble. It is the devils' playground. Once, my pile of matchsticks got down to a nub and I found myself wagering the Smell Museum itself as a stake to get back on top. One last chance. I was completely desperate. The news spread like wildfire throughout the tank of my despicable antisocial deed, the waves of shock and alarm and disgust were brought to me quickly. "Why, Jayum! Y'cain't violate a public trust, son!" I was reinstalled as curator only after a public shriving, the repeat of sacred vows, and the establishment of a blind trust.

We had medical problems with older rescuers, we had hasty whispered conferences through the bars trying to communicate with the women prisoners who were housed separately, but the main thing I remember of those days was getting to know the LIPIVITS and Good Ol' Boys crowd a whole lot better. Much has been written about the Last Greatest Generation, one of self-sacrifice. I had actually started to get to know them through my dad telling so many South Pacific stories around the fire when I was small, or camping in the Boy Scouts, but I got to know that generation much better when I started going to weekday Masses where all the widows and widowers hung out and went to coffee afterwards, in California, before I became a Catholic. But I got to know them best when we were all in the Green Hole. That generation is almost gone now, and with it, any earthly hope of stopping child murder. Baby boomers call child decapitation a "procedure" but LIPIVITS only and ever would refer to it as blasphemy, abomination, disgusting genocide. Sooner or later DeKalb and Cobb County sheriffs figured out who the ringleaders were, and they found space for us on a more ongoing basis, even to the point of opening a new part of the jail ahead of schedule. We couldn't get out to re-rescue. But the summer was coming to an end, and a lot of the people who had generously answered Randy's call had to go back to their jobs and families. The party was over. This led to Terms of Release negotiations, a sticky point in any large rescue, as we will see.

There are those who hate any terms of release, and I'm one of them, but practically speaking, we have to admit that we are in an extreme minority because we diehards tended to be young, unmarried and without any careers or houses or stuff like that to keep going, or L1PIVITS whose kids were all grown up and taking care of themselves already. The LIPIV1TS were natural coalition makers with the diehards, and some of them went as far as to say they didn't care if they lost the house in a siege type rescue, hanging out in jail and not giving in, as Joan did, and Martin Wishnavsky. Nowadays we must add Linda Gibbons, Mary Wagner, John Little and the tax refusenik up in Canada. Thank God for their continuing witness.

But the diehards tended to be the minority. Most people had "something to go back to" and that's exactly where a popular movement can run out of steam. It's a pity, really, since that always means unfinished business. What can 1 say? Paul can say "I wish all men were as I" but saying don't make it so. I have always believed that complete success has and should always be within the grasp of any dedicated group of lay people, but FACE killed that. This is Uncle Joe Stalin turf we are on now, and Mr. Redistribute-The-Wealth/Kill The Babies The Child Emperor and his fellow running dogs, and the Dowager Empress and her Slick Consort are extremely proud of exactly that. They aren't ashamed.

At one point in the Fall of '88, Randy said everyone still in jail had to give his or her name and come out. This would bring closure to the summer's campaign and those who had to go home wouldn't feel as if they were leaving someone behind. Failing to give our names was the only thing keeping us in jail at that point. As the summer wound down, the sheriffs were happy to see the back of us headed north. Or west, in the case of the Tennessee crowd. Or south, like the Deeper South crowd. Actually, I think it was the sheriffs who first realized that they could have a secondary problem on their hands even after Randy left town. Not everyone wanted to go home, even if Randy said so. I believe that this is why the up-to-then generous offer of give-your-name-and-we'll-let-you-go was extended even down to the bitter dregs of the diehards: the police didn't want a remnant hanging around in their jails, perhaps to be inspiring as martyrs, or a seed to yet another future series of rescues, maybe next year.

The sheriffs did well to be cognizant of that exact contingency because it was at this point in the fall when a remnant did in fact appear, part of it holed up in the Green Hole in DeKalb Co. Jail, right there with the Smell Museum, which had been entrusted to the G.P. The diehard holdout situation was the reason I received the toughest assignment I ever got in OR: I was told to go back in the Green Hole and talk the diehards out of holding on. I didn't like to do this because I fundamentally agreed with them, but I was officially working for OR and I'm a grunt, so I said I would try.

The core of the diehards were two codgers, Baby Doe No. 126, and Jim McWilliams. Jim has since left this vale of tears, R.I.P, shortly after having visited me in western New York, so I don't think he'll mind if I tell you his name, but NO. 126 was quite proud of his ID as a Baby Doe number, proof of diehard status, but proof also of something much more: a principal. We won't come out until you stop killing babies. Until then, we Baby Does clogging the jails is part of the price you must pay for your continued genocide. Shortly after I started carrying out my OR responsibilities with No. 126 I recognized this for what it was: perfect moral theology with twenty centuries of holy application and martyrs and resistance to wicked establishments and the Grand Coalition of the Status Quo behind it.

It is said of John the Baptist that he was not martyred for "preaching the gospel" in the happy happy joy joy teddy bear sense we are led to believe in these times. John got his head chopped off for standing up to Herod specifically in the area of sexual misconduct, precisely the same reason Thomas More got his own head chopped off by Henry VIII. Abortion treats of "sex," not real sex, but illicit sexual license, and folks don't appreciate advice from strangers on that subject, even if the license is obtained with the lives of innocent children. It's true the sex revolution kicked into high gear in the 1960's, but it was merely an acceleration of the decline set in motion in 1517 in Germany -- a priest self-dispensed from celibacy vows -- and 1535 England -- Henry seeking divorce from Catherine of Aragon. Sterile "sex" in both cases.

No 126 and Jim McWilliams were adamant on the point: the lives of children, and even the tiny ray of hope afforded to them by a reminding and prophetic resistance in jail, were not negotiable. Stop killing babies now, or we will stay here in jail. No. 126 and Jim and about a dozen others were the only ones who were in effect saying: this is not a summer internship or summer missionary post for us. This is a life calling. We will not go. We're in it for the long haul.

In the ensuing years this theme of stubbornness would infect all "terms of release" confabs amongst us rescuers for all subsequent large or long rescues. Those included the Dobbs Ferry Category Zero rescue (1990-1991), Wichita Kansas (91-92), West Hartford, Connecticut (91), Fargo North Dakota (91) and all of the Lambs of Christ rescues led by Father Norman. All of these rescues, and more, each of which threatened to become open-ended ongoing presences inside the local jails, can be said to have received their initial inspiration from No. 126 and Jim McWilliams sitting quietly on their bunks in the Green Hole and saying tell Randy no. We won't come out.

Looking back, it's a scream if you ask me. I sat and talked with 126 for four solid hours one day. At the start I said "Randy says come out. You're wrecking esprits des corps." After an hour or so, it was "Randy told me to tell you to come out." After a couple hours, it was "Look, 126, if he ever asks you, will you promise me you'll tell Randy that I told you to come out?" After that I began to see 126's vision clearer and clearer. I should've stayed my own self. We made up for it a little in Rome, but Atlanta was a missed missed to be sure. And even in Rome we should have stayed longer. Right now, in all the world, Linda Gibbons and Mary Wagner seem to be the only people willing to grow old and die in prison for the babies. What a shame there aren't more. This tragic lack becomes Reason No, 7,562 why we deserve so well what we've got coming right down the pike, straight at us.

No. 126 and his dear wife had more to lose than I. No. 126 and Jim stayed to the bitter end, true to their word. The Atlanta PD refused to stop protecting child murderers. This refusal is a very thinkable task, for any cop, don't let anyone tell you otherwise. If they had stopped protecting the killers, 126 and Jim would have given their names. But the cops didn't quit, and so one day they just let 126 and Jim out the back door. They never did give their names. I thank God for 126 and Jim, and Martin Wishnavsky in Fargo and Matt Trewhella in Milwaukee and Joan in

Florida and the two Canadian ladies and scores of others. Yeah, it didn't "work." Those few stubborn jailhouse witnesses did not "succeed," but it was not their fault. It's certainly not the fault of the God Who sent them, Who would never have dreamed of such an awful thing as child decapitation in the first place, and He said so.

That leaves you and me. We had perfectly adequate awareness of a brave and sacrificial movement that knew for a fact that some problems can't be fixed by just holding a picket sign, or blabbing on a microphone, or opening a new website, or mental prayer alone, or lobbying, or any number of all the other failed stuff, stuff we wouldn't allow for one second to be our only effort if our own son or daughter were hanging out of the window of a burning building and no fire truck in sight. In Atlanta '88 and all these other states and times of holy witness, Americans touched the plow and looked back even though they knew we were busy. If it hadn't been so, if we had picked up on the wonderful and most definitely sufficient start to a widespread and successful grassroots movement, guns and arson and all the rest would never ever have even been thinkable, let alone so obviously required due to the ongoing stubbornness.

America would, should and could have responded, and we did not. It's gonna be a hot spot on Judgment Day, whether that would be the Big One, or the little one all of us face when our eyes close for the last time. In addition to the Final Judgment or the particular judgments, there is a third "judgment" which has already started. It's the judgment which takes place when the Lord finally tires, as it were, of keeping on reminding us of our sins, in the face of our stubbornness about it. He says, in effect, well, have it your own way, then. He withdraws at least a little bit. I can't prove this, it's simply my belief. Sinners like us love to cry about how if God were really there, He'd make it more obvious, like the Swiss businessman who picked me up hitchhiking one day. Or, He wouldn't allow this or that if He were so loving. But in reality it is we who fail to take responsibility for being the direct and only cause of what is now a chilled relationship with Him and suffering on earth.

There comes a point where the peevish teen who keeps throwing things and saying I hate you I hate you I hate you, in fact, gets his way. He is left alone. Until a sullen dinner when he gets hungry, I suppose. We take the blessings God gives to all humans, but we don't like the rules, even when it's so obvious, As The Light Declines. Do you want irrefutable proof that these same rules properly understood are not only about keeping children and their heads intact but provide adults with happiness in their lives? Look around you. There is no joy in baby-killing Mudville, right now. None. The puddles of blood are just too deep. I do not fear you, but if I do not warn you, you will die in sin and the Lord will ask me to account for your life. Repent.

No one will ever be able to say that he didn't know, that there was not sufficient information or witness or human emotion. Ten thousand people from all over America left their homes and families and jobs and came to Atlanta and got their butts kicked on TV. We knew this. We all knew. We didn't do the needful, as we would have for our own child, and now we will pay for it. I absolutely guarantee it. It's already started if you just take off the blinders to look around. And when we see our own children in trouble, as they've already started to get there since they have no spiritual protection, perhaps we will remember how we hardened our hearts against other people's children, even if they were the children of those who did not love them enough. Let us repent by actions, not words, now. Hurry up, while there's still a little light left in the day. It won't be long, and in so many ways, it's already too late.

I suppose it's possible you or I could escape the wrath to come, already spilling from the overflowing cup. I personally don't believe it, but I suppose it's possible. Repent. For me, steel started in Houston in '87 a couple years after chain and Kryptonite rescues started in SF in '84 or '85. As soon as Atlanta was over, I rushed up north to start making the next lock. I loved the big rescues with no locks but they were too few and far between. Even so, I didn't want to get too wrapped up in a day job or a career in case another big rescue came along. As a result of all this, in between big rescues I wound up welding new locks and I did temp work or pickup construction jobs to pay for the welding rods and gases and scrap steel that we used to make the shielded locks with.

It was after one of these steel rescues up North that I heard about what had happened in Vermont. John Cabot was a family farmer somewhere in upstate New York, or maybe in Pennsylvania. How he wound up in a Burlington Vermont rescue I don't know, but people in Plattsburgh New York are known to talk to their neighbors in Vermont across the lake, meaning Lake Champlain and a rescuer over there on the Vermont side in Burlington probably asked for John's help to get some more rescue "numbers" in Vermont, which needed them. It's not their fault, those original Vermont rescuers, there's not a lot of anything up there except maybe trees and nice granite and maple syrup, and Vermonters like it that way just fine.

I think the Burlington cops held on to John after the first rescue he was in because he was out of state, or they gave him a bigger sentence than the locals. I think that was the original mistake the cops up there made.

Local Vermonters sent out the word: the cops are singling out John and a few other New Yorker friends of ours, come help us! I think that's how Vermont got started; something like that.

By the time I got up there fifty or so rescuers were in jail already and each successive rescue at the one or two mills in Burlington was adding to the number since everyone was going "Baby Doe," just as in Georgia. They refused to give their names and refused to walk. It's a Braille thing, OK? You can't hear us when we tell you in plain English to stop decapitating little babies, so we're going to try some show-and-tell. Pure street genius, straight out of the head and heart of Joan Andrews, the Tennessee cowgirl, thank God.

This reminds me that there is something else I need to tell you about Vermont before we can go any further. It is as gross as the mass autopsies I did in Phiily, in its own way. If you think about it, any abortion is gross. There's no such thing as a cool abortion. That's why they knock the moms out. No delivery room smiles caught on camera for this one!

After I got to Burlington, I tried to find out what was needed most. Locks, they said. They asked me to help make some locks because this rescue didn't look as if it were going to be another Atlanta with tons of people to block a door. They had been hoping to clog the jails enough to make them let us go and stop wasting our time with rigged trials. Then we'd move on to save some more babies. But it didn't look as if they were going to get the numbers. So, they needed locks to slow down the arrests of the few people who were showing up.

I'm telling you all this as a way of explaining how I could be sitting in Vermont with babies dying every day, and fifty fellow rescuers in the clink, and myself trying to help make some locks, and, uh, well, and sitting in a restaurant, reading a newspaper. Among those inside the jail, a minority faction emerged. They had given assurances that they would lead a rescue in another city in the spring and they needed to go back home for that. Further, that they would not leave Vermont if everyone else didn't leave with them; it was all or nothing. They were very persuasive. Most of this discussion took place among "leadership" behind closed doors. One Irish guy inclined toward action over words, I suppose, got so sick of the whispered intrigues and leaks from on high he actually made a little sign he pinned to his shirt: "See Leadership." He didn't want to talk about it. I'm still amazed at what happened next, but the minority ground everyone down, even the last of the diehards who would only go kicking and screaming. I'm a little bit sheepish to admit this, but I think the only time rescuers can relax and enjoy each other is in jail, strange to say. As long as we are in jail we can't rescue! All our plans and hopes and dreams about the next rescue fly out the window and we have a good time praying, singing, worshipping, making new friends, and catching up with old ones. Our "jail" in Waterbury was so porous that at one point a local smuggled in a couple half-gallons of ice cream through a temporary displacement of the window screen security system. It lasted about forty-five seconds, but everyone got a bite.

Vermont had variety in the rescuers, but it was a different kind than that of Atlanta, say, or New York. There was a young man in Vermont whose wife was in a coma but who believed very strongly that she wanted him rescuing rather than with her. There was a saint -- you don't get to meet many of those -- Renee Riddle, who was a paraplegic, and the sweetest thing on earth. You could say non-cooperation came natural for her, dear soul. She was the heart and soul of the entire rescue, especially in-custody, with all the peace and love that radiated from her, even if she couldn't get around. The hallways had a ton of people nearby who were happy to get things for her if she needed something. Also, Vermont was a chance for everyone to get a real good look at Fr. Norm's tremendous drive to save babies and to try to expand his notion of Gandhian non-violence. Fr. Norm was living proof that true satyagraha is not passive. It is not for dope-smoking, peace-sign making sissies or mere draft dodgers. It is quite arduous and painful and that was the truth of Gandhi, not the convenient and comfortable fiction that costs you nothing but lip service. Fr. Norm's ministry bore this truth out with the Lambs of Christ.

Fr. Norm was the most aggressive non-violent rescuer I ever met, exactly as Gandhi truly intended and practiced. There was a TOR (Third Order Regular) Franciscan monk there, in habit, who used to design planes. Real planes, on the street. He made paper planes like you've never seen, in Waterbury, that would swoop around a turn and land on a dime.

There was a local seminarian who was quite the intellectual. Fr. Norm was a retired Air Force lieutenant colonel who sounded like General Patton. Future Father Rosario was a quiet type, a faster who seemed to channel the Cure of Ars with a hippie lifestyle, to the extent that the hippie lifestyle is consistent with a priest's lifestyle, of course.

Most of the crowd was either New England, Philly or New York but we had some Good Ol' Boys from I'm not exactly sure where, but a little closer to the Mason-Dixon Line than Thet Holler, Caintuck. Once, the Good Ol' Boys holed up in a room, closed the door, and started sending out messages. The usual attacks on Catholicism (yawn). Some of the Irish New Yorkers got their brogue up and said, hmmmm, and sent back little notes about scripture, encyclicals and the history of the faith and every time without fail, the lock-in scholars would bounce out a reference to yet another Bible verse. It was a little bit like a correspondence chess game in real time. Great fun.

A couple times a week the police would send us up to "rec" through the tunnels underneath the complex. Rec was a gym. We'd play volleyball. After a while we started to mock the absence of a real jail and real jailers, especially during these tunnel moves, and one of the rescuers started to whistle "Bridge Over The River Kwai," the ditty from that classic prison camp movie about the pacific theater. We started to march in time in an exaggerated way and snap off snappy salutes to all the amazed bureaucrats we passed along the way.

I can still remember the befuddlement of a guard who came on duty one night, one of those Let's-Take-Charge black female guards whose attitude is I'm Not Tolerating Any Baloney! Shape Up! Army Regulations, or Its Tasers and Mace! kind of people. She had just come on duty after dinner time, poor dear, and she had just stepped out of the guard's "bubble," a glass-walled office, into the main room, which was a kind of inmate's day room. She had a stack of polaroids, and she meant business! No one was going to mess with her count! Her eyes were like flint as she surveyed the room. This is what she saw: Out on the porch, Red, the guy whose wife was in the coma, was playing the accordion as a one-man orchestra for what were ballroom dancing lessons taking place out on the porch. Some of the ladies had even smuggled in some long fancy ballroom dresses. Just inside the doorway, the Third Order Regular, in full Franciscan habit, was carefully tweaking his latest paper airplane design so that it would make a long swoopy turn around the room from just a gentle let-go. The airplane, which really looked like a complicated origami something, would float out across the room over and over as he tested it again and again, and each time it would finally come to rest at about the same point across the room, after its curving flight. Two ever-vigilant Japanese soldiers had a pretty good idea where that plane would land, and they had decided by foresight to install an anti-aircraft battery emplacement there, to defend the Home Islands. They were fanatically zealous about their duties and when the enemy aircraft hove into sight the gun operator would swing his gun toward the evil plane of the wicked American imperialist Satan, trying to shoot it down. He was assisted in this by a seminarian who would swivel the gun mount he was sitting on -- a collapsed folding metal chair -- in accordance with the commands of the gunner, both of them screaming out in intense bursts of incoherent Kill Bill Japanese. If they succeeded in downing the bogey, they would instantly have a joyful sake toasting ritual, but if they failed and the plane hit them, they would commit hari-kari on the spot with many a shouted dying curse against the Evil Empire. Either way, the monk would calmly step over and reload for another attack, adjusting the paper ailerons for another test. At the outer limit of the plane's attacking dive/curve, it just missed New York's Oldest Established Floating Crap Game, where the chips were candy from yet another successful run of smuggled contraband. The Baptists tried to pretend that gambling and dancing and other such mortal sins were not taking place in their holy and sanctified ministry, but occasionally they'd mention them in their little Bulls From Under The Door as yet more proof that the idolatrous Catholics were under the command of the Antichrist. Even so, they seemed to be the only Inquisitors I've ever heard of with a healthy sense of humor about it all and the New Yorker defenders of the Grail returned the favor by drawing the veil of modesty over the misdeeds of Martin Luther and Henry VIII.

    Behind the monk in the corner, just inside the ballroom/porch, was the quiet ongoing Bridge Club, ably taught by a former Wall Street investment banker-turned-priest who would instruct his philosophy professor partner, "Put a diamond on that, sweetheart" in his scratchy Bronxian voice. Squared off against that pair was North-South, a Bolivian missionary and a returned carpenter. Just off the main day room but behind a semi-closed door, a cradle Catholic was being baptized out of an immaculate mop bucket by a group of overarchingly zealous and anti-Catholic charismaniacs who didn't want to lose this one to the clutches of Satan.

## TO RECEIVE A CHILD

In the next room over, perhaps inspired by the Ineffable Other's sensing of a shift in the harmonic convergence, a suburban Philly mom of six listened with perfect attention to a yawningly hours-long and meticulously historically correct explanation of the Immaculate Conception. The I.C., according to the speaker, was not only not Mariolatry but rather an edification of the Divinity of Jesus, especially as a natural prerequisite to His Incarnation in real time. She wound up on board with the I.C. Just in time for court, slipping back inside the jail in the nick of time with the unerring preternatural timing of the Irish on the hunt was Joe Wall, fresh from refreshment at a local pub in downtown Waterbury. Supervising from a remote location, as it were, was Renee Riddle who was instantly informed about every single detail of it all with a stream of whispering palace informants even while her noble duties prevented her from leaving her happy and always joyful headquarters. The lady guard with her seriously trimmed afro and her stack of Polaroid's, fresh from some training session about how prison riots start and How Things Can Get Out of Hand, took all of this in with a sweep of her gimlet gaze: dancing, gambling, naval battles, scholars, bridge, encyclicals…all of it. I can still remember perfectly that in front of my eyes, I saw this dear woman go through the Seventy Seven stages of denial: anger, grief, What The Hey? and I must have missed the lecture about this at police academy, do I call the FBI? or the ASPCA?, etc., until finally she just broke out laughing. She knew she was in the presence of God knows how many federal crimes and Vermont state felonies flaunted by this incorrigible band of reprobates and she knew she was helpless to protect the virtue of the Vermont State Corrections meme. She was still laughing when she retreated with her polaroids back to the comparative safety of her guard station and remained there the rest of her shift, laughing and drinking coffee. She was paid the same either way, as the saying goes amongst guards.

Sooner or later in Vermont we ran out of new rescuers and the jail population in Waterbury after a month or so stabilized at just about ninety. It was at this time that a little discussion off in the corners started to erupt about terms of release, that old bugaboo of rescuers everywhere. I suppose one way it started was with information sent into the jail by lawyers who were in contact with the Vermont prosecutors. Most of the rescuers by far were content to let it all ride under the one Main Directive: we won't give our names. Let us go. Stop killing babies.

This Baby Doe status was not at all merely peevishness and still less an attempt to avoid the consequences of our actions, unjust as those consequences were. In addition to the sound moral basis of it -- we identify with children who are also nameless and denied process when they are torn to pieces and who also cannot walk -- it had a practical ring to it. We were tired of traipsing around all over the country to appear at trials wherein we were never allowed to talk about babies anyway. After a few rescues even the trial appearances alone could interfere with plans for a new rescue, and this is a crime against the next wave of children being mowed down. The primary purpose of life is not to send a message through the courts but rather to stop the killing now. These two things are not always the same thing especially when the courts are as crooked as a dog's hind leg. All of this in-custody stuff was a crusty Old-School Irish way with dealing with the establishment's efforts to grind down the resistance. Christians are happy to go to trial, of course, as a consequence of our actions, but not rigged trials. Waste of time. Time that could be spent saving more babies. Each one is worth it all.

So, the majority of us in Vermont sent the message out to the lawyers: we're standing pat. We won't give our names. Let it ride, status quo ante. This posture of the rescuers indicated an incredibly swift change from the Atlanta endgame of only a few months before. Now, everyone was staying as diehards. The heroic influence and pathbreaking sweat of No. 126 and Jim McWilliams, channeling Joan Andrews, and John Ryan before her, was finally bearing fruit in a large number of people. Before, rescue was the new thing. Now, it was rescue plus an in-custody protest which was a legitimate response to our being substantially frozen out of court, and the kids with us.

After a while, though, a minority faction emerged. They had given assurances that they would lead a rescue in another city in spring and they needed to go back home for that. Further, that they would not leave Vermont if everyone else didn't leave with them; it was all or nothing. They were very persuasive. Also, unlike Atlanta was the fact that all of this discussion took place inside the jail, even if most of it was among "'leadership" behind closed doors. One Irish guy inclined toward action over words, I suppose, got so sick of the whispered intrigues and leaks from on high he actually made a little sign he pinned to his shirt: "See Leadership." He didn't want to talk about it.

I'm still amazed at what happened next, but the minority ground everyone down even the last of the diehards who would only go kicking and screaming. and the whole bunch of us came out on one day, CIS, Credit for Time Served. No future trial. For Vermont, who had to pay the food and guard bills, it was a steal. But they tax baby killing, so...

For myself and a lot of diehards it was yet another missed opportunity. At the time I rolled along with everyone else and when leadership asked me to explain some legal details I did, but I wish I had just joined a little splinter group like No. 126 and Jim McWilliams had down in Atlanta. It would have been rough since they would have taken the smaller group back down to the Burlington jail and it would have been like starting all over again after we had made such an advance in bringing the principle of noncooperation to bear in a large group. Even as it was, Vermont was a tremendous step forward for that alone. Also, if we were repatriated, so to speak, to Burlington, what would this mean for the prisoners once we were split up? Communication becomes very difficult, and there is a huge burden on those out of custody who want to help, who are constantly running from one jail to another and getting the runaround from the authorities, who now "have us where they want us" and can sit back and let the normal routine of jail wear us all down.

Still, it was true that the nascent rescue movement had yet to engineer a way for the diehards to get along, over the long haul, with the mortgage and day jobs and career people, and bid them an amiable adieu when it came time to part company even if only temporarily, while still being at one with each other in our hearts.

The mortgagee's point was well taken about the smaller fraction being sent back downtown, but if I had to do it over again that's exactly what I would have done, and it's a shame since there were plenty of diehards willing to do the same. Plus, we don't know for sure that's what would happen. And if there was a higher punishment of the smaller group, we could just crank it all up again. The mortgagees protested that this would put them at a disadvantage since they would already have given their names, but there comes a point where you got to go for it, or, as Ruth Gordon said, you got nothing to talk about in the locker room. Vermont was a good time to remind ourselves that it wasn't a party after all. Lives are at stake, got to do what you gotta do, and also, make sure you don't interfere with that other guy trying to follow the Lord according to the lights provided him.

Goodbye mortgagees, we love ya, but this is what we gotta do and let's let the Lord work out the details. I think it wasn't until just a few years later that Martin Wishnovsky did precisely that: hung around in stubborn non-cooperation as a large passel of rescuers came and went from the jail. Amy Boissoneault did the same thing in Enfield NJ in the later 90's and Linda Gibbons and Mary Wagner, a couple more living saints, do the same thing right now in Canada. All of this was inspired by Joan's holy stubbornness in Florida. So, one diehard prophetic stance from in custody was all it took, and we can definitely say it was given a great try-out in VT, NJ, North Dakota and Canada. Ninety people doing ninety days non-cooperating in custody is nothing to sneeze at, and a huge step up, diehard-wise. And, not to forget, it did suffice as a People Power response to Andy Cabot getting thumped up in VT, shame on them. All told, we misapplied the Three Musketeers All For One, One For All rubric. It has its merits, on TV anyway, for people fortunate enough to be already born, but in real life the total axis of this principle needs to put the babies first. They are helpless. They need the help and solidarity more than you and I.

For all this angst, a shred of diehardism continued after everyone got out, even so, in Vermont itself, even before the North Dakota and Kansas City things got going. Even in Waterbury along with dancing and bridge lessons there had been some "welding" classes, and these bore fruit on the outside after we got out. A handful of us diehards got together after we were released from Waterbury and we just couldn't bring ourselves to leave town. We hung out for a few days and recuperated and watched Anne of Green Gables tapes and got to talking: why not do a steel rescue, up here in Vermont? Do we really have to traipse back to Manhattan in such a hurry? The cattle were lowing in the barn where we found an old welder and some scrap metal. It took maybe a week or two but we kicked out two or three "Dieters." We named them after Dietrich Bonhoeffer, the man Hitler executed for trying to get him, and for smuggling Jews out of Nazi Germany, and the man the Rev. Dr. Martin Luther King extolled as an exemplar of political action under the circumstances of a nefarious regime of evil, most definitely relevant when an entire nation pulls the heads off children. These locks were Kryptonite bike locks covered in two-inch mild steel Schedule 40 piping as opposed to the laminated plate/carbide-reinforced "Mahler" locks. What a difference that last Dieter rescue was from the one in Burlington the previous winter!

Everyone had left town and three diehards decided to see what a couple of Dieters could do to stretch out the efforts of the others.

We decided this time to rescue at the witch's mill where they drank murdered baby's blood at black masses. (It would be a wonder if that building is still there, one of the last freestanding all-wood mills in America.) We started out on the porch, just three of us diehard leftovers from Waterbury: Jim McWilliams, one of the original Atlanta diehards, your humble "author," and a philosophy professor from the Tri-State area. Lock and blockers had always hoped that the ménage of steel, concrete and humans would form a clump too heavy and awkward to move. Such a clump works best inside a building with narrow doorways and corridors.

At the witch's mill, however, they knew us by sight. There was no chance of getting inside and setting up. Locking into all the locks does take some time even if it's only a half-minute. I can't recall how they did it, but the police started by getting us off the porch with a huge investment of diabolical determination, manpower, witch nagging, and liability hubris. We were in a bedraggled heap in the driveway for an hour or so before someone hit on a plan of how to get us, still all in a clump and without cutting open any of the locks, onto the back of a truck. That took another hour or two, with the City Attorney of Burlington, I'm sure, on speed-dial that entire time with the City's liability underwriters about the risk of injury. Especially since one of the rescuers was connected to the clump by his neck, and another rescuer was in his 70's and not in great health to begin with. Even with all this, the fact is we still shut the mill for an hour, a great achievement thank God, for only three people who normally would have been scooped up in a matter of a few minutes, jailed, and this time, very likely, prosecuted by ourselves. No ninety brothers and sisters in solidarity this time. Unless they all came back. Surprise! We're baaaaaack! By noon or so they had us on the truck. Now what? By some inscrutable logic the authorities decided to play a huge joke on the Catholic Diocese of Burlington. It turned out that the chancery was located immediately across the street from the witch's mill and the cops dumped us on their front lawn and left us there. No locks cut, no arrests, no identifications, no nothing. Just dumped and left.

I still don't know whether to laugh or cry about all this. I mean, if we had to be pulled away from the mill, I suppose there are worse things that can happen besides being dumped onto private property and not being arrested. Also, we got a pass on all the sparks and noise and harm of people trying to open the locks for hostile reasons. But I can't help but wonder if God's own sense of humor prevailed, too, in a prophetic way. I mean, you could say we were now, like it or not, "protesting" the chancery, and perhaps, in a nicer way, inviting the bishop to come out and play. I mean, when you think about it, wouldn't it be logical for him to protest at the mill anyway? What is a witch's mill doing murdering babies and eating them, anyway, right across the street from a chancery? Anywhere in the world? Limousine liberals could coo about the cultural tolerance frisson of all that, but to hell with that. We're talking child cannibalism. Zero tolerance necessary for that. The bishop never did come out and that was also yet one more missed opportunity in New England. What would it have cost His Excellency to come on out and even do something simple such as make a short statement of solidarity with the "non-violent" protesters? Would that have spoiled some vast eternal plan? I doubt it. These are portfolio-protecting bishops; well, correct me if I'm wrong. I've met the lawyers who are hired to help them do it, and whose advice they slavishly follow, Jesus shoved in the background. These are the same ones who are the first to condemn what they call "violence," meaning, the Thomistic use of force, and yet when we are not forceful at all, just hanging out "protesting," they are cowards then, also. Either way, it helps child killing continue. This reminds me of the children in the square who wouldn't dance or grieve, flute music or funeral music, it's all the same. Either way, they're just dead. When you show atheists a picture of a child rendered limb-from-limb, they ask, "What's the question?" You see? Same-same. And you wonder why child murder has persisted so long.

As it was, in Burlington, there, on the bishop's lawn, after an hour or two a kindly secretary came out to tell us, "he knows you're here" in the hushed cultural tones of an NPR announcer as if I'd just been told Elvis can see me now in his dressing room. Only I was locomotively challenged at the moment, like my adopted children, and His Excellency never came out. Lockers are stubborn sorts and we decided to hang out right there. We at least were near the mill and our presence, even dumped on the lawn with no chance of blocking the door, still constituted our best effort to stop child killing even if only by appealing to people, calling out to moms, and reminding passersby what was happening in their midst with their passive consent and cooperation.

## TO RECEIVE A CHILD

In the middle of the night a bunch of witch sympathizers showed up and started singing what they considered to be diabolic chants. The joke's on them. At one point they sang Cherokee medicine chants, which are very healing, and are not at all diabolical, especially when you consider the number of current Cherokees who are Christian, very prolife and wary about forced abortions, dicey informed consent sterilizations, etc., on the reservation in the federal medical clinics there, and who are also traditionalist with regards to the language and legends of their tribes, including the Creation dances. Silly you, witches! You sure blew that one. Some counter protesters showed up in solidarity with the babies and we all said some rosaries and read some psalms and other Bible verses. We were there twenty-four hours altogether, a record that remained up until the fireside legend of Harrisburg '95. And. Harrisburg had a strong diabolic presence also. All child killing does but these two were pretty bad.

In the late 80's and early 90's I had some chronic health problems; not terrible, but I could feel them, and they were starting to limit my ability to move around. I remember after a steel rescue in upstate NY I was so battered I had to sit it a tub and sip vino and take ibuprofen for a good couple of days to keep the back from spasming up. Once it locked up so bad after the Rome rescue and torture, I wound up in the hospital with traction and all that; humiliating, a little, since here I was, at the mercy of staff, when I was usually the one putting people in traction. The doc said to me: no more protests for you, after the Rome thing. One more beating like that and you'll wind up in a wheelchair for the rest of your life.

Then there was the injury from the Ohio Lambs' rescue where the teenage counter protester just kept jumping up and down on my ankle until she snapped it. It wasn't hard for her, since I was immobilized by my other ankle being in a Mahler. Also, we were trained to be very still to avoid assault raps against us, so, bang. There it went. That injury never really healed up properly, resulting in a permanently stretched tendon, this meant that the foot would roll over without warning. When you make a living on a parapet thirty stories up, no lifeline, this is no good. One day shortly after that injury I woke up in the middle of the night realizing that I had spent the entire day walking along the edge of a cornice of a twenty-story building, no parapet, no nothing, just drop-off, and half the time my trick ankle was the outside ankle, meaning, if it went out, there was only one direction to go. When you act as a saboteur one or two stories up, it ain't good either. I used to joke to my fellow prolifers: when I wind up in a wheelchair, I will crash it into the mill at three miles an hour, if that's all I can do.

Maybe a little rehash, here, of the late 80's and early 90's will help. Rescues had died down to almost nothing. A few heroic stalwarts hung on. This was very noble, but most days the killers still killed anyway, even with a diehard rotting in jail a mile away, and even in Fargo. Some say rescue died due to FACE and Clinton and her appointment Reno, but local magistrates had already killed peaceful protests long before that. When rescue grew from Randy's appeal on TV in Atlanta, we were joined by, lets' face it, normal people with jobs and mortgages and lots of kids. Once the judges said to them "I see you one more time it's ninety days" that chilled any growth in the movement. So, you don't need a Dowager Empress to murder children, as long as her little slaves are willing to get their hands dirty to appease her.

Speaking of politicos, even FACE was passed by a majority Republican Congress. And Roe was written by a Nixon appointee. So much, in all three cases -- lesser magistrates, US Congress, and the Supes -- for a political solution. By the late 80's and early 90's, everyone had settled in with child killing, the same as if Hitler hadn't been stopped. Everyone was used to those funny smells and the dark smoke. No outrage if it's routine, and everyone acts as if it's routine.

How about educating? Docs, lawyers, pols…Everyman? It was the docs and lawyers in concert with Everyman's acquiescence over time that brought about Roe to begin with. At first it was liberal elitist genocide, with an anti-woman end-around, true, but if there were any good men or women around then, in the 30's or up until now, they sure didn't stop it. Jail food's crummy, and the couch and remote beckon.

"Steel rescue" itself flagged after time. Even if they last twenty-four hours, they can get the lock open if they want to, and then there's the arrest. Any given jurisdiction could say: Enough! And even if it didn't, all it takes is one single solitary bored overpaid selfishly ambitious Assistant US Attorney desperately avoiding unemployment in an overcrowded field. Let's face it. He or she can overpower each and every state and local elected official and chalk up a FACE scalp for their pathetic Wall of Honor to boot. Steel was invented to stretch out the efforts of a small number of rescuers, but what if you couldn't even get the smaller number, as they ratcheted up the punishment? Which was easier to do after the crowds went away and we no longer had "numbers" clout.

Schools? We were frozen out of speaking at public schools, while the pro-deathers breezed right past us there anytime they wanted. Then, at the mills. For the young mom the mill represented simply the last plopping off of the brainwashing conveyer belt that the schools consisted of. Sidewalk counseling effectiveness rates dropped accordingly. I can remember in the late 70's when sidewalk counseling was very effective, and women would come outside just to chat. They were bored waiting for their appointments. That was all gone, now. They even put Walkmans over the mom's ears as she was walking into the building. There's free speech for ya.

The same is true of any "daytime" or public endeavor, protest, march, rescue, speaking opportunity, radio guest appearance, you name it. They hardly put it on the air and the few times they do, they will cherry pick some liberal who calls himself or herself a Christian but then proceeds to denounce the Christian position. Then the media can claim they aired both sides.

Well, how about that whole nighttime work thing? Why not content myself for the rest of my life carefully doing stink or slow arson, meaning, no bombs? Lots of preparation, reconnoitering, surveillance, advanced research, high percentage, low risk of arrest, etc.

Been there, done it, and, yes, an option, just not for babies and moms. Not a closer. I had been doing sabotage since '87 and by the mid-90's it was clear to see that the abortion industry could absorb the losses, even though those losses were unbelievably higher, per man-hour of work and arrest risk, than protest stuff.

One guy who kept his mouth shut and came and went like a "donut" gypsy could save more babies and moms in seven or eight seconds of work than 1500 people in a week of protests, like Manhattan '88. He could hit half a dozen mills in one night and vamoose up the canyon. Also, the 1500 all faced losing their day jobs. The price of "peaceful protests" could get into man-months-and-years. And even though there are prolifers who argue that protest is better than sabotage because it is a "hearts and minds" approach, sabotage is not without its prophetic angle too. I never thought of it that way while I was doing it, but if you have ears to hear and eyes to see, a smoking building is a teaching moment as much as a thousand people sitting quietly singing "If you cross the burning desert, you will not die of thirst." If you don't have eyes to see or ears to hear or a working human heart, none of it will make a difference anyway. You hear me, Rachel and Chris? That's where Braille comes in. Show-and-tell. Talking alone won't cut it, as we now know with apodictic certainty. Talking, to the exclusion of all else, when someone's dying, is a sin.

There's something I've been wanting to tell my fellow prolifers for ages: you don't need to shoot everyone or burn up their buildings to get them to quit: many docs walked away quietly, just because they heard of a shooting or arson or stink. I also don't believe the more forceful approaches are the only ways to go. But I will say this: force is a pinch of salt. Even if it's just a small thing, without that pinch of salt, you don't have a cake. The current, bland, Can't We all Just Get Along Together prolife approach to things is so bland, considering how horrible it is at the sharp end, to babies and moms, it's just not a cake. You almost can't blame Everyman for turning his nose up in disgust. It's a fake. And it's easy to see. The prolifers have been accepting the cautionary warnings of their paid-to-be-there lawyers for so long, they assume it's dictum. We need to start listening to Higher Sources for our info. Don't forget what the Lord did to the lawyers when he was around. Nicer than Shakespeare, I suppose, true, but still… Even in the early 90's you could see it: every other option, taken all together times a thousand, was absorbable by the babykiller machine, which gained strength each year with increasing ossification of intent as enabled by the modern police state, with the NEA facilitating with young minds in each new generation. This is simply history. Ask any feminist.

It's the kind of history no one cares about, the same way he doesn't care about architectural improvements in sewage treatment plants over the years, provided nothing actually stinks. To their noses. Polonius, call home. I smelleth a stable nearby, and my nose is in great indignation. Do you see how this goes? What started out as a Josef Mengele lark, bit by bit becomes institutionalized, until you're not just facing one whacko; you've got an infrastructure that everyone regards as being as normative as a sewage treatment plant, as if humans weren't even worth Soylent Green. Which it will come to, of course. Already there in terms of vaccine culture tissue harvesting. If you ask the guy who brings spare parts in for the suction pumps, he'll aw-shucks and toe the ground and say he doesn't know anything about that, but he feeds his family with blood money just the same. Electricians, plumbers who clean up ghastly messes downstream from the garbage disposals embedded into the end of the tables in the morgues. Roofers, cement finishers, even the salt of the earth have been corrupted. People you expect not to be corrupted.

So, a gun attacks a man, not a building or an idea? Not true but to the couch clickers, it's close enough. I was not aware of it at the time, but babykillers are harder to replace than buildings. The point is, the babykiller industry was able to withstand everything we had done, and we tried everything -- what Aquinas calls "exhausting lesser means." Prolife fake "pacifists" will point to sidewalk counseling and say that babies can be saved that way without violence. What they don't understand is that the violence has already started. The only question is, are you trying to lessen it or increase it? If you announce to everyone it's tolerable, you are increasing the violence, even if you try to convince yourself of the opposite.

If you use Thomistic force, you are actually decreasing the real violence. From the prolifer's perspective, the baby must be included in the evaluation of how much violence is there. Added to that is the violence done to the bond between mom and child, which exists, like it or not, from the start. The violence to this bond is easy to see with the abortion sequelae: drugs, suicide, chronic depression, breast cancer, you name it. I'm happy to hear about babies being saved with sidewalk counseling. Been there, done that. When an increase in sidewalk counseling rises to the level of saving 99% of all children and moms, instead of the current far less than 1% rate, I'd consider laying down the gun.

But even then that less than 1% would still need help as much as the 99%, now, wouldn't they? A child's a child; a mom's a mom. If one thousandth of all the people who claim to be prolife did nothing but come to the mill and stand there, it would save 99% of all the babies without any violence, wouldn't it? If everyone stopped smoking in bed, and pan-frying, it would also stop 30% of all fire calls too, wouldn't it? But that isn't happening any time soon, and until it does, firemen have to keep checking the gas tanks of their trucks. In the case of abortion, there will always be a non-zero fraction of very determined people, pushed by pimps, coyotes, the Ring of Powerful Males or Mommy and Daddy or Buck v. Bell or black hater/global culler Maggie Sanger or whoever will walk past any "persuasionist" efforts whatsoever. If there were only one child and mom in the world about to die today, you or I must stop it today. There is no such thing as a mother or child who can be bartered over to death even to save the 99 %. Do you see what's going on here? That strange ancient concept of just self-defense, and the defense of your family, and the defense of any innocent third party subject to unjust attack, that all arose from a situation that started out as a confused, happy, natural, warm-hearted reaction to a clear and unavoidable evil. I didn't realize it when I was younger, growing up in the prolife movement, but I was exhausting lesser means. Exhaust lesser means before you go to using more force than exists in suasion, exactly as any moms or dads do, now, at any moment, watching over their kids. There is nothing mysterious or creepy about it. What's mysterious or creepy is a grown, red-blooded adult standing there, watching, as if it were a godammed TV show, any child whatsoever being rendered limb from limb.

Utterly helpless children, who have no place to run. Their mothers often bullied, as anyone knows who actually gets into this. From the perspective of mother and child, the lesser means were in fact exhausted, in 1974 and before. Everything else since then has been you and i, standing on the sidewalk with our hands in our pockets, watching the blood run down the gutters and the hamburger children get swooshed down the sewers from the garbage disposals in the morgues. Geez, it's a damn shame, we mutter. Now, imagine doing that while a house burns and children hang out of the windows, screaming. The shame is on you and me. Forty-one years and fifty-six million kids and moms later, we're still doing it.

In some ways, and in many ways, the moms have gotten the worst of it. Forty-five million or so of them, staggering around the place, still shocked, no one to talk to. Weeping suddenly at the sight of babies in the arms of other moms at the market, or, suddenly bumping into a child the exact age and sex of their own, but growing up. Can't you feel this sad energy? I do. Ask Jenifer O'Neill and her brave friends. It's like the high-pitched sound only dogs hear, but I hear it. Ask her.

Guns are a perfectly real attempt, however clumsy and strange to us effetes, at ending this, not merely resisting it in some politically correct or acceptable way. Black-hating, genocidal morons like Maggie Sanger and her pals will always jump up and scream if you actually try to bring their Satanic party to an end, instead of just wringing your hands and crying about it. No one, in the history of the world ever picketed some bureaucrat for better VFD budgets while his house was actually burning down. Never. Not once. It's his house. Pop culture and the killers with actual blood on their hands, are both splashed in the face with the latest blood sports, listening for screams, watching Jackass or truTV, carrying the bloodstained money to the bank. They can hardly be bothered to laugh at our efforts when we resist, and no more. There's a time for everything, even protest, but not when a child and mom are about to get it.

For this reason I don't hate abortionists. Spiritually they don't know any better, or they fake it really well. The ones who frost me the most are the mainstream prolifers who definitely know better and say so. They talk pretty, but underneath it all they are just couch clickers like everyone else. Roaming in the gloaming I saw the gray pasty flickers of TV light against the interior walls of every house in America after dark, just like the mud huts in Temuco. You don't fool me. And I watch TV myself sometimes. Just not when it's time to get busy.

Now, it is clearer to me. Even the level of shooting I was at was not sufficient since abortion is still going on. Even shooting, and even with four docs dead, it was insufficient force to stop the most stubborn killers, the ones whose consciences were so seared even personal danger would not stop them. The pro-aborts who make money and get votes from continuation of the child murder all heroize these jerks, of course. There are people who admire Jeffrey Dahmer, too, though. and Dahmer never touched little babies. But it begs the question, doesn't it? Even if only 30% of all the docs wouldn't quit, in the face of arson and shooting, and sub lethal shooting and Avon and state regulations and ultrasound requirements, this proves that all that shooting and arson will never never never never work on the stubborn ones, and many children and moms will still die and be messed up. For them, the stubborn ones, change the law, sure. But will that do? Will that do for the children exactly what you would do for your own kid? No more, no less? Especially since there are so many abortionists who have already publicly stated they will kill even if abortion is illegal again? It is the child's absolutely knowable and provable helplessness in and of itself which draws a human response, not the fecklessness of a bullied harassed mother.

As with Avon, advance homework was a good thing. All big cities have lots of mills, but some more than others. The 1968 battle lines are a helpful place to start looking: New York, California, Florida, Illinois. These four states jumped zealously ahead of "Roe." Just those four alone also cover almost all of the grisly "market," give-or-take a state boundary or two. I can still see the first shooting town in my mind's eye. Northern; yes. Lots of nice forests; yes. Upper class types like forests, especially to look at out of their back windows. Their big back windows. The yellow pages had already revealed all the mills in town, most of them (the ads) with no doc names and no mill addresses. I obviously couldn't consult with local prolifers, who would've known all the mill addresses and maybe even some of the doc names or residence addresses, from home picketing. Instead, I started with the phone.

If you call every mill and every ob/gyns listed under the ob/gyn yellow page section and ask them directly do you do abortions? And, who does your abortions? You'll get hackles, of course. This was middle 90's and I think one of the first doc shoots was maybe '93 or so, in Pensacola. The receptionists were nervous. But there's more than one way to skin a cat. After a while, another telephone approach emerged, an indirect one. It's kind of like the process of getting a lawyer on the phone. You never ask to talk to the lawyer. Everyone does that. You chat with the secretary like you've got all day, and when she finally asks if you want to talk to the big guy, say, no! Oh no! I know he's too busy. Then you proceed to explain the whole messy legal matter to the secretary in great detail, with plenty of digressions for aunty Nelda's latest cat scan, and other news weather and sports. Drive her nuts, politely. She'll put him on if she can, or next time, just to get rid of you.

Same with the mill. I'll spare you the intermediate phases, but suffice it to say that after a while a story emerged, like a snake-oil salesman's patter. I'm new in town, helping my wife look for a new ob-gyn, my wife's very busy at her job. (Get it? Receptionists subconsciously admire a man who's supportive of… blah, blah, blah.) There's something very important I need to tell you, though (sigh, pause). We had a terrible experience in the town where we just came from. Out comes a story that would give any modern woman nightmares: We had an ob-gyn we loved to death. He was the best. Then one day (pause, sigh) she got pregnant.

Here's where you throw in the dealmaker. I mean, sorry. Skinny white boys gotta work the con., right? My wife and I, we're good Christians, right? We know all about that. But we were stuck and we really prayed about it, and we decided to terminate. You see how this works? One by one, in a thirty second conversation with a stranger, you're hitting all the buttons. You've got to. This was the mid-90's; this lady had already been told a thousand times, never tell a non-patient that Dr. Jones does abortions. Never. Let me hit the pause button on this receptionist/phone/shooting house list story just for a second.

My self-righteous fake Christian brothers and sisters at his point are nodding their heads wisely to each other and saying, see, he lies, I told you it was not of the Lord for him to be doing something like this, he's in the flesh, now we know. I could answer this objection with any number of ways, most of them brief and unprintable. Now, pay attention, nice church ladies, and pansy church men. Tell ya what I'll do: I refer all this pious discussion to Miss Corrie Ten Boom. She had a sister who was murdered in the camps later on, who had an extremely scrupulous conscience about lying. The Lord will not bless it, Corrie, etc. Corrie, for her sister's sake, took this to heart. When the Gestapo searched her house and said "Where are the Jews? Tell us now!" Corrie felt a sudden inspiration. "Under the table," she answered. The cops looked under the table. No Jews. The cops thought Corrie was nuts and told her so. Corrie was glad she could tell her sister she didn't lie. The Jews were actually under the floor under the table.

But it could've gone another way, with Corrie being the betrayer channeling her sister's delicate conscience. Corrie would have betrayed Jews who would've been better off if they had been hidden in the house of someone who wasn't so falsely scrupulous. Conscience examination is good, but it gives me an enormous pain in the neck when criticism like this comes from the cheap seats, to boot. Church ladies? Hello? You don't have to deceive anyone to throw a brick or a 6 foot by two-inch pipe end through a window at three a.m. and chase it with a nice diesel/unleaded mix and a road flare, ok? Until you do that, just be quiet and keep hoping Jesus will still want to save you after you've sat on your backside and prayed in churches a thousand yards away from where kids are getting their heads torn off. Sat in your easy chair, the one with the Bible next to it? OK? Be quiet. G.K. Chesterton said any stick will do to beat the church with. For lazybones, one excuse is as good as another. The evil one's goal is to keep you sitting there in the nice soft chair with the Bible. Don't look behind the curtain. Don't step outside the synagogue, to the street below where the publican is doing business and crying out to God.

## Chapter 6

## Shooting Slepian

### Prelims

Jon Wells asked me in an interview if I did Canada, and I was flummoxed. I could simply have told him the truth, but at that moment a thought came to me that hadn't occurred before: I'm toast. Here I am, really done for in two jurisdictions, New York and the U.S., and at that point I was more and more upset with the idea of a technical defense that most of the lawyers wanted: be silent and let your lawyer deny everything.

What? After all I knew from looking in microscopes, looking in the eyes of moms walking back out of the mills with their broken hearts and broken souls? After all I knew autopsying babies in Phily, you could say that the courtroom was a kind of legal fiction, a drama, and that you just say or do whatever it takes to "win," and then deny it all outside on the street. After Roe, well, yes, all courts are fictional. But even so we have only gotten this far precisely because no one stood up for babies, even in such a fictional courtroom.

## TO RECEIVE A CHILD

Courtrooms, for all their lies, are still located on planet earth. They occupy part of the land and air that God made, and His rules still apply. To pay someone to say I didn't do it was lying as much as Roe is. Supreme Court justices know what a baby is just as you and I do.

 Looking at Wells in that awkward glass visit booth at the customs jail in Batavia New York that day, it hit me: don't deny it, don't say nothing, don't retreat behind a lawyer to cover the awkwardness of not doing the most natural thing in the world -- telling the truth. Let the inside the beltway (itb) fbi tell their story. People, especially in the media, but also their customers, are comfortable with experts in authority telling a story. Their concern is not so much with the truth, but with perceived attributability. This expert, that official, they and their media guests would be very believable with the Canada story.

Of course, Canada has pictures of such and such a car going through a toll booth on the border. This doesn't surprise me a bit. I'm surprised they don't have DNA samples and voiceprint there, too. Why not? The Vito squad are experts, why can't the itb crowd be experts, too? Barely a few hours later, back in my cell, the fruit of the squirrely intuition that hit me during the interview became apparent. Whoever did Canada, this takes the pressure off. The Canadian police and doctors can all breathe a sigh of relief believing the itb fantasy. Why mess with a perfect happenstance? It's not like agreeing to the story would do me any good, either. Why not let it ride just as it was? This would give the outside the beltway (otb) fbi guys, the Vito squad, a little breathing room, also. No, I can't say for sure it was they, of course. I don't know who did Canada. But based on my communications with the Vito squad in the 90's, and the anecdotes I heard about them from some retired assistant U.S. attorneys, they are my first candidates, without a doubt.

If they are not, the field narrows quickly. Where to find such a good shot? A guy who could shoot so accurately he could injure someone three out of three and not kill him? Military and hrt snipers, Olympic and other amateur match shooters. It's a short list. And most of those are not inclined to break the law. The Vito squad was supremely motivated to get a little payback for the dowager empress messing up their lives. Also, in their curmudgeonly Irish and Italian hearts, they probably felt God was on the side of the babies. Cops feel this, deep inside, I know. The older ones, I mean. They are granddads. They are old school. The worst cases they saw, outside of abortion, in their professional lives, were the cases that involved the torture of babies. and the older ones even remember arresting abortionists. Plus, it could sound a little cynical, but end-game thinking goes along these lines: an injured doc who's still alive and retired is a lot more helpful to his fellow doc than one who, sadly, has died.

I even heard a story from some prolifers in Portland to the effect that one of the Canadian doctors who was injured up there gave a speech to a med school class about the hazards of his "choice" profession. He was walking with a cane when he said this. We tend to ignore people who have died, but a living limping man in front of you who can answer questions about his experience is more "a teaching moment." To forget the dead is not good, either way, whether the dead we so ignore are children, or the former doctors who killed them, or, say, Paul Hill and John Salvi, to pick just two.

One last thing about the painstaking accuracy of winging versus the easy fatal shot. I just can't do it. Media flacks and proaborts (what's the difference?) gas on and on about this, but they weren't there. I can tell you. It's the simple truth. Only one man looked through that scope that night, and it wasn't some media pundit or proabort. Only one guy can testify on this subject. It's hard enough to aim at someone's arm or leg, but to aim for the head or chest! I simply cannot do it, and I thought about it a lot. Maybe I wasn't in the struggle long enough. Maybe, unlike Scott Roeder and others, I didn't have someone in my sights who had already been injured but still kept going like some weird demonic energizer childkiller bunny.

This is not to take one single thing away from Scott and others. In fact, for all I know, he quite simply has the courage I lack, to do what is necessary under the circumstances, what you would want done in a heartbeat for yourself or your own child. Do you want to come back from work or dinner with a cop, holstered weapon at his side, saying, sorry, I just couldn't do it? And your child is dismembered at his feet, tortured to death? All this yakking about pacifism, but why is it brought forward as an excuse for violence; i.e., standing by to enable violence? Gandhi himself wouldn't tolerate such a thing, for one second, and he said so. He specifically said such a thing was cowardice. I am sick to death of violent "pacifism." Give me forceful peace, peace that begins with helpless children.

The bad guys could've ended this at any time, including long before anyone had ever fired a shot or threw a flare, easy as pie. But they did not.

Put your hand on a child and watch out. You will draw a human response, and eternity with the millstone. Hold your breath! The proaborts and their media running dogs would say I'm lying about this. They say I must be covering up for some other thing, some deep dark problem. It doesn't bother me when they say this. To paraphrase Tolkien, I feel exactly the same way about them, especially when they cast their gaze heavenward and pine about "choice" when really it's about dollars and votes and demonic predation and control freakism.

But back to Canada. If the Vito squad didn't do it due to the obvious training and skill and equipment available to graduates of the fbi hrt sniper schools and all that, then who did? At this point I'm really guessing. All I can say is it would have to be a real sniper, a pro. This points to ex-military, the Olympics and other match competitors, or the non-military pros, such as the big city hrt snipers. All right boys and girls, can you say, "big city p.o. snipers"? Here's where the real story starts to look more feasible than the backyard plinker meme of the media surrounding the Buffalo story.

My mental environment on the shooting range was to avoid the two kinds of misses that bothered me: a lethal miss, and an air-miss. They both bothered me because they both meant someone could die. I was not emotionally equipped to kill anyone, even accidentally, as a result of trying to injure only. I only found that out after the fact. At the time I had no feeling about it because I wasn't going to kill anyone. If I wasn't a skinny white boy from the suburbs with no gang or street fighting experience, I suppose I would've been more into baseball bats or mob stuff, but I was not. Babies are helpless; i'm a lamb, so...

Add to that, the possibility of guns. My dad qualified as sharpshooter on a Springfield 30.06 in 1942 at Camp Lejeune N.C. and Quantico Va. On a couple of family vacations, Dad took us plinking. It was a hopelessly archaic Sears Remington 22 with an extremely hard to pull back cocking spring. If you're small -- we were eight -- and do not have much arm strength, this has the tendency to drive the muzzle into he dirt while you are cocking it with one hand and holding it with the other. Yes, I connect the smell of cordite with yet one more happy memory from childhood, hanging out with Dad. It's sadder than that now. But child killing has wrecked everything, not just kids, hasn't it? I started out on a range near the "y" in the road that goes over the bridge from Baltimore and lands on the eastern shore of Maryland. It was near Wye, Maryland, close to the mobile home I lived in near Milford, Deleware, but not too close.

It was mainly a handgun range, with a rifle range off to the side. The rifle part was not very improved, shooting at grass, sitting in the sun. I don't know why I wound up at Elk's Neck after that, but it was love at first sight. The rifle range was a huge improvement over the Delmarva one, and it was much more woodsy and remote. The 100 yards and lesser distances were well marked off and the shooting area well developed with benches and stations and lanes. The crowd seemed much more serious about rifles, also.

One day a man showed up, my size, and coloring, and ethnicity. When he first showed up, he was just another shooter in a bunch that included seasonal hunters who only came in to dial their scopes with a couple dozen rounds. Many of them had kids, either with them or waiting somewhere else; so, you can't blame them. This one guy, though, was different. After a while, I found myself unloading, standing over behind his bench and just watching, goggle-eyed. He was obviously used to observers, as if he were some kind of instructor, and he completely ignored me, focusing on what he did, which was unusual. For one thing, he didn't even use the bench. He shot mainly freestanding, his left toe pointing toward the target. Like the Salisbury guys, he was in no hurry. He was definitely one of those bolt-action guys. I know, I know, real snipers sneer at semiautomatic amateurs like me, but when you're an amateur, you might need a second shot some day. Cycling with a bolt and keeping on target is slower in a scope, and even then a skill acquired only with years and years of experience. When you throw in the kick of the ak/sk, it gets even harder. Professionalism like that was not a luxury available to someone like me with the baby body count number clicking away every 30 seconds.

After a while, the guy looked around and we chatted a little on his break. I only saw him two or three times. We never asked each other's names, but one day he shyly divulged to me that in fact he was a pro sniper, working for a big city hostage rescue team (HRT). In the big cities and the military there are snipers and there are snipers. Most of them qualify merely as a cross-train, while retaining expert status in something else, like bomb disposal or drug cache cracking, or opening my locks. This guy in front of me at Elk's Neck was totally different. He just had the stuff in every ounce of his body and he didn't care about anything else. He was a specialist, a purist. He was the kind of guy who would cross-train the other guys. It was only after he told me he was P.O. that I noticed his shoes. Off-duty cops always wear the perfect Nikes under stonewashed Levi's. They are more vain about it than million dollar endorsement NBA stars.

But here was this guy wearing his uniform boots on the rifle range. He wanted the same feeling in his feet as if he were at work, so the practice time wouldn't be different from on the job. This would not have mattered if he weren't also a freestanding shooter. For this guy with an actual job and a tripod and setting up lying down or shooting off a parapet, it would have felt like reaching out and touching a doorbell. He had prep, the stance, the drawdown and the breathing/aiming, all perfect parts of a whole, just like a welder who spends as long as it takes to grind up the prep for one perfect bead that will hold forever.

Watching this guy shoot, and remembering the Salisbury shooters so carefully arranging everything and relaxing to shoot reminded me of the decision to stop everything and learn how to weld, so many years earlier. The first time I saw him free stand and shoot, it took so long for the pull, it was as if he'd forgotten what he was doing. After a while I got used to that, or what the marines call "squeeze, don't jerk." Sometimes I would squeeze so slowly I would get a double fire just from that. Something to avoid because no matter how fast it comes, two bullets won't land in the same place. I could say more. They say professionals make it look easy.

This man made it look as if it were possible. Not perfect, for me, but possible. Relax, be like the pro welder who takes all day grinding and setting up for just one perfect smooth bead that will last forever, but is laid down like snot off a glass door knob, practice practice practice.

One thing I can tell you with a certainty: now, twenty years later, I get chills up my spine thinking about Elk's Neck. Knowing what I know now. I know I was standing in the presence then of one of the tiny handful of men in North America who for a certainty were capable of making each of the three shots in Canada and be 1000% successful to injure but not kill. All I know about Canada is what I have read in the FBI reports and warrant application material that I have read so far in my case, that three former doctors were shot, three were injured, three are still alive, and three are retired. That's not just good shooting, it's perfect shooting. I really think it has to be a pro, if I had to guess who it is, just like the guy I saw in Elks' Neck, who shot for an HRT team in a large east coast city.

One other thing happened in Elk's Neck while I was there. A hunter let his five-year-old son stray under the front of the firing benches. The boy was just looking for brass, especially bright shiny new ones in the piles of old shells. It was the most natural thing in the world for a little boy to do, but dad was the culprit. All that kid had to do was pop up from his crouching position at the same time a barrel tilted down, as they do, on a reload or a scope check. That, and one "negligent discharge." Like the two-year-old grabbing the bright blue m&m in the comb of the 50 horsepower escalator in Ireland, right in front of his mom; it was the same thing. Kids are kids. If you can't protect your own damn kid in the womb, don't tell me you're such a good mother or father to one of your surviving children. It all runs together.

Ok! So, let's assume you're good enough, three-inch clusters at a hundred yards with FMJ's, a stable scope mount, and we're off! Ok, what's the target? Avon was very good discipline for reaching out and touching someone, meaning, ballistics. A gun is a much more serious business for everyone involved; so, donuts and night-time street person and all the rest of it would come into play. Avon turned out to be the perfect learning experience for reaching out, where the price for failure is steeper. My preference would've been to move more quickly into the neglected areas (arson and guns) but looking back I sense the sublets process of a long winding road that gets where it's going only after slow daily labor and improvement one little step at a time. Daily quiet time is the arbiter, the crucial crucible in the matter of the million daily decisions. Push forward? Relax and regroup? Cross-train? Retire? Back to the sidewalk? Try to get rescue going again?

Others were doing those resistance actions, and a ton more, like lobbying and all that. No one was pushing for an end game. An end game that started with this one child, today's child. You shall not pass. Lose this one and you lose them all, into the future. Each child, lost or saved, represents the whole thing, all of it. You lose today's child, especially by not doing for him or her what you would do for your own child. You lose them all, even the future ones that you thought you might save, by today's appeasement and compromise. Over today's child. No. It doesn't work that way. Either each child is as good as any other, or they all are expendable. Heaven help you, heaven help us, if we bartered away even one child, for our own convenience. Today. My enemies of course will shout hypocrisy when I invoke quiet time and the Lord in what they call violence. To make this accusation is the only rhetorical option they have, since they are so violent, and they won't quit. They have to put up a smokescreen. As you know by now, to push a known serial murderer away from a child is the true non-violence, the true peacefulness. And the corollary bears saying: nothing is more violent than to permit his access. At any time, for any reason.

As with Avon, advance homework was a good thing. All big cities have lots of mills, but some more than others. The 1968 battle lines are a helpful place to start looking: New York, California, Florida, Illinois. These four states jumped zealously ahead of "Roe." Just those four alone also cover almost all of the grisly "market," give-or-take a state boundary or two. I can still see the first shooting town in my mind's eye. Northern; yes. Lots of nice forests; yes. Upper class types like forests, especially to look at out of their back windows. Their big back windows. The yellow pages had already revealed all the mills in town, most of them (the ads) with no doc names and no mill addresses. I obviously couldn't consult with local prolifers, who would've known all the mill addresses and maybe even some of the doc names or residence addresses, from home picketing. Instead, I started with the phone.

If you call every mill and every ob/gyns listed under the ob/gyn yellow page section and ask them directly do you do abortions? And, who does your abortions? You'll get hackles, of course. This was middle 90's and I think one of the first doc shoots was maybe '93 or so, in Pensacola. The receptionists were nervous. But there's more than one way to skin a cat. After a while, another telephone approach emerged, an indirect one. It's kind of like the process of getting a lawyer on the phone. You never ask to talk to the lawyer. Everyone does that. You chat with the secretary like you've got all day, and when she finally asks if you want to talk to the big guy, say, no! Oh no! I know he's too busy. Then you proceed to explain the whole messy legal matter to the secretary in great detail, with plenty of digressions for aunty Nelda's latest cat scan, and other news weather and sports. Drive her nuts, politely. She'll put him on if she can, or next time, just to get rid of you.

Same with the mill. I'll spare you the intermediate phases, but suffice it to say that after a while a story emerged, like a snake-oil salesman's patter. I'm new in town, helping my wife look for a new ob-gyn, my wife's very busy at her job. (Get it? Receptionists subconsciously admire a man who's supportive of… blah, blah, blah.) There's something very important I need to tell you, though (sigh, pause). We had a terrible experience in the town where we just came from. Out comes a story that would give any modern woman nightmares: We had an ob-gyn we loved to death. He was the best. Then one day (pause, sigh) she got pregnant.

Here's where you throw in the dealmaker. I mean, sorry. Skinny white boys gotta work the con., right? My wife and I, we're good Christians, right? We know all about that. But we were stuck and we really prayed about it, and we decided to terminate. You see how this works? One by one, in a thirty second conversation with a stranger, you're hitting all the buttons. You've got to. This was the mid-90's; this lady had already been told a thousand times, never tell a non-patient that Dr. Jones does abortions. Never. Let me hit the pause button on this receptionist/phone/shooting house list story just for a second.

My self-righteous fake Christian brothers and sisters at his point are nodding their heads wisely to each other and saying, see, he lies, I told you it was not of the Lord for him to be doing something like this, he's in the flesh, now we know. I could answer this objection with any number of ways, most of them brief and unprintable. Now, pay attention, nice church ladies, and pansy church men. Tell ya what I'll do: I refer all this pious discussion to Miss Corrie Ten Boom. She had a sister who was murdered in the camps later on, who had an extremely scrupulous conscience about lying. The Lord will not bless it, Corrie, etc. Corrie, for her sister's sake, took this to heart. When the Gestapo searched her house and said "Where are the Jews? Tell us now!" Corrie felt a sudden inspiration. "Under the table," she answered. The cops looked under the table. No Jews. The cops thought Corrie was nuts and told her so. Corrie was glad she could tell her sister she didn't lie. The Jews were actually under the floor under the table.

But it could've gone another way, with Corrie being the betrayer channeling her sister's delicate conscience. Corrie would have betrayed Jews who would've been better off if they had been hidden in the house of someone who wasn't so falsely scrupulous. Conscience examination is good, but it gives me an enormous pain in the neck when criticism like this comes from the cheap seats, to boot. Church ladies? Hello? You don't have to deceive anyone to throw a brick or a 6 foot by two-inch pipe end through a window at three a.m. and chase it with a nice diesel/unleaded mix and a road flare, ok? Until you do that, just be quiet and keep hoping Jesus will still want to save you after you've sat on your backside and prayed in churches a thousand yards away from where kids are getting their heads torn off. Sat in your easy chair, the one with the Bible next to it? OK? Be quiet. G.K. Chesterton said any stick will do to beat the church with. For lazybones, one excuse is as good as another. The evil one's goal is to keep you sitting there in the nice soft chair with the Bible. Don't look behind the curtain. Don't step outside the synagogue, to the street below where the publican is doing business and crying out to God.

The Act There are dozens of ways to track down a serial killer and I used one of them to Find Barnett Slepian. There are dozens of ways as well to stop him from continuing to kill, and I used one of them. I waited outside his kitchen window a long time before he gave me the shot I wanted. When I saw Dr. Slepian go down by a movement of his shoulder, I was pretty sure I had hit him, and I knew my job was done. If the first shot had been a miss, I might have tried a second shot for the shoulder again, but it wasn't necessary. I went to one hole and shed all my nighttime equipment except the rifle. This is called "sanitizing," so that you are hypothetically prepared as best you can for an arrest at any moment. Then I went back to the ground holster and holstered the rifle. In real time this took all of 30 or 45 seconds.

The immediate aftermath Just west of the Slepian's house is a funny little double-ended dead-end street called cricket something, Cricket Hollow, maybe. On the one hand no one ever walks on it so there's no one to see you by accident. On the other hand, if you are walking on it, you stick out. The backyards/commons I shot from bordered Cricket Hollow along its western extent, and directly across from that was a tennis court. In front of the tennis court, on the western side of Cricket, was a lone ornamental tree on a lawn, with low branches that came down to the ground and covered it, like Christmas tree. I hid the bike under that tree. I rode it in and out as I was surveilling so that if a given night was the night to shoot, I would be ready to leave. It also put the car farther away from potential eyewitnesses.

I like bikes because they tend to look innocent. If the call was "shots fired," a cop, hurrying to the scene, wouldn't think of a bike as something to look for. Crossing Cricket Lane required some waiting and watching since I didn't want to just walk out onto the street and right into someone. Also, the house to the immediate north of the tennis court was strange, a kind of ranch style set back with a long drive. I could never really be sure if someone were outside that house or not.

After the shooting crossing Cricket and getting out on the bike without being seen was probably going to take two-and-a-half or three minutes. Even though I had already reconned this route, this was the first time I would be going through the backyard of the people living on the eastern side of the street west of Cricket Lane. Before, I had just biked right out of Cricket. Behind the tennis court was the boundary of the houses on the next street over to the west. It's funny that I would feel nervous about a simple trespass after what I'd just been through, but I was. This one house could be a problem. They did not have a back fence, and I came from behind their garage and then slowly walked down their driveway, pushing the bike. I can't remember why, but I had the sense that this was an older couple. Maybe it was the lack of mess and toys in the yard.

All the fear I had felt creeping down their driveway was ramped up the minute I broke free from the shadow of being next to their house and was now effectively on their front lawn, on their driveway. You have to act as if you do this every day, as if it's your own house and you're out for a little night biking as a matter of routine. But I got a big jolt. Right across the street, and in the street, was an impromptu post-football game party. I love high school football, but let's admit that these things are a little bit narcissistic, right, -- the whole football team/cheerleader dynamic, impressing your friends, and so on? Also, gauging by the feel of this particular party, I'd say the home team had won.

It's utterly impossible for me to believe that these kids, every one of them, didn't hear the shot, since it was an a.k., and unsuppressed. It kicks out a real bark, it was three minutes earlier, and it was not even a hundred yards away. I suppose in this case the narcissism of high schoolers was in my favor, even if normally it is a large part of why I do what I do, sad to say. They completely ignored me as I got on the bike, rolled down the driveway of the house and onto the street, and right through their party and past them. It was surreal, like the officer who is drinking tea while the Gallipoli kids are being mowed down, or the party scene in Apocalypse Now. Part of the problem in America is there just seems to be no end to the partying, but in this case it was to my advantage. The irony of heaven, I suppose.

It turned out the pre-planned route back to my car led through their impromptu party, and as 1 rolled down the tiny incline of the entrance of the driveway into the street, and did it on an angle, heading toward my destination which was to my right, this made for an odd moment, steering and balancing the bike. Also, there was a flinch at that exact moment. What was I thinking? Riding right into a crowd of dozens of witnesses, three minutes after a de facto gun felony? Even if they let me pass, it still was a huge danger, witness-wise. But I decided at the last minute, as I rolled into the street proper that to turn the other way would be even more dangerous in terms of possibly drawing attention, so I did the counterintuitive thing, of riding right through them as if I were innocent and did this all the time. Like them, in other words. They didn't have anything to fear, even though every sidewalk counselor and CPV worker in the world knows that liaisons and parties alike generate dead babies like rain in Indianapolis in the summertime.

There was a slight crawl on my flesh riding past them, that little cringe of: maybe I'll get caught. But sure enough they were sufficiently into themselves. As I rolled into the crowd, which was in the street itself, I heard the first siren of the night. It sounded like an engine company headed eastbound on the latitudinal arterial road just south of the Slepian's neighborhood. I'd guess that truck was about half a mile west of my position. The sound was actually sweet to me, because it meant Dr. Slepian would survive a shoulder injury with a rapid medical response. It meant someone has called for an ambulance, something I wasn't completely sure of when I pulled the trigger, because I never saw anyone else in the house. It is a strange thing: you want someone nearby to call the wagon, but you don't want someone nearby to get frightened or accidently shot, since it's a residence. Yeah, yeah, my enemies will say I'm a hypocrite, but then, they aren't looking at the before and after activity picture of Slepian when he's not at home. And they know it.

Before the trial I heard of a witness who saw someone getting into a car driven by someone else and leaving the area, from the other side of the property. I have no reason to doubt that that happened. It sounds to me as if someone was in the area who wasn't supposed to be, such as a burglar. They heard the shot or a scanner transmission and decided to get out of there knowing the cops might come soon. I didn't see it, so I cant say either way. But a shot in a neighborhood like that is not like a shot in the South Bronx. The rest of the bike ride was uneventful; in fact, the rest of the entire leaving the scene and leaving Buffalo was calm. I never again heard sirens or saw lights after that one time. At the strip mall west of the development, I stashed the bike in a peculiar half-acre no-man's land in between a detached residence next to the tiny mall, and the back fence of the next street of houses. It was a tiny grove of beeches or aspens, with a tiny enfilade. 1 wiped down the bike with my cotton gloves the best I could and got in the car.

In the car it took a minute to calm down and to make sure I wasn't nervous driving. It really is true that if you can get a few minutes and a mile away from a scene, you might as well be in Mongolia, and I tried to convince myself of that. What a shame to do a simple fender bender a mile or two away and lose it all after a successful egress. I went back to the motel near Transit Road to get something and to sanitize the room. I cleaned the car, changed out of the throw-away clothes and into some driving clothes, and hit the road. I didn't know this job world be such a big deal, so I had no other plan but to drive home. Home at that time was in a crummy fixer-upper apartment in Jersey City that I was living in, rent-free, sort of, as a perk for being a hillbilly carpenter for the owner. He did everything on the cheap, fixing up so-called "dollar houses," houses auctioned off for back taxes, or less.

The plan was to just drive home, but they say when you and I plan, God laughs. The quickest way home was straight eastbound on the New York Expressway, back to the tristate area, but for some reason I headed south instead. 1 think it was the old Avon reflex of trying to get a border between you and the scene as quick as possible, meaning, a state border. Not that that makes any difference to the feds, for a fed crime, but in the beginning hours, I think a crime and its prosecution always starts with local jurisdiction, even if it is a fed crime. In the old days, anyway, the fed actually had to wait for permission to work a crime. Think of that. Can you imagine?

The other main route out of town was south, straight through the New York southern tier, and down into Pennsylvania. Maybe I also wanted to get out of the weather, in case the famous lake effect snow were to blow into the area. My car was not a good snow car.

I found a motel just across the state line and stopped for the night. Based on what I saw in the 'scope, Dr. Slepian was still alive, being taken care of, and being a doctor himself. I had absolutely no idea of any other outcome. I don't recall trying to get the radio to work.

The motel had a continental breakfast and there was no one there so I ate and hit the road, maybe about nine or ten a.m.

About noon I stopped for gas at a rest stop southbound, still in Pennsylvania. I don't know why I hadn't turned back east to home yet. The road goes down to Pittsburgh and maybe I was thinking I would simply get the Pennsylvania turnpike there and go east, and that's when I hit the rest stop.

It was a general public rest stop, not a trucker stop, and I was sitting in a room that seemed like a kind of big lobby. It had vending machines and bathrooms and drinking fountains.

As I was sitting staring at a tv I couldn't hear, a tv mounted up on a wall, it never crossed my mind that the story would show -- a man is injured. This does not make news. But then I saw yellow tape, the trunk of a white police cruiser, and Amherst written across the trunk.

The name Amherst stuck in my mind just a little bit. Where have I heard that name before? The target, in my thinking, was always in Buffalo. Also, the cruiser was white, and the only cop car I had ever seen in the target area was a kind of medium tone blue, not light and not metallic, and an older model than the cruiser on tv. It was blockier too than the smooth, swoopy model of the cruiser I was looking at.

It really took quite a few minutes standing there for me to even suspect that the tv story was related to the job. Even then, without hearing the story, I didn't know if it really was. But when I left the rest stop, I think I had the idea in my mind: I am on the run now. This could be serious. I decided to act as if it could be serious as I got back into my car and be careful.

I stayed in a midrange motel in Steubenville that night. I bought something to eat from a seven eleven type store and sat on the bed and turned on the tv.

## The Buffalo Gal

As sad as it was that Dr. Slepian died, not all of the news from Buffalo was bad. In the Summer of 1999 a baby was born as a direct result of the shooting. The baby's family contacted Jim and told him how much they appreciate her life, "the apple of their eyes," and his action. The mom was bullied into making the appointment with Dr. Slepian, but was then relieved to find out it wasn't happening. Just one canceled appointment turned into a child, alive all this time. She will never know how close she came.

One day Jim mentioned to me one aspect of prison life. Many times he is asked: Any regrets? Now that you are doing life?

When that happens, Jim told me, he always remembers the Buffalo Gal, and smiles. He tells them about her, and then he answers their question with one of his own: Should this baby be dead? Just to satisfy your private aesthetic about "peacefulness"? And what is true violence at the clinic: Protecting a child? Or ripping her head off?

In twenty years he's never gotten an answer for that one. Not once. All prisoners of all faiths, including Muslim, Protestant, Catholic, agnostic, pantheist, neopagans and New Age are all antiabortion.

Also, the whole thing is a mild reprise for him over his failure in Fresno in 1983 to stop the forced abortion he saw there. This one made it through. She is a brilliant and elegant African American woman in Western New York, just turned 23 this year. She's got a right to Maya Angelou's Tree of Life, like you and me.

## At Trial

But finding out about the Buffalo Gal came years later. In real time, what happened long before that was Kopp's closing arguments at trial. Kopp painted a picture of someone who stumbles out of his door in the morning heading to work and sees a total stranger beating the neighbor's kid to death on his doorstep.

You don't go Rambo, Kopp told the jury. In fact, at first you don't even think of attacking the attacker. You put your arms around the little girl you know so well. But he just keeps coming. Kopp froze the action.

Let's humor the pacifists who are willing to risk the life of a child to satisfy their own personal aesthetic about pacifism, or squeamishness, or cowboy movie fake fair play: you shoot the attacker with a spitball. In this scenario the attacker instantly proclaims: "My bad. What was I thinking! I quit!"

A nice dream. Could happen. Has happened, a lot.

For the rest who remain, yes, Virginia, every doc has already been spitballed. On notice. They know the science to apodictic certainty. They and the pathologists assemble the tiny bodies to make sure a mom doesn't deliver a perfectly formed term arm or leg seven months later. They've also been politely asked to quit, every one of them.

Suppose he doesn't? Back to the scenario in front of your house. The guy won't quit. Suppose you also recognize the attacker as a recently released mass murderer who you know won't quit? This makes the analogy stronger. As Kopp told the state court at sentencing, 25 thousand kids with their heads torn off is a pretty good idea we're talking mass murder, especially when most of those are black and brown (as the killer's family said). That adds genocide to the pile. A gentile Shoah, and race-based, like the last one.

But at closing argument, it was about one child only. Any religious or political angle is off point. It's simply a human thing, something all humans agree on. You cannot sit there and watch a child being murdered in front of your eyes. Small children are in fact killed in front of our eyes, Kopp said, no differently from the poor child on your doorstep, because mills operate in publicly advertised places at appointed times. It's not hidden or unpredictable.

Then Kopp said, "Suppose pure defensive shielding won't cut it, and you must turn to face the attacker. Also, the goal is not to do this or that to the attacker other than to make him stop, certainly never to kill him as a goal in itself. Everything else is on the attacker. The Canadian shooter most certainly operated on this wavelength."

Three witnesses at trial made this point just a day before the closing argument: John Tomaselli, a Buffalo contractor, Joan Andrews Bell, and John Dunkle all endorsed force, however reluctantly, to save kids. On the subject of reluctance, Tomaselli mentioned Sgt. York, who did what he had to despite his personal feelings. The York point also fell into the category of the case of Wicape Milk and gray area homicides.

The idea of a train track came up. If your daughter is tied to a train track and the next scheduled train isn't until seven AM, would you leave her there all night? Just because you believe in train schedules? No. This is why there is urgency, even if it's not immediately before the killing scheduled for the next morning.

You also would not abandon a child being killed on your doorstep, period. Any circumstance, any attacker.

In his closing argument Kopp got into fake pacifism. According to G. K. Chesterton, no one can be a private pacifist any more than he can be a private murderer. Also, when life is at stake, the abuse of "satyagraha" by cowards was specifically mentioned by Gandhi. Rev. Dr. Martin

Luther King made the same point, when one must analyze the intentions of your enemy before you consider pacifism.

MLK and Gandhi both said that nonviolent political movements are relevant for Jim Crow and salt taxes, respectively, but they are not universal. More is involved when life is at stake, but so many abuse the noble idea of nonviolence when really they are just lazy and won't help a helpless person under attack. Even H.E. John O'Connor, Archdiocese of New York refused to order the sidewalk counselors to stay away when the distraught bishop in Boston said to, after a shooting up there. O'Connor said we'll stay until the killing inside the mills is stopped. This is true pacifism. It must involve the safety of innocent helpless children and their moms.

Kopp mentioned Pastor Mike Bray who spoke more eloquently even than MLK or Gandhi: Justice first, then peace.

What happened next indicates that at voting time, each juror understood this perfectly.

## The Jurors Who Cried

The news about the Buffalo Gal came about the same time as the federal trial. The state trial was in 2003 and the federal trial in 2007, both resulting in life sentences.

The polling of jurors in the federal trial revealed some anomalies not unlike the Buffalo Gal's mother who went to the clinic expecting one thing and came away with another.

In the federal trial the clerk polled loudly and clearly every jury member and asked them to state "Yes or No" as to whether or not Kopp was guilty.

Nine jurors did say yes, and three did not. They did not speak at all. Of these, the most dramatic was Mrs. Woltz, who broke down weeping and could not speak, like the other two silent jurors. None of the three spoke a single word at polling. All three cried.

Kopp appealed this in an immediate post-conviction correction of the record when the Judge forged the word "yes" three times onto the record, as if the three jurors had spoken. On appeal the judge said he heard the three jurors speak. Kopp said, fine: let's hear the audiotape. The audiotape suddenly became unsubpoenable.

This was not the end of it. Mrs. Woltz wrote the judge, her fellow jurors, and gave an interview to reporter Michael Beebe explaining why she couldn't speak, and that the jury chambers process was rigged with bullying. ("Juror Tells of Her Distress," Buffalo News, 2007).

Courts are supposed to keep evidence for ten years, in case of appeal. Nine years later Kopp filed again. By this time, the tape had done a Watergate Oval Office. But if the tape shows the jurors answering . . . why suppress it?

Mrs. Woltz told the paper of other jurors who agreed with her that Kopp didn't intend to kill Slepian.

But Kopp remembers the courage of Mrs. Woltz. At the time, he said. "Mrs. Woltz is my hero. I had 20 years to slowly realize how much help babies and moms need. Mrs. Woltz, not a prolife worker, got it in ten days.

## More Recent Events

After checking the court record I read about and met a lot of people on both sides of the matter. These people updated Buffalo, 1998.

For example Peace Officer Chet Gallagher said in a pre-Covid NY Times interview (byline: Damien Cave): If all prolifers went to the mills and prayed it would end in seven days. The problem is: they don't. In the meanwhile, false pacifism does the opposite. Viet Nam protesters stopped the war, but only by flooding the streets while the news had body counts every night.

Also, immediately before Covid a petition was circulated at the Walk For Life in WDC requesting pardon for Kopp and the other so-called "Prisoners For Christ." On examination it turned out to be based on a "Defense for Life" statement promulgated by Pastor Paul Hill in 1993:

"Any force justified to protect a born child is justified to protect an unborn child."

The interesting thing about this statement is its elegance, instantly comprehensible to any parent. Many leaders of the time signed it, including Hill, Pastor Michael Bray, and Fathers Robert Pearson and Thomas Carleton and Regina Dinwiddie. Signors of the 2020 petition included non-coop pioneer Joan Andrews Bell and moral theologian Catherine Ramey.

In 2017 I sent a copy of the Waters letter to trained moral theologian and Thomistic scholar Joseph Scheidler. He immediately wrote back: "There is nothing anyone can argue with in this letter. It's the truth."

More recently a TV pundit said that the years after Dobbs would see no change in the national annual average number of abortions. So far she's on target.

Verifying facts for this book I contacted third world prolife leaders. For them, abortion is part of a larger picture. They sourced David Icke, no friend to Christianity. In Perception Deception (2014, population control chapter only) he details the 2004 UN Committee target: 90% elimination of total world population. Also, the old Georgia Guidestones (94%). In a recent public statement Bill Gates wants to start immediately with at least 25%.

These numbers are not unthinkable. One overseas source reminded me of Stalin- or Mao-era thinking, where massacre becomes tolerated over time. Humans are herds of sheep with anthrax. Or given it. Further, recent statements by Abp. Carlo Vigano (US Nuncio, Ret'd) indicate that solid confirmation of these large fraction targets is available, while the earth can hold 55 billion humans, living simply.

Getting back to the US, while I was fact-checking in Western New York, an acquaintance of Mr. Tomaselli told me that all of the school and other mass shooters since Columbine grew up all their lives in a world where the value of life was nothing. Take away all the guns and they'll use cars and knives. He said the shootings will not stop before the culture of death stops. Lose the guns and the communists will do the exact same thing quicker than the school shootings.

The Western New York source recalled Mother Teresa: Nuke war is the fruit of abortion. It is not certain Ukraine will lead to that. It is certain that even without it, Gates and the UN can achieve a similar result by other means. Then, surgical abortion retroactively could look like just a run-up.

Kopp insisted he did Buffalo for only one child. These other sources add the global dimension.

CHAPTER 7

# FRANCE, THE VITO SQUAD, LAVENDER HILL

To talk about France for me is to talk about the prison there. To talk about a prison anywhere is to talk about the country that built the prison since the prisoners in it represent those souls who have rejected the country. You can receive a false impression of the country, especially if the only part of it you see is the prison and the guys in it.

I suppose it's a natural temptation to form sweeping impressions of a country from small observations, whether you are in or out of prison, but there were a few things I ran into in France, even so, that threw me for a loop. Also, it's important to remember that all modernist countries share the possession of that fraction of their populations that was simply knocked out of society by modern mechanization, over technology and the industrial revolution, one of the few things Freud ever said that I happen to agree with. This cohort shows up in every prison, guys helpless to keep up with over technology and the heartlessness of the modern world, guys who would have been fine in the Medieval world, in an even slightly simpler world.

I was arrested in the tiny tourist/historical town of Dinan, in Bretagne. Bretagne, which means "Little Britain," as opposed to Great Britain across the channel, is steeped in wonderful history. The Battle of the Bulge was there. Patton turned east toward the Rheine there, just after Normandy. Joan of Arc beat up on the English there after she got the Dauphin to get up off his rear end to fight. Henry V said once more into the breach for King Harry there.

Now, as in all of Europe, they kill babies there, in Bretagne. *Selah*

Speaking of babies, I might as well start at the beginning in terms of importance about what threw me for a loop in France. As you might guess, it was what was happening outside the prison that interested me the most, in a sad way. But I found it out while I was inside the prison.

Here's how I found it out: In France I was absolutely blessed in prison by the weekly visits of the chaplain there, Msgr. L'Pasteur. Probably the most wonderful thing about L'Pasteur was that he wasn't French. Not that it's a sin to be French, I suppose, but his non-Frenchness was something we instantly shared. We were both expatriates.

We also shared the English language. L'Pasteur was completely fluent even to the point of subtle idioms and slang, This, plus any pastor's capacity to discuss profound things, meant he and I could talk about anything in depth. When you are in a foreign land and don't speak the language, this is something you really miss -- deep conversations. You really miss them. L'Pasteur also had a Swedish cosmopolitanism about him, which Byzantines have also. This made it easy to talk to him. His chaplain experience I suspect also added to his ability to talk freely to anyone, even an accused murderer.

Of course, I denied being a murderer, there, as I do now, by the way, but back then the denial took the form of "I didn't do it," meaning murder. More on this later.

In these casual conversations in France, a total lifeline to me, the subject turned to sodomites, a subject all prisoners are interested in. I mentioned to L'Pasteur a couple of old gray prisoners who sat in the back of the chapel on Sundays and talked incessantly, ignoring the Mass and to some extent, disrupting it.

"It's the only time they see each other," he said, reminding me of the Marion Rules of that French prison, namely, we were all locked up most or all of the time.

"Ahhhh," I said. It wasn't the first time I'd heard about prisoners who go to church only to get out of their cells. This is especially true in Marion Rules prisons.

I told L'Pasteur that I thought the two old guys were a little creepy even aside from the thing about disrespecting Mass. This is code talk for saying I thought they could be child molesters, in addition to merely being sodomites, what is usually called "homosexual."

"You think these guys are chomoes? Tree jumpers?" I asked L'Pasteur.

He looked at me with a look of complete stunned ingenuousness. L'Pasteur had the simplicity and directness of a child for all his European sophistication. But it was also a look of, are you the only one here who doesn't know what's going on?

He proceeded to tell me that not only were those two men chomos, but that seventy percent of all French criminal dockets were unresolved cases against child molesters.

Now I was the one who was stunned.

"Seventy percent? They can't all be priests." I tried to make a joke. It was the first thing I could manage to say. He made a dismissive wave of his hands. "Pah. Priests are only a tiny number of all the chomoes. And everyone thinks they are most of it. It's a distraction, a smokescreen. The courts are so clogged with the other ones they can't even prosecute bank robbers and rapists and murderers.

This was a huge wakeup call to me. France is not the only country with a reputation for hinky. Actually, many European nations have one and the quickest way to see it is to look for the nationality of passports at remote resorts in Bali and Borneo and Thailand and places like that, when there's a "gay tour" on. These tours are a cover for people who aren't looking for consenting adults. They can find that back home. They go far away from home to find little boys. And when they come back home, it is a help to them to know that most people are forming false stereotypes about priests, which happens "naturally" since the modern world rejects the highest standard, which is the Catholic. They're looking for an excuse to call them hypocrites. Then they can carry out their wickedness with less disturbance. The stuff you find out in jail.

Mamas, keep an eye on your boys. What I mean is, keep an eye on whoever is keeping an eye on your boys. Don't trust anyone. There are no real men left.

In progressive groovy liberal London, the grammas there do with a gallon of gas in the back door of a chomo's house. The firemen slow-walk it. They're not stupid.

Meeting with L'Pasteur and learning all these things was a big part of my time in jail in France, but I should say something about what life was like in general in prison.

When I was first arrested some detective tried to grill me about how I'd gotten into the country, but after a while I just clammed up. They put me in the local county jail in Rennes, which I gather is a kind of practical modern commercial center for otherwise folksy touristy medieval Bretagne with its castles, old monasteries and pretty spots like Mt. Ste. Michelle.

From the start I was "isolated." Solitary in jail is a plus/minus situation. It's nice to not have to deal with yard politics but after a while most people just get tired of it. We all need some fresh air and contact with others. If you think you'd be better off without dealing with some people, I bet you've never been in solitary. But if you have to, it's doable, grace of God. After a while in the clink-just-a-clink I mentioned it to the warden. He had asked to see me one day and I was escorted into some kind of staff muster room.

"Why am I in solitary?" I asked him, because in jail, you have to do something to get yourself put in solitary. They won't just put you there for no reason. The something is usually violence that takes place in custody. Versus staff, another inmate, or suicide risk. The warden knew I had done none of these things, not only not in France but not in my entire history of jail going back fifteen years before France.

French wardens are a trip. They are not like US or British wardens. A French warden is actually a sort of political appointee. He could be a friend of the president. He doesn't really have to know anything about running jails. That's all handled by an experienced Chef D'Garde who only operates inside the walls. Wardens are media spokesmen, and someone to fire if things go really bad.

By careful innuendo and delicate diplomacy the warden finally made it clear that my being put in solitary had nothing to do with my own behavior.

Why, then? I asked. I can't remember his exact answer but other scales fell from my eyes on this subject a few days later. I was back in my cell as usual and I happened to hear two guards talking to each other right in front of my cell door. They didn't know I could hear them because unlike US prisons, the cell doors in that jail were solid wood. I also suppose they assumed I couldn't speak French, which is certainly true, but I love listening to any language. You can still hear little waves of emotion in it, and maybe even catch a gist, especially since the European languages share so many cognates. The little gist I got plus the warden's hemming and hawing fell together and I suddenly got the point: the president of France or his representative had threatened the warden in Rennes: if the American dies in custody, you get a one way ticket to Devil's Island in the French Guyanas. I even gleaned the rest of it: France, like America, has a "mutt" problem.

This is what guards call kids raised on the TV. You can make a strong argument that it's not the kids' fault. Go ahead, but here's the result: a kid grows up on the box, and pretty soon he has no idea of reality except what's on the box. This applies to sports, history, politics, news, anything. If it's on the box, it's true, if it's not, it's of no interest because it's unverifiable by the box. Example: you can see a symphony on the box, but obviously this is not the same as playing a violin. Ergo, playing the violin really does not exist, even if there were a reality show about someone learning how to play the violin (don't hold your breath).

In combination with the dreary lives of the mutts, it isn't long before mutts see the TV as having avatars of their own unfulfilled wishes. This is isn't just true in sports, but it could be anyone on TV.

Suppose a mutt sees someone right in their jail, right with them, who was on the TV? The mutt knows enough about how the TV works to know that if he kills that guy who was on the TV, the mutt himself will then be put on the TV as being the guy who killed the guy who was on the TV. He will be famous. He will "be somebody," the somebody his drearily daily real life never seemed to be able to deliver, even if he is pretty good at sinking three-pointers.

No need even to say "morality aside" on the question of killing the TV person, because TV is drenched with no-consequence killing, the same way it's drenched with no-consequence uncommitted sex. No problem.

Anyway, no matter what you or I or even the mutts think about this, God bless their hearts, what matters in jail is what the wardens think about this phenomenon, and according to them, it is real, and has probably happened more than once. So, they need to protect themselves from the embarrassment of a killing on their watch. In all this, the mutts are to be the most pitied, since it is the trivialization of a human life, especially their own, but ramifying out to everyone's. It's not as if we don't deserve it since everyone lives by the box nowadays. Try pulling someone away from it. Better yet, try getting someone to just throw it away if you don't believe me. See?

So, if a mutt sees someone he saw on TV, the temptation is just too much. This is a great opportunity to step across the glass and enter into the only reality he knows.

That's why I was in solitary regardless of my own record of in custody good behavior. I even told the warden I would sign away my liability, but he just laughed. It wasn't about me, it was about him. The embarrassment he would have on his record forever, that he had allowed a predictable thing like this to happen on his watch. This matter of his personal reputation among other wardens and within his profession trumped any consideration about my rights. So here I am, stuck in the bucket, and no way out even with perfect behavior. All due to the mutt angle. Hmmm.

Even so, there was a surreal and even slow burn joyful aspect to the time in solitary in Bretagne. My cell faced east, and all morning that summer the sun would stream into it, a huge luxury for any prisoner anywhere in the world. The cell window which was huge faced out onto a large exercise yard, which meant there was no other prison wing to block the sky.

The yard itself was on the edge of the prison with only a wall beyond that. Past the wall you could see the nearby trees and apartment buildings of Rennes, a town the size of Pasadena, a hundred thousand or so people. For some reason 1 always seem to remember a morning star, there, in the blue sky.

For the "breakfast" in MAR, Maisonne d'Arrete Rennes, there was only coffee and a roll, but so many prisoners slept in, that you could get as much coffee as you wanted. I would fill up a bowl as big as a US-salad bowl with coffee, put my chair in the sun, and put the Second Chapter of Acts and other Christian music on the boom box.

L'Pasteur had brought me a CD which, as far as I was concerned, saved my life.

Abide With Me, Crown Him with Many Crowns, and a lot of other great hymns and songs by many evangelical groups were on the CD. These were hugely comforting to me since that music was all my background. I like the fancy Catholic and Byzantine stuff fine, but the old

Protestant stuff was so familiar and a great solace in that clink. Then there was fresh air and birds singing, too.

Fresh air? Birds? In France the windows were not like US prison windows which usually are tiny and permanently sealed. The windows in France were huge and you could open them inward like a pair of French doors. There were bars, of course, but you still got all that fresh air and you could hear the birds and feed them. There was a wide granite ledge. It was large enough to cook on. Even before the morning coffee came if I woke up at three or four, I would heat up some commissary coffee over a fire. I built the fire in a big aluminum disposable pan, the kind you cook a Thanksgiving turkey in. I would heat up the coffee in a commissary saucepan.

I even had cigarettes in France. At first I got them to give to inmates in the yard through the bars. The French are completely obsessed with cigarettes. If they could have figured out a way to smoke in a spaceship, they would have colonized the moon long ago. The first time they tried it they probably blew something up. I didn't really smoke the cigarettes myself, but I liked lighting them and the smell of them burning. Something to do in the bucket. I wonder if the cigarettes had anything to do with the change in heart which took place after a little while among the inmates.

At first my presence there was unpopular amongst them, at least one of them anyway.

"Die, American mother- _____! Great American Satan! I will kill you!," one young inmate liked to scream through the gap under my door, every morning when he went down the corridor to the yard. A nice little wakeup call, n'est pas? In the case of the young Muslim gentleman—I should really say Shiite, to be a little more accurate -- all he needed to know from the all-knowing TV was that I was an American for him to hate me and want to kill me. But even for any non-Muslim French, this was also sufficient. By French thinking all Americans are crude boorish bullies, neo-imperialists who have usurped the natural French position as cultural world leaders.

One day my erstwhile Shiite killer shouted under the door: "I love America! God bless America!"

Well, there's a changeup for ya, huh? Was this merely because of cigarettes coming out of the window during rec. time?

How I wish it was. I found out later that our Shiite friend had just discovered that poor Dr. Slepian was Jewish. According to this logic, then, I was now his best friend. What a pity I never ran into him after I was released from solitary so I could tell him about my own Jewish background. Well, whatever, as they say. I've told every Muslim I've met ever since, and I'm still here. A God thing, do you think?

I need to tell you about commissary in France. Well, and about coffee, too. They go together in this story.

When I first got into jail on this "bit," I was amazed at what soap-opera gossips red-blooded males can be, but gossip pales compared to the amount of time we spend talking about food. Prisoners worldwide missed the Sunday School class about Jesus saying don't worry about food and clothes. They talk about clothes, too, and they'll obsess over ironing a shirt -- a dumb prison uniform shirt -- and they'll point out the tiniest spot of grease on your shirt from repairing a lawn mower. And don't even start me on shoes. They're worse than women, if such a thing were possible.

This is all part of what Shiites worthily describe as the American obsession with the superficial and our abandonment of moral substance. What I mean is a prisoner's obsession with food and clothes is not a prison vice, but merely a concentration of a "street" vice, concentrated due to the apparently limited horizons of jail itself. Men in jail about food are as bad as women about clothes. Men in jail can talk about a meal they cooked on the street, just once, twenty years ago, with certain spices and certain fresh foods and with such-and-such to drink, with the same measured and patient tones as a talking stock ticker or the NOAA weather frequency. This is why what I am about to tell you about French commissary is unbelievable to prisoners in the US, who are all foodies for the duration, to make Julia Child a rank amateur.

Most prison commissaries are about one one-hundredth of what you see in a really badly stocked 7/11 or Piggly Wiggly. A dusty gas station in West Texas that has Moon Pies still in stock from the seventies. And a real CocaCola machine out front with glass bottles in it. Like that.

Top Ramen, maybe a tiny sausage, some spaghetti noodles, toothpaste, shampoo, a candy bar, if you lucky some Mrs. Dash and some hot sauce, and that's pretty much it. Oh, and some rice. Just enough to make "crackhead soup" and eat it with chips and soda. If Slim Jims come into the commissary, it's a stampede.

By comparison, prison commissary in France was simply not to be believed. A typical commissary order list in the US has maybe fifty things on it, and half of them soap and toothpaste. In France, there was so much stuff for sale they couldn't fit it all on one list. They had separate lists for the days of the week and some lists only showed up once every two weeks.

There was one stand-alone list just for tobacco. Remember? The French and tobacco? It had fifty kinds for sale including Dutch pipe tobacco, every kind of US readymade, and bags of rollup including the stinky Turkish stuff and cheap-o Bugler, the most popular. There were British and French ready-mades like Pall Malls and Gitanes. There were cigarette lighters, kitchen matches, paper matches. The French are into smokes. If you could've invented rocket science and brain surgery while smoking, the French would have done all that ages ago.

There was the usual list of what American BOP prisoners call "cosmetics," meaning, soap, shampoo, deodorant and toothpaste. On that list there were things never heard of in a US jail, like saucepans, glass bowls, knives and forks.

Even the food count fit on one list. There was a list just for package goods including lots of fancy readymade meals in a pouch. There was a separate entire list just for fresh fruit and vegetables, unheard of in US prisons, and more than just apples and bananas. You could get an entire fresh pineapple and kiwi fruit and leeks and some African stuff I still am not sure exactly what it is. It also had nuts and sultanas, or what an American would call a golden raisin. There was even a tiny list to send out to a local restaurant for a meal cooked by them. The guards would bring it in.

It was the sultanas that got me in trouble one night. Beware the sultanas!

When I deck-handed the ferry and landing craft on Angel Island in San Francisco Bay in the early 70's I had a skipper, Lance Green, who smoked Dutch pipe tobacco. It always smelled like cherries. Loved that smell.

In France I made a pipe out of a metal shaving cream tube and a ballpoint pen barrel. What can I say? Jailbirds got time on their hands.

One night, no one to talk to, nothing to read and nothing to do, locked up in solitary with a dread feeling about the Buffalo charges. I was sitting on the bed and smoking my crusty old Navy skipper pipe and eating sultanas. And then...well, and then the funniest thing happened. I stood up at one point to get a glass of water or something, and I collapsed back on to the bed, totally off-balance. I was stoned! Totally buzzed and blitzed, just on Dutch pipe tobacco and sultanas!

Now you must understand: I'm a good boy. I'm an Eagle Scout for heaven's sake. I cleaned my room when I was a boy, and helped my mom with chores, and got all my merit badges and did my homework. My own mom was a Juvenile Justice Commissioner and my dad was the navy equivalent of an M.P. in the Big One. I was not into drugs. Except, now, for wicked sinful sultanas and Dutch pipe tobacco in France, I never have done drugs. I also hate what they make people do, enough to tell anyone: Don't do drugs.

However, that night in France even after I gyro-ed back onto the spinning rack. I forgot about the spinning after a while once I got on the bed, and I said to myself, well, what's up? And I still had half a pound of sultanas and tons of tobacco left, and I said to myself, gee, if a little's OK, more could be better! I went over the moon.

To this day if I tell this story to a typical jaded US junkie jailbird, who kills to put the equivalent of a Walgreen's back shelf, and more, into his veins every day, I get this slow, knowing nod, accompanied by a wistful smile immersed in the rhapsody of memory of their first high, and a You Sly Devil You look. Excuse me, but these guys know something about sultanas and Dutch pipe tobacco, something you and I don't know. They're keeping it a secret. It sure as heck was a secret to me, in solitary, in France that night.

Nighttime in solitary is something. No birds, no sun. What to do? One thing we'd do is stand an old paperback novel on end, twirl it so it fanned out, and light it up. We'd turn the lights off in the cell and the novel on the granite ledge burned very slowly like a big candle. It was a nice feel, like a log fire at home. When I ran out of French novels, which I couldn't read anyway, I made an Aladdin's lamp out of soda cans and melted butter. Later, I found paper and pen to write, and even novels in English, but if you ever find yourself in jail, don't hesitate to think outside the box for ways to amuse yourself, especially if you're in solitary. I believe you owe it to God, to yourself, and your fellow jailbirds to try to stay occupied as best you can. Of course, Jesus is the best cellie, especially if He gets you there to begin with! Just go easy on the sultanas and Dutch tobacco.

Oh, and coffee.

One night, nothing to do, I cooked up some coffee and drank that even before the house coffee showed up, and there was tons of that since most prisoners sleep in. I never drank coffee on the street and I had no idea what it could do to you.

One afternoon the Chef D'Gard himself showed up on my doorstep.

"Meseur Kopp, are you aware zatyou have ordered half the commissary list?" he said, as drones of trustee prisoners pushing carts dropped off tons of stuff.

I dimly remembered a caffeine-induced all-nighter frenzy of checking off everything that looked interesting on the lists. 1 even checked off stuff I had no clue what it was, just to see what I'd get. I don't speak French, you see. It's all Greek to me.

That day, red-faced in front of the Boss Himselfness, I resolved to quit drinking coffee cold turkey. From that day forward until forever -- well, OK, now and then on a really big feast day I'll put half an ounce in a carton of milk -- and I remember Bretagne when I do.

That same summer in France I remember a court hearing. I hope you never wind up in a criminal courtroom one hundredth of the times I've been there, but even in French it slowly dawned on me that I was being indicted.

The French judge read out parts of the extradition instrument, a big fancy thing with seals and ribbons on it and all kinds of smarmy language in it about how much the American people loved and respected France, when everyone in France knows the FBI are just self-appointed international bullies who get off into everyone's business nowadays.

It was sad to hear the name of a "law and order" USAG on the extradition papers, a man that my family would have helped get into office. No law and order for babies, though, I would discover, on the sharp end of things, there in France.

The proceeding was "gist" translated to me, and at one point my bilingual French lawyer, Msgr Herve LeBouef, a great guy, asked me if I wanted to say anything. 1 asked him to repeat the gravamen of the charges.

"Murder, Msgr. Kopp."

Please take note: not blocking a doorway, the essence of FACE, under which I was being charged. Not obstructing this or that, just plain murder.

Murder is the taking of the life of an innocent person, or more specifically, a person who is not in the act of murdering someone else. For example, yanking the head off an utterly helpless child.

Whatever other subtle prolife points that could be made later I realized suddenly I was innocent of murder, and I told the court that. When the press quoted the denial of the charge, they morphed it into statement from me that the FBI had the wrong man, something I didn't say. Though this was not what I said, even that misstatement had a kernel of truth to it for the simple reason that the guy who needs to be in jail is the one jerking the head off a child, not the guy stopping it. Even with this media mix-up, and the media always get it wrong, they did have the wrong guy after all, come to think of it. At that moment there in France I decided I was done talking to anyone but lawyers, since everyone else had a way of getting it all wrong. I let the statement stand, exactly as I was misquoted. In the years since then I have come to the firm conclusion that it is not accidental that the press, or anyone in the public sphere, get it wrong. To tell a child murderer, or his running dog, that child murder is wrong is like telling your kid to get his hand out of the cookie jar. When he responds that space aliens took him over and commanded him to do it, you know you are dealing with willful ignorance. With the press or politicians, with anything connected to child murder, they will always get it wrong, a hundred percent of the time. This is not accidental, it's willful confusion surrounding the obvious evil. Deer-in-the-headlights, Duuuuuuuh, What? You get that every time.

When I was still in solitary I met a most remarkable man. How do you do that in solitary? Every day the yard filled with prisoners. They were curious about the guy in the bucket and they'd come over to talk through the window. Usually it would be a short conversation a few words of English from them and a very few words of French from me, but when I'd offer them a cigarette the news spread like wildfire and there would be quite a contingent of smokers each morning. Unlike US inmate youth, the French kids were the height of courtesy when I offered them a cigarette. They would hang around and smoke them right there in front of my window even though we couldn't communicate much. It was in this manner, both of us searching for words, I found out the kids were nuts about US rap. When I myself got sent out to a tiny solo yard for my own rec time, I'd put French rap on the boom box before I left the cell so they could listen to it. After a while I found out that the brigadier sergeant would come in to turn it off. No loud rap in solitary!

One day an English speaking gentleman showed up at the window. He was fiftyish with a strong Midlands accent and he proceeded to distance himself from the other prisoners by declaring that they couldn't fly a helicopter, as he could.

Drug pilots in stir are usually not in a hurry to talk about it but my new friend was not shy. He was in France awaiting extradition back to England in connection with something involving the English Channel and white powder. We were in the same cell for a while when I got into GP and he had an enormous burden to teach me Cockney rhyming slang, the British equivalent of banlieu. I've forgotten every word, God help me.

Banlieu is like Cockney in that both dialects were invented to flummox the police. Bainlieu is named for the poor high-rises surrounding Paris which house primarily Algerian youth, the ones who regularly burn the cop cars.

This bainlieu interfered with my paltry attempts to learn French because I assumed I was hearing French out on the yard. But I could never correlate the stuff I heard there with what I saw in the French books I was reading at night, or the Rosetta Stone CDs the jail had me looking at. By the time I figured this all out and stuck to the books, I could barely order dinner in a restaurant even though I'd been immersed in the culture for a year.

At one point I figured I'd try comics to help learn some French, lots of pictures, short phrases. Who knows? It did help, especially Asterix, but this is how I bumped into French "graphic novels," a baloney name for comic books with literary pretentions. Not all such fake novels are bad I suppose but among these I found what is by far the most blasphemous disgusting anti-Catholic stuff I've ever seen. It's sad enough when someone begins the description of his criminal career by saying "I was an altar boy," as if that alone would rescue him, but in these grownup comics in France there was active loathing for Catholicism such as I'd never seen before. There, in the country called the "eldest daughter of the Church." The older I get the more I believe all of it's just backlash against the last community that's trying to hold a line somewhere, the highest standard against old-fashioned sin. The line not only involves respect for marriage and children, but the way to find the medicine and food to do "all that." As far as the disgusting novels are concerned, in my mind that would go a long'way to explain all the chomoes in France and elsewhere. But wherever, the more pagan anyone becomes, the more backlash. Selah. I'm no saint, but I've seen a few in action, and the peace they have in the midst of all this mess is really something. And the retirement plan is out of this world.

Up in the library one day I found the door to a store room in the back. Wow! Guess what -- a dozen large grapefruit boxes filled with spy books, action, adventure and mystery stuff, all in English! There were even some classics and some Inklings stuff in there. Bless me Father, I have sinned: the discovery of those books set back my French lessons worse than the Big Red One crossing the Rhine. But it sure helped "killing the bird."

Life in jail was not all a picnic. Sooner or later the American situation came into the forefront. At first I fought extradition on the simple logic that the American charges were unjust. Msgr LeBouef never ceased reminding me that not only was there no capital punishment in France, but the "cap" for any murder was ten years. If I managed to stave off the Americans that long, I could be released by the French, having served my sentence by their way of looking at things.

The next thing I must tell you brings me a lot of sadness and shame but I think God brought some good out of it anyway. It took a few years and some international borders but it came out right in the end.

A rescue friend in the US wrote to me. He was raising money for my defense and he wanted to know from the horse's mouth: did I do it or not?

There are two problems with this, known to every inmate in the world. One, you never get a lawyer for a friend on conditions. Two, you never ask a suspect outright if he did it or not, especially if not face-to-face, and even then it's tricky.

This well-intentioned and goodhearted rescuer violated both principles, and in a way that put me in a bind, a bind that was a burden on top of being charged with a capital crime, which is binding enough.

By contrast another rescuer sold literally all her family heirlooms just to raise enough to retain Mr. Cambria, a criminal defense lawyer from Buffalo, who showed up in France later. Yet another extremely generous soul on the Left Coast sent an enormous contribution and only diffidently asked an intermediary, "Well, do you think he did it?" If you're going to help out a guy in stir, that's how it's done, poor guy!

Anyway, the one zealous helper wrote and asked me outright if I "did it." He wrote that he was asking point blank because he was talking to several big donors and they wanted to know. (Huge mistake, this curiosity thing.)

I struggled with this quite a bit. It was the worst time I experienced in France. I was used to being in on misdemeanors that would get us six months at the very longest, and we never got that. I also was not used to dealing with all of this in and out of custody awkwardness. When I was in, I was in, and the affairs on the outside took care of themselves. I didn't concern myself too much with them. But this was different. I also believe the Holy Spirit was working in this situation. I had an idea of the end He was working toward, but I didn't want to go there. It was a bad time.

As one of the lawyers, an old friend, put it, I still had a right to a trial, and if I told this guy my complete involvement even with a denial of guilt due to obvious justification of saving the life of a child -- which Buffalonian child was saved, one or more, by the way -- I would effectively get no trial.

But if I denied everything to this persistent guy, it would be a species of lie.

This is a perfect example of well-meaning amateurs getting all twisted up in matters they know nothing about but think they do. You want a mortgage? You want to pay taxes and live in the 'burbs and roll along with the baby killing-now Obamacare-juggernaut? OK, well, do it! But leave us honest criminals who are trying to do something alone. Stop slumming. Don't take the "A" train, so to speak, unless you know where you're going. If you do want to throw in, for God's sake, be quiet, keep your head down, and go to work on your own. Stop "sharing" about it so damn much.

I think this is why II Cor 7 is so delicate about this matter of celibacy. I was not a professional celibate, as the Catholics call it, but I was certainly a gifted amateur. Long before this moment in France I had voted with my feet, even if I wasn't completely aware of it, that I was married to my work. When I had a chance to marry, the thought of leaving my work or making it second fiddle was an idea I simply could not live with. It will never cease to sadden me that history will show that the involvement of all-or-nothing prolifers in night time work never rose above the level of those who seriously worked with the Marquis in France or the

White Rose in Germany. More's the pity. In my mind, the catastrophe of child dismembering is big enough to include sincere involvement of everyone, married or single. The missing element is the attitude of Dietrich Bonhoeffer, a man who had a chance to marry in a troubled time and delayed it:

"When Christ calls a man, He calls him to die."

My own transformation into night work I talk about in another section of this book, but suffice to say here that in France I wrote this guy and told him that I did not do this, this horrible thing, a perfectly true statement since, as a rescuer, I was innocent of murder. I did not do what I was accused of.

This Jesuitical casuism came back to haunt me when I got back to the States, but I'm getting ahead of the story. Of course, the friendly guy back home interpreted my precisely worded statement to mean I didn't pull the trigger. And I knew he would do that. Ahhhh, the amateurs, God bless 'em.

## The Marras

To tell more about what happened next in France in jail I need to tell you a little story. I first met Dr. William Marra at the Washington, NJ Marian Shrine in 1989 or so. I think it had to be after '88, since I saw Fr. Norm Weslin down there too, and I first met Fr. Norm in seminary in the Bronx in '88.

Dr. Marra is a crystal clear perfect example of an unsung hero of the prolife movement, all the more since I don't recall him ever rescuing. But what a cheerleader for that, and such an eloquent defender of Thomistic force.

Dr. Marra taught philosophy at Fordham University in the Bronx. A, ahem, Jesuit school. Need I say more? If only all Jebbes were taught by the likes of Dr. Marra, we wouldn't even be in this mess. But even aside from Thomistic prolife thinking, Marra was one of those extremely rare breaths of fresh air in academia who could speak plainly and with infinite common sense even on a complicated matter. Schaeffer was the exact same way in his own intellectual circles. Both men could cut through argumentative tons of baloney with a few simple declarative words, words so badly needed in a world where child decapitation is thinkable, and debatable when it is not.

Compassion for moms, of course! All day long. And the Catholics pay for most of the shelters that way.

Dr. Marra's daughter Loretta, it turned out, was interested in steel rescues and I had met her in Vermont in the Bridge club. The daughter had an influence in her life that even Dr. Marra himself had not: her own mother was a French Resistance fighter. Yes, Dr. Marra married the Resistance worker, Marcel, but Loretta grew up with her as a mother. This is where it gets interesting, I think, because this influence on Loretta, the daughter, was a little bit similar to the influence my parents had on me, the Pacific Campaign Marine and my mom the wartime nurse.

Just for the record: there are still can-do people in our world, today, who do the right thing when life is at stake. It used to be that anyone would, but now we are specialized. Still, we have some left: firemen, cops, EMTs, construction people, truck drivers, farmers, hospital workers, manual laborers, soldiers, cowboys, ranchers, mothers, and more. A faithful remnant still remains that jump up and get busy when life is at stake.

Except a baby's life, of course, sad to say.

Anyway, since Vermont Loretta married a great guy, a marine and a prolifer, a real Marine not just a wannabe like us "devil pups." He was a Viet Nam vet.

When Loretta heard the news about the warrant for me as a witness in the Buffalo case -- for the first six months, I was only wanted as a witness, not a suspect -- she began to think like her Mother thought during the war. What to do with a flyer downed behind enemy lines? That is what the Marquis, the French Resistance, did. Downed flyers were hunted by the Nazis and the Marquis would search for them and smuggle them out to Spain or wherever.

We established a little contact when I was on the lam.

Looking back, of course, this was a disaster, completely my fault. When you go on the run, you go all the way. You don't look back. I know that. Still, you think you might get away with it. Plus, we are all humans and humans like to hear a friendly voice when the media only spouts hatred.

As Francis once said, however, you can have regrets but no doubts. God is certainly aware of all these subtleties and our own foibles and if He wanted to keep me out there another few years He most certainly would have.

I don't think about it much, or perhaps not at all. We are in God's hands, and if it was time for the clink, that's His business, not yours or mine to speculate about. In my humble opinion I still had another 50,000 miles left in me to try to save a few more babies, and I would have been happy to. On the other hand, I must admit I was starting to slow down a little bit especially considering the typical Lavender Hill Mob conditions we worked under. Not much food or sleep, lots of weather, and then there was the bad back, the bad ankle, and migraines. If I could have saved babies sitting in a chair by the fire, it wouldn't have been so bad, but the Mob conditions didn't have an MOS/job spec like that.

With more regular conditions in jail, I started to perk up a little, but that's not a realistic picture of life in the field.

The FBI and the powers that be celebrated when I was picked up. They should have wept instead. Wept for their sins. And they know about them, I told them. They think everything's clear sailing now, now that they've locked us all up, but they'll change their tune when the Lord brings his accounting for all the mess. None of us will bypass that.

So, Loretta decided to do what her own Mom would have done during the war -- she tried to send me some money. You and I would call this simple compassion. The feds call it "harboring" after the fact, a crime in itself, according to them, since they admitted Dennis and Loretta never had anything to do with Buffalo. As a realist of this and due to the infiltrating by the ITB feebs of a snitch masquerading as an old friend, Loretta, and her husband Dennis for good measure, and their two kids and I were all arrested at the same time on the same day in the Spring of 2001.

At this time Dennis and Loretta had two small kids, one still nursing. No matter! The feebs arrested the kids too! Plenty of room for everybody down at the FEMA camps, comrades! Twenty four hours later they handed the babies off to Loretta's extended family. Twenty-four hours is twenty-two hours too many for a baby to be in the clutches of a baby-killing beast.

It was a source of much sadness to me, in France, to hear that my Vermont Bridge partner was in the clink on my behalf, and her tiny young family too. At first my French lawyer played the resist extradition card, but one day I got a letter from a US priest to the effect that Loretta would be punished in my stead if the US could not get their hands on me.

How could they do that? you might ask, Since she was innocent of everything except trying to send a few dollars to help an old Bridge partner? And the money never was sent to me anyway.

The more I hang around the federal prison system and hear stories here the more I tend to cut off any discussion that begins with "they can't do…." They can and will, a government that genocides the entire black race by millions, year after year, can do anything it wants, especially if we don't stop it. Where does a five hundred pound gorilla sit?

So, I contacted the US about waiving extradition to make sure I got back to the US but linking the waiver to the Malvasi family getting back to being a family. I was single, after all, and busy doing things where you could hardly say you were surprised at being arrested and exposed to life in the clink, or worse. It would be awful if this young family were dragged into that by the clutching babykillers, especially whipped into bloodlust by the Dowager Empress. (I was remembering the press conference of the night after poor Dr. Slepian died.)

The first news I got back from the US about waiving extradition was don't. Not yet. The deal needed to be secured on the US end or it would be a wasted gesture on the French end.

One day that finally did come about, the securing of the benefit connected to the waiver, and it was au revoir, France!

## Jail 1

The first time I was ever in jail was in '84, after the chain rescue led by the biker angel who came and left San Francisco so mysteriously. I felt sad that I had been forced to stand up with a compliance hold, and I was already thinking how to beat that the next time so I wouldn't give in.

We were taken to a local police station, right there in the Richmond district. I was there for two hours only and let go. During that two hours I was cuffed to a ring in the wall behind a bench, and it was a very small lockup, just a holding cell, as opposed to a cell with a bunk and phone to the warden (prisoner's slang for a toilet).

But all I remember was the color of the cell: it was the most wonderful shade of blue, something not light, and not dark, leaning toward an aqua, the color of a wave that surfer's see, when its lifted up in the sun, and instead of being dark blue green it winds up aqua.

On the one hand, I felt like a horse who was tied up in front of a saloon in the old west. But also I was so at peace and relieved. We had done our best, and it was all over. I wasn't the slightest bit worried about how much jail I might get.

## Getting More Familiar

The first time I ever spent a night in jail was I think for the sewer pipe rescue. This was the one where I was booked for a felony. I had had four thousand dollars bail on me, though I was not aware of it at the time.

There's a scene in a Dirty Harry movie where Harry says "make my day" to some criminal. That scene, if I recall correctly, plays out i'm tempted to say on Mission Street, but in any event, it's across the street from the front door of the San Francisco Police Department headquarters near Mission south of Market. It's a white blocky building, a little Corbusier looking. There is an open corridor through the building, front to back. One story down from the back end of that corridor is the prisoners' entrance, from the garage.

We were asked to stand against the wall, and I noticed a splat of blood just at head height on the white wall behind me, right behind my own head. Since then, I have noticed the scars on the backs of the skulls of many career criminals, where perhaps their heads had a close encounter with concrete.

What a trip. When I was booked, there was a voluble cheerful black desk sergeant, and at one point I corrected the spelling of my name (this is how naive I was). "Well, your ass is in the computer and your ass has a c on it." That's the last time I ever corrected a booking sergeant. Of course, i've prayed ever since for poor James Copp who keeps getting pulled over for an old warrant he knows nothing about.

Finally, I was ushered into a room on an upper floor of the jail that probably was a gym. I seem to remember a wood floor. I'm not sure, because every single inch of that floor was covered with Spanish people sleeping; no mattresses, no sheets, no pillows, no nothing. Just you and wood.

The place was so crowded -- experienced prisoners will attest to this -- there was no room except immediately in front of the toilet, which was in constant use all night. This was, after all, a makeshift drunk tank. All night long, I had to move every time anyone of the one or two hundred guys had to go to the bathroom.

I don't know if I got any sleep. I don't think so. But I do recall, when it got quiet, that there was a fellow prisoner on drugs, or drunk, who seemed to be particularly concerned with what time it was. Experienced prisoners never ask anyone what time it is. Why? Because half of us are lifers, and we know when we're getting out. Not today. So why ask? We tend to ignore the clock.

But in the case of this prisoner, he would shout over to his friend, who would answer him (it was eleven). Then, the questioner would fall asleep for an instant, according to the vagaries of his drug or drugs of choice. Then he'd bolt awake and instantly ask his friend, again, "What time is it?"

This went on for several cycles. Then, finally, the man answering the question got angry at being woken up and being asked the same question every few seconds.

"It's eleven o'mother****ing clock, godammit, now shut up!"

Welcome to the world of the Lord's sense of humor. There is no dank corner of the world where you can be incarcerated without being accompanied by this joy, perhaps enabled by the sans souci environment of jail, where everything kind of just goes loose. The normal rules of social protocol are suspended.

For some reason, the idea of my urbanically gifted speaker interposing the particle "mother***ing" in between the phonemes "o'" and "clock" struck me as literary comedic genius, interposing as he did the modifier on the exact piece of information he wished to draw his slow-to-get-it interlocutor's attention to. I started laughing so hard I could barely keep it in, laughter i'm sure the guy with a watch would not appreciate. I still laugh now when I think of it, and i've been laughing ever since.

Strange to relate, but the worse jail gets, the better it gets. Paul Hill was unmistakably happy his last day on this earth. It's like that.

## And Now It's Old Time

In 1985 or so we did another crude "metal" rescue, like the pipe, when we were trying to figure things out. It involved trying to connect two knees together with an off-the-shelf kryptonite lock. Yes, yes, I know. But it seemed like a good idea at the time, and it turned out to be the right idea in the long run, and produced many children, but that day, with the bare lock, the apologetic cop slid it off our legs pretty quickly.

I remember that rescue. The cop got down on his knees and apologized for having to arrest us. This was not code words: he told us in plain English that he hated abortion and knew it was wrong. But he also said, it's legal and what can he do?

Trial and sentencing were set on different days. In the previous rescue, the pipe rescue, when I was asked in court to agree to stay away from the mill, my conscience instantly told me: don't do it. I did it anyway, bullied by a cheap appointed counsel, but later decided I should never do it again, because it's agreeing in principle that babies are not in an emergency situation. You would never agree to stay away from your own pool if the neighbor's kids were swimming in it and at risk of drowning. You would never agree to stay away from any house that might catch on fire and have children in it. It's like that. I only found out later that the East Coast crowd had come to the same conclusion, but back in California my earlier agreement still rankled, and in this case, down in Daly City, I was stubborn. No stay away.

Before sentencing the appointed counsel told me he'd be surprised if I did even a day in jail. The judge walked up to the bench, said "In the matter of James Kopp the sentence is 90 days," and he brought the gavel down and asked for the next docket. I looked around me, and suddenly there was a vacuum where the moment before there'd been a lawyer and others. In one instant the place was not the place to be.

Then the funniest thing happened. I realized that the closest person to me was a deputy sheriff whose job it was to take me into custody. I didn't try to run away; all I did was turn my body to look back into the gallery where my backpack was sitting in the first row. That motion produced a flinch on the part of the deputy, as if he thought I was trying to run away and he would have to tackle me. It was the strangest feeling. One minute, a certain amount of respect for the suburban white boy who was somewhat out of place in the nice suburban county, and the next instant, after the judge spoke, I was trash. I turned back to the sheriff to assure him I wasn't running. This was the first time in my life I had ever walked into a courtroom by one door, and out by a different one. It's a funny feeling. I still can't remember if my backpack was arrested also.

Now begins the hardest time I have ever done in my life. I have been in lockups with centuries old stone walls, no toilet and a bucket. I have been in cells with broken windows and snow falling onto the floor of the cell. I have been in solitary with no windows and no yard for weeks at a time, and other solitaries for years at a time. I have been in more county jails in America than I can remember. I have ducked as quietly as possible while a fistfight revolved near me. I have been tortured in Italy, thrown into a laundry hamper with other rescuers in the tombs in Manhattan, and dragged along more corridors than I can remember. In Manhattan I once spent the night with a dozen rescuers in a cell designed for one-person. We sat on the concrete in shifts. I have been sentenced to life twice and had my family insulted by strangers in the press.

None of this, times a thousand, comes close to the agony of the fifty-four days and a wakeup I spent in Daly County Jail.

Did anyone beat me up? Absolutely not. Was I tortured? Nope.

Imagine a room twice the size of your bathroom. Instead of a sink and a mirror, the walls had bunks bolted to them, three high, like bunks in a submarine, to hold 18 guys.

Now (here's the important part): bolt a TV to the wall and run it 24/7. And have the channel and volume on that TV set by junkies who grew up in a project with a TV on in their house 24/7, such that it is impossible for them to sleep without it. Also, that junkies have a funny thing about their burned out sensations: they need something loud or hitting them all the time to give them a feeling they are still alive. But especially when they don't have any drugs right at this moment which is the only moment that exists for a junkie.

Sad to say, my parents, back then, after 40 years of marriage, were "going through" a divorce. Would you believe that the TV show that they put on every day was divorce court? With commentary from the inmates as to this or that nasty quality of the women in the drama? I only found out later that the reason so many urbanic gentlemen hate women is that they never had a dad, and they resent that mom was mom and dad to them.

Whatever. But as a rescuer, when we are always trying to appeal to moms to trust, trust anyone, and to love themselves, this shouting on the TV was like a knife in a wound, all the time.

One time at about 3 am I snuck up to the TV and turned it down just a little bit. And then a little bit more. I should have been happy with that. I got greedy and decided to try for totally turning the sound off. The minute I did, an urbanite was woken by the absence of sound, got up, turned up the TV, and promptly went back to sleep. When you are in the distinct minority and a skinny white boy from the suburbs to boot, you don't have a say in the TV. It is an urban sacrament in a church you don't belong to. It is also all the "family" any of these guys ever had, like it or not. Huxtable (at best) reigns.

A bright light happened one day. A huge black guy strode into the tank and announced to all he was the new top dog. He proved it by setting the poker ante on the spot. Later on, he asked me what a skinny white boy was doing there, etc.

"I protest abortion at the abortion mill."

He was stunned. "You mean, you left that place and got arrested without blowing it off the map?" It turned out he was on my side. From that moment forward, everyone treated me a little better.

I did some in-custody protests, trying to imitate the little I had heard about Joan back east, but for a man, and, after you've already been cooperating, this is rough. I was in the bucket a day or two, and then they just muscled me to my feet with force and pain. They had no time for pansy protests clogging up their jail.

One day an inmate shouted "f*** you" to a passing guard. Without looking back, he shouted over his shoulder, "Oh, no, don't do that. You'll never go back to women."

The day I got out of there we were queuing up for hookup (cuffs) and I realized I wasn't being let straight out onto the street. I was being "transported." I asked a sheriff where I was going?

"Don't worry Mr. Kopp. Wherever you're going, there's room for you there."

It turned out it was an old warrant in Oakland. I got out after one night because my neato brother bailed me, and also, due to the tender mercies of a large slow moving urbanically gifted clerk of the court who took one look at me and told my mom, "Oh no. He doesn't belong in here"

## Going East Again

In about '86 I went to the East Coast. I had gotten a samizdat about Joan Andrews being in jail in Florida, five years for a simple rescue, and her non-cooperation while in custody, not just going limp at the scene, which was the usual thing back then.

When I got to Delaware, the big thing was a rescue coming up in Georgia. We all piled into cars and went down. Southerners were there too, but it was mainly a carpetbagger thing.

At a meeting before the rescue, I remember that John Ryan or Jcoke had put out two simple clipboard lists asking for volunteers for a future rescue. At the top of one of them it said, you sign up for this rescue on the condition that you only do it if a 100 people go with you. At the top of the other one, it said, you sign up for this rescue on the condition that you only have to do it if a 1000 people go with you. I have always believed this was the most elegant idea in the history of rescue. With a 1000 people together, the fear factor goes way down, both in terms of what could happen at the scene, and the jail time.

Then, that same week, they gave a little demonstration of the idea of what "numbers" could do.

Poor Chamblee, Georgia! A tiny town, and not such a bad town, I suppose, but they had a mill.

I think about 70 had come to the meeting, and maybe 50 went to the rescue. We even cooperated once they had us loaded into cruisers. They had to borrow a van from a neighboring town. Don't ever call them "paddy wagons"! The Irish contingent said this is a no-no, so we called them vans.

Here's how it played out: they put us in some kind of day room for their cop shop. It wasn't even a gym for prisoners as we had wound up in many times, because that town didn't have anything bigger than a couple of drunk tanks, like most small towns.

To transfer us to the county jail would involve a charge to the tiny town of Chamblee.

But the best part was when one cop sheepishly admitted to one of our leadership: we've just exhausted our entire budget for feeding prisoners for the entire year, and they had done that by ordering a hamburger and a cup of coffee for each of us.

They fed us at noon. They had to, sort of, you know? and we were out by 2 PM. They couldn't afford dinner.

As far as jail time, I think we hinted to them that if they docketed us, we'd all come back in a group and do it all again. I don't recall being asked to appear before a judge in Chamblee Georgia.

Numbers. Got to have numbers. This was a holdover from the students of the Irish troubles of 1926 that were among us. You should see Michael Collins, the movie, if you haven't.

I can't remember if it was the same trip as the Chamblee rescue, but we all swung over and did another one at the mill Joan had been arrested at. You could say it was protesting Joan's arrest, which isn't as high a motive as rescue itself, which is not a protest but rather an attempt to save a life. Secularists always assume anyone who gets arrested willfully is in it for the media, but this isn't true. Rescue and protest are two different things, and either one could involve an arrest.

I will always remember this: sitting in the driveway of the mill in Pensacola Florida, the rumor spread that the mill was not even scheduled to kill that day, which would mean that no rescue was needed. See the difference? But while we were processing that, I think some women did try to come in. We clogged the driveway, which also served as an entrance for moms. The nice thing about that crowd was that many of them were not risking arrest. So we had lots of sidewalk counseling capacity, i.e., lots of older moms with families who were right there available to talk to moms coming in. Mom to mom kind of thing. This is great, and it's unfortunate that it isn't always so. Counseling is more important than mere blocking. The point is mother and child, not some statement or power move.

Whether or not the place was open, the director of the place decided to force the issue by simply driving his truck into the driveway. He didn't crash into the crowd, though he could have. He nudged the bumper up against us, and we didn't move. A little nervous-making. Was he some whack job?

But at one point I looked up and saw the face of the truck driver/clinic owner, and it was chilling. Total fish eyes, complete dispassion, and here he was driving his truck into a crowd of men women and children sitting on the ground. He was waiting for the police to clear the place out, and he wanted to prove that he was boss. I heard a rumor later that he was a marine. Hmmmm. Marine to marine.

The cops dragged me out into the middle of the street. Since the rules of behavior were that we didn't move for fear this would be taken as aggressive behavior, I just went limp wherever they dragged me. Then another cop with different uniform and different jurisdiction came along and arrested me for simply blocking route 9 or whatever it was.

The trial I remember also, in voir dire, one after another of delicate sensibility, Bible Belt housewives came to the stand and said they absolutely couldn't be an impartial juror since they were good Christians and they were against abortion.

After a while the judge saw how it was going and began to plead with the housewives: well, even with your beliefs, isn't it possible you could still keep an open mind?

This is how it happens. Seventeen centuries ago, and every century since, Christians have been tossed to the lions and such like for simply saying "no!" to this question, but that day, they all said, well, OK, open-mindedness, without balance, without limit, is now some cmc virtue. That's how we got here.

The judge even let me try to put in a justification defense. I totally winged it. They sent a special prosecutor from Tallahassee just to prosecute my little misdemeanor, a super ambitious Irish firebrand traitor from the state attorney general's office. This is how Ireland was lost in 1798, and earlier. Someone had to open the door for Cromwell.

After all that delicate handwringing in voir dire, the jury convicted in less time than it takes to mix sugar into a cup of coffee.

Before this trial, I had always believed that somewhere in the bible belt some would come to their senses and help. They talk about Jesus so much, can you blame me? After this trial I quietly discovered that most folks down there like abortion as a backup in case their daughter is raped by a black man. It's not about Jesus after all, is it? I've been disappointed about the South ever since. All those experienced hunters down there. But then, recently, country music TV switched over to soft porn, so it's too late. And Houston has no-fooling, sho-nuff porn on their TV out there in front of God and everyone. I have been disappointed in the alleged virtues of the South, ever since. We needed you!

## The Lavender Hill Mob

The Lavender Hill Mob started in the Deep South in 1987 and my little contribution to it came to an end in Bretagne, France, in 2001 when the silver bracelets went on for the last time.

What happened in-between? Those fourteen years?

The Lavender Hill Mob was not a person, place, or thing. Well, OK, it was all of that, but it was mainly an idea. The idea swam up out of the longsuffering rescuers who got tired of waiting around for the cops to show up and arrest them. Tired of ghost dockets a thousand miles away, judges who lied about the ghost dockets, running around all over the country on our nickle when judges would fake-notice us. All of it. We were tired of the whole idea that if you stand up in court and plainly state your case, that goodness will prevail. Kid-wise, it obviously did not. And we prolifers weren't doing so hot, either.

Of course the lefty leftovers from the anti-Viet Name war protest movement -- peace to all sides, calm down, that cohort of the pro-life movement -- wrung their hands and cried and cried about sabotage. They went on the tube glibly agreeing with the enemy's deflection of our normative and descriptive accusation of violence, and using that word instead to describe damage to property. Which, in the context, is not violent at all, it's non-violent. If you care about humans, that is.

Gandhi will win out, the lefties said. Just wait a little longer. They clucked their tongues, instead of shouting Hallelujah, when they opened up the paper, sitting in their arm chairs, eating their tea and crumpets, and reading about another mill that had been burned down.

When they said "This is bad for the movement!" they meant it. It was bad for them, the people who were always taught by their mothers in the fifties: if you get in trouble, run to the police. If you asked them if it was bad for the babies and moms scheduled to die that day, you'd get Deer-In-The-Headlights Ummm.

The Lavender Hill Mob kept its own counsel about all this. But they said to themselves, hey, can we just skip the whole arrest thing? Been there, done that.

## The Vito Squad

Speaking of arson -- about the same time the Lavender Hill Mob was kicking into high gear, another group that did the same stuff also got going: the Vito Squad. The Vito Squad was a bunch of disgruntled, aged, ethnic RC feebs forced into early retirement by Janet Reno and her boss and mentor, The Dowager Rodham Empress. Those two had tasked the new FBI, their own personal police force, to focus on the little old gray-haired ladies with rosaries and Bibles praying in front of the mills. After all, they were just standing there, right? Throw 'em in jail, steal their houses, done by lunch. A perfect task for the kind of cowards who protect people who rip the heads off children.

It was The Squad that started sending me messages in the early 90's about the circling wolves that were feigning and dodging deeper and deeper into the movement after they got tired of chasing after Grandma. But more about the Squad later.

### The First Lavender Hill Mob Gig

The first specifically Lavender Hill type job I ever did was in the South. I was squatting on a fourteen-foot-high roof over a strip mall venue, and I heard a siren.

Maybe I should say a word about the word "mill." What our enemies call "abortion clinics" we call mills. This is because a clinic is someplace where you go when you are sick, and when you come out, you are better. A mill is someplace where you go when you are healthy and when you come out, you are dead. Every sidewalk counsellor in this benighted country has had to watch at least one dead mother pulled out of a mill, or near-dead. So: mill.

Remembering this memory of the siren sound gives me the chills. It was bad enough at the time, but now, it's doubly scary. Why?

In the early Oughts I heard the story of some poor guy who dropped his wallet on the roof of a mill while he was "busy." In the wallet was his driver's license and membership cards to various prolife groups. Hearing the laughing cops had to be as bad as doing the time.

In my case, when I think back to squatting under the parapet on the roof of that strip mall, it scares me twice, like the time I woke up in a cold sweat in the middle of the night after I'd been walking twenty stories up on the outer edge of a building cornice all day, no lifeline. The ankle I'd been walking on near the edge all day was the same one that was broken by the teenager who'd bounced up and down on it until it broke. That ankle. The one that tends to roll over with no warning at the most inappropriate times.

So. That night, on the other roof, the mill roof, I didn't lose my wallet. Thanks Pronto! They also didn't find a tool that I had thrown off the roof into the bushes when I was done with it, and which I lost, fingerprints and all. Also, I didn't fall off, clinging, with no arm strength, to the fourteen foot southern roof gutter, the storm catcher kind.

A soundproof grapple hook? Anti-print tools? Nothing in pockets? These were all worked out later, but "later" only happened because Heaven spared us that night, the night we made every mistake in the book.

It turns out that we didn't even hurt the mill too much, either; but that training job was inside a donut of sorts, so interns of a future career, maybe even that was part of the blessing.

"Donut?"

Take a Krispy Kreme and center it on your house, the place where you actually sleep and pay taxes. Do this on a Rand McNally's trucker's map, the kind that's on the back pages; the US map.

Don't get busy inside that donut, OK? We're talking a radius of about 500 miles. Also, even outside the donut, never go to a town where you've been before, or where you're known.

If you follow this rule faithfully, no exceptions, you create what the FBI calls a "gypsy crime." They hate them. The crimes, that is. All the usual stuff that works on TV doesn't work solving a gypsy crime.

"Round up the usual suspects," or, "Danno, call every hardware store on the island and find out who bought duct tape last week" just doesn't cut it.

Like gypsies, then, we were.

## Mob Street Bum Rules

The Donut Rule brings up a bunch of other rules we learned in the early days, making so many mistakes but, thank God, getting away with it.

One of the most central of these Mob Rules was the Street Bum Rule.

You see, if you dress up like some Mutant Ninja Turtle with throwing stars and coils of rope and black kung fu robes, it's a little rough explaining all this to an inquiring cop.

Especially if it's not Halloween.

On the other hand, if you wear nice clothes, the kind that would make a cop think you're a taxpayer, that might not work either. Nice taxpayers don't hang around in alleyways at three AM. What to do?

Enter the street bum. If you dress and act like a street person, this at least gives you a chance, in the night-time world. You can blend in with an urban landscape, the part that taxpayers are used to avoiding anyway.

Cops arrest street people every day, often just for being street people. But then again, they don't, lots of times. If they see one who's minding his own business at that moment, he might want to take a pass on what would otherwise involve a lot of talking, a long story, or even what cops call counseling, which they hate. If you are silent with the Lord at Quiet Time every day, and you do the street bum rule thing, you just might get through the job without an arrest.

God can do anything, of course, and he can do it with you in jail, too. It's really up to him, isn't it?

My beloved Evangelical brothers and sisters who equate the protection of the Lord (Psalm 69, let's say) with never going to jail, or never losing your job for the babies, give me a giant pain in the neck. It's because of them that we are in the place where we are. And in this regard, of course, we would have to include the liberal US Catholics, sadly.

[Liberal US Catholics are worse. There's no Evangelical Church implying to Evangelicals they're going to hell unless they do something about this shoah, is there?]

But Street Bum Rules are more than just the clothes. Suppose you were interviewed by a cop. You've got to play it out a little bit. Burnt out on drugs like some Southern California surfers, or a kind of Cheech and Chong vibe of irrelevant trivia when law enforcement wants specific answers. Maybe it's a little bit like Verbal Kint and Agent Keyon in Usual Suspects.

[My oldest son, Matt, was mentally ill: I love him and he loved Usual Suspects. He died four years ago. I cry when I read things like this.]

But even in a case like that, there is a point where the irrelevancy has to wait. Wait for the cop to actually take the hook. Gotta give him a chance. And this is where the Eagle Scout/John Bircher thing has to take a back seat. Pride goes before a fall. Gotta play along with the street thing.

A big part of it is patience, I think. A street person lives on the street. He's not in a hurry to go get a shower somewhere and watch TV. He's got all the TV he needs right there on the street, and his panhandling access to drugs, which is like breathing to him.

When you're not in a hurry, outside, in the dark, you just might find that you have time to watch.

Watch what?

Why, a mill, silly!

RALPH M. GABRIEL

## Surveillance Mob Rule

I bet you've heard this story before, from the Armchair General set, who haven't the slightest idea how hard it is to actually save a baby and mom, and if you told them they'd cry and run away like Calvin's friend Suzie. There's a little bit more to it than giving speeches and hiring corporate lawyers to give you Nervous Nellie advice.

The story is this: how can you burn a mill?

Ewwwwwww! they'd say. How horrible! Someone could've been inside it, like a janitor! You could've killed him!

I will detail a specialized form of arson in this book. I've never done bombs: I'd probably blow myself up first. Bombs make sense when the killers moved over into masonry structures, but the form of arson in this book is as good or better. Also, most bomb material accessible to amateurs is home made or some other kind of unstable. This is not good for anyone, me thinks.

One very dear armchair lady whose cousin was a fireman went further: the fireman could die, trying to rescue someone he believes is inside.

The Surveillance Rule fixes all this.

See, arsonists don't need to go inside a building they torch.

And if it's not necessary, they might not like to. It could be more like a smash-and-grab thing, where you're gone before the cops get there. As in, long gone.

So, how do you know the building's empty? How do you know? For sure?

If you want to be an armchair hypocrite, I suppose you can always ask that. It keeps you home, safe and sound, doesn't it? And isn't that what all the oh-so-delicate sensitive concern is about? Right? That same level of concern is most certainly not directed toward babies and mothers. Not by the armchair critics, anyway. Oh, I almost forgot: you'll pray for the babies. Good for you.

For Lavender Hill types, that posture doesn't cut it, for the precise reason that it wouldn't for our own kids.

Surveille. Hour after hour. Not words, or rhetoric, but simple work. After a while you know to a very high level of certainty who's in and out of that building. And the nice thing about whoosh versus bang is that whoosh gives just about anyone a chance to get the flock out of there. Armchair people drive through green stoplights all day long, not knowing for certain no car will come the other way, yet this is somehow not good enough for children who will be dead for a certainty if we do nothing, or the insufficient little we've already done.

 Parking lots, cars, faces, janitors, shifts, whatever. Twenty-four/seven. Every "business" has a rhythm. The surveiller would never do a job without knowing it.

And when the firemen show up? They know the exact same information. They live there. They know, much better than the gypsy, exactly who's in the building and who's not. They act accordingly

All this philosophy about 99.99% safety for a baby-murder-helper who is a janitor, and no one wants to go to the trouble to do the night-time homework, to give a one percent chance to an utterly helpless kid. As I say, the armchair critic can sit back and click the remote in peace now, having imparted his wisdom that costs him nothing. This "wisdom" certainly doesn't have anything to do with what it takes to actually save a baby, or they'd be burnt as a nut standing in front of the mills, people with whom I have no problem, and they usually none with me. Makes you mad, huh? Or, want to get even. Baby-wise. We think about janitors. Give the kids a break, too, though.

## Lavender Hill Mob 3 – Butyric Acid

I first smelled butyric acid in lab at Cal. We just wiffed it, we didn't synthesize it, but that was enough. The vomit inside the stomachs of ten thousand people wouldn't smell at all except for a tenth of a drop of this stuff. My tuition at school sure paid off.

In the beginning we were buying it a quart at a time, scientific grade, from scientific supply houses with a story about a high school teacher who forgot to get his purchase order in on time for a lab coming up tomorrow, plus an ID that would not have survived Chapter One of Catch Me If You Can. But this becomes a problem after a while. A quart is a nice amount to cook one mill, especially if you water it with a medium trickle from a garden hose through a bashed copper pipe through the doorsill air seal.

So? Quantity. As in, a barrel. From the factory.

Doping reminds me of the time we got into welding. We were spending so much time coming up with stories to tell a real welder, and watching him give us funny looks when he worked on our, uh, "motorcycle lock."

It took time to learn to weld. But it moved the lock thing way ahead when we finally buckled down and did it.

Same with the barrel of sauce. When you've got a barrel of it, you start thinking of six mills in a night, instead of one mill in six months.

Efficiencies of scale, streamlining, optimization, experience and confidence start to kick in. Also, surveilling six mills in one town, outside the donut, of course, is also more efficient. We'd just keep rolling around town, eyeballing them one after another until it all seemed like hometown.

Storage is another problem connected with scaling up, but also worth it. But it takes prayer and thinking and the help of heaven. Remote but accessible. You need to put the sauce in just the right place.

Just like with welding, buying quantity was essentially a con, like The Sting, say. The reason people go for it could be that it never occurred to them that someone would go to so much trouble just for a bucket of stinking stuff.

When the marks walked into the betting parlor in the movie, whatever doubts they have, it would never occur to them that all of the people and equipment was in place just for them. Same thing with stink buying. We created an entire paper shell just for the purchases.

Many stories might work, but one that did involved a fake chemical engineering company that was developing some new "process" that could involve a railroad tanker of the stuff as a precursor once the process was perfected for large production. Production of what? Ahhh, I don't know, I'd tell the salesman. That's chemist stuff. I'm just in Purchasing. Sorry. Can't help ya. No salesman in his right mind wants to interrupt the flow of a sale with unnecessary glitches.

Then we would haggle back and forth about the price per barrel, but based on a tanker load. This sets the hook. It creates an environment of big dollar signs swimming in the head of the factory salesman, as he calculates commission based on tanker loads of stuff.

Then, in a casual move one day, a memo from the "chemist" shows up: Send me just a barrel so I can do QC on the technical grade, and we'll get back to you on the tanker load if everything else works out all right. When you do it this way, the main event is anything but the silly little old barrel. Instead, the worry is the company's competitor that might have a slightly better price on their tech. grade. Or, it's about some unseen "process." What could it be? Is this guy making shells for some new iPhone? A salesman could break out in a sweat thinking about those things. Give him what he wants. Hurry. Make everything smooth for this guy, so he thinks about you when the gravy train comes in.

The paperwork on the P.O. was absolutely everything. After that it was only a matter of a dolled-up pickup truck with fake magnetic signs, and those hazmat cards from the welding shop, a fake clipboard with one fake P.O. on it and an old janitor's uniform from Salvation Army. Hi, Bob! Keep the name label on.

Then there's the other end. Delivery. A snap, really, once the bigger picture is in place, meaning, supply, storage, target surveillance, street presence, target-rich environment in a big city increasing the efficiency of your in-the-field costs, and, of course, donut.

In the eighty's killers were forced by insurance underwriters into masonry or cement buildings when it became too easy to burn the wooden ones. Multi-tenant office buildings forced them into single detached buildings when the other tenants complained about the stench and how they were innocent. Most modern brick buildings have modern sealed windows and HVAC systems. This is actually an advantage to the stink operation. No one ever aired out a stunk building. Not that it would do them any good, mind you; but an ounce of stink sure goes far with a contained system recirculating it all night for a nice, even distribution. The garden hose helps, too.

Imagine a modern fixed window in a modern building with AC. Imagine the aluminum frame being invisible. What do you see? Glass, suspended inside a masonry hole, with a half inch gap all around. Half inch is way more than you need with a stinger that fits into a three-thirty secondth hole, when you know how to hit the gap. We clipped the needle copper off the back of a reefer in an unofficial dump.

Drilling is another one of those things that is a lost art, especially since you can't farm it out, not even at first. When I was tiny, I spun an entire electronics chassis because I snagged it with an oversized, under speed bit. But that was fifty years ago. I had been drilling ever since. There is a knack to not breaking bits, going as fast as you can, knowing the material, etc. But come on. This is aluminum, too.

Depending on the mill layout and neighborhood, you never know where the weakest point will be. There's a murder cabal of non-doc women, for example, who swear up and down they'll still do child-killing if abortion becomes illegal again or restricted, and in fact they killed before it became legal.

Currently, they kill without doctors all the time and train others to do it. I think it's called the Feminist Women's Health Operation or something like that. They're not shy about it. Come to think of it, the Kumbayah-singing part of the prolife movement should really look at these people before they fantasize any more about that "just one more" supreme they say they need.

Anyway, mention the FWHO because they are very touchy about their mills. If they can do private doctoring, they can do private policing, and this means they sleep in their cars in front of the mills all night. This means that the weakest part of that mill, that night, might be in the back or on the roof, when, if the ladies weren't in their cars, it could be the front door. See what I mean? The weakest point is a fluid concept that could change moment to moment, like the way some mills under a flight path can't set their alarms too well, or, in a hurricane area, because all the alarms might go off at once.

The weakest spot on a given structure could be a half inch of plywood on the roof, two layers of 20 ga. steel in an alley fire door, an aluminum door sash, or the window frame. Personally, I like window frames. They're everywhere.

After a while the underwriters might put z-deck plus conk, up high, which just moves the weak spot to flashing fittings or the AC. Bell-hanger's bits could come into play when we were dealing with soffits or thick walls. They even come in handy in masonry walls, as I found out when I wired up a Scotch castle in Kenya one day. Sometimes it took some creative welding, or purchasing.

Once I came around the corner looking for the first time closely at the curbside plan of a job, and lo and behold, someone had already smashed a sidelight on the doorknob side of the jamb, one of those cutesy things architects do to brighten up a place they've been ordered to design around. I had to laugh. It was laminated and still in place, so drilling through an existing crack was one second of work. One man sows, another reaps.

Usually I would drill and inject on two separate walk-ups to the mill. That does a few things. You're carrying fewer tools at any given instant, which reduces your criminal liability exposure just a smidge if you were to get popped at one point or another.

Also, just in case you trigger an alarm with the drilling, it gives you a chance to hang back and check it out. Scanners optional. But even scanners don't do everything and they shouldn't be looked at as a magic protector anymore than a radar jammer on the road. Plus, on a roadside pullover and shakedown, it would be a big uh-oh to the cop. Thank God, we never were shook down. Some trust in horses, you know? I don't believe it's smart to get too wrapped up in technique, certainly no more than in closeness to the Lord. If you are close to Him, trying to be busy as His servant, you'll always be OK even if you do get popped.

## Lavender Hill 4. franchise

I remember the time I got as far as wanting to franchise the Lavender Hill Mob. I believed in high quality of course, meaning there's only so many saboteurs to go around. Be sure to protect them so they can save babies and moms. A lot of training and experience could be wasted if a skillful operator wound up in the clink.

I don't deny that a significant part of the operation was staying out of jail. The child rescuing mission came first, yes, but staying out of jail means a lot toward accomplishing the part of the mission at the next mill. We'd paid our dues with the Gandhi thing. Or I should say the fake Gandhi thing. Gandhi himself would never have applied passive response to life-and-death, and he said so. And we'd had it with judges who notified us for court dates a thousand miles away and then, when we showed up on our own nickle, presto-chango! Disappear them and re-docket. (Hello, Atlanta!)

Still, I had a hankering to try to franchise the whole deal.

This began with an experiment to see if two teams could operate in the same town on one night, side-by-side, but independently.

It seemed like a good idea at the time, or, as my old Wycliffe boss used to say just before we would cut over a switch in the jungle, "If it doesn't work, we'll always think it should have." Ahhhh

Well, at least some experienced Lavender Hill types would be there that night, right? Keep an eye on things?

What a disaster. Not that I wouldn't try again. And there were even moments when I came very close. But that night, wow. As my Dad used to say, some days are longer than others.

Even attempting it was a neat trick, a blessing, I believe, because finding a good solid half dozen Mobbers ready to go at one time is hard.

Why? Because a Mobber absolutely can't be a talker. An explainer. A bragger. A justifier. He knows in his heart why he does what he does. You can talk, and you can do, but you can't talk and do in a hostile regime like ours.

And he must be a prayer warrior. Otherwise, the Lord could just believe he needs a little more time in the clink for all that. Or any other kind of slow-down.

He pretty much needs to be a hardcore rescuer, too, because without that he might be scared of the cops and that's no way to go into the field. Rescuers don't fear police contact as the newbies do.

Single? On the whole, sure. Of course a married guy could do it, but he'd have to be more careful. Also, there are peripheral tasks that have basically zero arrest exposure, like over-the-road driving. Some mobbers confined themselves to that, and the operators were in better shape when they got there.

Mobbers need to be a real prolifers, too, in the sense that they've already seen dumpster babies and aren't just intellectual or neo-Platonic about the whole thing. And they can't be drenched with all the fake Gandhi stuff. The stuff Gandhi himself refuted in life-or-death situations. In those cases, it's more than salt-tax and water fountain protests, important as those things are. MLK said the same thing. Look carefully for his Bonhoeffer quote. You will find it. Are you listening, Eric, pal? Dr. King had you in mind.

We all camped out by a beautiful lake. Late afternoon to dusk seemed to be the time we would all wake up, get together, decompress from recon the nights before, look at maps, look ahead to the evening's work, do quiet time. Urban areas have that advantage, being target-rich. Once you get some familiarity with the town and its mills, you can get busy and hit them all in one night -- no maps, please God, and be gone in the morning. That way you could avoid the prospect, say, of an owner or mill operator camping out one night because of something he heard on the TV happening across town. The hardcore ladies with the amateur operators and no MDs are real big on camping out. It's tedious to work around them.

Our stuff didn't always hit the media, especially if they didn't catch us, and thank God, they never did. The media cooperated with the child killers in that regard, as they did most of the time. It would be bad for industry morale if news of a hit without an arrest got out. But when you throw in the Vito Squad, a hit without an arrest was a much more common occurrence than the lamestreams would care to admit. The Wall Street Journal concluded this about the mainstream, in the early 90's. The Vito's were that good. They were…how shall I put this? federally trained professionals. You were the best, guys. *Sigh.*

What a hell-hole, that night, the first time I tried to field a franchise team. Dawn would never come, and even when it did, we still had work to do. Not good, that!

My miseries started when I was still sitting in a diner.

All-night diners are cool, the saboteur's friend. Every Mobber needs one. Every worker needs a break, right? We'd sit down in a diner right next to a uniformed on-duty cop who'd stopped in for coffee, radio perched on the table. Kind of like you're own personal scanner, huh? We'd be the first to know.

There are limits, however, to how much eccentricity can be ignored, even in an all-night diner. Wide limits, yes, but, still, limits. Gotta keep an eye on your "Target ensemble" and keep tuning up your legend as you eat.

A nice lunch break at two or three AM helps to give the entire night a workaday feel. Let off some strain.

That night, the Night from Hell, our little sub-team had done two or three targets (Avon calling, I recall) and we were taking a break.

It may have been a mistake, but I told the other team where our diner was. On the one hand, of course it's not good to have not-quite professionals who don't quite have the street presence to roll up on you where you're sitting at three AM to try to make it look like a coincidence, or at worst, some kind of a frat house treasure-hunt thing on steroids. Even a jaded third shift waitress can start to ask herself, "What's up here?"

On the other hand, I hated to send out the first experimental team on its own, without a panic-spot to come to. We actually had a cascading tier of panic assembly spots, each farther and farther from the crime scene, in the event of an unintended separation of team members. This tier ended up with: get out of town! Go home.

Sometimes the mama duck pushes the baby duck farther out into the pond. Is that what I'm saying?

Diner mash-up was Mistake Number One. Looking back, I should've known something was up when a bedraggled member of the B team showed up at our diner before we could even finish lunch.

"I don't know, Jim," he said, "we didn't hit all the places on the list."

"Uh-huh.'"

"One just looked scary.'"

"and then?"

"Well, then the next one looked scary."

Hmm, I thought. Well, we'll just shove this duckling back into the water.

It would've been too complicated to try to set up another all night diner meet-place. Messages into and out of the field, with radio silence, is tricky, especially with some comparatively new faces in the crowd. So, I took my sub-crew back out for the bottom of our sub-list and told the B team to look for us in the diner if there were any more problems. This was Mistake Number Two.

We finished our sub-list in a couple hours and returned. First light at that latitude and season was still two or three hours away. On a one-team night we'd have been back in the rack already, or at least on the road out of town, but that would've made that town a two-nighter. Not good. Would the B team come through?

The same tired messenger straggled up the aisle of the diner. Somehow – I didn't want to know – he'd gotten separated from his team during panic flight from some kind of real or perceived police presence.

Remember my cowering on the rooftop the first time I heard a siren? Like that.

## Lavender Hill 5. Franchise 2

This was very understandable. But in this particular case, in the panic, this guy ran off, and in the process, distanced himself from the perceived danger so far that he lost contact with his team entirely. Even this can make sense, to diminish risk. Someone could survive.

Whatever the real danger that night, no one was arrested or ID'd, thank goodness. It's hip to be scared.

The separated team member had gotten two blocks away from the kerfuffle – good -- and caught a cab to the diner. Mistake Number Three. Sort of.

We hung out a minute, dreading further news, or hey, a cop tail that figured it all out and popped us in the diner, for all we knew. I broke out in a sweat. "Hey, pal, where's your car parked? Can you show me?" That would've been fun.

It was either Bad News Messenger Number One or Two, but about a half hour before dawn a picture emerged: the police scare happened after the hit (successful), but we still had a Mobber, a vehicle and a boom box that were all AWOL, lost in the panic. Not good.

I still am not sure exactly how this all worked out. There was miraculous intervention for us to survive a screw-up this bad. Anyway, somehow a hierarchy of values coalesced in our minds: Mobber, car, boom box.

We sent out a rescue car with a B team member to lead the way to the site and found the last AWOL member walking the streets nearby. Blessing Number One.

On the way back to the diner, he told me about the location of the car that was still AWOL.

After delivering the Mobber to the diner, we went back out and got the car, all of this with no visible cop presence. Blessing Number Two.

But first light had come and gone by now. It was after dawn, a time no Mobber should ever be seen outside of a motel room or, say, a car on the interstate, one or two states away. Nervous-making, to be sure.

After the car rescue, the tattered remains of the B Team picked that moment to remind us that a boombox was still missing, a boombox being the crude home-made PVC fire-extinguisher-like thing that we pressurized and used to deliver the sauce. The one with the needle from the junkyard reefer. We had attached the needle thing to the four inch PVC pipe by a miracle of modern plumbing from the open bins at Home Depot. We went from a four inch diameter pipe down to about one and a half mm. inside diameter, in about two or three longitudinal inches, inches that mattered a lot when you are trying to stuff something into your coat and walk normally. A lot of work had gone into those boomboxes, but on the other hand, they had been designed to be dumped in a panic, with no prints or DNA in skin from your hands or any of CSI stuff. Better to arrest a boombox than the person holding one, right? It's just that this was the first time anyone had actually done what I had always said they could do: dump it off. Better they get away; still, I'd rather the cops not even get the boombox. The less they knew about our operation, the better. Hate to see a nationwide APB on boomboxes go out. Could make for a swifter roadside arrest on one of these recurring amiable pullovers.

So. How to rescue the boom box. We drove back to the police scare target for the third time that morning. Fifth blessing, actually, for the B Team.

Blessing Number Three was something I was not prepared for at all. I had never been within fifty or a hundred miles of a target when the sun came up, and so this was a whole new experience for me, driving back again, hoping to recover a boombox.

One of the differences was that now there was a regular morning commute going on. Who knew, tooling around empty streets all night that this or that road would be a commuter artery? At night they all looked the same: desolate. But there it was, and not only that, but as I got closer to the target mill, the traffic slowed down more and more.

Traffic jam. Morning commute fender-bender. What could be more commonplace.

We inched along. A glimpse up ahead of some fire trucks. OK, an accident. Four lanes, two directions, like a dual carriageway, were all compressed over to one side of the road. About a mile of backed up traffic going two or three miles an hour.

Finally, we got up close to the fire trucks and then past them. The traffic eased up and shot ahead.

But wait a minute! No wreckers! No ambulances! And guess what, Virginia? One of the huge trucks said HAZ MAT RESPONSE TEAM on it.

An entire Class A rig, as big as the biggest urban hook-and-ladder, completely dedicated to putting on sawdust and Dustin Hoffman moonsuits? That's funny..

Then someone whispered, "Hey! We just passed the mill!"

All that fuss and bother, over just one mill? My knees buckled.

We did not always trip the alarms doing these jobs, and even if we did, a police drive by might not detect evidence of an injection. This meant that the first indication of a hit might not come until someone came to open up the mill at the beginning of regular business hours, for another day of baby decapitation and incineration. Since it was now dawn, the time normal people wake up and go to work, this must have been what happened.

Recovery of the Mobber and the car (he'd been too scared to go back to it at the time) all took place with no obvious police presence. The cops had driven by in the night (the cause of the cop scare) but then gone away. The building had appeared intact and unharmed

What a shocker. After all the years of sauce-and-go, here, for the first time, I had an indication of what it was like for baby-killing civilians and the bystanders who let them do it, to deal with sauce.

We took a deep breath and spun around the block. That's an old trick, by the way -- three right turns done automatically, if you think someone's following you. Right turns are easy and they don't involve too much stress. Watch out for New York City, though. They don't like that so much up there.

What the heck. We still were not under arrest, and maybe everyone was focusing on the building right then, not the surrounding area. And there the boombox was, on a civilian's lawn, right out in front of God and everyone in plain view and full sunlight; probably the first sunlight that baby had ever seen. It had been thrown up there in a second's panic by a Mobber, and good thing he did. He was following protocol.

But, damn! There it was, right out on some guy's lawn, obviously something that didn't belong, and if it had been the post 9/11 environment, that silly boombox would have already gotten way more attention than the stinky building a half a block away. Anybody could've seen it and called the real bomb squad. Phew! Blessing Number Three.

Yes, we would field other second units. But before you look for quantity, get the quality thing down, first.

On another run, a B Team got created, but quite by accident. Three seasoned vets were doing our thing in yet another big town, and one of them said, hey, can you pull in this parking lot? OK? Just a sec. A little too much coffee at the diner, and no time to go find another diner. This dumpster behind a grocery store would do, right? Street people do this all the time.

Having attended to business, I turned back to where the car had been sitting one second earlier to discover, no car. Later, I found out it was yet another cop scare (a driveby) and the driver was convinced that it was one of those driveby, the kind where the cop says to himself, OK, weird, but I'll let it go. Now if it's still there the next time I come by, I'll investigate.

So the driver went off thinking that he'd just circle the block and come back to pick me up, revolving doors like in a French bedroom farce.

That was the plan, anyway.

The problem was that on our driver's trip around the block, he encountered yet another cop scare and decided for a circle just a little bigger, intending to still come back to the original spot by the grocery.

That was just about the time I got a creepy feeling about the grocery store lot so I backed off and tried to watch it from a distance. In the woods this is a snap, but in the urban environment it's tricky business, A pedestrian can stick out even more than a car. But now we were truly separated and the only spot we had in common to rendezvous was hot as a pistol.

If that had been the end of it for the crew still in the car, it might not have been so bad. Somehow they got truly waylaid by an unholy congruence of third shift cruisers who simply wouldn't buy the legend, And they were bored.

"Two pretty girls like you? Out alone like this? In this part of town?" It was Galahad Redux, a time when even a Mobber might wonder if it were better if the cops returned to Cop Task Number One: Arrest the Guilty,

An argument between the cops ("Nope, nope, I just don't buy it. This is a crime scene."), more lecturing about how the Mobbers needed to be more careful, which tended to morph into less-disguised flirting, and finally a motorized escort Off My Turf.

So. No arrests so far, and those cops had to be kicking themselves at dawn when they realized what they really had been looking at (a crime scene). But the next problem was that by the time all this was resolved, a rendezvous anywhere near the original panic spot was just about impossible. Both sides were very nervous about going back to that spot. The car team searched as much as they dared, considering that they had just been thrown off that turf, but it was no dice.

Thirty-six miles travel by foot back to the surburban hideout fixed it (i was broke) but not without a price. We were shattered, as they say on the Auld Sod. Time for a day off! We hit the ponies! I won twenty cents on a two dollar bet, Favored-To-Show (Don't tell the Baptists! Shhhh).

Sun, turf, trumpets in the open air, appaloosas, cash , gotta love it. Suffering for Christ in the missions we were. He takes away, He gives, Job tells us. Sigh.

## Toasted Marshmallows

Marshmallows…toasted marshmallows.

Nice, right? But you gotta have a heat source for toasted marshmallows. Well, in the history of the Lavender Hill Mob, toasted marshmallows came about much the same way as butyric acid.

I encountered butyric acid for the first time in a lab in school. I heard about homemade napalm reading a book on the 1/9 Cav. about Viet Nam. Once, they were so hard up for napalm they made some up out of tank automatic transmission fluid and I forget what else. One day we were hanging out in between jobs but in the field, in other words, outside the donut, and you could say we had a little time on our hands. So, we took a day off where you could sleep in the dark like normal people. The campsite was extremely remote, and large, and our campsite was out in the boonies, out of sight of the owner's house and the place where the fancy RVs hook up. We were mere tenting customers, like the peanut gallery. I brought up the Viet Nam story and the synthetic napalm. Enthusiasm reigned. It was not -- I came, I saw, I got blowed up, like Ernest Worrell, but it was a close thing.

A tiny historical note might be in order. In the 80's insurance companies nudged baby killers out of wood structures and into masonry/concrete. Building supervisors threw killers out of multiple business buildings when the legitimate lessees, usually real doctors, got wind of the first whiff of sauce in the lobby areas of their buildings. Or picketers.

Blowing up something, without blowing yourself up, without all the professionally made caps and stuff, without blowing up a bystander, is actually tricky, I believe, especially when you're dealing with a hardened structure. Fine for others, perhaps, don't get me wrong, but I passed.

So, how to disable a hardened building when you can't burn it down and blowing it up is problematic?

Well, sauce, for one. But 1/9th Cavalry provided a new angle with the improvised napalm story. Pure ATF might not get off too quick, and pure gas has too little smoke, as we quickly discovered at our remote camping site combustion laboratory.

A marvelous combination appeared after a modicum of experimentation -- 50/50 diesel and unleaded, with a simple road flare to get the marshmallows going. Road flares cover all sorts of different circumstances for ignition, rain or snow, an awkward spot, or a puddle of stuff already delivered fifteen vertical feet down some shaft , exact configuration unknown

When the road flare hit the ATF/unleaded mix, it was Eureka! Watson, I need you! A B.F. Goodrich moment.

It was now just a matter of tweaking the formula, logistics, and delivery.

On another occasion we got real close to perfecting an idea which we got standing in a marine chandlery: a simple emergency marine signal flare that would enable a touch-off from a slight distance, a crucial distance. Suppose everything was ready to go, for example, but for the sake of snappy egress you'd just as soon not touch it off from the top of a ladder or even the ground.

The flare gun would help that way, especially since avoiding a stumble or fall in the first few second of a marshmallow whoosh, in the panic of it, would drive up your chances of success. It would be a real drag to be caught just because of a twisted ankle. Don't you just hate that? It would also save the nuisance of hand-striking a real flare while you are standing so much closer to the woosh. Singed eyebrow gonna be a big giveaway in that midnight line-up, you know. But obtaining and using the flare gun would change the foresic profile a little bit. There's that.

Ahhh, so many mills, so little time.

## Highway Patrol--Gotta Love 'Em!

That's a funny thing for a prolifer to say. Cops are cops. Cops nowadays protect child murderers when just a few decades ago they tossed 'em in the clink.

But the state troopers rarely mess with that. Not directly, anyway. Plenty of cultural breakdown can show up on a highway breakdown, but by and large, troopers are a little more avuncular than the city cops who moonlight on private duty guarding kid slaughterhouses. A state trooper's more like Uncle Bob.

Uncle Bob's that way because much of the time he's carrying out Cop Task Number Two: Protect the Innocent.

The first time we were pulled over outside the donut on an interstate, it was Change Your Shorts time. We were utterly convinced that Smokey Servant of the People was carrying out Cop Task No. 1: Arrest the Guilty. Especially with stuff burrowed away in the car that just might not have a ready explanation.

When Cheech and Chong were sidelined by the likes of Stacey Reach, their exposure was six months, say. Under FACE, our stuff would start out at five years and go up from there. If Democrats were in office, maybe more like 10 years for a starting point.

As a matter of fact, we felt like changing our shorts the first dozen times we were pulled over to or from a job, until, finally, a kind of Thermidor Shorts-Changing ennui set in.

Why do we have to keep changing our shorts? Here we are, a dozen pullovers into this, and we've still never been arrested. Could it be that it's an us thing? That we need to get our heads around the idea that pullovers aren't necessarily game stoppers?

Could it even be a, a God thing? Hi! Fooled ya, Huh?

Shoulda seen the looks on your faces. Hopefully avoiding the twin perils of Calvinism and presumption, we began to wonder -- maybe God does have a sense of humor. Or at least, a kind of short leash on the whole existentialist thing. As in, Stay Close. Don't go running off, or thinking you can do it all alone. Something to think about anyway.

Along about the same time the Shorts Changing/Thermidor Ennui set in, another idea came along: we gotta work on our story.

The Legend. So important. Plenty of time to work on your legend, the story you tell a cop, coming and going from your donut. Almost like, the more you work on it, the deeper it gets, and after a while, it could withstand several follow-up questions, if it had to. Cops usually don't get that into it on roadside pullovers, but it still adds to confidence, to have a deep legend. I suppose you could say it was like a John Le Carre thing. He could spend half a book on a legend who's only purpose was to support a thirty second exchange. At a border kiosk, say.

The core of the legend has to have a kernel of truth to it, we discovered, so it could come out more convincing.

Suppose I have Connecticut plates on my car. Suppose "outside my donut," for today, happens to be the Midwest, or the Near South. Or the Cold M's (Minnesota, Montana, Michigan, Missouri). Or the Plains. My story is that I'm driving out to visit my sick Mom/Grandma in California.

Cops in the Middle are very familiar with native Right Coasters who migrate to California and then want to go home for Christmas, but the reverse story -- could be true, in my case -- is unusual enough to have a ring of quirky authenticity to it. The Left Coast accent and demeanor and Right Coast tags all help the story along.

The sunny California demeanor, by the way, helps, on the road. It helps in a general way no matter what your legend is. But beyond friendliness, or even optimism, cops like something a little different, a task imposed on native Californians at birth, like it or not. I can't help but wonder if all cops aren't just a little bit Californian. Even in an isolated or rural part of the country, the cop that works there is going to be the first one to have to encounter something just a little bit different. And I think the whole country is tilting a little more in the direction of gypsy-ish every day. The poor cop catches a little bit of this, even if his only exposure to it is the swatch of interstate that rolls through his turf. Texas and Florida are close runners-up in that whole gypsy, or newcomer thing. Carpetbaggers. But the carpet baggers sometimes turn out to be local taxpayers.

You, your tags, your car, and everything in it must match the legend. If I were poor, a trash bag full of Salvation Army throwaway clothes (big, dark, disposable immediately after a crime) in the back seat kind of fits the story. Snacks wrappers are closer to Giant Eagle and Mickey D's than five-star dining. Tools in the back fit the itinerant handyman; and so on.

Big Smile, and never pass up a sincere opportunity to convert a me-you challenge into an "us" moment of water-cooler talk:

"How do you deal with being out in this cold all night, officer?'" said to a Montana trooper in winter, goes down a lot better than "I got my rights! How dare you!"

On all these pullovers, even with trunk inspections, no cop ever found sauce or a boombox. Some things are just The Lords. "Some trust in chariots." I mean, do your best, but in the end it's His show.

Once a cop shone his light in back where a big tub of boom boxes and vials of sauce were all in plain view. I saw the light play over it. The cop knew mills in that town had been stunk the previous night.

This was more than Change Your Shorts. Change your burnt to a crisp pacemaker battery, get a new tube of Fixodent when your choppers fly out, speed dial F. Lee Bailey, put your cat's kennel in the will, write a will, tell Mama you loved her and put a fork in it. We were so toast.

But we weren't. I saw the cop see it; I saw his face. It was a cluttered alleyway in a town miles from an interstate, no legend here! What is this tag doing in this alley at two-thirty AM?

"I told you this was not the way to the freeway, dammit!" I fumed at the driver.

She fumed back. Being of one X and one Y chromosomal entities, the two vehicle passengers rapidly drove the cop away from the clearly niggling thought that this was the felony of the century right under his nose for which he'd get a big citation. Now, it was just another domestic dispute, which he settled with elaborate directions to the interstate. Mom? Sick? California? Remember?

Never pass up a change to nudge a cop off of Task No. One and on over to Task No. Two: Assist the Taxpayer. They love it. Less paperwork, too.

As I say, I saw the look on the cop's face just before the fake fight. Was he smiling a tiny RC grandfatherly smile, a Vito Squad smile, like the Engine Brigade Captain back in San Francisco? The one who said he would never be able to undo a Chinese finger puzzle?

They're all gone, the Last Greatest Generation, Woe is us.

On the subject of clothes, the phrase "'Target Ensemble" can have a meaning that transcended even Ernest P. Worrell. Salvation Army clothes, cheap enough and clean enough. You could buy lots of it, including "throw-aways." Dark enough to be black at night but colorful enough that you wouldn't look like a Grateful Dead roadie or a Ninja Turtle if you happened to pass under a street light or were hanging out in a diner. Nice enough or close to new enough you didn't look like an outright bum if you moved like one in the Red Zone -- the slice of time from the last bar closing until the first garbage truck run, in any town.

A tired glance of a cop taking all of it in – you, your car, your stuff -- would tend to paint this kind of a picture:

Just enough money to be employed and paying taxes somewhere and not be a bum, but nowhere near enough to be a true suburbanite who would never be out slumming, this time of night, in this part of town.

These are the thoughts you want running through a cop's mind. Irritated, disgusted a little at having to deal with the white trash, but not enough to arrest you.

Move along. This is not the droid you seek.

The story, the Legend. You. Your appearance. The car. The tags. The contents of your pockets and the car. Story. Your exact relationship to passengers, and how that appears to him. It all must match and God protect too for it all to work.

Coming and going from donuts we practiced the story and prayed to God, long, long prayers and lots of listening silence.

## Lavender Hill Mob [transformers]

At one point the Lavender Hill Mob began to expand their horizons beyond armomatherapy, ultimately into marshmallows. As in roasting them. That, in turn, led to Reach Out and Touch Someone, which wasn't really Mob work, more like freelancing.

One interesting stop along the way to all that was transformers. We tend to ignore them even though without them, we'd be stuck dead in the water. Modern technology-wise, anyway. Suction pump-wise, to be a tad more specific about it.

Stuck dead in the water. That's the goal of saboteurs. Shut down the killing factories, just as the Air Force did in World War II. Same deal. Only we go after the actual camps, and the Air force did not. But since we are obviously a smaller force, we can't do it with B-17s, so we started to look at the utility step-down transformers close to the mills.

We called them flyers, walkers, or swimmers, depending on if they were on a pole, surface mount, or buried, respectively.

All transformers share a weakness. They must be somewhat separated from a structure, in case of fire, and a little bit like water heaters, which have their own little closets unalarmed and essentially open to the outside world.

Hot water heaters are also, by the way, yet another underexploited weak link in the infrastructural chain required to murder a child.

But back to transformers. Engineers and architects don't like to put them too close to buildings, just in case they catch fire, which they tend to do all by themselves, now and then.

We just wanted to speed it up a little. The whole random thing was a little too slow for us.

The other weakness transformers have is that they must have cooling fins, and these must be exposed to function as heat exchangers. Any attempt to shroud them could be self-defeating because any shroud would tend to defeat the passive cooling function. Just a little tidbit for you electrical engineers out there when the babykillers come knocking.

The original theory was to use the highly carcinogenic and polluting PCB oil inside the transformer as a fuel to burn the transformer itself, or at least the insulation on its connecting cables, something that we did on a few until we discovered that simply letting the oil out would often achieve our goal just about as well. We didn't even need to light them off.

In a way it reminds me of the decision toward Avon when the insurance underwriters herded the killers into masonry structures: explosives is one way to deal with it, but was it the only way? How about some things with a little more finesse but the same impact?

We never got quite deep enough into it to do the after-report, but it would've been nice to double check to make certain some bureaucrat somewhere had declared the soil underneath a sabotaged transformer to be a toxic site by virtue of the PCB oil leaked onto it from a few holes drilled in the cooling vanes, which are made of very thin sheet metal. Don't forget some vent holes in the top! Small holes would do the trick fine by morning, an eighth of an inch or so. The little double-headed Ace bits work wonders.

We even considered an anonymous tipster who'd let the Sierra Club types know, after a drilling, to make sure our tax dollars were at work protecting the comrade citizens from this horrible toxin. Give a hoot, don't pollute!

Of course there is always the danger that the otherwise thoroughly liberal pollution monitors of a given town might decide that this particular toxic site deserves a pass, for obvious political reasons. That's when yet another citizen needs to step up to do his civic duty! Madame Lafarge of the Superfund sensitivities, sharpen up your knitting needles! And if you're a Republican, get an alibi, too.

But what a boon! To give a mill, or its owner, or the landowner, a big Bambi/Save The Whales headache with just a few minutes' worth of drilling.

As I understand it, when properly done, restoration would involve excavation of all the dirt under a transformer spot, whether it was a flyer, walker or swimmer, and I bet that would, in turn, involve re-pulling the connection to the high voltage utility. Oh boy. Lotta bang for the buck on that one. We never quite got there, but if it had been worked up to the level of Avon logistics and planning where we'd research a dozen sites and then hit them all in a night, that would be even easier since you don't need to deal with alarms. Not that we did, very often, with Avon, but still.

One story I do remember in the learning curve days. I think we were fooling around trying to collect the oil to cook the vanes with. Anyway, a bunch of vapor accumulated in the shroud that protects the cable terminations, and the density of the vapor was just enough to ignite when we lit off the collected oil underneath. The liquid oil burned nicely, perfect for marshmallows, but the vapor trapped in the shroud went with a pop, not a really big one, but big enough.

Bang! I checked my face, my torso, whatever, and I was uninjured, but it woke up the old ticker in the old man. It also made more noise than we needed.

After that we tended to just drill a few holes and put up a hazard tape to keep people out of the mud and away in case of a burnup from overheating. Now there's a nice little bonus, on top of the whole Erin Brockovich thing.

To this day I'm sure there are some soil contaminations that were swept under the rug by the utilities. Erin! We need you!

Also, lighting off the oil should always be on the table to fry the cable insulation in case the town doesn't give a hoot.

Stopping all child dismemberment, today and no later, is obviously the best, especially if you're the next one on the conveyor belt. But to drive 'em out of business with increased insurance premiums or utility surcharges works too. Flo only goes so far with the cheerful thing.

Once, in the South, we saw a really tempting flyer, the poles surrounded by private property, off the road, out of view in a kind of loose common courtyard behind many businesses. That was also just about the time Home Depot was kicking out their eighteen volt cordless equipment. We were thinking of just "permitting" the pole at eye level until it came over, without even touching the transformer itself. Replacing the pole itself would have to take time too. Or, drilling the can once it sagged down, a kind of two-fer.

Now, the funny thing about "swimmers" is that the keyed sockets needed to spin the bolts on their grilles. Some of these could be gotten through a post-office box shell company, like buying bulk Avon, or like being a locksmith as we once did to get some ready-made lock picks. In this case we'd be some start-up co-op utility that need the pentagonal bolt sockets to spin them

There are also now "keyed" bolt heads with very explicit randomnish patterns to fit with a marked key socket, but none of those have been made that can beat a CAD milling machine, or, heck, a little creative manual Dremel tool die-grinding.

Plus, you can put the resultant key socket in your pocket and just test to see if it works before you tool up for the main event. It only needs to grab once and then we'd throw it in the river. The feebs have a whole unit for "toolmarks." In fact, all tools that touch death-camp metal are one-use. ALL.

RALPH M. GABRIEL

Afterward

# James Kopp, In Defense of Others

By Elizabeth McDonald

Most news reports described the scene in these terms:

Barnett A. Slepian, 52, an obstetrician and gynecologist who also performed abortions stood in the kitchen of his house, warming soup in a microwave. On the evening of October 23, 1998, Dr. Slepian had just returned from a synagogue service honoring his late father. He chatted with his wife and one of his four sons who was watching TV in an adjoining room.

As Slepian waited for the timer to call him back to the microwave, a sniper in the woods behind the house waited too. Through an unshuttered rear window, which provided a view of the kitchen, the sniper had watched as Slepian placed the soup bowl in the microwave. Bracing himself against a tree, he trained the sites of his rifle on the spot where Slepian's left shoulder would be positioned when he returned for his soup.

How terrible to be a vulnerable person in the warmth and security of his own home unaware that a stranger watches, poised to strike. But Dr.

Slepian's experience was not unique. Sallie Tisdale, an RN at an abortion "clinic," wrote this chilling, first-hand account of her own, similar stalking:

> It takes practice to read an ultrasound picture, which is grainy and etched as though in strokes of charcoal. But suddenly a rapid rhythmic motion appears – the beating heart. Nearby is a soft oval, scratched with lines -- the skull. The leg is harder to find, and then suddenly the fetus moves, bobbing in the surf. The skull turns away, an arm slides across the screen, the torso rolls. I know the weight of a baby's head on my shoulder, the whisper of lips on ears, the delicate curve of a fragile spine in my hand. I know how heavy and correct a newborn cradled feels. The creature I watch in secret requires nothing from me but to be left alone and that is precisely what won't be done.1

How terrible indeed to be a vulnerable person in the warmth and security of his own home, his mother's womb, unaware that a Tisdale or a Slepian awaits. And what precisely would "be done"? Dr. Paul Jarrett explains:

> My 23rd abortion changed my mind about doing abortions forever. This patient was a little overweight and ultimately proved to be a little farther along than anticipated. This was not an uncommon mistake before ultrasound was readily available to confirm the gestational age. Initially, the abortion proceeded normally. The water broke, but then nothing more would come out. When I withdrew the curette, I saw that it was plugged up with a leg which had been torn off from the baby. I then changed techniques and used ring forceps to dismember the 13- or 14-week size baby. Inside the remains of the rib cage I found a tiny, beating heart. I was finally able to remove the head and looked squarely into the face of a human being — a human being that I had just killed.2

Unlike this unborn child, however, Barnett Slepian was no innocent victim. He did not find himself in the crosshairs of a rifle that night because he was a husband or a father or a doctor or a Jew, but because he was a killer who would kill again in a few short hours. The hands that so carefully placed the soup bowl in the microwave that night would be busy in the morning deftly crushing and shredding the bodies of live babies -- perhaps 25 or more.

Oh, the banality of evil. Just before the listing for "abrasives," a modest display ad on page 2 of the Erie County Bell Atlantic Yellow Pages solicited murder of unborn children in the age range of "4 to 19 weeks" with "Medicaid/Insurance Accepted" at the "clinic" where Slepian worked on Saturdays. Now all the appointments had been scheduled with the age of each inconvenient and unwanted child carefully recorded beside the name of his/her mother. Our sniper, James Kopp, knew that these little ones would be no match for Barnett Slepian. For how can any small child, whether a three-month babe in the womb or a three-year-old playing in the park, defend herself from an adult assailant?

Since the intentional killings of innocent human beings can never be justified, the abortionist Slepian was, in moral terms, an unjust aggressor. For the sake of the innocent, justice requires that an unjust aggressor be restrained and restrained with force, when necessary.

Jim Kopp saw 25 babies in imminent danger of death and, being a good man, he saw his duty to defend them. The shot was fired around 10 p.m. and no babies died at the hands of Barnett Slepian on Saturday, October 24, 1998. The life and career of one very prolific serial killer had come to an end.

But shooting Barnett Slepian was so extreme and so terrible. There must have been a better way -- a nonviolent way -- to prevent him from killing more babies. Yes, of course there was a better way. In fact, there were several better ways, which, in previous years, had served quite effectively to restrain killers like Slepian. New York, along with every other state in the union, had laws which provided penalties including incarceration for those found guilty of committing the crime of abortion. Compliance, of course, was never perfect; there were always some who were willing to kill babies for money. But, to paraphrase Dr. Martin Luther King: although laws cannot change the heart, they can and did restrain the heartless. A nation is rightly judged by how zealously it safeguards, through the rule of law, the lives and rights of those least able to defend their rights themselves. So, it is to our great shame that New York legalized abortion in 1970. Three years later, the Roe v. Wade decision effectively struck down the abortion laws in every state. Thus, the most vulnerable member of the human family, the unborn child, was officially cast out of our protected circle.

A second line of defense began to form in the late 1970's. Small groups of citizens, responding to the unborn child's urgent need for protection, began peacefully interposing their bodies between the abortionist and his victims at abortion "clinics." These rescuers recognized that pro-life work in such areas as education and legislation, though worthwhile and necessary, could not save the life of a child scheduled to die by abortion in their community that day. By the late 1980's this rescue movement had spread across the country. In some cities, over 1,000 citizens risked arrest and made good on their promise -- "No babies die here today!" There was much to commend in this approach. It demonstrated that even when government fails to protect a vulnerable group of people, a community has the duty and the power through sheer force of numbers to secure the safety of those no longer protected through force of law. Unfortunately, after more than 50,000 arrests and many lives saved, this other "better way" to restrain abortionists and protect babies was also abandoned. Failures in the movement's leadership and draconian civil and criminal penalties imposed under The Freedom of Access to Clinic Entrances Act combined to stall and then kill the rescue movement. All the summer soldiers fled the field and their rallying cry --"If abortion is murder, act like it!" -- died in the air.

So, in considering the shooting on October 23, 1998, the question to ask is not: Wasn't there a better way? The proper question is: Was any better way actually available to Jim Kopp and to the babies whose lives were in danger? Sadly, the answer is "no." The police were not at the "clinic" that night cordoning it off with crime scene tape in conformance to a wonderful, new government edict, perhaps a Supreme Court ruling or Human Life Amendment, which had restored protection to unborn babies. Nor were Bishop Mansell and Rev. Behn in a church hall rallying the good citizens of Buffalo and instructing them in their duty to protect their littlest neighbors. On Saturday morning there would not be 500 or 1,000 caring adults to stand between Barnett Slepian and the babies he was scheduled to kill.

Only one person, Jim Kopp, saw the terrible deaths awaiting these babies and resolved to defend them effectively. Decades of "legalized" abortion had left many good people feeling defeated and even desensitized: for how can anyone relate to a toll in human lives lost which is now in the range of 45 million? Jim knew that he could not save the million or more killed annually and he could not save all 4,000 who would die on October 24, 1998. But he could be faithful to the truth that each unborn child is an irreplaceable, innocent human being by focusing on one individual killer and on the little ones who would be that killer's next victims. For those babies in Buffalo, their defender, Jim Kopp, was the last good man and true -- the only one who would not abandon them.

When the duty to protect a group of innocent people in imminent danger of death has been left to one private citizen, that person is justified in using whatever degree of force he reasonably believes is necessary to effectively defend them. This should be obvious to all. In fact, the laws in every state recognize that "conduct which would otherwise constitute an offense is justifiable and not criminal when…such conduct is necessary as an emergency measure to avoid an imminent public or private injury." (Section 35.05 New York State Consolidated Laws)3

On the basis of this "defense of justification," also known as the "necessity defense," pro-life rescuers in the past routinely pled innocent to charges such as trespassing which arose from their blockades of abortion "clinics." They asserted that their actions at the "clinics" were not crimes because they were necessary to prevent the killing of unborn children, just as a person is justified in trespassing to pull a drowning child from a neighbor's pool. It is important to understand that these rescues were not essentially acts of protest or civil disobedience. Unlike civil rights activists sitting-in at a lunch counter in violation of an unjust, segregationist law; the pro-life rescuers were not disobeying unjust laws: laws against trespass are not, in themselves, unjust. Their conduct, while not conforming to the requirements of the trespass laws, was made lawful by its necessity as an emergency measure to avoid an imminent private injury, i.e., the killing of unborn children.

Although most courts refused to consider the necessity defense in these cases, across the country there were a number of good judges who acquitted rescuers on the basis of this defense. In St. Louis, over 200 cases either ended in acquittal or dismissal of charges after Judge Harold Johnson, Judge Arthur Miorelli, and Judge George R. Gerhard, acquitted rescuers on the necessity defense. The "Judgment and Opinion" entered by the Hon. George R. Gerhard, Division 31, St., Louis County Circuit Court, dated August 16, 1989, states, in part:

> This Court finds that the credible evidence in these cases establishes justification for the Defendants' actions. Their violations of the ordinances involved here were necessary as emergency measures to avoid the imminent private injuries of death and maiming of unborn children, which imminent deaths and maimings were

occasioned through no fault of the defendants but occasioned by the operation of a lucrative commercial endeavor. The desirability of avoiding death and maiming of unborn children — persons — obviously outweighs the desirability of avoiding the injury sough to be prevented by the ordinances.4

Judge Gerhard's opinion mirrors the language of both the Missouri and New York laws on the defense of justification and would serve as a fine model for Judge Michael L. D'Arnico as he considers Jim Kopp's case. And, yes, the defense of justification is available to Jim Kopp in the shooting death of Barnett Slepian.

Many who would deny Jim Kopp the defense of justification believe that unborn children scheduled for death are unworthy of any form of defense -- forceful or non-forceful. They have accepted the fallacious notion that a certain class of human beings, unborn children, can be designated "nonpersons" under the law and treated as property to be disposed of at the discretion of their owners. This odious idea, promulgated by Roe and its progeny, simply echoes the holding of Dred Scott V. Sandford, 60 U.S. (19 How.) 393 (1857) that black slaves were "nonpersons" under the law, a decision the 14th amendment was intended to reverse. The Rev. Jesse Jackson understood these bigots well:

> Don't let the pro-choicers convince you that a fetus isn't a human being, he warned: "That's how the whites dehumanized us, by calling us niggers. The first step was to distort the image of us as human beings in order to justify that which they wanted to do -- and not even feel like they'd done anything wrong." . . . "There are those who would argue that the right to privacy is of a higher order than the right to life," he said, "but that was the premise of slavery. You could not protest the existence or treatment of slaves on the plantation because that was private and therefore outside of your right to be concerned."5

Of course, this was the "old" Jesse Jackson speaking; before, blinded by political ambition, he became just another Step'n Fetchit on the abortion plantation. Nevertheless, his words remain good and true and worthy of consideration. Another voice from the left, Ken Kesey, called abortion "fascism": "How can abortion be anything but fascism again, back as a fad in a new intellectual garb with a new, and more helpless, victim?"6 Speaking of the "un-dead old" and the "un-born young," Kesey said, "[t]hese beings, regardless not only of race, creed and color, but as well of size, situation or ability, must be treated as equals and their rights to life not only recognized but defended! Can they defend themselves?"7

The condemnation heaped upon Jim Kopp by fellow pro-lifers is harder to understand. What is wrong with these people? Having proclaimed the humanity of unborn children and demanded their full protection under the law, many pro-lifers now agree with the bigots that unborn children are not entitled to the same effective, forceful defense that the law permits to born persons in the United States. Many of these pro-lifers erroneously believe that the justification defense is not available to Jim Kopp because that defense is, in its application, limited to the commission of minor offenses such as trespass. In fact, there is no such limitation. The nature of the conduct which may be justified under this defense is principally limited by the nature of the injury which that conduct seeks to prevent. For example, Sec. 35.25 New York State Consolidated Laws provides for the use of "physical force, other than deadly physical force" to prevent the crimes of larceny or criminal mischief. However, Sec. 35.15 permits the use of "deadly physical force upon another person" when "such other person is using or about to use deadly physical force." Once the Court recognizes, as Judge Gerhard did, that the injury sought to be prevented is the "death and maiming of unborn children -- persons", it follows that conduct which may be justified ranges from trespass up to, and including, the use of deadly physical force.

Jim Kopp's shooting of Slepian in defense of the babies in Buffalo is justified under the same law and legal theory that were employed by the pro-life rescuers in their trespass cases. The essential threshold question in all of these cases is: Does the killing of unborn children by abortion constitute a grievous private injury -- i.e., the taking of innocent human life, or is the killing of unborn children by abortion merely the disposal of property abandoned by its owners? The method of rescue or the degree of force employed is not the central issue. If abortion does not pose a "threat to life and/or safety of community"8, not even minor infractions such as incommoding or trespassing can be justified. Pro-lifers should understand that if Jim Kopp's conduct was not justified, then their own use of the justification defense was, likewise, illegitimate, and the 50,000+ rescuers and all the judges who acquitted them were wrong.

One element of the justification defense on which pro-lifers must agree with Jim Kopp is the "reasonableness" of his belief that Slepian "was about to use deadly physical force" upon the babies he was scheduled to abort on Saturday. Case law in New York has held that "Jury must determine whether defendant believed that other person was using or was about to use deadly physical force and whether defendant's belief was reasonable, in determining whether defendant was justified in using deadly force."9 Actually, Jim Kopp's case comes at a time when, not only pro-lifers, but the general public as well, acknowledge that every abortion takes a human life.

It was not always so. Many were deceived in the early years [for sure -- the first public pro-deathers I encountered were teen-age girls calling us "friends of the fetus, tee hee."] A medical journal article, published in 1970, provided this helpful tip on how to make abortion palatable to a Nation historically grounded in the Judeo-Christian ethic:

> Since the old ethic has not yet been fully displaced it has been necessary to separate the idea of abortion from the idea of killing, which continues to be socially abhorrent. The result has been a curious avoidance of the scientific fact, which everyone really knows, that human life begins at conception and is continuous whether intra- or extra-uterine until death. The very considerable
> semantic gymnastics which are required to rationalize abortion as anything but taking a human life would be ludicrous if they were not often put forth under socially impeccable auspices.1O

Indeed, this proved to be the pro-abortionists' most successful tactic in winning the right to kill. We were constantly assured that the unborn child was "just tissue", "uterine contents", "potential life" -- nothing more. To counter this, pro-lifers poured their efforts into education, convinced that, if only the public could see the full humanity of the unborn child, abortion would be rejected. In his book Aborting America, published in 1979, former abortionist Dr. Bernard Nathanson wrote, "If wombs had windows . . . If the abdominal wall of the pregnant woman were transparent, what kind of abortion laws might we have?"11 The answer seemed self-evident. Of course, the American people would never tolerate the killing of babies!

A strange thing happened, though. As the decades rolled by, the pro-lifers won the argument over the humanity of the unborn child, but the killing continued. Actually, the argument was largely won for them through amazing advances in the field of fetology, a medical sub-specialty first recognized in 1973 -- ironically, the same year that the patients of this new sub-specialty were declared "nonpersons" by the U.S. Supreme Court. We have seen the distinction between "born" and "unborn" dissolve as we watch TV specials featuring surgery on unborn children in which the uterus is opened, the baby partially removed, surgically repaired, and tucked back in for 3 or 4 more months in the womb. And, of course, through the wide availability of ultrasound technology, wombs now have windows, so to speak. For the last 15 years or so, the first treasured photos in every baby book have been baby's first sonograms. Abortion apologist, Naomi Wolf, in a 1995 article "Our Bodies, Our Souls" acknowledged the challenge presented by these images and by the explosion of information derived from the fields of fetology and perinatology: "So, what will it be: Wanted fetuses are charming, complex, REM-dreaming little beings whose profile on the sonogram looks just like Daddy, but unwanted ones are mere "uterine material"?12 In the same article, she asked another good question:

> The pro-choice movement often treats with contempt the pro-lifers' practice of holding up to our faces their disturbing graphics. We revile their placards showing an enlarged scene of the aftermath of a D & C abortion; we are disgusted by their lapel pins with the little feet, crafted in gold, of a 10-week-old fetus . . . and we are quick to say that they are lying: "Those are stillbirths, anyway," we tell ourselves. [But] many of those photographs are in fact photographs of actual D & Cs; those footprints are in fact footprints of a 10-week-old fetus; the pro-life slogan, "Abortion stops a beating heart," is incontrovertibly true. While images of violent fetal death work magnificently for pro-lifers as political polemic, the pictures are not polemical in themselves: they are biological facts . . . How can we charge that it is vile and repulsive for pro-lifers to brandish vile and repulsive images if the images are real?"13

Still, Wolf, the loyal pro-abortionist, declared that, "sometimes the mother must be able to decide that the fetus, in its full humanity, must die"(emphasis added).14

So, even Naomi Wolf's words support the reasonableness of Jim Kopp's belief, restated in Wolf s terminology, that Slepian was about to cause the "violent . . . death[s]" of 25 "charming, complex, REM-dreaming little beings" in their "full humanity." It seems that only the poor U.S. Supreme Court has been left behind -- stuck in a time-warp, doggedly clinging to the gee-whiz-who-can-tell-when-human-life-begins ignorance feigned by the Roe Court back in 1973.

Of course, the biggest problem mainstream pro-lifers have with Jim Kopp concerns his use of deadly force. But these pro-lifers, in demanding that the defense of innocent lives be accomplished by non-forceful methods only, have added a requirement not found in the law and which is, in fact, quite contrary to the law. Sayings such as: "killing is always wrong," "violence just begets violence," and "violence never solves anything" may sound nice, but they are not legal precepts in American law. Rather, the laws on the defense of justification recognize that the use of physical force, even deadly physical force, does indeed solve problems where human life is in imminent danger such as murder, kidnapping, forcible rape, forcible sodomy and robbery. (See Sec. 35.15 New York State Consolidated Laws). Our legal system is rooted in the Judeo-Christian ethic, which holds the preservation of innocent human life to be of paramount importance. Our law reflects the understanding that the 5th Commandment prohibition against murder contains an implied affirmative duty to prevent murder.

With the protection of innocent human life as its chief concern, the law does not require that conduct in defense of others be "nonviolent." Rather, it requires that the conduct be, among other things, effective. In New York, case law holds that "[t]he requirement that the conduct be 'necessary as an emergency measure' to avoid the injury contemplates conduct which is not only warranted by the circumstances as an emergency response but is also reasonably calculated to have an actual effect in preventing the harm." (emphasis added)15 It is strange, but true, that Jim Kopp could have enjoyed the approbation of many pro-life friends if he had responded to the impending deaths of the babies in Buffalo with a quixotic gesture such as dashing to the clinic door and briefly blocking Slepian's entrance – never mind that all the babies would have died that day. Instead, Jim chose a course of action, which was, as the law required, "reasonably calculated to have the actual effect in preventing the harm."

## No Babies Died, But His Action Was Roundly Denounced By the Very People Who Call Abortion Murder

As a result, no babies died, but his action was roundly denounced by the very people who call abortion "murder." Do they believe their own words? How have so many pro-lifers managed to get it so wrong when it comes to the just defense of babies?

First of all, it must be said that pro-lifers are, in general, exceptionally kind, peace-loving people with a deep aversion to violence. This is why they hate the slaughter of unborn children by abortion. They are not motivated by a desire to abuse or dominate women, as their detractors charge. In fact, more than half of the pro-lifers are women. They are simply good, decent, tenderhearted people who, in John Donne fashion, genuinely feel the deaths of strangers. Take the elderly woman who faithfully stands with her hand-lettered sign at the "clinic" entrance week after week. Her chief desire is that the words on her sign and her prayers for each mother and unborn child as they arrive at the "clinic" might touch the heart of a mother and give her the wisdom and courage to reject death for her baby. She sees each tiny, unwanted child as a person of worth and dignity, created in God's image, whose death is an immeasurable loss to the world and a personal grief to her. Many such dear souls find it excruciatingly difficult to consider the possibility that killing can ever be justified.

Not only is nonviolence the natural inclination of most pro-lifers, but it has also been held up to them by their leaders as an essential element in opposing abortion. In the earliest days of the rescue movement, Gandhi's philosophy and practice of passive resistance to evil was adopted as the model for rescues at abortion clinics. In a pamphlet, which promoted rescue, entitled "Nonviolence Is An Adverb," John Cavanaugh-O'Keefe wrote:

> What Mahatma Gandhi demonstrated -- based on what Christ taught -- is that active love, a campaign of nonviolence, can be a proportionate response to the greatest of evils. Because Gandhi brought about India's independence without going to war with the British, we can hope that a campaign of nonviolence will protect the unborn, now and in the future.16

Since they were not seeking to create riotous mobs, it was wise of the leaders to emphasize nonviolence in their efforts to recruit good, law-abiding citizens to act as a community in defense of unborn children. And the rescue movement, at its height, did prove that a "campaign of nonviolence" can be a proportionate response to the evil of abortion.

When the rescue movement died, however, pro-lifers who had made "nonviolence" the sine qua non of opposition to abortion were at a complete loss. They thought they had constructed a consistent ethic by denouncing not only the violence of abortion, but all forceful opposition to abortion, as well. It sounded so high-minded and virtuous to declare, "No violence period."

But that is cheap talk indeed when the violence is being visited 4,000 times a day upon other people. Since the practice of "drawing and quartering" passed from favor centuries ago, no born person is in danger of being subjected to a government sanctioned "procedure" whereby he is eviscerated, dismembered, and decapitated. (If any reader somehow missed what abortion does to an unborn child, he should go back to page 1 and read Dr. Jarrett's description again). In fact, this pacifist "ethic," with all its pretensions to spiritual and moral superiority, does not even meet the standard of the golden rule -- that most basic, homely, universal guide to moral conduct. Consider: Would any of these pro-lifers truly want what they do unto unborn children to be done unto themselves and their own families? I will only believe it, when I see a transcript of a 911 call that looks like this:

> Dispatcher: What is your emergency?
>
> Pro-lifer: Help! My home has been invaded by a serial killer! My wife and my five children and myself have all been tied up. I just managed to wiggle one finger free to dial my cell phone. Now he says he is going to kill us one by one! But, whatever you do, Operator, don't send any armed men who are prepared to use deadly force in our defense. Violence never solves anything, ya know. Just send an old station wagon full of picketers to stand out front while my wife and five…Oops! Dang!…four children are killed. We have to remember that he has only been a serial killer for 13 years, so repentance must be just around the corner.

Gandhi, himself, would be appalled. While he promoted nonviolent action, he certainly never endorsed nonviolent inaction. In fact, "Gandhi taught that violence is better than apathy and cowardice, but that nonviolence is better than violence."17 Have Cavanaugh-O'Keefe and the other old rescuers forgotten that "nonviolently is an adverb" -- a word describing action? How tragic that, in pro-life circles, "nonviolence" has now become merely a pleasant state of mind that serves the emotional needs of pro-lifers and the p. r. needs of their movement, while helpless babies go to their deaths undefended.

By looking to India for a role model, did these pro-lifers imagine that Western Civilization had never before been confronted with the problem of how to deal with an unjust aggressor? Guided by the Judeo-Christian ethic, Western Civilization long ago concluded that an unjust aggressor must be resisted and resisted with force when necessary. This is why we provide soldiers and policemen with guns. And, this is why our law provides the defense of justification. Certainly an unjust aggressor should be restrained with little or no physical force when possible. The pro-life rescue movement and state laws against abortion were both, in this regard, "better ways." When necessary, however, the killing of an unjust aggressor is clearly preferable to permitting the killing of the innocent by withholding forceful defense required for their survival. This is not extremist, radical rant. It is part of basic training in every branch of law enforcement. At its best, our foreign policy is also based on this principle: our participation in World War II was certainly an example of resisting unjust aggressors with force. When properly viewed within this moral framework, all of Jim Kopp's actions in defense of others have been moral, lawful, and highly commendable. While he recognized that the imminent killing of unborn children constitutes a true emergency, he consistently used the least amount of force necessary for the defense of these children. Jim devoted many years to the rescue movement, participating in over 100 rescues and working to promote rescue here and abroad. He also developed a variety of locks, which were very difficult and time-consuming to remove. These were used to join small groups of pro-lifers together, so that even a small number of people could stop the killing. When numbers dwindled to the point where not even a handful of friends could be rounded up for a "lock and block rescue," Jim knew that the use of force was the only way that an individual, acting alone, could protect every baby who was scheduled to die on a given day at a given location. Even then, when deadly force was justified, he still tried to use the least amount of force necessary. "I didn't intend to kill Dr. Slepian," Jim said in an interview, which was published in The Buffalo News on November 20, 2002. "I made every effort possible to make sure Dr. Slepian would not die. It's the easiest thing in the world to kill somebody with a rifle. You aim at the head or upper body. It's very, very difficult just to wound somebody if that is your goal . . . The truth is not that I regret shooting Dr. Slepian. I regret that he died," Kopp said. "I aimed at his shoulder. The bullet took a crazy ricochet, and that's what killed him. One of my goals was to keep Dr. Slepian alive and I failed at that goal." Jim also explained why he shot Slepian in his home on Friday night, rather than waiting for his last opportunity, which would come when the abortionist walked from his car to the "clinic": Kopp said he did not want to risk shooting bystanders, and he felt he had a better chance of wounding Slepian at home. "Why do you think I used force against Dr. Slepian when he was within 10 hours of taking the lives of 25 babies? The question answers itself."

The second count of the State's indictment against Jim Kopp contains this curious phrase: "evincing a depraved indifference to human life." Now, who does that phrase best describe -- the accused or the "victim"?

The "victim," Barnett Slepian, was, according to the press, "the mainstay of Buffalo's only abortion clinic" and "an abortion provider for 13 years." Can anyone do the math? 200 abortions per month (which would be a bare minimum for such a "provider") over a 13-year period of time, adds up to a staggering body count of 31,200 human lives lost. These are the Disappeared: the children who will never come to your door selling Girl Scout cookies, who will never learn to catch a fish, or wish upon a star, or even take their first steps. In an article for WorldNetDaily, Jack Cashill reported:

> Within a year of his arrival in Buffalo, Slepian would boast "that he could do an abortion in the time it took Billy Joel to sing a song. . ." He could "take out 15 an hour," Slepian told his niece, Amanda Robb, who, despite her pro-choice views, worried that Slepian sounded too much "like a boy who thins deer populations." He described the process "as American as supply and demand . . . part and parcel of keeping the minority quotient manageable."18

The photographs Naomi Wolf described as "vile and repulsive images . . . of violent fetal death" were not, to Slepian, just pictures on a placard that he passed as he drove to the "clinic." They were scenes he re-created with his own hands every Saturday. The carnage wrought by Slepian was truly the ultimate expression of "depraved indifference to human life."

The two men, Jim Kopp and Barnet Slepian, could not have been more different. In his interview with The Buffalo News, Jim explained the genesis of his conviction that "every baby is valuable":

> While studying for his master's degree in biology from a California university, Kopp said, he became fascinated with the development of embryos. By 1980, he was becoming a pro-lifer, he said, for both religious and scientific reasons. One particular incident, he said, forever influenced him and turned him into an ardent

abortion foe. Kopp said he was doing research that year at a hospital in California, when he encountered a doctor who took him to the morgue. According to Kopp, he saw a long metal table with a paper bucket at one end. Inside the bucket was a fetus with "a few minor birth defects," he said, including six fingers and genitalia that had not developed properly. "(The doctor) was flipping this baby back and forth, like a rag doll," he said. "She was proud that she and her boss had detected some of these defects in-utero. The woman told me, "When you see stuff like this, you really start to believe in abortion." This was the first time I had ever seen a baby who had been killed, and this woman was proud, happy. I was stunned. I changed in that moment."

Far from being "indifferent to human life," Jim devoted the majority of his adult life to preserving the lives of those least able to defend themselves. He did this at great personal cost to himself and he did it for strangers -- for little ones who could never thank him and whom he would, most likely, never meet. Countless children are alive today because of Jim Kopp's altruism.

When abortions have been cancelled because of blockades of "clinics" or, in the case of Slepian, the shooting of the abortionist, many people assume that all the abortions are simply rescheduled and take place on other days. Pro-lifers and abortionists have known for years that this is not true. One of the major abortion groups, I believe it was either The National Abortion Federation or The Alan Guttmacher Institute, conducted a study in the mid-1980s to determine why many women who miss abortion appointments do not reschedule. It was found that 20% of women who missed their appointments for any reason — even reasons as prosaic as "the car wouldn't start" or "the baby-sitter didn't show up" -- would not reschedule and would carry their babies to term. Their reasons varied; for instance some found unexpected support from the baby's father or from their families, but the bottom line was that cancelled abortions translated into lives saved. For this reason, abortionists, suing pro-lifers, complained bitterly to judges about income lost -- not merely deferred -- due to pro-life rescues.

It will no doubt provoke howls of indignation from fans of Barnett Slepian to point out that there are children alive today because of the shooting. But what reasonable person could look at little boys and girls who are now three years old and wish that Slepian had been available to kill them on October 24, 1998?

Jim Kopp's defense of these children was a true expression of respect for human life because it put the lives of the innocent first and because it was commensurate to the danger posed to their lives. Jim did not stage a little protest at the "clinic" on the day the children were scheduled to die, as if their mothers were entering a fur store to buy mink jackets. Instead, he acted appropriately -- defensively -- and in a timely manner; because he saw clearly that abortion is first and foremost a deadly attack on a helpless baby, not an issue for debate or protest. Did the misguided soul who opined to The Buffalo News that "violence ends debate" think Barnett Slepian was going to the "clinic" on Saturday to debate abortion -- or to "take out" babies at the rate of "15 an hour"? Having a true respect for human life, Jim knew that the killing of the innocent must stop first. Then, we can all debate to our hearts' content, although, it goes without saying, that no civilized society should ever seriously debate the propriety of intentionally killing innocent human beings.

How then can so many good people tolerate terrible, government-sanctioned injustice when the victims are, of all people, helpless children? I was introduced to this question in a powerful way when I was a child. My paternal grandmother was born in 1889 in Nashville, Tennessee, a descendant of the early settlers of that region. She had a remarkable memory and could repeat, word for word, stories that her grandmothers told, which included reminiscences of everyday life that are so often lost to formal history. The story, which made the deepest impression upon me, was of her own paternal grandmother's earliest childhood memory. This grandmother was born into a prosperous family in 1831, one of 14 children. They lived in the country near the Gallatin Road, four miles from Nashville. She recalled that in her earliest memory in life she had just stepped out onto the front porch of her home on a beautiful morning in early summer. With her mother beside her and the big, exciting world of her front yard laid out before her, she experienced a moment of pure happiness. Before she had taken another step, though, her ears pricked up at a strange, new sound -- very faint at first. As it grew louder and closer, she realized in horror that the sound she heard was a chorus of children's voices wailing and crying. And she, herself, was suddenly filled with fear. She could not see the children, but she could pick out individual voices now -- anguished cries of "Mama! Mama! Mama!"

She buried her face in her mother's skirts and wept. My grandmother said, "they were driving slaves on the Gallatin Road" -- "driving," as in "driving cattle." Among the slaves were a number of children who had recently been separated from their mothers and were being taken away for sale. She said her grandmother told her that the terrible lament of these children could be heard for nearly a mile. Being a child, myself, I naively hoped for a happy ending. Even as I asked the question -- "What did her mama do?" -- I imagined all the adults in the household rushing to the aid of the children and I pictured the joyful reunions with their mothers. But my grandmother replied, "her mother scooped her up in her arms and carried her in the house." Then she closed the front door and the windows on the front of the house, so they could not hear the slave children anymore.

I remember very well the sorrow and profound disappointment I felt. Then I thought indignantly, "If only I had been there!" Isn't that what we all think, when confronted with injustice in another age? We would all be heroes in that other time and place. The injustice is so clearly evil and those who acquiesced so obviously contemptible. Identifying with the victims, we accept no excuses and the only response we find appropriate is that which we would want to be done for ourselves. We like to think that, as "good," "nice" people, we have unfailing moral compasses which would guide us true under any circumstance, but we underestimate the power of the law. As the saying goes: the law is a great teacher. Certainly, the law is a very powerful teacher. And what terrible lessons are taught when the legal system is turned against an entire class of vulnerable, innocent human beings. Even the "nicest" people can learn bigotry and apathy. We have only to look at the experience of black Americans to see how thoroughly the law can inculcate contempt for the lives and rights of others. As late as the 1960s, to any child growing up in the South, as I did, segregationist laws represented the collective Wisdom of the adult world that blacks were inferior. The message was brutally clear: because the law and so many nice people treated blacks as inferior, they were inferior. It followed then that no one needed to feel bad about treating blacks as they deserved to be treated. The sad truth is that, unless one happened to be black, segregation "felt" just fine to most people.

Like slavery and segregation, the peculiar institution of abortion can only exist because of bigotry and apathy. It can only exist because society is still willing to assign a lesser value to a certain class of human beings based on their physical characteristics. In the case of unborn children, they are deemed not only inferior, but expendable, because they are small and dependent on their mothers. Bigots today love to dress their contempt for the lives and rights of unborn children in the righteous robes of the civil rights movement -- as if a wonderful, new "right" for women could be fashioned from the broken bodies of helpless babies and written into law in their innocent blood. But who can seriously believe that Dr. Martin Luther King's "dream" included Barnet Slepian "keeping the minority quotient manageable" by exterminating black children in their mothers' wombs? Was this really the "dream" Dr. King had for his children and for all children? As evil as the kidnappings and forced servitude of black children were, that slave trader in Nashville was an Angel of Mercy compared to Slepian who killed the black babies whose mothers came to him for the "reproductive health service" of abortion. He killed them "quick as Billy Joel could sing a song." He killed them by the thousands. And he killed them for money. If we judge my ancestors and their neighbors in the South as cruel and heartless people, what does our own tolerance for the evil of "legalized" child-slaughter make us? We should remember the words of Abraham Lincoln: "I tremble for our Nation, when I consider that God is just."

But it doesn't "feel" like abortion is as bad as all of that. The fact that the killing of unborn children is "legal" and supported, or at least tolerated, by so many "nice" people seems to represent the collective wisdom of society that unborn babies are inferior and different and unworthy of protection. The abortion nurse, Sallie Tisdale wrote:

> We make the powerful assumption that the fetus is different from us, and even when we admit the similarities, it is too simplistic to be seduced by form alone. But the form is enormously potent -- humanoid, powerless, palm-sized, and pure, it evokes an almost fierce tenderness when viewed simply as what it appears to be. But appearance, and even potential, aren't enough.19

That, in a nutshell, is the bigots' creed in every age. For them it is never "enough" that a fellow human being has a human "form" and human "potential." To be admitted into their protected circle that form must be the "right" color, or the "right" size, or the "right'" something else.

Who can forget the image of four, little black girls walking into their new school in Mississippi flanked by National Guardsmen? The Guardsmen were there because bigots cannot be "seduced by form alone." No, you can't fool them. The fact that those little girls had the "potential" and the "form" of human beings was just not "enough." With bigots, it never is. But a truly just society would insist that simply being human and alive is "enough" to be counted as "one of us" -- a full member of the human family. And if the dream of equality means anything at all, it means that the smallest and most vulnerable among us deserve our greatest care and protection. They do not deserve to have their helplessness offered up as proof of their inferiority. If our Nation's sad history of bigotry and injustice has taught us anything, it should be this: the fact that the legal system and many "nice" people will tolerate terrible injustice says nothing about the worth and humanity of the victims. But it does say everything about the humanity, or rather inhumanity, of the society that tolerates it. Once established by law and custom, of course, injustice can "feel" just fine to those who are not its victims: hardness of heart is an inevitable by-product of institutionalized injustice. And when the killing is done quietly and discretely behind the closed doors of a "clinic," it is all too easy to leave that unfailing moral compass at home in a sock drawer and to go about our business, heedless of the brutality and injustice inflicted upon, of all people, helpless babies.

Where are the heroes today? Where is the person who sees clearly the evil of injustice, who truly identifies with the victims, who makes no excuses for inaction, but does for the victims what is moral and lawful to do for any valued member of society? The correct response to injustice is to do justice -- not to wish for justice, or hope that justice will "happen," or wait patiently for justice while new victims are killed daily. On October 23, 1998, Jim Kopp did justice by protecting those who could not defend their lives and rights themselves.

The day after the shooting, scores of law enforcement agents scoured the Slepian's property and neighborhood for evidence, collecting every hair and fiber. Neighbors were interviewed and evidence technicians took measurements and photographs. Hundreds of miles away, FBI agents confiscated boxes of Jim Kopp's property from the home of a friend. But by the end of the day that Saturday, they had all overlooked the most important piece of evidence -- the bucket. Nurse Tisdale concluded her article with a description of the bucket and its contents:

> Maggie, one of the nurses, received a call at midnight not long ago. It was a woman in her twentieth week of pregnancy; the necessarily gradual process of cervical dilation begun the day before

had stimulated labor, as it sometimes does. Maggie and one of the doctors met the woman at the office in the night. Maggie helped her onto the table, and as she lay down the fetus was delivered into Maggie's hands. When Maggie told me about it the next day, she cupped her hands into a small bowl -- "It was just like a little kitten," she said softly, wonderingly. "Everything was still attached." At the end of the day I clean out the suction jars, pouring blood into the sink, splashing the sides with flecks of tissue. From the sink rises a rich and humid smell, hot, earthy, and moldering; it is the smell of something recently alive beginning to decay. I take care of the plastic tub on the floor, filled with pieces too big to be trusted to the trash. The law defines the contents of the bucket I hold protectively against my chest as "tissue." Some would say my complicity in filling that bucket gives me no right to call it anything else. I slip the tissue gently into a bag and place it in the freezer, to be burned at another time.20

On Saturday afternoon the bucket stood empty at the "clinic" where Slepian worked. Dozens of babies, who would have filled that bucket, transformed by "choice" into a gory stew of arms and legs and headless torsos, had been granted a reprieve. Because of Jim Kopp's intervention, those little ones were still alive and "everything was still attached." They would all sleep safe in their mothers' wombs that night. The empty bucket, which no one thought to collect as evidence, testifies to the many, precious lives saved that day and to the horrific deaths so narrowly averted. Without words, it declares the justice of Jim Kopp's action and trumps every piece of the prosecution's evidence.

A Strange Objection

Still, some believe that Jim's forceful defense of these babies was not justified, because he could not guarantee that each baby saved on Saturday would continue to live in the coming weeks and years. This is a strange objection. Since we are all mortal, the one thing that is certain is that any person saved from danger on one day will die another day. Many, such as those severely injured, die shortly after their rescues. It is patently unjust to withhold life-saving aid from fellow human beings based on the cynical calculation that not all of them are good bets for long-term survival.

## A Particularly Vile Concoction

Others denounce Jim for not making as his top priority Barnett Slepian's spiritual conversion. To these pro-lifers, Slepian's possible, future repentance was worth more than the lives of all the babies he would kill while he remained the unwilling subject of their spiritual reclamation efforts. This is a particularly vile concoction because it presumptuously purports to know the spiritual needs of unborn children and weighs them against the spiritual needs of the abortionist. In this contest, the abortionist is found to be needier, so he gets to keep his life, while the babies are killed. This is a bizarre variation on the argument that mercy is better than justice. Certainly, mercy is a wonderful thing, but it can never be dispensed at the cost of innocent human lives. That is injustice. In fact, this is the central error of the Roe v. Wade decision. Roe is premised on a low view of women which holds that women cannot hope to function fully in society as long as they are afflicted with a lousy biology that constantly threatens to make them mothers.

The all-wise and merciful Roe court sought to correct this defect by generously granting women a special dispensation from the time-honored prohibition against the intentional taking of innocent human life. The Court exceeded its authority: the innocent lives of unborn children were not the Court's to give away. It is shocking and sad indeed to see pro-lifers fall into the same error. How many more babies were these pro-lifers generously willing to sacrifice in the interest of an abortionist's hoped-for conversion? If more than 30,000 dead babies were not enough, was there truly no limit? Encouraged by these foolish "friends of the unborn," society at large would lavish every consideration and all its concern on the welfare of the killers, while the innocent victims are denied justice altogether.

While Jim Kopp would not join in this error, he certainly never denied the humanity of Barnett Slepian. "To pick up a gun and to aim it at another human being, and to fire, it's not a human thing to do," Kopp said in the opening statement of his interview [with the Buffalo News]. "It's not nice. It's not pleasant. It's gory, it's bloody. It overcomes every human instinct. The only thing that would be worse, to me, would be to do nothing, and to allow abortions to continue."

Barnett Slepian was a human being. He was "one of us," but he was one who chose to use his license to practice medicine as a license to kill innocents. He killed with impunity for 13 years and, at the time of his death, he was scheduled to kill again within 10 hours. Jim Kopp had the opportunity and the duty to defend Slepian's next victims. Just as the lives of those innocent babies were not Slepian's to take, those innocent lives were not Jim's to give away. He could not grant mercy to a serial killer at the expense of that killer's next victims.

The shooting of Barnett Slepian shocked the sensibilities of a Nation grown comfortable with the practice of "legalized" child-slaughter. To treat as equals the most despised and disenfranchised members of the human family, of course, seems "radical" and "extreme" to such a society. But Jim Kopp will be honored and praised by those who truly love justice.

## Sources

1. Sally Tisdale, "We Do Abortions Here: A Nurse's Story," Harper's Magazine, October 1987, p. 73.

2. Dr. Paul Jarrett, "Abortionists Speak," Students for Life, Vanderbilt University. http://www.vanderbilt.edu/SFL/abortionists_speak.htm

3. Section 35.05 New York State Consolidated Laws. http://www.assembly.state.ny.us/leg/?cl=82&a=l2

4. "Judgment and Opinion", Hon. George R. Gerhard, Division 31, St. Louis County Circuit Court, August 16, 1989.

5. Nat Hentoff, "Pro-choice bigots: a view from the pro-life left." ASAP, November 30, 1992. http://www.no-violence.net/

6. "Can They Defend Themselves?", Excerpts from "An lmpolite Interview with Ken Kesey" by Paul Krassner, The Realist, Vol. 90, December '71.

7. ibid

8. People v. Shenker, 2001, 187 Misc.2d 521, 725 N.Y.S.2d 519.

9. People v. Comfort, (4 Dept. 1985) 113 A.D.2d 430, 496 N.Y.S.2d 863.

10. "A New Ethic for Medicine and Society", California Medicine, 113 p.67, 68 (1970).

11. Bemard N. Nathanson, M.D., Aborting America, Doubleday and Co., 1979, p. 206, 211.

12. Naomi Wolf, "Our Bodies, Our Souls," The New Republic, October 16, 1995, p.32.

13. Ibid, p.29.

14. Ibid, p.33.

15. People v. Craig, 1991, 78 N.Y.2d 616, 578 N.Y.S.2d 471, 585 N.E.2d 783 at 623-24.

16. John Cavanaugh-O'Keefe, "Nonviolence is an Adverb", Prolife Nonviolent Action Project, 1985, p.10.

17. Ibid, p.9.

18. Jack Cashill, "Slepian softens before his death", WorldNetDaily, May 9, 2002. http://wwwworldnetdaily.com/news/article.asp?ARTICLE_lD=27546

19. Sallie Tisdale, "We Do Abortions Here: A Nurse's Story," Harper's Magazine, October
1987, p. 68, 69.
20. Ibid, p.70.

# ADDITIONAL SOURCES

Bonhoeffer, Dietrich. *Cost of Discipleship*
Cavanaugh-O'Keefe, John. *No Cheap Solutions*
Cohen, David and Connor, Krysten. *Living In The Crosshairs*
Cowden-Guido, Richard. *You Reject Them, You Reject Me; History of the Prolife Movement*
Cruise, Tom. *Valkyrie* a movie based on an insider's account of the plot to kill Hitler in Volume 2 of *Bis zum Bittern Ende*
Faber, Eberhardt. *Biography of Dietrich Bonhoeffer*
Hill, Pastor Paul. *You May Mix My Blood with the Blood of the Unborn*
Jackson, Matthew. *Lock & Block and the New South*
Jefferson, Professor Mildred, MD, Harvard and USSG (Ret'd) Everett Koop, MD, Weill. *Anaheim 1979 L'Abri Tour Lectures* DVD
Maxson, Lt. Col. Ronald, USA (Ret'd). *Lambs of Christ and the Freeway Radio Car Blitzes*
Miller, Dr. Monica Migliorino. *Abandoned*
Nathanson, Bernard, MD. *Aborting America; Silent Scream* DVD
Ramey, Catherine. *In Defense of Others; A Time to Kill*
Risen, James and Thomas, Judy. *Wrath of Angels: the American Abortion War*
Schaeffer, Francis A. *How Shall We then Live?* DVD
Scheidler, Joseph. *99 Ways to Stop Abortion; Meet the Abortion Providers*
Solzhenitsyn, Alexander. *Gulag Archipelago; Cancer Ward*
ten Boom, Corrie. *The Hiding Place*
Teresa of Calcutta, Mother. *Nimraal Hriday Tertiate Talks* (Brian Coladieczyk, Ed.)
Waagner, Clay. "Autobiography"
Wells, John. *Sniper*
Willke, Jack, MD. *A Matter of Choice* DVD
Wurmbrandt, Richard. *God's Smuggler*

RALPH M. GABRIEL

## Acknowledgments

Grateful acknowledgment is made to those who were so generous with their time in the making of this book, without whom it would never have happened and who graciously answered my e-mails, calls and letters. Among them also were the friends, acquaintances, family and survivors of those below who had an impact on the story that found its way into this book.

First among these is the 1968 NYC chain-lock-and-blocker and parish secretary I ran into in Sandy Springs, Joe Scheidler, Andy Scholberg, Gateway City John Ryan and Judge "Mick McMurphy" who cut him loose 450 times, Anne O'Brien, Tim Dreste and the other Tim, Drs. Nathanson, Schaeffer and Willke, Father of Rescue John Cavanaugh-O'Keefe, Tom Herlihy and Co-op City, George "Can't Stand Ya" and the Magnus Opus Chess Club, Roosevelt Field chapter, Guadalcanal Construction Battalion chainsaw craftsman and Dark Pope of Long Island Hugh McEneaney, Joan Andrews Bell, Boston College Dr. Scott Austin, Frs. Pearson and Carleton, the aboriginal and Novus Ordo LIPIVITS, Italian rock star on Jesus/Tarzan hair/Maxwell Smart shoe-talking RT who needs his own book, Pastors Childers and Joseph Foreman and the Surf City Street Prophets, Denny Sadtler, Joe Wall, Jose Lina, Bob and Anna Brothers, Cpt. Steve Lang and John Broderick, USMCs and PFCs Rich Bruno (101st Airborne) and George "Scottie" Welsh, USA (Ret'd), Deputy Sheriff Chet Gallagher, LVPD (Ret'd) and the other V-Twin Ghostrider from Apache Junction and Ghostrider's prophetess acquaintance.

Acquaintances of Lt. Col. Fr. Norm, MC Post., USAF (Ret'd) and LOC were also very helpful. He also needs his own book. Sr. Carolyn, SJOC, Sr. J. and the Valencia Street Shelter MC Sisters, Lt. Col. R. Maxson, USA (Ret'd), Paul DeParrie and the Northern Exposure Expert Spacey, ERT Tac Squad and the "Fort Apache" 13th Precinct ESU/NYPD, Tenor Dan, A F of M, Refusenik Col. T.A. O'Conner, MD USA (Ret'd), JP II (both of them). Then, Fix-It-Again Tony, who turned me on to "The Scarlet and the Black" which led naturally to the White Rose, Sophie Scholl, Elie Wiesel, Polish death camp survivor and post-Collapse of the FSU Warsaw and Gdansk rescuer Eva Edel, rescuer Corrie ten Boom in Placentia, California, Rabbi Martin Buber, to-his-face Schicklegruber denouncers Fr. Max Kolbe and the Bishop of Cologne/Koeln and the Sobibor block of priest resistors, and then to Bonhoeffer, the babies he saved living now in NY and his memorial on the Avenue of the Righteous and Golda Meir who put it there, In Western New York there was the mother who got a forced abortion from BS MD and the DDS Sikh with the inside baseball on that same illegal cross-border advertising scheme. Also, bumping into the last eye witness to Pedophile Island still alive, the off-Caneel Bay plantation IBEW worker, and Hetty Pasco, and the old street prophet guy thrown out of court in Buffalo by the US Marshals, and Linda and her truck sign pals who walked and drove all around it.

The hospitality of Alphabet City Dan Brusstar and the Dobbs Ferry crowd and the Chief of DFPD (Ret'd) must be mentioned, and Pilar, Sr. Pilar, RGS, 'Lito and the Quezon City Mom and Dad Irregulars and all the Verzoga truck and jeepney drivers, Blue-eyed "Thumbs" Rescue, Cissy Ann and the Guardini crowd, the Precious Feet people and the Houston and Arizona morgue photographers, Nellie Gray, "B1- Bob," Jacob Koppensteiner, USN, artist and cinematographer par excellence Frankie S. and the four Huemoz daughters and their heroic spouses. The two crying cops in DCPD and SLPD (Manchester Precinct), hoping they finally get their conscience clause. The real Atomic Dog: Danny Ainge. Or maybe Daman Wayan. You decide. Raphael T's maybe Mini-Me Ed and Monica, Commodities "Professor" Trader Joe, Dr. Germaine Griszez and the other Ivy League moral theology wonk, H.E.'s Burke, Mueller and "The Vig.", Clay Waagner and pioneer Michael Griffin and all the POC's. Herve Rouzad-LeBouef, Pierre Constant, Paul Cambria and the Coverts, Bruce Barket and John Human, Thomas Patrick Monaghan, Esqq., legal eagles.

Enfield "Judy! Judy! Judy!" sparkled as usual and her baby and the other Judie and her tireless better half, and Fr. Morrow of Huntly, Communione & Liberacione and their on-time cameraperson, the La Scala Intermission Drinking Club and their Vatican mole, H.E.A. Stickler, Ginny Smythe, MD, CHO, Anzio Beach sidewalk counselor Maria Mara, H.E.s Fr. Vig. and the Atlanta Josephite, the rural Georgia Orthodox, the Alabama Charismaniacs, Walt Gies, Regular and Ethyl in the Rare Auld Times, the Sunday morning tea-after clubs, friends of Ginger Rogers commuting on the Pasadena Freeway, Meredith Willson, AF of M and the Pasadena Playhouse, Marlborough L'Abri staff, lab wonks Drs. Larry

# RALPH M. GABRIEL

Eng, Dixon and William Hurlbut MD, SUMC, and Dr. Friend, UCSF, the Stanford University Sociology Department Far East Program, Dr. Kennedy, Wolf's Lair in Montana, UGLI physics study group, Santa Fe soprano, light opera and the City of Lights, Anaheim Mem. ER, ICU and Med/Surge staff. Tuba City Dr. Charlie "Tuna" Lambert, lab techs of Drs. Donal Grant and Todd Newberry, Birgitte Kahnert, Timchen, Candace, Tom, students of Herbert Marcuse, Baby Shoppe Pam, and Drs. Stephan Fuchs and Karl Folkers at the IBR in Austin. Pastors Walter Mees, Sr., Michael Bray and the Missouri Synod, PCA Reformed, Fr. Paul Marx, OSB, Maurice Lewis, H.E. Fr. LeFebvre, and Rabbi Yehudi Levin and his pals Rabbis Gruener and K. and the Brooklyn Hasidim.

Back in California again Escondido Daniel Gorman was very helpful, Kitty Agegian and other members of the SoCal Armenian Community, the Brentwood Chaldeans, the Byzantines, Fr. Thomas Loya, Light of the East, Tom Ashcroft and his cool ride with the fleas in the seats and J Mercer and the Travolta sweatshirt he wore there, Fanny, Shostakovich's Fifth/Key Largo and the Whitefriar Street Temple Bar Pub Singing Association, Captain and Expert Pilot Bernie Green, USN, (Ret'd) CSDP, the third shift sub rosa workers, Drs. John Pearse and Doyle and Joel Hedgepeth and his harp . . . not the kind you drink, EEs Bill Dixon, Al Paeth, Mark Mimnaugh, Sunnyvale, Dave, Bruce and all the Middlefield Manor Home for Unwed Fathers residents, and the Placentia Guys' House guys, Bob Smith, M. Barati and the Mahler's Fourth soprano, Islander magnate Bob Pearson, John and Bea, "Dutch" Pete and Delores, the "Does Anyone Care?" Jebbe, Lone Star Chet Pelletier, USN, (Ret'd), And to those whom I have forgotten or who spoke on background.

Finally, I have mentioned in this book several acquaintances of Mr. Kopp. Their inclusion or mention of their statements or actions does not imply their endorsement of Thomistic force to save children. Any inference of such from their inclusion here would be false.

R. M. G. Advent 2022

## Author's Note

Would you like your rescue, crisis pregnancy center, or sidewalk counseling story included in an upcoming book?

If so, please send it to johndunk@ptd.net.

Proceeds from the sale of this book will go to fund free ultrasound projects for distressed moms worldwide.

# RALPH M. GABRIEL

*Arranged and edited by John Dunkle*

Credit must also be given to the Rev. Michael Bray, author of A Time to Kill and Actors in the Kingdom. Not Clappers in the Audience. His ideas on the just use of force in defense of unborn children appear frequently in this essay.

www.ingramcontent.com/pod-product-compliance
Lightning Source LLC
Chambersburg PA
CBHW071949070526
44583CB00015B/1116